A STANDARD GUIDE TO
CAT BREEDS

A STANDARD GUIDE TO CAT BREEDS

CONSULTANT EDITOR
Richard H. Gebhardt
President and Chairman, The Cat Fanciers' Association, Inc.

GENERAL EDITORS
Grace Pond
Fellow of the London Zoological Society

Dr Ivor Raleigh
Chairman of the Governing Council of the Cat Fancy

McGRAW-HILL BOOK COMPANY
NEW YORK · ST LOUIS · SAN FRANCISCO · TORONTO

Contributors

Feline Genetics: Roy Robinson F.I. Biol.

The Design and Management of Stud Quarters:
Alison Ashford, Feline Advisory Bureau, London

The Design and Management of Boarding Catteries:
S. M. Hamilton-Moore
The Feline Advisory Bureau, London

Feline Medicine: P. A. Flecknell, Vet MB, MRCVS
Clinical Research Centre of the Medical Research
Council

Feline Behaviour: Randall Lockwood, Ph.D.,
State University of New York at Stony Brook

Published in the United States 1979 by
McGraw-Hill Book Company

Created, designed and produced
by Trewin Copplestone Publishing Ltd, London

Phototypeset in Great Britain
by Keyfilm (Trendbourne) Ltd, London

Printed in Italy by New Interlitho Spa, Milan

Published in Great Britain by
Macmillan London Limited 1979

Library of Congress Cataloging in Publication Data
Main entry under title:

A Standard guide to cat breeds.
   1. Cats – Standards. 2. Cat breeds. I. Gebhardt,
Richard H. II. Pond, Grace. III. Raleigh, Ivor.
SF445.37.S7 1979 636.8 79–14602
ISBN 0–07–023059–5

Contents

Foreword

The cat fancy throughout the world is dedicated to the welfare of cats, and particularly to promoting an understanding of the perpetuation of established breeds and the development of new ones. It is for this reason that the organizations within the worldwide cat fancy have evolved standards of perfection for the various breeds.

Most cat breeds are recognized internationally, although the standards set for them by different associations may differ in some respects. For example, the Persian, or Longhair, bred in the United States is a bit more extreme in type than that bred in Britain. This is not to say that one is *better* than the other; it is simply a matter of preference.

Similarly, the Burmese cat in Britain is longer and more foreign in type than its American counterpart, which is a rounder, cobbier cat, because British breeders have chosen to preserve the type of the early Burmese. In addition, the six-month quarantine in Britain tends to restrict the importation of cats and, therefore, makes it necessary to crossbreed many cats. Thus many new colors have been introduced within the Burmese breed.

Far more important than the superficial accomplishment of producing winning cats and collecting trophies is the cat breeder's responsibility to interpret the standards and to develop breeding programs that will produce cats to those standards. Health and vigor are undoubtedly of the utmost importance. All other qualities are undermined if the line proves to be one that produces weaknesses or encourages undesirable features. The breeder's wisdom is reflected in his or her careful selection of sound, healthy stock for mating in which all the component parts are compatible and without defect, in the planning that ensures the necessary introduction of new blood into the line, and in the willingness to share with others interested in the breed new discoveries and knowledge gained from experience. The greatest reward is to know that your efforts have benefited others in perfecting the breed.

Breeders also have an important responsibility in selling the kittens they have reared. In my opinion it is better not to select a kitten for a buyer, but to let him take his choice. However, it is essential to inform a buyer of the particular characteristics of the breed and to stress the type of care involved, and the amount of time it will take. Animals with an abundance of coat, such as the Persians, are always crowd pleasers. Too often the novice owner assumes that the animals simply grow up this way. The buyer must be made aware from the beginning of the time and care involved to maintain a luxurious coat. There is no point in selling a kitten to an unsuspecting buyer who then becomes discontented with the cat when he finally realizes all the work and effort that is involved. An unhappy customer means an unhappy home or, in many cases, a short-term home for that precious kitten, which may even be neglected or abandoned to become a stray. All breeders have a responsibility to take back any kitten or cat that they have sold when it is unwanted.

For many years the Cat Fanciers' Association had taken the position that a breed was determined by what it was bred from and not by how it looked. Today more careful study and the growing interest in, and understanding of, genetics has altered some of the earlier thinking. And with the increasing import and export of cats around the world, we are beginning to see a more universal attitude to standards and ideals.

It is hoped that this *Standard Guide to Cat Breeds*, with its informative articles on genetics, feline medicine, catteries and stud quarters, and descriptions of each breed of cat as well as the full official standards of the Governing Council of the Cat Fancy and the Cat Fanciers' Association, will interest you, inform you and guide you in the world of cats.

Richard H. Gebhardt

The Cat Fancy

Blue Persian/Longhair with Cream kitten

The cat may have been domesticated many thousands of years ago, at least as far back as the nineteenth century BC in ancient Egypt, and perhaps even earlier, but the deliberate breeding of cats to maintain, improve or perfect certain characteristics – that is, the establishment of pedigree cats – only began a little over one hundred years ago.

The interest in pedigree cats and cat shows throughout the world started through the foresight of Mr Harrison Weir, a Fellow of the Horticultural Society, an artist, and a cat lover. There had been cats on show at exhibitions and fairs, but, Mr Weir said, 'I conceived the idea that it would be well to hold Cat Shows, so that different breeds, colours, markings, etc, might be more carefully attended to, and the domestic cat sitting in front of the fire would then possess a beauty and an attractiveness to its owner unobserved and unknown because uncultivated heretofore.' He wasted no time in setting to work, and within a matter of days had worked out a schedule, classes, prices and prizes for just such a show. Most important of all, he also set out the first 'Points of Excellence', standards by which cats could be judged.

His next step was to find a suitable hall, so he approached Mr Wilkinson, the manager of the Crystal Palace. The Crystal Palace was the brainchild of Prince Albert, Consort of Queen Victoria. Built entirely of glass, it was erected in Hyde Park for the Great Exhibition of 1851, and was moved to a site in south-east London some years later. It was used for many shows and exhibitions, and dog shows had already been held there.

The Crystal Palace appointed Mr F. Wilson, who may have been the manager for the dog shows, to be responsible for this first cat show. When the great day, 13 July 1871, arrived there were approximately 160 exhibits. Mr Harrison Weir, his brother, John Jenner Weir, and the Reverend J. Macdona officiated as judges. After the show Harrison Weir was presented with a large silver tankard for his services. John Jennings, in his book *Domestic or Fancy Cats* written in 1895, said 'Many will remember the sensation created by this first Cat Exhibition, which opened up a channel for the feline race never hitherto dreamt of. Many who then were seized with "cat fever" will recollect how this first programme was subject to criticism. . . . The usual wisdom after events have been successful was of course strongly in evidence.' This first show attracted great interest, and eventually proved to be the forerunner of cats shows throughout the world today, and was responsible for the birth of the Cat Fancy.

In 1873 a show was held at the Alexandra Palace and one in Birmingham, and in 1875 a show in Edinburgh had an entry of 560 cats, a special attraction being a cat rescued from the ninth storey of a building after a fire. In the same year the Crystal Palace show had 325 pens, and there was a class for the 'Wild or Hybrid between Wild and Domestic Cats', in which an ocelot won the first prize. (The National Cat Club continued to hold shows at the Crystal Palace until it burned down the night before one of their shows in 1936. The show manager found another hall, sent telegrams to all exhibitors informing them of the change of venue, and the show went ahead as usual.)

Dr Gordon Stables, another early cat judge, was a true prophet when he wrote in 1876 that 'cat shows are only in their infancy and anyone who chances to have a good cat may nowadays take prizes. In future years there will be no chance work about the matter at all, and those only who study the breeding and rearing of cats in a scientific and sensible manner will be the winners.' Then he

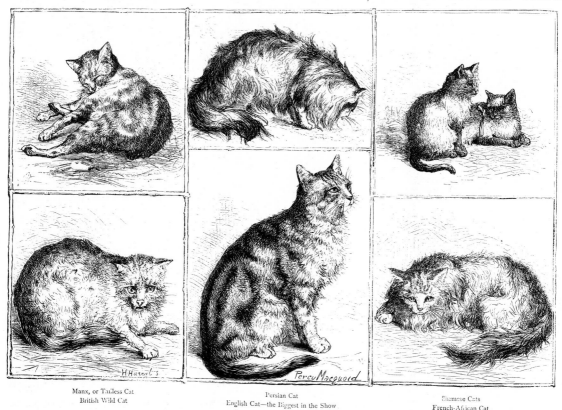

Manx, or Tailless Cat
British Wild Cat

Persian Cat
English Cat—the Biggest in the Show

Siamese Cats
French-African Cat

PRIZE CATS

Prize cats at the cat show of 1871

gave good advice to would-be fanciers that still applies today: 'Having made up your mind as to what particular breed you mean to go in for, stick by that breed for a time, at least, and go in for no other.'

Cat shows became fashionable, particularly as they were patronized by Queen Victoria, who owned a pair of Blue Persians, and by the Prince of Wales, later Edward VII, who presented photographs of himself to the owner of the winning cat at a show.

The first shows were composed chiefly of short-haired cats divided into different colours. These were Mr Harrison Weir's first love, and some years

Looking at the exhibits at the first cat show

1. Mrs. Yarborough's silver Persian "Silver Charm," highly commended.
2. Miss F. Moore's silver Persian "Columbine," first prize.
3. Mrs. Vallance's silver Persian "Pearl," commended.
4. Miss Southam's long-haired brown tabby, second prize.
5. Miss E. Emming's long-haired red tabby "Sam," first prize.
6. Mr. J. W. Townsend's blue Persian "Goblin," third prize.
7. Miss L. Abbott's white Persian "Beauty," first prize.
8. Mrs. T. Weightman's white short-haired cat "Samson," first prize.
9. Mrs. V. Swan's white short-haired cat "Dot," second prize.
10. Miss Beddington's white Persian "Ba-Ba," first prize and silver medal.
11. Miss Bulpitt's white Persian "Jumbo," first prize.
12. Mr. H. Smith's Persian "Ross."

Prize cats at the cat show of 1890

later he complained that the cats from the East (the longhairs) were taking over from the resident British cats.

Cats from Britain were soon being sent all over the world, forming the foundations of new cat fancies. In 1895 the first official cat show was held in Madison Square Garden, in New York, to be followed by many others all over the country.

After the very successful early cat shows and the ever-growing interest in the exhibits, it was realized that in order to produce specific colours some knowledge was needed of the parentage of the cats. In 1887 the National Cat Club was formed, with Mr Harrison Weir as its first president. The Club started to keep a stud book and became the first registering body for pedigree cats in the world. It continued in this capacity until 1910, when the Governing Council of the Cat Fancy came into being and took over this function from the National, which was given the right always to have four delegates on the Governing Council.

The British cat fancy suffered a severe set-back during the First World War. Fewer shows were held and less cats bred than in the preceding years; at the National Cat Club show held in 1920 there were only 236 cats. The numbers increased gradu-

ally after the war, but the fancy was again hard hit by the Second World War. During the war years there were no shows, very little breeding was done, and many cats were put to sleep. Only two hundred exhibits were entered in the National Cat Club show in 1948.

Apart from the war, the drop in numbers can also be blamed to some extent on the fact that over the years violent outbreaks of feline infectious enteritis took their toll, with some catteries suffering an almost total loss after a show. Fanciers became unwilling to risk losing their stock, and so refrained from showing. With the introduction of vaccines, and vaccination against feline infectious enteritis (see page 300) becoming almost a general practice, shows began to build up again, until today, more and more show managers have to return entries, so great is the interest in exhibiting pedigree cats.

The Points of Excellence, or standards, that Mr Harrison Weir drew up for the first cat show were as important for the development of pedigree cats as the establishment of the registering bodies themselves. The primary purpose of standards, then as now, is to promote sound breeding practices by approving those characteristics that can only be

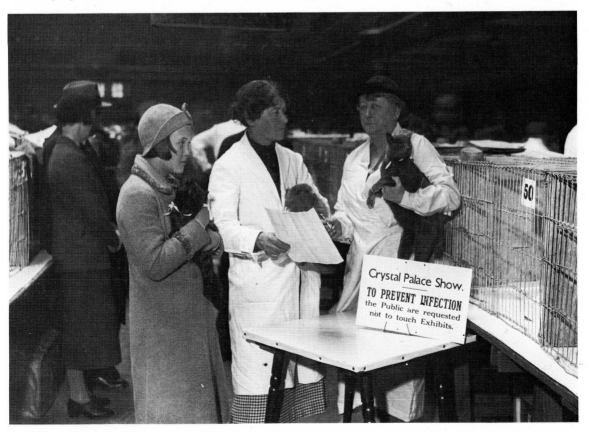

1936: Crystal Palace burned down, but the show went on

Russian Blue

Cornish Rex

Persian/Longhair

Himalayan/Colourpoint Longhair

achieved in this way. And, of course, they provide the basis for uniformity in judging.

Mr Harrison Weir had built up his Points of Excellence gradually, basing them on his vast experience of more than fifty years of studying cats. In his book *Our Cats*, published in 1889, he gave comprehensive Points of Excellence for British Shorthairs of many colours, Abyssinians, the Royal Cat of Siam – with a light body and black points – Persian, Angora and Russian cats. He allocated one hundred points in judging each cat, dividing them between the various characteristics required according to their relative importance to the overall appearance of the cat.

Some of these standards have been changed very little since they first appeared. Of course, as new varieties are introduced, new standards must be established. This process begins with the cat clubs and societies and is completed by the registering body with which they are affiliated. The way in which this is done may vary slightly from one registering body to another, but the basic procedure is the same. A cat club or society proposes a provisional standard to its registering body, which may then require evidence of true breeding and a number of awards or merit certificates in Any Other Variety or Assessment classes before granting official recognition.

Since Britain had the first organized registering body, it is interesting to note how its recognition system developed. At the first cat shows in Britain there were few breed classes, as there was no planned breeding, and so cats were put into classes more or less according to colour. There were classes for some specific colours, such as Black, White and Tabby longhairs, but the majority of cats was entered under the heading of 'Any Other Colour'. Judging was difficult, and the prize-winners were usually entirely dependent on the particular judge's preference for certain colours. For example, even the first Blue Persians appeared in the Any Other Colour class. In those days most of these had some white and tabby markings, and it was not until 1889, when they had been improved by careful breeding, that they were given a class of their own.

Gradually, more colour classes were introduced and the numbers in the Any Other Colour class decreased. Many fanciers thought that the class should be withdrawn, but the Governing Council of the Cat Fancy decided that this would be unfair to any cat not conforming to a set standard, as it would mean that it could not be shown. The Governing Council decided that these cats should be continued to be registered as Any Other Colour and that there should still be these classes at the show.

Undoubtedly, this decision proved an asset to breeders in that cats produced by crossbreeding or resulting from experimental breeding could be shown as pedigrees. No challenge certificates were given, however, and these exhibits could never become champions. Even if the variety was ultimately recognized, wins in the 'AOC' class did not count.

In the mid-1970s the Governing Council and many of the breeders decided that the situation was not really satisfactory, and so Assessment classes were introduced. An official cat club proposes a provisional standard for a new variety and, if accepted by the Governing Council, cats are then entered in the Assessment class in a show. The cats do not compete with one another: each cat is judged individually by three judges, who do not confer with each other. The judges write their comments on special assessment forms, remarking on the head shape, body type, coat colour and condition, etc., referring to the provisional standard displayed on the pen. If the cat is considered worthy, the judge may award a merit certificate. When the cat club applies to have the provisional standard recognized as an official standard, the number of merit certificates is taken into consideration. In order to be granted recognition the variety must have proven three generations of pure breeding, show that a reasonable number of the variety is being bred and, that a sufficient number of breeders is interested in producing them. Once recognition is granted, the cats may be re-registered and may then be entered in their Open breed class.

Mr Harrison Weir hoped that interest in pedigree cats would be created by the first show, but even he could never have foreseen how successful he would be. With shows being held all over Europe, throughout the United States and Canada, in Australia, New Zealand, Japan, South Africa and in many other parts of the world; with pedigree cats and kittens being exported and imported from one country to another, and with cat judges being invited around the world to officiate at each other's shows, and international friendships being formed for life, the cat fancy is a way of life to a great number of people who love and care for cats.

Registering bodies

In Britain there is one registering body, the Governing Council of the Cat Fancy, composed of delegates elected by members of the affiliated cat clubs throughout Britain. The Council grants

Siamese kitten

licences for shows, keeps a record of all registered cats and transfers, awards challenge certificates, and Grand Champion certificates, approves new judges, and recognizes new varieties or breeds of cats. It may also take disciplinary action, if necessary, against clubs and members.

In North America there are a number of registering bodies. The largest is the Cat Fanciers' Association, Inc., which has over six hundred clubs under its jurisdiction in the United States, Canada and Japan. The next largest is the American Cat Fanciers' Association, which is also responsible for a number of clubs throughout the continent. Others are the American Cat Association, the Cat Fanciers' Federation, the United Cat Fanciers' Federation, the Independent Cat Federation, and the Canadian Cat Association.

The various registering bodies run shows under their jurisdiction, and all aim to promote the interest in pedigree cats and their welfare.

In Europe the largest registering body is the Federation Internationale Feline de l'Europe, known as FIFE, which controls clubs in twelve European countries. The member clubs in each country keep their own registers, but send delegates to the Annual General Meeting, where various matters concerning cats are discussed. There are a number of independent cat organizations throughout Europe that are also registering bodies. The majority organize cat shows.

There are several registering bodies in Australia. The varieties of cat recognized, the standards of points, and the rules regarding shows and registration of kittens and cats are all very similar to those of the British Governing Council of the Cat Fancy, on which they are based.

The cat fancy in South Africa began slowly, mainly with cats imported from Britain, and now there are many breeders throughout the country. There is one registering body, and its standards and rules are based on those of the British Governing Council.

Silver Tabby Persian/Longhair kittens

Feline Genetics

The principles of heredity were discovered in 1866 but, for reasons that may seem inexplicable at this time, did not become common knowledge until 1900, when it became evident that these were applicable to both plants and animals. In particular, this knowledge revolutionized animal breeding. In place of notions like percentage of blood and influence of the paternal (maternal) line, a number of simple rules could be formulated to govern the transmission of traits from parent to offspring. The science of heredity is known as genetics and the basic laws that consistute elementary genetics are fundamental to cat breeding.

The material basis of heredity are the chromosomes, tiny bodies present in the cells and just large enough to be observed under the microscope. It is important to appreciate this fact because the rules of heredity are determined by the behaviour of the chromosomes and are not a theoretical abstraction. The cat has 19 pairs of chromosomes, each pair being different from other pairs. Each body cell contains the full complement of 38 chromosomes (i.e., 19 pairs) but the germ-cells (sperms of the male and ova of the female) have 19 chromosomes (only one of each pair). This reduction is necessary so that, when the germ-cells fuse to create offspring, the normal complement of 38 chromosomes is restored. The rules of inheritance follow from this fact – and it is a fact, not a supposition, because the chromosomes can be observed under the microscope.

Chromosomes are the bearers of the genes, the unit of heredity determining all the characteristics of the cat. The genes are borne on the chromosomes like beads on a string. This is an apt description because the chromosome is a thread-like body and the genes occur at definite points along its entire length. Each chromosome carries some thousands of genes, each of which controls some function of the cat's growth and well-being. Normally, the genes reproduce themselves in a remarkably exact manner, duplicating themselves to be passed on to the offspring via the germ-cells.

However, on rare occasions, the duplication is inexact and a new gene comes into being. This is how mutant genes arise. The effect of a mutant gene may take any form: a new coat colour or a coat type, as for example in a self black or the Cornish Rex. Mutant genes are grouped according to the effects they produce and the two most important groups for cat breeders are coat colour and type. These will be used to outline the principles of inheritance and, later, to show how they feature in the creation of breeds of cats.

Basic principles

The rules of inheritance are those describing how mutant genes are handed on from parent to offspring and the effects they produce either by themselves or in combination with each other. This may be illustrated by following the inheritance of the self colour black versus the self colour chocolate. Black is the normal pigment of cats and chocolate is a mutant form (as in the Havana breed). Should a black cat be mated to a chocolate, the offspring will be expected to be black. Should the first-cross offspring be mated to each other, they will be expected to produce black and chocolate in the ratio of 3:1. But should the first-cross offspring be mated to a chocolate, black and chocolate offspring will be expected in the ratio of 1:1. The question is: why these particular ratios and how are they produced?

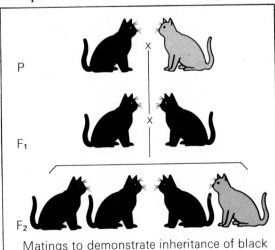

Matings to demonstrate inheritance of black versus chocolate. Pure black mated to chocolate will produce black progeny. These mated together will produce black and chocolate kittens in the ratio of 3:1.

At this stage it is necessary to introduce some symbolism. The genes have been given universally recognized symbols in precisely the same manner (and for the same reason) as chemical atoms. The symbols are a convenient shorthand. The gene for black pigment is symbolized by B and chocolate by b. The two genes are on one of the chromosomes and, since the chromosomes occur in pairs, it follows that the black cat will be BB and the chocolate cat will be bb. The germ-cells contain only one of each pair of chromosomes, hence the germ-cells from the black will carry B and the germ-cells from the chocolate will carry b.

So far so good: the mating of black and chocolate means the fusion of B germ-cells from one parent with b germ-cells from the other. Therefore, the constitution of the offspring will be Bb. These are black in appearance because the effect of B is stronger than that of b. Gene B is said to be dominant to b; conversely, gene b is said to be recessive to B. The choice of symbol is an indication whether a gene is dominant or recessive since the former are represented by capitals and the latter by small letters. This is a universal rule.

Now, the first-cross offspring have the constitution Bb and the germ-cells will be of two sorts, namely, B and b. The germ-cells can carry only one gene and the Bb constitution implies that these will be either B or b in equal numbers. Therefore, when the Bb blacks are mated together, B germ-cells from one parent will have an equal chance of fusing with B or b from the other parent, to produce offspring BB and Bb, respectively. Similarly, b germ-cells from the same parent will have equal chance of fusing with B and b germ-cells from the other parent, to produce offspring Bb and bb, respectively. This gives a total of four offspring: one BB, two Bb and one bb. Since both BB and Bb are identically black, this gives a ratio of 3:1 of black (BB and Bb) to chocolate (bb).

The 1:1 ratio of black and chocolate offspring from the mating of the first-cross black to chocolates follows immediately from the above remarks. The Bb black will be producing B and b germ-cells in equal numbers, whereas the bb chocolate will be producing only b germ-cells. Thus, the expectation is 50 per cent Bb and 50 per cent bb or 1:1 ratio of black to chocolate.

The different generations and matings have been given precise names in order to avoid confusion. The initial generation of black and chocolate is the parental or P, the first-cross is the first filial or F_1 generation, and the F_1 mated to each other produce the second filial or F_2 generation.

The F_2 is also known as the intercross, and the mating of the F_1 black to the chocolate is the backcross. The various types of individuals produced by these crosses have been precisely defined. The genetic constitution (BB, Bb and bb) is the genotype, while the appearance is the phenotype. It is important to appreciate that the same phenotype may have different genotypes. Thus, BB and Bb are both phenotypically black but have different genotypes because of the dominance of B to b.

It should be apparent that individuals with different genotypes will breed differently. This is recognized by terming those individuals with two similar genes (BB and bb) as homozygotes and individuals with dissimilar genes (Bb) as heterozygotes. Particularly note that there are homozygous dominant (BB) and homozygous recessive (bb). Since b arose from B by mutation, it means that each occupies the same point on the chromosome. This is recognized by saying that B and b show alternative inheritance. Each cat must contain either BB, Bb or bb in its genotype.

The expectations for any mating can be worked out easily and systematically by the aid of chequerboard diagrams. The expectations are formed by writing the different types of germ-cells produced by one parent along the top of the diagram and those from the other parent down the left side. The diagram is then ruled off into as many cells as dictated by the number of different types of germ-cells at the top and left side. In the case of the F_1, this

Expectations from mating two blacks heterozygous for chocolate.

Expectation from mating black heterozygous for chocolate to chocolate.

gives a 2 × 2 square and for the backcross, a 1 × 2 oblong. The composition of each cell is found by entering the gene symbol at the head of the column and side of the row in which the cell resides.

The chequerboard diagram is valuable because it compels the compiler to think carefully about the relevant genes in a given mating and how the expectations are derived. This is more obvious when two mutant genes are involved in the same cross. The chequerboard below shows the expectations for a F_2 of a parental mating of a chocolate and a blue. Not only is the usual pigmentation of the cat black, but the pigment granules in the hairs are also densely packed. However, a mutant gene is known that causes the pigment granules to be less densely packed. The effect to the human eye is a blue colour.

black **BbDd**

		BD	bD	Bd	bd
black **BbDd**	BD	BBDD black	BbDD black	BBDd black	BbDd black
	bD	BbDD black	bbDD chocolate	BbDd black	bbDd chocolate
	Bd	BBDd black	BbDd black	BBdd blue	Bbdd blue
	bd	BbDd black	bbDD chocolate	Bbdd blue	bbdd lilac

Expectation from mating two blacks heterozygous for chocolate and for blue. Note how the germ-cells determine the composition of the offspring.

The symbols for these two genes are D for dense and d for dilute pigmentation, respectively. By themselves genes D and b are inherited exactly as for B and b. Gene D is dominant to d so that DD and Dd are dense coloured cats, while dd is a dilute. Substitution of D and d for B and b in the diagram on page 16 will show how the genes are inherited. A different letter is deliberately employed to denote the dense-dilute pair of genes to indicate that they are independent of the black-chocolate genes and reside on a different point on another chromosome.

Since two pairs of genes are now involved, this means that the genotypes will consist of four genes. The chocolate cat is densely pigmented, hence its genotype is bbDD. The blue cat is not chocolate but clearly diluted, hence the genotype is BBdd. The germ-cells will carry one of each pair of genes; that is, bD from the chocolate and Bd from the blue. Mating chocolate to blue will produce BbDd offspring due to the fusion of these germ-cells. Remembering that B is dominant to b and D is

dominant to d, implies that BbDd is a black. Mating these F_1 blacks together should produce an interesting F_2 and the full expectation is shown in the chequerboard on this page. The germ-cells from BbDd must contain one of each pair of genes, and four different combinations are produced: BD, Bd, bD and bd. This is because the pairs of genes are inherited independently and the chances of B and b entering the same germ-cell as D or d are equal.

The four different kinds of germ-cells are written along the top and left side of the chequer-board, indicating that the chequerboard will consist of sixteen cells. Each cell will represent an expected offspring. The genotype of each cell is determined by the genes at the top of the column and at the side of the row in which each resides. These should be entered in each cell. The phenotype is found by considering the dominance of B to b and D to d. All B-D- are black, all B-dd are blue, all bbD- are chocolate and the solitary bbdd is lilac. What this cross has demonstrated is that the colour known as lilac is genetically dilute brown. Counting the number of colours reveals that there are 9 black, 3 chocolate, 3 blue and 1 lilac. The 9:3:3:1 is merely an extension of the basic 3:1 ratio of genetics.

The nine blacks are identical in appearance but examination of the genotypes will reveal that these are composed of four different sorts. Similarly, it may be seen that the chocolates and blues each have two different genotypes. These facts should emphasize the vital difference between phenotype and genotype for animal breeding. Cats of identical phenotype will not necessarily breed true. The reader is urged to pick out genotypes at random from the chequerboard and build up the relevant germ-cells and chequerboards for imaginary matings. This is useful exercise in gaining confidence in working out expectations for any crosses. A particularly interesting mating would be to cross BdDd to bbdd. The expectation is black, chocolate, blue and lilac in equal numbers, reflecting the output of germ-cells.

Mutation is a rare event but if a gene can give rise to a new mutant gene on one occasion, it may do so on a second, third, etc. Each mutant gene need not be the same as the previous, and in this manner a series of mutants may be produced by the original gene. The various mutants are known as alleles and the group as a whole as an allelic series. Several allelic series have been discovered in the cat, reason enough to be aware of their occurrence and how they are inherited. Since only one gene may be present at any point on the chromosome, no matter how many alleles there may be in a series, only two can be carried by the individual (one of each chromosome) and only one transmitted by the germ-cells. This may be illustrated by an example.

Burmese and Siamese are colours produced by two recessive genes c^b and c^s of a gene C present in fully black cats. (Note the symbolism: since both Burmese and Siamese are recessive to full colour, they are represented by the small letter c, but are distinguished from each other by a superscript b and s, respectively. This is a general rule for denoting recessive alleles.) Accordingly, the black is CC, Burmese is $c^b c^b$ and Siamese is $c^s c^s$. Suppose a black heterozygous for Siamese (Cc^s) is crossed with a Burmese heterozygous for Siamese ($c^b c^s$). The black will produce germ-cells C and c^s while the Burmese will produce germ-cells c^b and c^s. The expectations from the fusion of these germ-cells is shown in the chequerboard below. There will be a

	black **Cc^s**	
	C	**c^s**
c^b	Cc^b black	c^{b}c^s Burmese
c^s	Cc^s black	c^{s}c^s Siamese

Burmese **c^{b}c^s** (row label, left side)

Expectation from mating a black heterozygous for Siamese to a Burmese heterozygous for Siamese.

ratio of 2 black: 1 Burmese: 1 Siamese; the ratio of 2:1:1 is due to the fact that the three genes are alleles of the same point on the chromosome and no individual offspring can receive more than two from its parents. Apart from this, there is no difference in the inheritance, whether two or three alleles are involved. The chequerboards on pages 16 and 18 can be compared to verify this statement.

All breeds and varieties of cats display variation, be this the depth of colour in chocolates and blues, intensity of yellow pigment in the red tabby, length or fullness of coat in longhairs or quality of coat in Rex. This variation is due to two factors; either to accidents of development (in the uterus prior to birth or during kittenhood to maturity) or to heredity. With a character such as colour, most of observed variation is due to heredity. These genes are called modifiers because they alter the expression of a character rather than change it abruptly, as in the case of mutants considered up to this point.

Modifiers are inherited in the same manner as major genes. Indeed, the terms major and minor genes sums up the situation very well. Modifiers are genes with minor effects that cannot be individually identified. This is not to say that their effects are insubstantial. One group of modifiers is so influential that it has been termed the rufus group. The rufus modifiers are responsible for deepening the colour of the ginger cat to the flaming colour of the red tabby, changing the colour of the yellow-grey tabby to chestnut-brown and modulating the tone of the cream. All characters of the cat are modified to some extent by minor genes. These will be the subject of further comment in following sections. The best method of dealing with modifying genes is selection, namely by breeding from those cats that come closest to the ideal animal.

Sex-linked inheritance

Sex is determined by a pair of chromosomes designated as X and Y. The male has the formula XY, and the female XX; consequently, Y is called the male and X the female chromosome. The germ-cells can only transmit one chromosome; hence the male will produce two sorts, X and Y, while the female will produce only one, X. The fusion of X and Y with X will give offspring XX (female) and XY (male) in equal numbers. This is the explanation of equal numbers (on average) of male and female kittens.

The cat is almost unique in having a sex-linked gene O for orange pigmentation. The phenotypes produced by the O and o genes are OO, ginger or red female, Oo tortoiseshell female, oo normal coloured female, OY ginger or red male, and oY normal coloured male. The O gene is said to be sex-linked because the gene is on the X chromosome. The above genotypes show this directly. Males are either red or normal, almost never tortoiseshell because this colour is the heterozygote Oo and requires two Xs.

There is no real difference in the inheritance of ordinary (non-sex-linked) and of sex-linked genes, except that the sex of each parent must be specified in the latter case. This is to take account of the fact that the genotype will differ between the sexes for sex-linked genes. Table 1 opposite shows the expectations for the heredity of orange for the six possible matings. The diagrams opposite show how the chequerboards are constructed for sex-linked genes.

The rare occurrence of tortoiseshell males is due to the animal accidently receiving two X chromosomes, one X carrying O and the other carrying o.

Table 1. Expectations for matings of cats carrying the sex-linked orange gene.

| MATING | | OFFSPRING | |
Queen	Stud	Males	Females
Orange	Orange	Orange	Orange
Normal	Orange	Normal	Tortoiseshell
Tortoiseshell	Orange	Orange Normal	Orange Tortoiseshell
Tortoiseshell	Normal	Orange Normal	Tortoiseshell Normal
Orange	Normal	Orange	Tortoiseshell
Normal	Normal	Normal	Normal

Orange means red, cream or orange-based colour. Normal means tabby, black or any non-orange colour.

Table 2. Standard symbols for known genes of the cat.

Symbol	Designation	Symbol	Designation
a	Non-agouti	O	Orange (sex-linked)
b	Brown		
c^{ch}	Silver	p	Pink-eyed dilute
c^b	Burmese	Pd	Polydactylia
c^s	Siamese	r	Cornish Rex
c	Pink-eyed albino	re	Devon Rex
c^a	Blue-eyed albino	S	Piebald White Spotting
d	Blue dilution		
Fd	Folded ears	T^a	Abyssinian tabby
h	Hairlessness	T	Striped tabby
l	Longhair	t^b	Blotched tabby
M	Manx	W	Dominant white
		Wh	Wirehair

Some, in fact, are masculinized females, with the curious XXY constitution. Nearly all tortoiseshell males possess a chromosome anomaly of one sort or another. This is why the majority are sterile.

Colours of cats

The various known mutant genes combine and interact to produce the many breeds and varieties of cats. The inheritance of individual genes (or even two or more simultaneously) has already been explained. Always remember that the orange O gene is sex-linked and must be handled a little differently from ordinary genes. All of the symbols have international status and should be used in any discussion on feline genetics.

Any discussion of colour in cats should start with the tabby. Everyone is familiar with the tabby cat! In fact, the tabby is a complex colour. It is made up of two components, the agouti or ticked background and an overlay of dark pattern. Strictly speaking, it is only the dark pattern that is the tabby pattern. If this seems curious, reflect on the fact that while four types of tabby pattern are known, the agouti background is the same in each one.

The four types of tabby pattern are striped or mackerel, spotted, blotched or classic, and Abyssinian. The striped tabby is the wild pattern of the European wild cat, *Felis silvestris*, and is characterized by vertical, slightly curving, stripes along the body. The spotted tabby is similar except that the stripes are not continuous but are broken into short bars or spots. There is some variation: the spots may be ovoid or round, large or small. This breaking-up of the more regular striped pattern is typical of the North African wild cat *Felis lybica*, from which the domestic cat descended some 4000 years ago. Both patterns are common among the oriental or foreign type breeds.

The blotched tabby, on the other hand, consists of a heavy pattern of bars and whorls on the sides of the body. The pattern is very variable, often with the whorls coalescing into large splotches of pigment. This pattern is usually found in the long-haired and European type shorthairs. It is the so-called classic pattern of these breeds and should conform to a recognized standard.

In contrast to the above, the Abyssinian tabby is almost devoid of dark pattern on the body. Not entirely, however, for some barring is often present

Expectation from mating a tortoiseshell to an orange male.

Expectation from mating a tortoiseshell to a normal coloured male.

on the forelegs, low on the flanks and on the tail. The pattern forms the basis of the Abyssinian breed, where breeders have by selective breeding eliminated the barring from the forelegs and body. The pattern of markings on the head is less pronounced for the Abyssinian compared with the striped or blotched tabby.

The various tabby patterns are due to three allelic genes, symbolized as T^a (Abyssinian), T (striped), and t^b (blotched). The order of dominance is T^a to T to t^b. It is thought that spotted is probably not due to a distinct gene, but is basically TT with modifying genes causing the stripes to appear as bars. There is evidence that selective breeding is changing the bars into spots and making the spots more defined – all of which goes to show that the placing of the tabby markings is open to genetic manipulation.

The greyish background that is apparent between the overlay of tabby pattern is known as agouti and is composed of hairs that are banded with yellow. The effect is clearly seen in the Abyssinian because of the absence of body pattern. The Abyssinian was affectionately known as 'bunny-cat' in its early days because of the resemblance to the agouti domestic rabbit. The ground colour may vary from yellowish-grey to a rich reddish-yellow, due to the rufus modifiers. Breeders prefer the richer coloration. Agouti is due to a gene A, which, however, has mutated to non-agouti a. Non-agouti lacks the yellow band to the hairs, producing a self black cat. Non-agouti is a very ancient mutant, probably reaching back into the Middle Ages, if not beyond, and is known throughout the world.

An interesting situation now arises. The black colour obscures the tabby pattern so that while AATT is striped and AAt^bt^b is blotched, aaTT and aat^bt^b are both black. An exception is that tabby pattern can often be discerned in young kittens as a 'ghost' underlay of darker pigmentation. This aspect confirms that gene a obscures the effects of T^a, T and t^b. This obscuring effect is known as epistasis and should be distinguished from dominance. Dominance is the term to be used when the effect of one allele is stronger than another, whereas epistasis is the term to be used when the effect of a gene can obscure the presence of an independent or non-allelic gene.

The normal pigment in the coat of the cat is black, but this may be replaced by a dark chocolate. The gene responsible for black pigment is B while that for chocolate is b. However, gene B has produced two mutants, b for chocolate and b^l for light chocolate. The first mutant is found in the Havana

combined with non-agouti, aabb, while the second occurs in the red Abyssinian $AAb^lb^lT^aT^a$.

The effects of dense D and dilute d genes on pigmentation have been discussed. The four colours produced by the combinations of B, b, D and d are the basic colours of cats. This is most clearly seen in conjunction with non-agouti and is worth setting out in full:

Colour	Genotype	Breeds
Black	aaBBDD	British Shorthair, Foreign Black
Blue	aaBBdd	British Shorthair, Russian Blue, Korat
Chocolate	aabbDD	Havana
Lilac	aabbdd	Foreign Lilac

Breeds of cats with the same colour genotype are not necessarily identical. They usually differ in such characteristics as coat quality, head shape and body conformation.

The four colours may be found in all of the various tabby patterns and the Abyssinians are the best known:

Abyssinian variety	Genotype
Normal	$AABBDDT^aT^a$
Blue	$AABBddT^aT^a$
Chocolate	$AAbbDDT^aT^a$
Lilac	$AAbbddT^aT^a$
Red	$AAb^lb^lDDT^aT^a$
Cream	$AAb^lb^lddT^aT^a$

The brown tabby is a breed description of the black pigmented tabby $AABBDDt^bt^b$. The name does not mean that the breed has the chocolate allele b. To avoid confusion $AAbbDDt^bt^b$ could be called chocolate tabby.

All cats must possess a gene known as full colour (C) if they are to exhibit the colours discussed above at full intensity. This gene has produced the following series of alleles: c^b Burmese, c^s Siamese, c^a blue-eyed albino and c pink-eyed albino. The reason why gene C is called full colour is because the c^b, c^s, c^a and c genes cause the amount of pigment to be produced at less than full strength. The result is a distinct weakening of the colour.

The Burmese ($aaBBc^bc^bDD$) is a dark sepia-brown, with the points darker than the body (this is especially noticeable in kittens, but less obvious in the adults), despite the fact that animals have the B gene. The reduction in intensity is obvious in the Siamese ($aaBBc^sc^sDD$), for, while the points are dark, the body fur is a medium to light sepia. The pigmentation of the eye is so reduced that the iris is a deep to medium blue. The inability to produce pigment in the blue-eyed albino (aaBBc^{a}c^{a}DD) is so pronounced that the coat is white (even on the points) and the iris is a pale, translucent blue. In the pink-eyed albino (aaBBccDD), there is a complete absence of pigment, the coat is white and the iris is a translucent pink. The pupil may be dark red or ruby in some pale coloured Siamese and albino cats. This is due to reflection from the blood circulating in the eye.

The Burmese gene c^b is incompletely dominant to c^s, so that a Burmese heterozygous for the Siamese gene (c^{b}c^s) is often of an intermediate colour – noticeably darker than the Siamese but not quite as dark as the typical Burmese on the body. The contrast between the intensity of the points and the body is greater and considered by some breeders to be more attractive. These cats are known as Tonkanese. Two Tonkanese mated together will be expected to produce a ratio of 1 Burmese: 2 Tonkanese: 1 Siamese. This ratio can be confirmed by writing out the appropriate chequerboard, as shown below:

Tonkanese **c^{b}c^s**

Tonkanese **c^{b}c^s**

	c^b	c^s
c^b	c^{b}c^b Burmese	c^{b}c^s Tonkanese
c^s	c^{b}c^s Tonkanese	c^{s}c^s Siamese

Expectation from mating two Tonkanese.

Incomplete dominance is rare in the cat; most dominant genes display full dominance over their recessive alleles. In fact, even in the present instance it is possible for some heterozygotes (c^{b}c^s) to appear as dark as lighter-coloured Burmese.

Both the Burmese and Siamese are recognized in the same four colours as self cats except that the colour is paler in Burmese, and paler and restricted to the points in Siamese:

Burmese	Genotype	Siamese	Genotype
Brown	aaBBc^{b}c^{b}DD	Seal	aaBBc^{s}c^{s}DD
Blue	aaBBc^{b}c^{b}dd	Blue	aaBBc^{s}c^{s}dd
Chocolate	aabbc^{b}c^{b}DD	Chocolate	aabbc^{s}c^{s}DD
Lilac	aabbc^{b}c^{b}dd	Lilac	aabbc^{s}c^{s}dd

The above genotypes may seem complicated, but these are built up step by step as each new

mutant comes into play to produce a series of colours. All that is necessary for understanding is to observe carefully the effect of each mutant and note how the effect behaves in conjunction with other genes. For example, gene c^s produces the Siamese pattern, regardless of the genes with which it may be combined; all these other genes produce colour changes on the points exactly as they would if not combined with Siamese. This mutual interchangeability is a common principle for almost all of the colour varieties of cats. There are exceptions and these will be discussed later.

The dominant inhibitor gene I has the curious effect of drastically inhibiting the production of pigment in those areas of the coat that are least pigmented, that is, in the tabby areas between the tabby pattern and the undercolour. The result is the silver, which is tabby pattern against a white ground. Silver may be striped or spotted (AAIITT), or blotched (AAIIt^{b}t^b). Some outstanding silver spotted tabbies have been bred because the I gene helps to clarify the spotting.

There is variation in the expression, with some silvers showing a yellowish suffusion, but breeders have selected against this defect to make the background colour as white as possible. In combintion with non-agouti, the smoke (aaII) is engendered. The hairs are tipped with black over a white undercolour. It is not an easy task to breed animals with the correct amount of ticking over a distinctive white undercolour.

The orange gene O is mainly responsible for the red tabby, but not entirely, for the richness of colour is due to rufus modifiers. Without these, the red tabby would be a ginger alley-cat. Most red tabbies are of the blotched form OOt^{b}t^b. The cream is the dilute version of the red (ddOOTT or ddOOt^{b}t^b). The sex-linked red Abyssinian (OOT^{a}T^a) has been evolved recently and has proved to be a brighter coloured variety than the original red variety. Similarly, the sex-linked cream (ddOOT^{a}T^a) is a clearer and brighter colour than the original cream.

The red Burmese (c^{b}c^{b}OOTT) is lighter in colour but distinctive from the ordinary red. Breeders are attempting to produce a uniform colour by selection for a cat with diffused tabby markings. The red Siamese (c^{s}c^{s}OOTT) has red points and yellowish-cream body fur. Both cream Burmese (c^{b}c^{b}ddOOTT) and cream Siamese (c^{s}c^{s}ddOOTT) are most delicately coloured.

The tortoiseshell (aaOo) is a brindled mosaic of black, red and yellow. The variety does not possess three colours, of course; the red is produced by the intense tabby pattern (usually blotched) while the yellow is produced by the paler areas between the pattern. The blue-tortoiseshell is the dilute form (aaddOo), being a mixture of blue and cream brindling. Tortoiseshell Burmese (aac^{b}c^{b}Oo) and Siamese (aac^{s}c^{s}Oo) are produced by suitable combinations of genes and are recognized varieties of these breeds in Europe. As a point of interest, Burmese breeders have all four colours of the tortoiseshell: black (as above; aaBBc^{b}c^{b}DDOo), blue (aaBBc^{b}c^{b}ddOo), chocolate (aabbc^{b}c^{b}ddOo) and lilac (aabbc^{b}c^{b}ddOo).

The bicolour is produced by a dominant white spotting gene, S. The gene causes white patches on the face, stomach and sides of the cat. Extreme animals may be almost all-white. However, these do not conform to the ideal bicolour, in which the coloured areas should be solid (not brindled with white hairs) and evenly distributed. The bicolour is recognized in any self colour, the black (aaDDSS) and blue (aaddSS) being the more common. Bi-coloured animals may or may not be true breeding because the S gene is incompletely dominant, so that Ss has less white than SS. However, the variation of white is so great that it is almost impossible to separate one from the other. Bicolours should be bred on the principle of mating the better marked cats to each other.

Bicolour Persians/Longhairs

The tortoiseshell is recognized in two guises, the ordinary tortoiseshell and the tortoiseshell and white, which is called the calico in the United States. The tortoiseshell and white is created by the addition of S to the genotype (aaOoSs), usually as a single gene because (aaOoSS) may have too much white. A fascinating aspect of tortoiseshell and white breeding is that the presence of white causes the orange and black areas to become 'segregated', resulting in a more patchwork effect of colours instead of brindling. The greater the amount of white, the greater the patchwork effect.

The all-white cat is produced by the dominant gene W. This gene is dominant to the normal gene w (present in all normal coloured individuals) and epistatic to all other colour genes. Thus, for example, the white carrying tabby (AATTWW) or white carrying black (aaTTWW) are indistinguishable. Some W white cats have patches of coloured fur on the head as kittens but this disappears with age. On occasions it is possible to identify certain genes carried by white cats from the colour of the patch. For instance, a blue patch could signify that the cat is a blue under a white coat (aaddWW).

Tortoiseshell Persian/Longhair

The eye colour may be yellow or orange, blue, or even odd-eyed – one eye orange and the other blue. The occurrence of blue or odd eyes is one of the effects of the W gene. The gene also induces deafness, either in one or both ears. Not all white cats are deaf, but quite a high proportion may be. There is a slightly higher risk that a blue or odd-eyed animal will be deaf compared with an orange-eyed one. The reason for this is that the W gene has a three-fold effect.

It will produce a white in all individuals but blue eyes or deafness in only some, and then not necessarily together. Because of this, the inheritance of blue eyes and deafness is erratic. If blue eyes are preferred, then blue-eyed cats should be given preference for breeding. Deaf animals should never be used for breeding unless they are really outstanding in a compensating feature.

The W gene also features in the Foreign White, or genotype $c^s c^s WW$. Many years ago, a foreign type breed was envisaged that would breed true for blue eyes. The eye colour would result from the c^s gene while the W gene would remove the points that would normally be present in all $c^s c^s$ individuals. The breeding programme was successful and the Foreign White is now an established and charming breed. Deafness is a hazard, due to W, but neutering of deaf animals appears to be keeping the defect under control.

Long hair

The coat is made up of three types of hair. The underfur, consisting of soft down hairs, whose function is to insulate the skin from excessive heat loss, and the top coat, consisting of the guard hairs, whose main function is to protect the underfur. There are two sorts of guard hairs. The primary guard hairs are straight, stout hairs. In addition to protecting the coat, they have a tactile function. They are controlled to some extent by erector muscles and are responsible for the coat 'standing on end' whenever the cat feels threatened. The second type of guard hairs are the awn hairs, so-called because they have a bristle-like tip. Awn hairs have both an insulatory and protective function. The down hairs are extremely numerous and make up most of the coat, followed by the awn hairs and then the primary guard hairs, which are the least numerous.

All shorthaired cats possess a gene L for short hair, but this has mutated to a gene l for long hair. The coat is made up of the same hair types as above but all are longer due to an extended period of growth. The quality of the coat varies greatly, from the shorter, somewhat coarse coat of the mongrel longhair with prominent guard hairs, to the exquisite coat of the exhibition Persian/Longhair. The coat of the latter is very long and full, with the guard hairs submerged in the long silky down hairs. All longhaired cats are ll and the variation is due to modifying genes controlling the actual length of hair and probably the proportion of down to guard hairs. Similar variation (due to the same modifiers) produces the different hair types found in the shorthairs, but the effects are magnified in the longhairs and more easily appreciated.

The long hair mutant is inherited independently of the colour genes, hence all of the colours discussed earlier may be bred with long coats. In most instances the colour is known under the same breed name but in several cases under entirely distinctive names. The best example is that of the Colourpoints, which are longhaired cats with the Siamese patterns. These may be produced in seal ($aaBBc^s c^s DDll$), blue ($aaBBc^s c^s ddll$) and other colours. They are not simply longhaired Siamese because the body type is completely different. In the United States, the Colourpoint is known as Himalayan, and the longhair with Siamese body type is known as Balinese.

The Birman are generally similar to the Colourpoint/Himalayan, but have white gloves on all four feet. These are probably due to the S gene with diminished expression.

The Turkish breed is an interesting breed. These are longhaired orange animals with extreme spotting (llOOSS). The coat is nearly all-white with small red patches on the head and body. A cream Turkish (ddllOOSS) is one of the latest developments of pedigree cat breeding.

A litter of Birman kittens

The longhair silver ($AAIIIlt^bt^b$) is similar to the shorthair silver in possessing a distinctive tabby pattern over a white ground colour. However, a remarkable development is the chinchilla, which is almost pure white except for black tipping to the hairs and a rim of black around the eyes, nose and lips. At birth, when the hair tips are erupting, the chinchilla appears as a silver, but, as the hairs continue to grow, the kitten matures into the chinchilla. Crosses between the chinchilla and silver produce a 'shaded silver' animal with an intermediate amount of hair tipping. It is uncertain if the chinchilla differs from the silver by a major gene but the current theory is that the variation is due entirely to modifying of the white undercolour due to I.

The beautiful longhaired cameo is the outcome of combining the orange and inhibitor genes as $IIllOO$. The undercolour is palest cream or white, with variable amounts of red hair tipping. The variation is so great that three varieties of cameo are recognized: the shell, which is the lightest; the shaded, which is more heavily veiled; and the smoke, which is the darkest with abundant red ticking. An apt description of the darkest cameo is the red smoke, a name that is now out of favour. The variation of amount of white undercolour is comparable to that found in the longhair silver and chinchilla and seemingly due to the same modifying genes.

Rex

The two Rexes do not have exactly the same type of coat. Admittedly, both are rex in the sense that the coat is shorter than normal, probably as a result of a slower rate of growth. However, although the

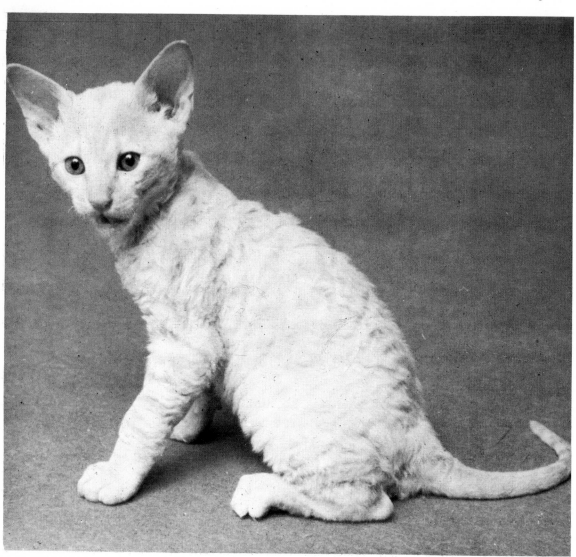

Cornish Rex kitten

Cornish Rex has the better coat, there is an absence of primary guard hairs. The coat is composed of down and awn hairs, and is the main reason for soft texture and the inclination for marcel waving. This is a variable feature, with some Rexes having little wave, others a loose wave, and yet others covered in tight curls.

On the other hand, the coat of the Devon Rex has all three hair types, but these are more abnormal than the Cornish. The hairs are of uneven diameter, with constrictions along their length and a propensity to breakage. This is most evident for the whiskers, which are often reduced to a few stubs. There is frequent loss of hair from the shoulders, chest and stomach. Every effort should be made to improve the fur quality by selective breeding of those Rexes with the fullest and most well-developed coats.

The two rex mutants, Cornish (r) and Devon (re), are of comparatively recent origin. Both are inherited as recessive and are independent of each other. A cross between the two would be of the form: rrReRe (genotype of Cornish) mated to RRrere (genotype of Devon) to produce RrRere (normal coated). This is the proof that the two rex genes are recessive to normal coat and independent. These crosses are not recommended and, in fact, are strongly depreciated by the Rex breed societies. Each of the Rexes may be bred in any of the colours found in normal coat cats. There is, however, a preference for the well-known and established colours.

The longhaired Rex (llrr or llrere) is rather an unbecoming cat. The whiskers are curled or missing, depending upon the type of Rex, while the coat is shorter than that of the usual Longhair. It is also very fine and inclined to hang limply. A few have been bred from time to time, particularly in the early days of Rex development as a consequence of the accidental introduction of the longhair gene. They never became popular.

Manx

The Manx is an unusual breed in several respects. Firstly, the breed is founded upon an anomaly (absence of tail) and, secondly, the homozygote is a pre-natal lethal. All Manx are heterozygotes Mm, where M is a dominant gene for taillessness. Therefore, Manx bred to Manx will be expected to produce a ratio of two Manx (Mm) to one normal tailed (mm) offspring. The most highly regarded cats are those that are completely tailless, but others are bred that have stump or half-formed tails.

The majority of matings in practice are of Manx to normal, which produces a ratio of half Manx and half normal tailed offspring. These normal kittens are sometimes called 'tailled Manx', which merely signifies that they are bred from Manx matings and has little genetic meaning. Manx may be bred in any colour or hair type. In the United States, the longhaired Manx is known as the Cymric.

The Manx has a peculiar stilted gait, which is due to abnormal fusion of the sacral and pelvic bones. A proportion of kittens regularly suffer from spina bifida and abnormal anus (imperforated or too small an opening, which can cause partial constipation). It is unfortunate that the most highly prized tailless Manx is the most prone to these defects. The homozygote MM dies early in gestation.

Scottish Fold

The folded-eared cat has the tips of the ears bent forward in a characteristic manner. The young kitten has normal soft ears but as the cartilage stiffens, the tips turn over. The unusual ears are due to a dominant gene Fd and the folded-eared animal is the heterozygote Fdfd.

Scottish Fold

Although the heterozygote is apparently normal (except for the ear cartilage), the homozygote FdFd suffers from an overgrowth of the cartilage around the joints and tail. This interferes with normal movement, is probably painful and distresses the cat. To avoid breeding these homozygotes, all matings should be of Scottish Fold to normal eared cats: the expectation is half Fold and half normal. Scottish Fold are bred in the United States, but their breeding is discouraged in Britain.

Inbreeding and selection

Inbreeding is the mating together of related animals. In general, the closer the relationship, the closer the inbreeding. Brother to sister mating is clearly the closest possible while breeding animals collaterally related via a distant common ancestor is the least possible. Close inbreeding may be unavoidable (even desirable) on occasions, but usually it is not a process to be carried too far. The reason is that genes with small deleterious effects can accumulate and produce somewhat sickly cats.

Experienced breeders are aware of this and keep a watchful eye open for any decline in the health of their stock that could be attributed to inbreeding.

Strictly speaking, inbreeding is a neutral process: it can bring out both good and bad qualities with fine impartiality. Is there any means of harnessing the process to advantage? The secret is not to inbreed too closely. A breeder seeking to improve his cats must pick and choose among his animals, selecting certain of them for future breeding and rejecting others as unsuitable. The

An Abyssinian: selective breeding has almost eliminated the dark tabby pattern

Blue Tabby American Shorthair

breeder hopes to perpetrate good points in preference to the bad. Mild inbreeding can assist in uncovering the latent qualities of the animals. After this, it is up to the breeder to pair his charges to encourage the development of the best possible characteristics.

There is no hard and fast rule in this respect; each case has to be considered on its merits. Straightforward selection is the simplest and most efficient system of breeding as a general rule. It is better to assess the probable outcome of any pairing by the appearance of the prospective mates, rather than by appraisal of a high-standing pedigree. The difficulty with pedigrees is that, unless one has seen the listed ancestors, these are just names. To be sure, a pedigree sprinkled with champion this or that carries some weight, but these are still just names unless one is familiar with the individual cats.

The breeding of cats to a high standard of perfection is far from simple: in fact, it is a life's work, for each peak of attainment is but a stepping stone to the next. As the quality of the breed improves, the task of breeding the superlative animal becomes more difficult season by season. However, the rewards in terms of prestige is that much greater. Outstanding male cats should be placed at public stud in order that the genes that have produced the animal can be handed on to his progeny. This is not to imply that the offspring of champion cats will necessarily be outstanding. Alas, animal breeding is not that simple.

The problem is that superior individuals are formed from chance combinations of genes, which may not be immediately duplicated. Nevertheless, the genes are handed on and the more a stud cat is used, the greater are the chances that the genes will recombine in later generations to produce individuals as good as, if not better than, earlier generations. It is only by breeding from superior animals that the general level of a breed can steadily be raised. Owners of superior male cats should feel obliged to place them at stud, subject to certain veterinary safeguards.

The quality of the queen is just as important as that of the male as regards breeding ability. Emphasis is placed on the male because he is capable of siring many more kittens than a queen can hope to mother. It will be appreciated that fewer males are bred from than females, hence it is wise to insist that their quality be above average. This is mere breeding prudence. Therefore, if the queen is of only moderate quality, it would be desirable to locate a male that is superior in as many features as possible. Obversely, it would be unwise to accept the services of an inferior male unless this cannot be avoided. Knowing which studs to choose for mating with a queen is the art and science of cat breeding, and can only be acquired by judicious reading and practical experience.

Coat Patterns

Variation of white patterns. The various steps in the amount of white are known as grades. There is wide individual variation of pattern within grades. Grade 0 would be a cat with no white. The top left cat, grade 1, merely shows spots of white on the chest, stomach or toes.

Tabby patterns

According to the dictionary, tabby is 'a watered fabric, especially silk; also a brindled or mottled or streaked cat, especially of grey or brownish colour with dark stripes; cat, especially a female'. The word 'tabby' is said to be derived from the Attibiya quarter in Baghdad where the weavers of a material known as 'Atabi' worked; in time the name became corrupted to 'tabby'. Harrison Weir in *Our Cats* said that gradually the word was used to mean the markings, rather than the material.

In some parts of Britain a tabby cat used to be referred to as a 'Cyprus', and in some dictionaries 'Cyprus' is still defined as: 'dark, tabby as a cyprus cat: a delicate transparent black lawn'. Bailey's Dictionary of 1730 defined 'Cyprus' as a kind of cloth made of silk and hair, showing wavy lines on it, and coming from Cyprus. Some experts maintained that the cat's coat pattern resembled the markings on the material, hence the name tabby, although others considered it to be the other way round.

There are millions of cats with tabby markings throughout the world; the majority are short-coated, non-pedigree cats, whose markings do not conform to any set pattern. Even in the shortcoated pedigree varieties it is not always possible to produce the required pattern. A similar pattern of markings is required in the Longhair or Persian Tabbies, but is much more difficult to produce and to see the true pattern in the long fur. In the British standard only the Classic Tabby pattern is recognized for Longhairs, but in the United States the standard of the Cat Fanciers' Association also lists the Mackerel Tabby Pattern, although it is only fair to say that these are comparatively rare.

Harrison Weir, to whom we refer often because there are so few others that could write with authority about the early days of the cat fancy, discussing the Longhair tabbies, said that he had never seen strong-coloured Angora tabbies, nor did he believe that such were true Angoras. Of the Persians he wrote that 'The colours vary very much, and comprise almost every tint obtained in cats; though the tortoiseshell is not, nor is the dark marked tabby, in my opinion, a Persian cat colour, but has been got by crossing with the short-haired tortoiseshell, and also the English tabby.' Apparently cats were also imported from Russia, and he said that 'the coat was long and coarse and the colour was of dark tabby, though the markings were not a decided black, nor clear and distinct.' In his

Points of Excellence, Weir gave quite a list of possible tabby colours, including brown, blue, silver, light grey and white, chocolate, mahogany, red and yellow, and mentioned spotted tabbies with long coats. None of the latter have appeared at shows for decades, and there would obviously have been great difficulty in producing cats with distinct separate spotting showing up clearly in the long fur.

John Jennings, in his *Domestic or Fancy Cats*, published in 1893, told of a cat with long fur found in India and known as the Tiger cat, 'with striped markings of red and black; with long hair, but coarser in textures than either of the other long-haired varieties, [that is, the Angoras and Persians] and its ears are larger and less furred internally than the Persian, whose tail, however, it closely resembles'. He also wrote about the Russian cats with long fur, saying that they were 'the most woolly of cats'.

At the early shows there were classes for Longhair Tabbies, a separate one for the Silver, and, until 1894, another class for Brown or Red Tabby, with or without white, but the descriptions given varied from 'brown and red' to 'Sandy Persian'. There was a change in 1895 and the Orange (later Red) and Cream cats were given another class. The first shows too had a class for Blues, self-coloured or tabby, but the tabby was dropped as the Blues became more popular, and became definitely self-coloured. For a while Blue Tabbies were included in the Silver Tabby class, and were probably used in producing the early Chinchillas, whose colour was frequently referred to as lavender. Blue Tabbies are recognized in the United States today, but in no way resemble the early variety.

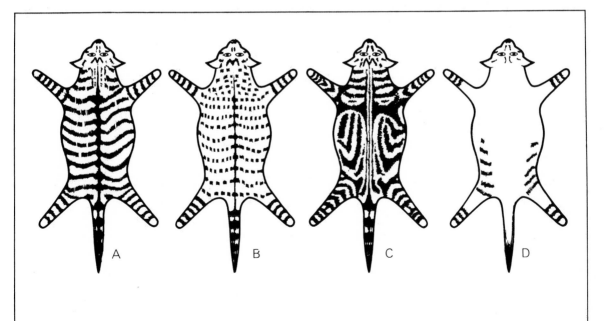

The four tabby patterns : A striped, B spotted, C classic and D Abyssinian. All of the basic patterns display individual variation.

Coat Colours

It is exceedingly difficult to describe the colour of a cat's coat in a word or two, as the colouring may change with the light and time of year. The chart lists the names used to describe the fur and points of the recognized varieties, with the appropriate colours.

Pure white	Off white, Magnolia	Bluish white, Glacial white	Pale bluish ivory	Ivory
Rich cream (Burmese)	Buff cream, 'Cool' rich cream	Lilac, Lavender, Pinkish dove grey	Pale lavender	Rich lavender
Light tangerine	Red	Orange red, Flame, Bright reddish gold	Copper red, Warm glowing red	Deep rich red, Deep rich brilliant red
Silver	Silver grey, Soft silver grey	Silver blue	Light blue, Lavender blue	Blue grey
Medium blue	Bright blue	Deep blue grey	Very deep blue	Deep steel blue
Pale cream fawn, Pale warm fawn	Warm beige	Warm fawn, Tawny buff	Light bronze	Rich tawny sable, Rich tawny brown

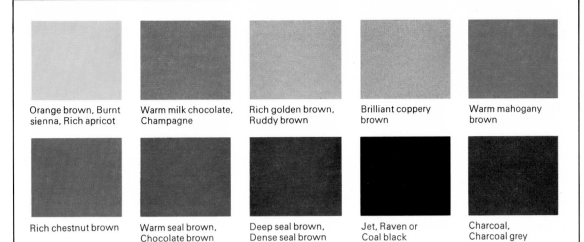

Orange brown, Burnt sienna, Rich apricot

Warm milk chocolate, Champagne

Rich golden brown, Ruddy brown

Brilliant coppery brown

Warm mahogany brown

Rich chestnut brown

Warm seal brown, Chocolate brown

Deep seal brown, Dense seal brown

Jet, Raven or Coal black

Charcoal, Charcoal grey

Eye Colours

The colouring of cats' eyes varies according to the variety, but frequently may be the same whether long-or short-haired. The chart endeavours to convey the eye colouring as given for the pedigree varieties' standards, but it should be appreciated that the colour varies considerably according to the light.

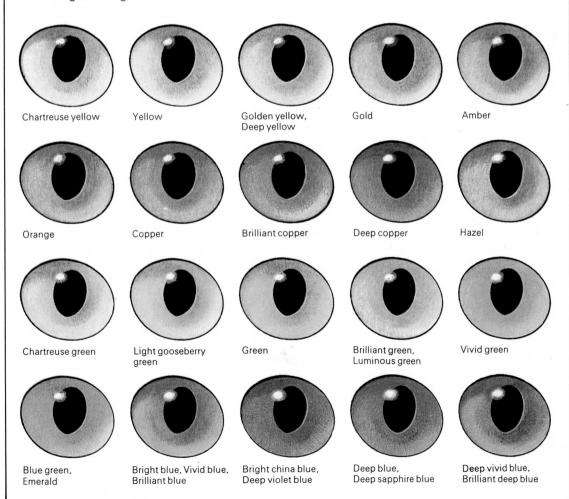

Chartreuse yellow

Yellow

Golden yellow, Deep yellow

Gold

Amber

Orange

Copper

Brilliant copper

Deep copper

Hazel

Chartreuse green

Light gooseberry green

Green

Brilliant green, Luminous green

Vivid green

Blue green, Emerald

Bright blue, Vivid blue, Brilliant blue

Bright china blue, Deep violet blue

Deep blue, Deep sapphire blue

Deep vivid blue, Brilliant deep blue

Glossary

Affix: The name of a registered cattery that is used after the name of all kittens bred there.

Alter: A neutered or spayed cat.

Angora: Originally, the name given to the first cats with long fur seen in Europe, so called after Angora (now Ankara) in Turkey, from where they were thought to have come. Now a recognized breed.

Blaze: Distinct marking of white or contrasting colours to body on the cat's forehead.

Breed true: To produce a kitten exactly the same as the parents.

Brindling: Hairs of the wrong colour mixed in with those of the correct colour.

Brush: A bushy or plume-like tail of a longhaired cat.

Butterfly: The pattern of markings seen on the shoulders of correctly patterned tabbies.

Button: A white, or contrasting colour, patch anywhere on the body.

Calling: The noise made by a female cat when in season.

Cat fancy: A term used to refer to pedigree cats and their breeding, cat clubs and societies, and anything associated with them.

Challenge Certificate: In Britain, an award given to the adult winner of a breed class if it is thought worthy.

Champion: In Britain, a cat winning three challenge certificates at three different shows under three separate judges. In the United States, a cat that has won six winner's ribbons under at least four different judges. In both cases the relevant registering body must approve the title before the cat can bear the name Champion.

Characteristics: Distinguishing features in the standard of points for which marks are awarded.

Cobby: Short sturdy on low legs.

Condition: General health and fitness.

Cross-breed: The mating of two pedigree varieties.

Cryptorchid: A male cat whose testicles have not descended.

Dense: Thick, full coat.

Entire: A full male cat, having both testicles descended.

Feline: Of a cat or the cat family.

Foreign: Certain varieties of shorthaired cats.

Frill or ruff: The fur around the head that is brushed up to form a frame for the face.

Fur ball: Fur that may be swallowed by a cat when cleaning itself and may form a felt-like mass in the stomach.

Genotype: The constitution of an animal in terms of its genes; see Feline Genetics, page 15.

Grand Champion: In Britain, a Champion cat winning three grand challenge certificates at three shows under three judges. In the United States, a Champion cat that has been awarded the equivalent of seven Grand Ribbons by accumulating points in Best Champion competition; see CFA Show Rules (page 252).

Grand Premier: The equivalent of a Grand Champion for a neutered or spayed cat.

Haw: A transparent third eyelid at the inner side or lower lid of the eye, which keeps the eye clean and moist; also called the nictitating membrane.

Hot: Term used to describe the incorrect reddish tinge sometimes seen on the back of cream cats.

Interbreed: The mating of two closely related cats such as mother and son, or brother and sister.

Intermingled: Fur of two colours mingled together, as required in the Blue-Creams.

Kink: A malformation or thickening of a joint in the tail.

Kitten: A cat up to the age of nine months in Britain or eight months in the United States.

Locket: A white, or contrasting colour, patch under the neck.

Longhairs: A term used in Britain and other countries for all cats with long fur.

Mask: The dark colouring on the face seen on the face of some cats, such as the Siamese, Colourpoints and Himalayans.

Monorchid: A male cat with only one testicle descended.

Muzzle: The projecting jaws and nose of the cat.

Neuter: A castrated male cat or kitten.

Oriental: The name of some specific shorthaired varieties; also the shape of some cats' eyes, for example, the Siamese.

Patched: Fur that has patches of different colouring, as in the Tortoiseshell and Whites.

Pedigree: Having at least three generations of pure breeding.

Pencillings: The delicate, pencil-like markings on the faces of Tabbies.

Persians: A breed of cats with long fur, referred to as Longhairs in Britain.

Phenotype: The appearance of an animal; see Feline Genetics, page 15.

Points: The darker colouring on the head, paws and tail, as seen in the Siamese and other varieties; also the marks given in the set standards.

Prefix: Registered name of a cattery used before the name of all kittens and cats bred there.

Premier: A neuter or spayed cat that is equivalent to a male or female champion, having won its title in the same way.

Queen: A female cat used for breeding.

Rumpy: A completely tailless Manx cat.

Self: The same colour fur all over.

Spaying: The neutering of a female cat or kitten.

Spraying: A male cat's habit of micturating anywhere, probably to establish his territory.

Snub: The short noses seen in some of the longhaired varieties.

Squint: Cross-eyed, with the eyes so placed that they seem to look permanently at the nose.

Standard: The characteristics required for each variety, for which one hundred points are given.

Stumpy: A Manx having a stump of a tail, instead of being completely tailless.

Ticking: One, two or three bands of contrasting colour on each hair of the fur, as in the Abyssinian.

Type: The structural appearance of the cat.

Tufts: Hair growing from the ears or between toes.

Wedge: Head shape seen in some foreign varieties.

Whip: A long, thin tapering tail, as seen in the Siamese.

Whiskers: The long bristles protruding from the cat's face.

Shorthair Cats

There are millions and millions of domestic cats throughout the world, all more or less the same size, but having multifarious coat colours, patterns and personalities. Some have long fur, some have neither particularly long nor short coats, but by far the majority have short fur. Of those shorthaired cats, some have fine, silky and close-lying fur, and others have short but dense fur.

The Egyptians are usually given the credit for having the first domestic cats; the early Phoenician travellers are thought to have been instrumental in introducing them to many parts of the world, and the Romans for bringing this much valued creature to Britain. The cats featured by the Egyptians in their wall murals, statuettes, amulets, scarabs and those found in tombs mummified are obviously shortcoated. It is assumed that those taken to Britain by the Romans were also shortcoated but, as only bones have been found in the burned-out ruins of Roman villas in Britain, this cannot be proved. The wild cat that was known then, not only in Scotland as now, but also in England and Wales, was hunted for its fur, but the rare domestic cat was much prized. In AD 948 Prince Howel the Good compiled laws for its protection. A kitten before its eyes were open cost one penny, and after it was older and had caught a mouse it was worth two pence, a great deal of money in those days. Anyone who dared to steal or to go so far as to kill a cat that guarded the Prince's own granary

was fined a lamb or even a sheep, or the amount of wheat that would cover the dead animal when it was suspended by the tail with its nose just touching the floor.

Documentation about the progress of the early domestic cats is practically non-existent, but it is certain that over the centuries their numbers increased throughout the civilized world, and they were much appreciated for their prowess in keeping down rats and mice.

The Middle Ages saw the start of a very unhappy time for the cats, with superstition and Black Magic playing their parts in transforming the admiration for, even the adoration of, these animals into dread and hate. Cats now were looked on as familiars of the devil, companions of witches, and even witches themselves. Shorthaired black cats particularly were feared, as people thought these cats were able to change their form at will. It is known that Louis IVth of France presided at the then annual inhumane practice of burning cats alive on the day of the Feast of St John. He apparently opened the festivities by dancing around the bonfire, carrying a bunch of roses.

Gradually, superstitions like these died, and the true worth of the cat became appreciated once again. It was realized that they served a useful purpose in keeping down vermin and they did make ideal companions. It was in Victorian times that they really came into their own, with the first Official Cat Show held in 1871 at the Crystal Palace. For the first time it was appreciated that domestic cats could be produced in different breeds and varieties and pedigrees could be built up. As both Queen Victoria and Queen Alexandra were animal lovers, many members of society became interested in possessing and breeding pedigree cats. In fact, to own a pedigree cat was almost a status symbol.

At the first shows almost all the entries had short fur, and included Tortoiseshells, Tortoiseshell and Whites, a few Siamese (although these were black-pointed rather than brown, according to early judges), some Manx and Self-coloured Blues. There were a few with long fur too. Gradually, the resident domestic cats almost disappeared from the shows, as the cats from the East (referred to as Eastern cats) with long fur became more popular. The longhairs themselves were later overtaken in popularity by the Siamese. The British Shorthairs are only now enjoying a renewed popularity, with the British Blue in particular being in much demand. The Tabbies, Torties, and Tortie and Whites are perhaps the oldest, being produced from the original domestic cats frequently found in farmyards long ago. The pure Whites, the Blacks, the Blue-Creams, and the Creams are still comparatively rare, but many of them have outstanding type.

The first Blue Shorthairs were said to have come from Archangel in Russia, and were referred to as Archangel cats, and then as Foreign Blues. For a time the classes were very mixed up, with the resident British Blues and the Foreign Blues all being shown in the same class regardless of type and characteristics. Indeed, some were neither one breed nor the other. Gradually, the breeders realized that there should be two definite varieties, and after the end of the Second World War, the name 'Russian' was adopted officially in Britain for the shorthaired blue cats with foreign type, and the British Shorthairs were referred to as British Blue, as before.

Nowadays the foreign varieties, such as the Siamese and Abyssinians, have very little to do with the country after which they are named. The story of the origin of these and other varieties is strangely similar, however, with the tale of such and such a cat or cats having been brought from a particular country, having been given as a rare gift to some person of note. There may be a grain of truth in these travellers' tales, as undoubtedly any cat of striking and different appearance may well have been presented as a special gift to a reigning prince or High Priest, and it would then have been bred from and made much of, and even been specially protected.

Whatever their true origins, it should be appreciated that it has taken years of patient and careful selective breeding to produce to perfection the breeds and varieties recognized today.

SIAMESE

Seal–Point Siamese kitten

The origin of the Siamese cat is lost in antiquity. Some experts believe that it developed over the ages from the Temple Cat of Burma while others trace its development from the Sacred Cat of Ancient Egypt, a theory that finds support in the close resemblance that the typical specimen bears to statues of Bast (also known as Bubastis and Pasht), the Cat Goddess. Whichever of these theories is correct, there is no doubt that this cat flourished in Siam more than two hundred years before its introduction to England. In Siam ownership of this beautiful cat was restricted to members of the royal family. It is said that it took several years of careful negotiation conducted through diplomatic channels by General Walker with the King of Siam for Miss Walker, the general's daughter, to receive permission to take one male and two female cats to England. Soon after, Lady Dorothy Nevill succeeded in bring out several others. The cats were first shown to the general

Blue-Point Siamese

Seal-Point Siamese

Lilac-Point Siamese

Lilac Tabby-Point Siamese

Tabby-Point Siamese

public at the Crystal Palace exhibition in 1886, and although initially very delicate, they soon became acclimatized and began to thrive.

At its best, the Siamese is a svelte, medium-sized and beautifully balanced animal in which, due to the operation of a recessive gene, colour is limited to certain well-defined areas referred to as the 'points': the mask, ears, tail, lower legs and paws. The coat colour in the original Seal-Point varieties is cream, shading to a light, warm fawn on the back, where it is connected to the dark ears by a light but well-defined tracing. In the best show specimens the light body colour and the uniformly dark points should be in strong contrast.

Originally only known in the Seal-Point variety, in the course of the last fifty years Siamese having other points colours appeared and became popular. Some of these, like the Blue-Point and possibly the Chocolate-Point and Lilac-Point, were natural mutations or dilutions. Others, including the Red-Point, the Tabby-Point, the Cream Point and the Tortie-Point, were artificially derived by cross-breeding with cats of the desired colour and by refining and establishing the new varieties by a process of selective and line breeding.

The Siamese cat is the supreme extrovert of the feline world. It is very active, enormously 'talkative', hugely affectionate if it likes you and utterly independent when it chooses to be so. In feline terms, it is hugely affectionate if it likes you and utterly inde-warm and temperate climates.

Most of the early Siamese brought into Britain possessed squints (when both eyes seem to look at the nose permanently) and kinked, or bent, tails. Originally, it was thought that these characteristics were natural and desirable. Although some people still consider them to be rather charming, they are looked upon as being serious faults when seen in the show cat.

Soon after being established in Britain Siamese cats were exported to the United States and very soon became extremely popular. Although the American standard for Siamese is rather different from the British and European standard, the essential appearance of the variety is the same everywhere. The standard of the Cat Fanciers' Association requires the cat's skull to be flat in profile instead of slightly rounded as in the British standard. It also favours a longer head; the ratio of head length to head width in many American champions is greater than in the best British specimens. This configuration looks very attractive providing that the long nose and muzzle are matched by a proportionately long lower jaw. For this reason the standard calls

Seal-Point Siamese

Seal-Point Siamese

for the chin to line up with the tip of the nose in the same vertical plane. When the lower jaw is not sufficiently long the head may look very striking when seen from above, but gives the impression of a weak chin when seen in profile. It may also lead to an unevenness of bite, a fault which can interfere with the ability of the mother cat to bite cleanly through the umbilical cord after giving birth to a litter.

Unless the concept of a very long head is interpreted with understanding it can result in the breeding of Siamese with a somewhat snipy appearance; and this is amplified by calling for a flat instead of a slightly rounded forehead when seen in profile. Such a forehead possesses certain advantages viewed as an engineering structure, the slight curve acting as an arch to support the longer head.

American breeders have maintained in their darker-pointed lines a most attractive contrast in colour with the body coat. This may be due in part to the ambient temperature; a warm temperature favours the growth of a lighter-coloured coat. It is also due to selective breeding to cats with light bodies when they are fully mature, as contrast is a quality that can be passed on.

The Cat Fanciers' Association standard is more explicit than the British standard in its list of faults. For example, it treats spotted or off-colour nose leathers and paw pads as faults and condemns a soft or mushy body. These characteristics are not explicitly given as faults in the British standard, although every judge regards them in that light when they detract from the overall beauty of a cat.

The CFA standard for Siamese includes only the classic colours: Seal, Chocolate, Blue and Lilac. The British standard includes both the classic colours, which are given the breed number 24, and many of the new colours, such as Cream, Red and Tabby, which are given the breed number 32 and which the American governing bodies classify as Colourpoint Shorthairs (see page 52). The American practice seems more logical than the British. By allocating two breed numbers the Governing Council of the Cat Fancy implies that it has some reservations in calling the new varieties Siamese. Nonetheless, the cats are recognized as Siamese and are allowed to breed with the latter without penalty and without any distinction being applied to the progeny arising from such matings where they conform to standard Siamese colouring.

In nature, character and type the Siamese and the Colourpoint Shorthairs are identical. In Europe, where the British standards are generally accepted, both varieties are known as Siamese.

OFFICIAL STANDARD

Cat Fanciers' Association, Inc.

SIAMESE

POINT SCORE

Head (20)	
Long flat profile	6
Wedge, fine muzzle, size	5
Ears	4
Chin	3
Width between eyes	2
Eyes (10)	
Shape, size, slant and placement	10
Body (30)	
Structure and size, including neck	12
Muscle tone	10
Legs and feet	5
Tail	3
Coat (10)	10
Color (30)	
Body color	10
Point color—matching points of dense color, proper foot pads and nose leather	10
Eye color	10

General

The ideal Siamese is a svelte, dainty cat with long, tapering lines, very lithe but muscular.

Head

Long tapering wedge. Medium size in good proportion to body. The total wedge starts at the nose and flares out in straight lines to the tips of the ears forming a triangle, with no break at the whiskers. No less than the width of an eye between the eyes. When the whiskers are smoothed back, the underlying bone structure is apparent. Allowance must be made for jowls in the stud cat.

Skull

Flat. In profile, a long straight line is seen from the top of the head to the tip of the nose. No bulge over eyes. No dip in nose.

Ears

Strikingly large, pointed, wide at base, continuing the lines of the wedge.

Eyes

Almond shaped. Medium size. Neither protruding nor recessed. Slanted towards the nose in harmony with lines of wedge and ears. Uncrossed.

Nose

Long and straight. A continuation of the forehead with no break.

Muzzle

Fine, wedge-shaped.

Chin and jaw

Medium size. Tip of chin lines up with tip of nose in the same vertical plane. Neither receding nor excessively massive.

Body

Medium size. Dainty, long, and svelte. A distinctive combination of fine bones and firm muscles. Shoulders and hips continue same sleek lines of tubular body. Hips never wider than shoulders. Abdomen tight.

Neck

Long and slender.

Legs

Long and slim. Hind legs higher than front. In good proportion to body.

Paws

Dainty, small, and oval. Toes, five in front and four behind.

Tail

Long, thin, tapering to a fine point.

Coat

Short, fine textured, glossy. Lying close to body.

Condition

Excellent physical condition. Eyes clear. Muscular, strong and lithe. Neither flabby nor boney. Not fat.

Ideal Siamese type showing points

CFA OFFICIAL STANDARD continued –

Color

Body: Even, with subtle shading when allowed. Allowance should be made for darker color in older cats as Siamese generally darken with age, but there must be definite contrast between body color and points. *Points:* Mask, ears, legs, feet, tail dense and clearly defined. All of the same shade. Mask covers entire face including whisker pads and is connected to ears by tracings. Mask should not extend over the top of the head. No ticking or white hairs in points.

Mask covers entire face

Penalize

Improper (i.e., off-color or spotted) nose leather or paw pads. Soft or mushy body.

Squint, or crossed eyes

Disqualify

Any evidence of illness or poor health. Weak hind legs. Mouth breathing due to nasal obstruction or to poor occlusion. Emaciation. Visible kink. Eyes other than blue. White toes and/or feet. Incorrect number of toes. Malocclusion resulting in either undershot or overshot chin.

SIAMESE COLORS

SEAL POINT

Body even pale fawn to cream, warm in tone, shading gradually into lighter color on the stomach and chest. Points deep seal brown.

Nose leather
Same color as points.

Paw pads
Same color as points.

Eye color
Deep vivid blue.

CHOCOLATE POINT

Body ivory with no shading. Points milk-chocolate color, warm in tone.

Nose leather
Cinnamon-pink.

Paw pads
Cinnamon-pink.

Eye color
Deep vivid blue.

BLUE POINT

Body bluish white, cold in tone, shading gradually to white on stomach and chest. Points deep blue.

Nose leather
Slate colored.

Paw pads
Slate colored.

Eye color
Deep vivid blue.

LILAC POINT

Body glacial white with no shading. Points frosty gray with pinkish tone.

Nose leather
Lavender-pink.

Paw pads
Lavender-pink.

Eye color
Deep vivid blue.

OFFICIAL STANDARD
Governing Council of the Cat Fancy

SEAL-POINTED: VARIETY 24

Shape (body and tail)
Medium in size, body long and svelte, legs proportionately slim, hind legs slightly higher than the front ones, feet small and oval, tail long and tapering and free from any kink. A visible kink shall disqualify.

The body, legs, feet, head and tail all in proportion, giving the whole a well-balanced appearance.

Head: long, narrowing to a fine muzzle

Head and ears
Head long and well proportioned, with width between the eyes, narrowing in perfectly straight lines to a fine muzzle, with straight profile, strong chin and level bite. Ears rather large and pricked, wide at the base.

Eyes
Clear, brilliant deep blue. Shape oriental and slanting towards the nose. No tendency to squint.

Body colour
Cream, shading gradually into pale warm fawn on the back. Kittens paler in colour.

Points
Mask, ears, legs, feet and tail dense and clearly defined seal brown. Mask complete and (except in kittens) connected by tracing with the ears.

Coat
Very short and fine in texture, glossy and close-lying.

Definition of squint
When the eyes are so placed that they appear to look permanently at the nose.

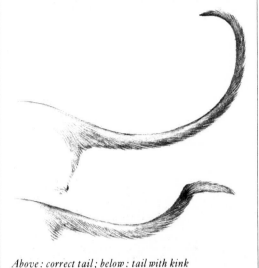

Above: correct tail; below: tail with kink

Notes
The Siamese cat should be a beautifully balanced animal with head, ears and neck carried on a long svelte body, supported on fine legs and feet with a tail in proportion. The head and profile should be wedge shaped, neither round nor pointed. The mask complete, connected by tracings with the ears (except in kittens), the eyes a deep blue, green tinge to be considered a fault. Expression alert and intelligent.

White toes or toe automatically disqualify an exhibit. It is important to note that the Standard with regard to type is the same for all Siamese cats.

SCALE OF POINTS

Type and shape	
Head	15
Ears	5
Eyes	5
Body	15
Legs and paws	5
Tail	5
Total	50

Colour	
Eyes	15
Points	10
Body colour	10
Texture of coat	10
Condition	5
Total	50

OFFICIAL STANDARD
Governing Council of the Cat Fancy

BLUE-POINTED: VARIETY 24a

The standard is the same as for Seal-Pointed with the following exceptions:

Colour
Points blue; the ears, mask, legs, paws and tail to be the same colour. The ears should not be darker than the other points.

Eyes
Clear, bright, vivid blue.

Body colour
Glacial white, shading gradually into blue on back, the same cold tone as the points, but of a lighter shade.

Blue-Point Siamese

The late Kathleen R. Williams, formerly secretary of the Siamese Cat Club in Britain, recorded that a Mr Speakman exhibited a Blue-Point Siamese in the 1890s, but that the judge refused to recognize it as being a true Siamese. In the present century Major and Mrs Rendall were responsible for developing this colour to perfection in Britain. The cats bred by them possessed perfect points colour and extremely light coats. Unfortunately, in many of them the heads were too round by modern standards. This defect has largely been overcome by breeding them with Siamese of other colours. Some breeders believe that there is a genetic relationship between the ideal colour contrast and purity and the slightly rounder head shape, but this has not been rigidly demonstrated. Today Blue-Points are of the same quality as the Seal-Points, and both varieties may appear in the same litter.

OFFICIAL STANDARD
Governing Council of the Cat Fancy

CHOCOLATE-POINTED: VARIETY 24b

The standard is the same as for Seal-Pointed with the following exceptions:

Colour
Points milk chocolate: the ears, mask, legs, paws and tail to be the same colour, the ears should not be darker than the other points.

Eyes
Clear, bright, vivid blue.

Body colour
Ivory colour all over. Shading, if at all, to be colour of points.

Chocolate-Point Siamese queen with kittens

Chocolate-Point Siamese

The Chocolate-Point Siamese was known in England in 1900, and there was a good deal of debate as to whether it was a new variety or only a bad form of the Seal-Point. The matter was resolved when it was shown genetically that the new colour represented a true mutation in the dominant B gene present in the Seal-Point Siamese.

In Britain Chocolate-Points are allowed to have some shading in the same colour as the points. In the United States the Chocolate-Points do not have any shading and the points stand out sharply against the much lighter coat.

OFFICIAL STANDARD
Governing Council of the Cat Fancy

LILAC-POINTED: VARIETY 24c

The standard is the same as for Seal-Pointed with the following exceptions:

Eyes
Clear, light vivid blue (but not pale).

Body colour
Off white (Magnolia) shading, if any, to tone with points.

Points
Pinkish grey, nose-leather and pads faded lilac.

Lilac-Point Siamese

Lilac represents the response of the eye to the presence of chocolate and blue in the correct proportions. The Lilac-Point Siamese is free from dominant colour genes and manifests simultaneously the recessive genes for both the blue and the chocolate dilutions. It is difficult to breed a good lilac shade of coat; in many cases the nose appears blue while the tail appears chocolate. For the points to appear uniformly lilac the two components must be present in the correct proportions. This cannot be achieved by selective breeding, which merely results in the occasional production of a fine specimen. To fix the two colours in the right proportion to display a uniform lilac-points colour it is necessary to line breed.

OFFICIAL STANDARD
Governing Council of the Cat Fancy

TABBY-POINTED: VARIETY 32

Type and shape
As for Seal-Pointed Siamese.

Colour
General body colour: pale coat, preferably free from body markings including back of head and neck and conforming to recognized Siamese standard for the particular colour of points.

General points colour: same colour essential, but varied tones of same colour acceptable, i.e. Seal, Blue, Chocolate, Lilac, Red and Cream. The standard for Tortie/Tabby Points is given below.

Ears: solid, no stripes. Thumb marks as clear as possible.

Nose leather: conforming to recognized Siamese standard for the particular colour of points, or pink.

Mask: clearly defined stripes, especially around the eyes and nose. Distinct markings on cheeks, darkly spotted whisker pads.

Eyes: brilliant clear blue. The lids to be dark rimmed or toning with the points.

Legs: clearly defined varied sized broken stripes. Solid markings on back of hind legs.

Tail: many varied sized clearly defined rings ending in a solid tip.

Coat
Very short and fine in texture. Glossy and close lying.

TORTIE/TABBY POINTS

As above, with the following exceptions:

Ears
Mottled.

Nose leather and pads
Mottled.

Tail
As above, but mottling permissible.

Points
Patched with red and/or cream over tabby pattern. Distribution of patching on points immaterial (as in Standard for Tortie Points).

Note
These cats usually resemble Tabby Points rather than Tortie Points.

SCALE OF POINTS

Type and shape (as for Seal-Pointed Siamese)	50
Colour and condition	
Ringed tail	10
Eyes	10
Body colour	15
Points and thumb marks	10
Texture of coat and general condition	5
Total	100

RED-POINTED: VARIETY 32a

Type
As for Seal-Pointed Siamese.

Colour
Restricted to points.

Body
White, shading (if any) to apricot on the back. Kittens paler.

Nose leather
Pink.

Ears
Bright reddish-gold.

Mask
Bright reddish gold.

Legs and feet
Bright reddish-gold or apricot.

Tail
Bright reddish-gold.

Eyes
Bright vivid blue.

Note
Barring or striping on mask, legs and tail is not to be deemed a fault.

GCCF OFFICIAL STANDARD continued –

TORTIE-POINTED: VARIETY 32b

Type
As for Seal-Pointed Siamese.

Colour
Restricted to points as in all Siamese: basic colour seal, blue, chocolate or lilac, as in Breeds 24, 24a, 24b, 24c.

Body
As in equivalent solid colour Siamese.

Nose leather
As in equivalent solid colour Siamese (see note).

Mask
Seal, blue, chocolate or lilac as in Breed 24, 24a, 24c; patched or mingled with red and/or cream.

Ears
Basic colour as in mask, patched or mingled with red and/or cream, which must be clearly visible.

Legs and feet
Basic colour as in mask, patched or mingled red and/or cream.

Tail
Basic colour as in mask, patched or mingled with red and/or cream.

Eyes
Blue, as in equivalent solid colour Siamese.

Coat
Very short and fine in texture, glossy and close lying.

Note
Distribution of patching on points colour and leathers of all tortie point Siamese is random and immaterial. Barring and ticking shall be deemed a fault.

PROVISIONAL STANDARD
Governing Council of the Cat Fancy

CREAM-POINTED: VARIETY 32c

Type
As for Seal-Pointed Siamese.

Colour
Restricted to points as in all Siamese.

Body
White, shading (if any) to palest cream.

Nose leather
Pink.

Mask
Cream, with tracings to ears, except in kittens.

Ears, legs and feet
Cream.

Tail
Cream.

Eyes
Bright vivid blue.

Coat
Very fine and short in texture, glossy and close lying.

Modification
Barring and striping on mask, legs and tail, is **not** to be deemed a serious fault.

Note
A hot cream is not desirable.

SCALE OF POINTS

Type and colour	50
Body	10
Nose leather, mask, ears, legs and feet, tail	10
Eyes	15
Coat	10
Condition	5
Total	100

Tortie-Point Siamese

COLOURPOINT SHORTHAIR

Seal Lynx-Point

Colourpoint Shorthairs were produced by mating Siamese cats with cats of other varieties, such as the Abyssinian and the shorthair tabby, to achieve new colours and patterns that would be restricted to the points. The F2 generation of cats from the original crosses was mated back to Siamese repeatedly, and for several years since the resulting cats have been mated exclusively to Siamese. A line in which all the offspring have been mated back to Siamese for as few as ten successive generations will carry only 0.1 per cent of the non-Siamese gene inheritance. This figure is too small to be mathematically significant when one considers random errors in pedigrees and apparently 'pure' Siamese genotype structures. Nonetheless, because the new colours and patterns are known to have been 'manufactured' in this way rather than having occurred as the result of a natural mutation, they are given a separate variety name by the American governing bodies, but only a separate variety number within the Siamese category by the British (see page 42).

In general, Colourpoint Shorthairs conform to a very high grade of Siamese phenotype. There are, however, two respects in which they sometimes fail to come up to the highest standard. First, Red-Points and Cream-Points tend to show little colour on the front paws and only a little more colour on the back ones, and, second, Seal Tabby-Points, or Lynx-Points, tend to exhibit areas of markings where the seal colour has a habit of appearing as chocolate. This duality of colour on the cat can be unattractive. It is due in part, or possibly entirely, to the phenomenon known as epistasis, where a particular gene is either wholly masked or modified by the presence of another. The Siamese colour restriction gene acts in this way to lighten the colours due to other genes. For this reason the Chocolate and Blue Tabby-Points, which are already dilute in colour, tend to exhibit a more monochromatic appearance.

OFFICIAL STANDARD
Cat Fanciers' Association, Inc.

COLORPOINT SHORTHAIR

POINT SCORE

Head (20)	
Long flat profile	6
Wedge, fine muzzle, size	5
Ears	4
Chin	3
Width between eyes	2
Eyes (10)	
Shape, size, slant and placement	10
Body (30)	
Structure and size, including neck	12
Muscle tone	10
Legs and feet	5
Tail	3
Coat (10)	10
Color (30)	
Body color	10
Point color—matching points of dense color, proper foot pads and nose leather	10
Eye color	10

General

A Colorpoint Shorthair is a separate breed. The type description and scale of points is the same as for the Siamese. A svelte, dainty cat with long tapering lines, very lithe, but muscular. Excellent physical condition. Eyes clear. Strong and lithe. Neither flabby nor bony. Not fat.

Head

Long tapering wedge. Medium size in good proportion to body. The total wedge starts at the nose and flares out in straight lines to the tips of the ears forming a triangle, with no break at the whiskers. No less than the width of an eye between the eyes. When the whiskers are smoothed back, the underlying bone structure is apparent. Allowance must be made for jowls in the stud cat.

Skull

Flat. In profile, a long straight line is seen from the top of the head to the tip of the nose. No bulge over eyes. No dip in nose.

Neck

Long and slender.

Nose

Long and straight. A continuation of the forehead with no break.

Muzzle

Fine, wedge-shaped.

Ears

Strikingly large, pointed, wide at base, continuing the lines of the wedge.

Eyes

Almond shaped. Medium size. Neither protruding nor recessed. Slanted towards the nose in harmony with lines of wedge and ears. Uncrossed.

Chin and jaw

Medium in size. Tip of chin lines up with tip of nose in the same vertical plane. Neither receding nor excessively massive.

Body

Medium size. Dainty, long, and svelte. A distinctive combination of fine bones and firm muscles. Shoulders and hips continue same sleek lines of tubular body. Hips never wider than shoulders. Abdomen tight.

Legs

Long and slim. Hind legs higher than front. In good proportion to body.

Paws

Dainty, small, and oval. Toes, five in front and four behind.

Tail

Long, thin, tapering to a fine point.

Coat

Short, fine textured, glossy. Lying close to body.

Color

Body: Even, with subtle shading when allowed. Allowance should be made for darker color in older cats as Colorpoint Shorthairs generally darken with age, but there must be definite contrast between body color and points. *Points:* Mask, ears, feet, legs, and tail, dense and clearly defined. All of the same shade. Mask covers entire face including whisker pads and is connected to ears by tracings. Mask should not extend over the top of the head. No ticking or white hairs in points.

Penalize

Lack of pigment in nose leather in part or in total.

Disqualify

Any evidence of illness or poor health. Weak hind legs. Mouth breathing due to nasal obstruction or poor occlusion. Emaciation. Visible kink. Eyes other than blue. White toes and/or feet. Incorrect number of toes.

CFA OFFICIAL STANDARD continued –

COLORPOINT SHORTHAIR COLORS

RED POINT
Body clear white with any shading in the same tone as points.

Points
Deep red, lack of barring desirable.

Nose leather
Flesh or coral pink.

Paw pads
Flesh or coral pink.

Eye color
Deep vivid blue.

CREAM POINT
Body clear white with any shading in the same tone as points.

Points
Apricot, lack of barring desirable.

Nose leather
Flesh to coral pink.

Paw pads
Flesh to coral pink.

Eye color
Deep vivid blue.

SEAL LYNX POINT
Body cream or pale fawn, shading to lighter color on stomach and chest. Body shading may take form of ghost striping.

Points
Seal brown bars, distinct and separated by lighter background color; ears seal brown with paler thumbprint in center.

Nose leather
Seal brown or pink edged in seal brown.

Paw pads
Seal brown.

Eye color
Deep vivid blue.

Red-Point

Red-Point

Chocolate Lynx-Point

Red Lynx-Point

CHOCOLATE-LYNX POINT
Body ivory. Body shading may take form of ghost striping.

Points
Warm milk-chocolate bars, distinct and separated by lighter background color; ears warm milk-chocolate with paler thumbprint in center.

Nose leather
Cinnamon or pink edged in cinnamon.

Paw pads
Cinnamon.

Eye color
Deep vivid blue.

BLUE-LYNX POINT
Body bluish white to platinum grey, cold in tone, shading to lighter color on stomach and chest. Body shading may take form of ghost striping.

Points
Deep blue-gray bars, distinct and separated by lighter background color; ears deep blue-gray with paler thumbprints in center.

Nose leather
Slate colored or pink edged in slate.

Paw pads
Slate colored.

Eye color
Deep vivid blue.

LILAC-LYNX POINT
Body glacial white. Body shading may take form of ghost striping.

Points
Frosty gray with pinkish tone bars, distinct and separated by lighter background color; ears frosty gray with pinkish tone, paler thumbprint in center.

Nose leather
Lavender-pink or pink edged in lavender-pink.

Paw pads
Lavender-pink.

Eye color
Deep vivid blue.

RED-LYNX POINT
Body white. Body shading may take form of ghost striping.

Points
Deep red bars, distinct and separated by lighter background color; ears deep red, paler thumbprint in center.

Nose leather
Flesh or coral pink.

Paw pads
Flesh or coral pink.

Eye color
Deep vivid blue.

SEAL-TORTIE POINT
Body pale fawn to cream, shading to lighter color on stomach and chest. Body color is mottled with cream in older cats.

Points
Seal brown, uniformly mottled with red and cream; a blaze is desirable.

Nose leather
Seal brown to match point color; flesh or coral pink mottling permitted where there is a blaze.

Paw pads
Seal brown to match point color; flesh or coral pink mottling permitted where the point color mottling extends into the paw pads.

Eye color
Deep vivid blue.

CHOCOLATE-CREAM POINT
Body ivory, mottled in older cats.

Points
Warm milk-chocolate uniformly mottled with cream; a blaze is desirable.

Nose leather
Cinnamon; flesh or coral pink mottling permitted where there is a blaze.

Paw pads
Cinnamon; flesh or coral pink mottling permitted where the point color mottling extends into the paw pads.

Eye color
Deep vivid blue.

BLUE-CREAM POINT
Body bluish white to platinum gray, cold in tone, shading to lighter color on stomach and chest. Body color is mottled in older cats.

Points
Deep blue-gray uniformly mottled with cream; a blaze is desirable.

Nose leather
Slate colored; flesh or coral pink mottling permitted where there is a blaze.

Paw pads
Slate colored; flesh or coral pink mottling permitted where the print color mottling extends into the paw pads.

Eye color
Deep vivid blue.

LILAC-CREAM POINT
Body glacial white, mottling if any in the shade of the points.

Points
Frosty gray with pinkish tone, uniformly mottled with pale cream; a blaze is desirable.

Nose leather
Lavender-pink; flesh or coral pink mottling permitted where there is a blaze.

Paw pads
Lavender-pink; flesh or coral pink mottling permitted where the point color mottling extends into the paw pads.

Eye color
Deep vivid blue.

Lilac-Point

ABYSSINIAN

Usual or Ruddy Abyssinian

In the opinion of many zoologists, and judging from mural paintings, the Abyssinian cat resembles the Sacred Cat of Egypt; and there is no doubt that cats very similar to the modern Abyssinian in general configuration and markings existed in many parts of Asia. Dr Gordon Staples writing in 1882 tells how a Mrs Barrett Lennard brought such a cat back with her from Abyssinia at the end of the Abyssinian War.

In contrast, Harrison Weir, himself a naturalist of some standing, rejected the view that the Abyssinian cat had a definite place of origin and insisted that the variety was created as a result of experimental work done on tabby breeding lines. The truth is probably that several native varieties occurred naturally in many parts of Asia and Eastern Europe and were obtained by selective breeding aimed at achieving an idealized type, which was then fixed by a process of line breeding.

Since the Second World War a good deal of experimental work has been carried out on this variety and has produced several distinct colours other than the usual rich, golden brown. The Red Abyssinian is now recognized by the governing bodies in Europe and America. In Britain a provisional standard has been granted for a blue variety, and a silver and a sorrel Abyssinian have been produced, but have not yet received recognition. The Cat Fanciers' Association of America recognizes only the Ruddy and the Red Abyssinian. The American and British standards are fairly similar, but differ in that the British prefers the ears comparatively large and tufted while the American makes no mention of tufts.

Ideally, the Abyssinian should be completely free from white markings of any kind. In practice, all the cats possess white markings on the lower jaw and usually on the throat. In many specimens the white extends in a more diffuse form down the chest, and even appears on the stomach of poor specimens. In this respect the Red Abyssinian is usually less contaminated with white than its normal, or Ruddy, counterpart. The presence of a necklace, usually of dark-tipped, but sometimes light-coloured, hairs, appears to be almost unavoidable in the normal Abyssinian and frequent in the Red. The standards regard an unbroken necklace as a serious fault.

The cat that started many of the American lines of Abyssinian was a female bought by Dr Ward Price in 1931 or 1932 from Mrs E. Menezes, a well-known British breeder. Another Abyssinian bred by Mrs Menezes was sent to Canada in the 1940s to a Mrs Burnford (whose Siamese made the 'incredible journey' in the book of that name). While on holiday in Miami, the Abyssinian, Rasamba by name, was stolen from Mrs Burnford, and nationwide press and television coverage failed to achieve her return. There are now a great many Abyssinians of very high quality in America.

Very fine specimens of Abyssinians abound in Europe, particularly in Holland; and one seen in Finland possessed hardly any white at all and had not a

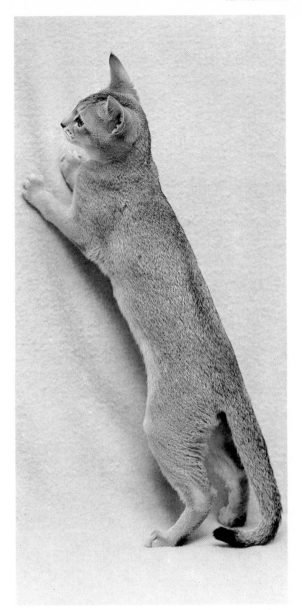

Red Abyssinian

trace of a necklet. Other tabby markings, such as bars and stripes on the legs, have been much more easy to lose and are rarely seen.

There has been a decline in the quality of Abyssinian cats in Britain in recent years. This is particularly sad when one considers that the Abyssinian cat was one of the first to be recognized in England, in 1882, and that until the early 1960s some of the world's finest specimens were regularly to be seen on the British show bench. Breeding has been affected by the fact that Abyssinians are small breeders and produce more males than females. They have also been shown to be particularly susceptible to feline leukaemia virus and less resistant to other viral infections than before.

OFFICIAL STANDARD
Cat Fanciers' Association, Inc.

ABYSSINIAN

POINT SCORE

Head (25)

Muzzle	6
Skull	6
Ears	7
Eye shape	6

Body (30)

Torso	15
Legs and feet	10
Tail	5

Coat (10)

Texture	10

Color (35)

Color	15
Ticking	15
Eye color	5

General
The overall impression of the ideal Abyssinian would be a colorful cat of medium size giving the impression of eager activity and showing a lively interest in all surroundings. Lithe, hard and muscular. Sound health and general vigor. Well balanced temperamentally and physically; gentle and amenable to handling.

Head
A modified, slightly rounded wedge without flat planes; the brow, cheek and profile lines all showing a gentle contour. A slight rise from the bridge of the nose to the forehead, which should be of good size with width between the ears and flowing into the arched neck without a break.

Muzzle
Not sharply pointed. Allowance to be made for jowls in adult males.

Ears
Alert, large, and moderately pointed; broad, and cupped at base and set as though listening. Hair on ears very short and close-lying, preferably tipped with black or dark brown on a ruddy Abyssinian or chocolate brown on a red Abyssinian.

Eyes
Almond-shaped, large, brilliant and expressive. Neither round nor Oriental. Eyes accentuated by dark lidskin, encircled by light-colored area.

Body
Medium long, lithe and graceful, but showing well-developed muscular strength without coarseness. Abyssinian conformation strikes a medium between the extremes of the cobby and the svelte lengthy type. Proportion and general balance more to be desired than mere size.

Legs
Proportionately slim, fine boned.

Paws
Small, oval and compact. When standing, giving the impression of being on tip-toe. Toes, five in front and four behind.

Tail
Thick at base, fairly long and tapering.

Coat
Soft, silky, fine in texture, but dense and resilient to the touch with a lustrous sheen. Medium in length but long enough to accommodate two or three bands of ticking.

Penalize
Off-color pads. Long narrow head. Short round head. Barring on legs. Rings on tail. Coldness or gray tones in coat.

Disqualify
White locket, or white anywhere other than nostril, chin, and upper throat area. Kinked or abnormal tail. Dark unbroken necklace. Gray-black hair with no ruddy undercoat. Any black hair on red Abyssinian. Incorrect number of toes.

Head: modified, slightly rounded wedge

ABYSSINIAN COLORS

RUDDY

Coat ruddy brown, ticked with various shades of darker brown or black; the extreme outer tip to be the darkest, with orange-brown undercoat, ruddy to the skin. Darker shading along spine allowed if fully ticked. Tail tipped with black and without rings. The undersides and forelegs (inside) to be a tint to harmonize with the main color. Preference given to **unmarked** orange-brown (burnt-sienna) color.

Nose leather
Tile red.

Paw pads
Black or brown, with black between toes and extending slightly beyond the paws.

Eye color
Gold or green, the more richness and depth of color the better.

RED

Warm, glowing red, distinctly ticked with chocolate-brown. Deeper shades of red preferred. However, good ticking not to be sacrified merely for depth of color. Ears and tail tipped with chocolate-brown.

Nose leather
Rosy pink.

Paw pads
Pink, with chocolate-brown between toes, extending slightly beyond paws.

Eye color
Gold or green, the more richness and depth of color the better.

Abyssinian

OFFICIAL STANDARD
Governing Council of the Cat Fancy

ABYSSINIAN: VARIETIES 23, 23a and 23b

Type
Foreign type of medium build, firm, lithe and muscular, never large or coarse. The head to be broad and tapering to a firm wedge set on an elegant neck. The body to be of medium length with fairly long tapering tail. A 'cobby' cat is not permissible.

Head and ears
Head is a moderate wedge of medium proportions, the brow, cheeks and profile lines showing a gentle contour and the muzzle not sharply pointed. A shallow indentation forming the muzzle is desirable but a pinch is a fault. Ears set wide apart and pricked, broad at base, comparatively large, well cupped and preferably tufted. In profile the head shows a gentle rounding to the brow with a slight nose-break leading to a very firm chin.

Eyes
Well apart, large, bright and expressive in an oriental setting. A squint is a fault. Colour, amber, hazel or green. A light eye colour is undesirable.

Tail
Broad at base, fairly long and tapering. Neither a whip nor a kink is permissible.

Feet
Small and oval.

Coat
Short, fine and close lying with double, or preferably, treble ticking, i.e. two or three bands of colour on each hair.

Markings
It is required that the appropriate darker hair colour extends well up the back of the hind legs; also showing as a solid tip at the extreme end of the tail, and the absence of either is a fault. A line of dark pigmentation is required round the eyes and absence of this is also a fault.

Undesirable markings are bars on the legs, chest and tail. An unbroken necklet is not permissible. The Abyssinian cat has a tendency to white in the immediate area of the lips and lower jaw and it is a fault if this white area extends on to the neck. A locket and other white markings are not permissible.

Abyssinian

Usual or Ruddy Abyssinian

GCCF OFFICIAL STANDARD continued –

COLOURS

USUAL: VARIETY 23

The body colour to be a rich golden brown, ticked with black and the base hair ruddy-orange or rich apricot. A pale or cold colour is a fault.

The belly and inside of legs to be a ruddy-orange or rich apricot to harmonize with the base hair on the rest of the body. Any spinal shading to be of deeper colour. The tip of the tail and the solid colour on the hind legs to be black. Nose leather to be brick red and pads to be black.

RED: VARIETY 23a

The body colour to be a lustrous copper-red, ticked with chocolate and the base hair deep apricot. A pale or sandy colour is a fault.

The belly and inside of legs to be a deep apricot to harmonize with the base hair on the rest of the body. Any spinal shading to be of deeper colour. The tip of the tail and the solid colour on the hind legs to be chocolate. Nose leather and pads to be pink.

Abyssinian

PROVISIONAL STANDARD
Governing Council of the Cat Fancy

BLUE: VARIETY 23c

The body colour to be blue-grey with a soft warm effect, ticked with deeper steel blue and the base hair pale cream or oatmeal.

The belly and inside of legs to be pale cream or oatmeal to harmonize with the base hair on the rest of the body. Any spinal shading to be deeper colour. The tip of the tail and the solid colour on the hind legs to be steel blue. Nose leather to be dark pink and pads to be mauve/blue.

Note

Any cat displaying a **feature** which is **not permissible** (i.e. cobby type; whip tail; kink in tail; unbroken necklet; locket; other white markings) shall not be awarded a first prize, nor a challenge certificate nor a premier certificate.

Any cat displaying a **fault** may be awarded a prize but any cat displaying two or more faults shall not be awarded a challenge certificate nor a premier certificate.

SCALE OF POINTS

Colour	
Body colour	25
Ticking	20
Type	
Body shape, tail, feet, coat, carriage and general condition	30
Head and ears	15
Eyes	10
Total	100

Abyssinian kitten

BURMESE

Blue Burmese kittens

As in the case of so many varieties of domestic cat, the origins of the Burmese are open to considerable doubt. The first Burmese to reach the United States was imported from Burma by Dr Joseph Thompson and exhibited at a cat show in San Francisco in 1930. This brown female cat, called Wong Mau, was a roundish typed cat, and the one from which the American standard developed after breeding to a Siamese male and subsequent selective breeding.

There is some evidence to support the view that the Burmese cat was not an original breed, but that it was 'manufactured' by breeding together two or more varieties commonly found in India and Burma. It is likely that the Siamese was one of the varieties, for the Burmese, like the Siamese, carries a colour restriction gene. The Burmese gene is less effective as a colour restriction than the Siamese and although Burmese kittens show clearly defined points, these tend to disappear or to become greatly reduced in intensity as the kitten becomes an adult. Nevertheless, except in the darkest of the Brown Burmese, the points remain more or less in evidence.

The Burmese was formally recognized by the Cat Fanciers' Association of America in 1936. After the war, Sydney and Lillian France imported the first specimens into Britain. Shortly afterwards, Mr V. Watson, the well-known judge and breeder, imported Champion Laos Chili Wat, an outstanding American female, and Cas Gatos de Foong, a fine male, who did much to start this breed in Britain.

Brown Burmese

The Governing Council of the Cat Fancy in Britain recognized the variety in 1952. Other fine specimens were imported, including Champion Cas Gatos Darkee, a useful outcross who helped to maintain vigour in the breed, and Champion Darsham Kudiram, who introduced an entirely new strain. Darkee was later mated with his daughter, Champion Chinki Golden Gay, who belonged to Lillian France. The resultant litter included the first British Blue Burmese.

The cat fancy in America recognizes only the Brown Burmese, which should not have any points colouring, but in Britain championship status has been granted also to Red, Cream, Blue, Lilac and Chocolate varieties as well as the Brown Tortie, Blue Tortie, Chocolate Tortie and Lilac Tortie. Blue Burmese often appear on the show bench with very dark blue fur tinged with brown, but this is a serious fault.

The two governing bodies also tend to see Burmese type in a different light, the American Burmese having a rounder head and slightly cobbier body than its British counterpart.

The Burmese cat is generally recognized as being one of the most difficult to judge; and what is known among judges and breeders as the 'Burmese look' is extremely subtle. Many judges of Burmese have confessed that when they first started to judge them they would become quite disheartened by seeing a class of perhaps twenty kittens, all looking as alike as peas in a pod, staring at them with curiosity from their pens. Some of the difficulty experienced by judges arises from the fact that the Burmese is a brown cat in which the entire gradation in depth of colour is allowed. In addition, the type of the Burmese is in no sense extreme, like that of the Siamese and Siamese-related

Brown Burmese

Brown Tortoiseshell Burmese kitten

Chocolate-Tortie Burmese

varieties, and so it takes a long time for the judge's eye and heart to develop the inner vision that is necessary to see into the very nature of an animal's being. Only when this coordination of eye and mind has been achieved does the true beauty of this variety become poignantly evident and only then may one call oneself a judge of Burmese.

Another difficulty in judging Burmese is that the eye colour often changes when viewed in artificial light. This difficulty does not occur in many other varieties and is possibly due to a special internal characteristic of the cat's eye. On numerous occasions judges have seen Burmese cats that seem to have green eyes when viewed in the comparatively poor illumination that is the curse of most show halls. On taking the same cat to a window or to another source of white light, the green hue often disappears and is replaced by an acceptable yellow colour. Of course, this does not occur in cats having an ideal eye colour intrinsically free from green.

Cream Burmese

OFFICIAL STANDARD

Cat Fanciers' Association, Inc.

BURMESE

POINT SCORE

Head (25)

Roundness of head	7
Breadth between eyes	4
Full face with proper profile	8
Ear set and placement	6

Eyes (5)

Placement and shape	5

Body (30)

Torso	15
Muscle tone	5
Legs and feet	5
Tail	5

Coat (10)

Short	4
Texture	4
Close lying	2

Color (30)

Body color	25
Eye color	5

General

The overall impression of the ideal Burmese would be a cat of medium size and rich solid color; with substantial bone structure, good muscular development and a surprising weight for its size. This, together with its expressive eyes and sweet face, presents a totally distinctive cat which is comparable to no other breed. Perfect physical condition, with excellent muscle tone. There should be no evidence of obesity, paunchiness, weakness, or apathy.

Head

Pleasingly rounded without flat planes whether viewed from front or side. Face full, with considerable breadth between the eyes, tapering slightly to a short, well developed muzzle. In profile there should be a visible nose break.

Ears

Medium in size and set well apart on a rounded skull; alert, tilting slightly forward, broad at base with slightly rounded tips.

Eyes

Set far apart and with rounded aperture.

Body

Medium in size, muscular in development, and presenting a compact appearance. Allowance to be made for larger size in males. An ample, rounded chest, with back level from shoulder to tail.

American Burmese

CFA OFFICLA STANDARD continued –

Legs
Well proportioned to body.

Paws
Round. Toes, five in front and four behind.

Tail
Straight, medium in length.

Coat
Fine, glossy, satin-like in texture; short and close lying.

Color
The mature specimen should be rich, warm sable brown; shading almost imperceptibly to a slightly lighter hue on the underparts, but otherwise without shadings or markings of any kind.

Nose leather
Brown.

Paw pads
Brown.

Eye color
Ranging from yellow to gold, the greater the depth and brilliance the better.

Penalize
Green eyes.

Disqualify
Kinked or abnormal tail. Locket or button. Incorrect number of toes. Blue eyes.

Chocolate Burmese

OFFICIAL STANDARD
Governing Council of the Cat Fancy

BURMESE: VARIETIES 27–27j

The Burmese is an elegant cat of a foreign type, which is positive and quite individual to the breed. Any suggestion of either Siamese type or the cobbiness of a British cat must be regarded as a fault.

Body, legs and tail
The body should be of medium length and size, feeling hard and muscular, and heavier than its appearance indicates. The chest should be strong, and rounded in profile, the back straight from the shoulder to rump. Legs should be slender and in proportion to the body: hind legs slightly longer than front: paws neat and oval in shape. The tail should be straight and of medium length, not heavy at base, and tapering only slightly to a rounded tip without bone defect. A visible kink or other bone defect in the tail is a fault, precluding the award of a challenge certificate, but an invisible defect at the extreme tip may be overlooked in an otherwise excellent specimen.

Head, ears and eyeset
The head should be slightly rounded on top, with good breadth between the ears, having wide cheek bones and tapering to a short blunt wedge. The jaw should be wide at the hinge and the chin firm. A muzzle pinch is a bad fault. Ears should be medium in size, set well apart on the skull, broad at the base, with slightly rounded tips, the outer line of the ears continuing the shape of the upper part of the face. This may not be possible in mature males who develop a fullness of cheek. In profile the ears should be seen to have a slight forward tilt. There should be a distinct nose break, and in profile the chin should show a strong lower jaw. The eyes, which must be set well apart, should be large and lustrous, the top line of the eye showing a straight oriental slant towards the nose, the lower line being rounded. Either round or oriental eyes are a fault.

Eye colour
Eyes should be any shade of yellow from chartreuse to amber, with golden yellow preferred. Green eyes are a serious fault in Brown Burmese, but Blue Burmese may show a slight fading of colour. Green eyes with more blue than yellow pigmentation must preclude the award of a challenge certificate in Burmese of all colours.

Coat
The coat should be short, fine, satin-like in texture lying close to the body. The glossy coat is a distinctive feature of Burmese, and is indicative of good health.

*Above left: American Burmese body type;
lower right: British Burmese body type*

Lilac Burmese

Brown Tortoiseshell Burmese kitten

Brown Burmese and kitten

GCCF OFFICIAL STANDARD continued –

Condition

Cats should be well-muscled, with good weight for size: lively and alert.

COLOURS

General considerations

In all colours the underparts will be lighter than the back. In kittens and adolescents, allowances should be made for faint tabby barring and, overall, a lighter colour than adults. The presence of a few white hairs may be overlooked in an otherwise excellent cat, but a noticeable number of white hairs, or a white patch, is a serious fault, precluding the award of a challenge certificate.

BROWN: VARIETY 27

In maturity the adult should be a rich, warm, seal brown, shading almost imperceptibly to a slightly lighter shade on the underparts; apart from this and slightly darker ears and mask, there should be no shading or marking of any kind. Very dark colour, bordering on black, is incorrect.

Nose leather
Rich brown.

Foot pads
Brown.

BLUE: VARIETY 27a

In maturity the adult should be a soft silver grey only very slightly darker on the back and tail. There should be a distinct silver sheen on rounded areas such as ears, face and feet.

Nose leather
Very dark grey.

Foot pads
Grey.

CHOCOLATE: VARIETY 2

In maturity the overall colour should be a warm milk chocolate. Ears and mask may be slightly darker, but legs tail and lower jaw should be the same colour as the back. Evenness of colour overall very desirable.

Nose leather
Warm chocolate brown.

Foot pads
Brick pink shading to chocolate.

LILAC: VARIETY 27c

In maturity the coat colour should be a pale, delicate dove-grey, with a slightly pinkish cast giving a rather faded effect. Ears and mask may be slightly deeper in colour.

Nose leather
Lavender pink.

Foot pads
Shell pink in kittens, becoming lavender pink in adults.

RED: VARIETY 27d

In maturity the coat colour should be light tangerine. Slight tabby markings may be found on the face, and small indeterminate markings elsewhere (except on sides and belly) are permissible in an otherwise excellent cat. Ears should be distinctly darker than the back.

Nose leather and foot pads
Pink.

Head: slightly rounded, with wide-set ears

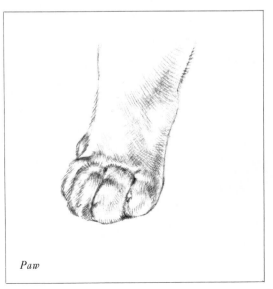

Paw

Lilac Burmese

PROVISIONAL STANDARD

Governing Council of the Cat Fancy

BROWN TORTIE: VARIETY 27e
(Normal Tortie)

The coat should be a mixture of brown and red without any obvious barring. The colour and markings are not so important as the Burmese type, which should be excellent.

Nose leather and foot pads
Plain or blotched, brown and pink.

OFFICIAL STANDARD

Governing Council of the Cat Fancy

CREAM: VARIETY 27f

In maturity, the coat colour should be rich cream. Slight tabby markings may be found on the face, and small indeterminate markings elsewhere (except on the sides and belly) are permissible in an otherwise excellent cat. Ears should be only slightly darker than the back coat colour.

Nose leather and foot pads
Pink.

PROVISIONAL STANDARD

Governing Council of the Cat Fancy

BLUE TORTIE: VARIETY 27g (Blue Cream)

The coat should be a mixture of blue and cream without any obvious barring. Colour and markings are not so important as the Burmese type, which should be excellent.

Nose leather and foot pads
Plain or blotched, blue and pink.

Blue Burmese

PROVISIONAL STANDARD
Governing Council of the Cat Fancy

CHOCOLATE TORTIE: VARIETY 27h

The coat should be a mixture of chocolate and red without any obvious barring. The colour and markings are not so important as the Burmese type, which should be excellent.

Nose leather and foot pads
Plain or blotched, chocolate and pink.

LILAC TORTIE: VARIETY 27j (Lilac Cream)

The coat should be a mixture of lilac and cream without any obvious barring. The colour and markings are not so important as the Burmese type, which should be excellent.

Nose leather and foot pads
Plain or blotched, lilac and pink.

Note

In the case of the four tortie colours 27e, 27g, 27h and 27j, the coat may display two shades of its basic colours and **may thus appear to display three or even four colours.** The colours may be mingled or blotched: blazes, solid legs or tails are all permissible: therefore additional marks are awarded for type, which is of far greater importance than coat colour and markings.

SCALE OF POINTS

	General	All Torties
Body shape, legs, tail, feet	30	35
Body colour, coat texture and condition	25	20
Head and ears	20	20
Shape and set of eyes	15	15
Colour of eyes	10	10
Total	100	100

Chocolate Burmese queen and kittens

RUSSIAN BLUE

Russian Blue

Russian Blue

The Russian Blue cat was well-known in Britain in the late nineteenth century. It was said to have originated in the neighbourhood of Archangel in northwest Russia and to have been brought over by merchant sailors from ships trading with England. Very similar cats may be found in the colder regions of the Soviet Union today.

Russian Blues were shown extensively at the Crystal Palace shows in the 1850s. These differed considerably from British cats in that they had longer heads and were, even then, more of what is now called 'foreign' type. The standards set for these cats in the early days were very similar to those used today, except that the eye colour was given then as deep orange.

During the Second World War Russian Blues would probably have disappeared from the British scene had it not been for the devoted work of Mrs Rochford, who kept two or three breeding cats throughout the war period. The orange eye colour was maintained in the standards well into the present century and was then

changed to green. After the war, several breeders worked hard to regenerate the variety, using Mrs Rochford's remaining stock augmented, very much to the detriment of the breed, by the use of British Blues and Blue-Point Siamese. A white variety of the cat has been produced but it never became popular and is very rarely seen today.

The preservation of the Russian Blue in Britain was undertaken by the Short-Hair Cat Society, which still maintains an overall responsibility for the variety. There is also a small specialist club devoted to it.

The Russian Blue cat recognized in Britain in addition to possessing a double blue coat having a silvery sheen like its American counterpart, is marked by two essential characteristics: a pair of pronounced whisker pads and the ears set rather close together and held high up on the head. The standard of the Cat Fanciers' Association of America for the Russian Blue makes no mention of the pronounced whisker pad characteristic and does not emphasize the ears high up on the head.

OFFICIAL STANDARD
Cat Fanciers' Association, Inc.

RUSSIAN BLUE

POINT SCORE

Head and neck	20
Body type	20
Eye shape	5
Ears	5
Coat	20
Color	20
Eye color	10

General
The good show specimen has good physical condition, is firm in muscle tone, and alert.

Head
Top of skull flat and long. The face is broad across the eyes due to wide eye-set and thick fur.

Head: eyes set wide apart

Ears
Rather large and wide at the base. Tips more pointed than rounded. The skin of the ears is thin and translucent, with very little inside furnishing. The outside of the ear is scantily covered with short, very fine hair, with leather showing through. Set far apart, as much on side as on the top of the head.

Eyes
Set wide apart. Aperture rounded in shape.

Neck
Long and slender, but appearing short due to thick fur and high placement of shoulder blades.

Nose
Medium in length.

Chin
Under-chin is level.

Body
Fine boned, long, firm and muscular, lithe and graceful in outline and carriage.

Legs
Long and fine-boned.

Paws
Small, slightly rounded. Toes, five in front and four behind.

Tail
Long, but in proportion to the body. Tapering from a moderately thick base.

Coat
Short, dense, fine and plush. Double coat stands out from body due to density. It has a distinct soft and silky feel.

Color
Even bright blue throughout. Lighter shades of blue preferred. Guard hairs silver-tipped giving the cat a silvery sheen or lustrous appearance. A definite contrast should be noted between ground color and tipping. Free from tabby markings.

Nose leather
Slate gray.

Paw pads
Lavender-pink or mauve.

Eye color
Vivid green.

Disqualify
Kinked or abnormal tail. Locket or button. Incorrect number of toes.

OFFICIAL STANDARD
Governing Council of the Cat Fancy

RUSSIAN BLUE: VARIETY 16a

Colour
Clear blue and even throughout. In maturity free from tabby markings or shading. Medium blue is preferred.

Nose leather and pads
Blue.

Coat
Short, thick and very fine, standing up soft and silky like seal skin. Very different from any other breed. Coat is double so that it has a distinct silvery sheen. The texture and appearance of the coat is the truest criterion of the Russian Blue.

Body
Long and graceful in outline and carriage. Medium strong bone.

Tail
Fairly long and tapering.

Legs and feet
Long legs. Feet small and oval.

Head
Short wedge with flat skull; forehead and nose straight forming an angle. Prominent whisker pads. Strong chin.

Eyes
Vivid green, set rather wide apart, almond in shape.

Ears
Large pointed, wide at base and set vertically to the head. Skin of ears thin and transparent, with little inside hair.

Faults
White or tabby markings. Cobby or heavy build. Square head. Yellow or blue in eyes. Siamese type is undesirable.

Withhold certificates
White anywhere. Incorrect eye colour. Siamese type.

SCALE OF POINTS

Colour	20
Coat and condition	25
Body and tail	25
Eyes	15
Head and ears	15
Total	100

Russian Blue

Russian Blue

HAVANA BROWN

British Havana

This extremely handsome, brown 'foreign' type was developed from the Siamese by Baroness von Ulman in the early 1950s. It has the type and some of the temperament of the Siamese, but does not carry the Siamese colour restriction genes and is not quite so noisy. The type is ideally Siamese and the cat is characterized by having pink foot-pads and the green, oriental eye common to nearly all the Siamese-type shorthairs. The kittens are the same colour at birth as at full maturity. They show no shading on any part of their bodies, although sometimes in the summer the old, moulting coats may look rusty. The true Havana has a

Havana kittens

wistful and gentle face, which expert judges of the variety refer to as the 'Havana look'. This gentle and beautiful cat has steadily gained in popularity since its recognition.

Originally recognized in Britain as the Chestnut Brown Foreign, this cat is now known internationally as the Havana. Havana is an appropriate name, for its coat has the colour and matt appearance of a Havana cigar; and although the colour appears to be matt, the coat is close-lying and glossy. The type of this cat differs slightly in America and Britain, as can be seen by comparing the two standards. The American Havana, for example, has a shorter wedge than the British cat and the fur is medium in length. The British Havana has Siamese type and a very short glossy coat. The Oriental Self Brown recognized by the Cat Fanciers' Association is more or less identical to the British Havana.

British Havana adult

OFFICIAL STANDARD
Cat Fanciers' Association, Inc.

HAVANA BROWN

POINT SCORE

Head	20
Coat	10
Color (40)	
Coat color, paw pads, nose leather	25
Eyes	10
Whiskers	5
Body and neck	15
Eyes	5
Legs and feet	5
Tail	5

General
The overall impression of the ideal Havana Brown is a cat of medium size with a rich, solid color and good muscle tone. Due to its distinctive muzzle shape, color and large forward-tilted ears, it is comparable to no other breed.

Head
The head is slightly longer than it is wide, with a distinct stop at the eyes. The break at the whisker pad is about the same width overall. A strong chin forms a straight line with the nose. Allowance will be made for stud jowls in the male.

Coat
The coat is medium in length, smooth, and lustrous.

Body and neck
Body and neck are medium in length, firm and muscular. The general conformation is mid-range between the short-coupled, thick-set and svelte breeds.

Eyes
Oval shaped.

Ears
Ears are large, wide set, round tipped, slightly tilted forward, not flaring, giving an alert appearance. They have little hair inside or out.

Legs and feet
Medium in length, ending in oval paw pads.

Tail
Medium to medium long, tapering.

Color
Rich warm, mahogany toned brown. Solid to the roots; free from tabby markings or barring in the adult.

Nose leather
Brown with a rosy cast.

Paw pads
Having a rosy tone.

Eyes
Ranging from chartreuse to green, with the greener shades preferred.

Whiskers
Brown, complementing the coat.

Disqualify
Kinked tail, locket or button, incorrect eye color, whisker, nose leather or paw pad color.

Left: American head type; right: British head type

OFFICIAL STANDARD
Governing Council of the Cat Fancy

HAVANA: VARIETY 29

Havana Foreign shorthaired, cats are of the Siamese type. Fine in bone, lithe and sinuous and of graceful proportions. The coat is a rich brown in colour, even and sound. Whiskers and nose leather to be the same colour as coat. The pads of the feet are a pinkish shade of brown. The eyes are green.

Coat
Rich chestnut brown, very short and fine in texture, glossy and close lying, even and sound throughout.

Head and ears
Head long and well proportioned, narrowing in straight lines to a fine muzzle. Ears large and well pricked, wide at base with a good width between. Strong chin.

Body, legs and tail
Medium size body, long and lithe, well muscled, graceful in outline. Slim and dainty legs with small oval paws, hind legs slightly longer than front legs. Long whipped tail. No kink.

Eyes
Oriental in shape and setting. Green in colour. No squint.

Faults
Tabby or other markings. White spots or hairs. Any tendency to British type. Yellow or copper eye colour. Kinked tail. (Allowances should be made for kittens showing 'ghost' tabby markings which should not be held against an otherwise good kitten).

Withhold certificates
Incorrect eye colour.

SCALE OF POINTS

Head	15
Ears	5
Body	15
Legs and paws	5
Tail	5
Eyes	20
Coat	20
Texture of coat	10
Condition	5
Total	100

American Havana Brown

British Havana kitten

British Havana adult

FOREIGN AND ORIENTAL SHORTHAIR

Foreign Lilac

Generally, the term 'foreign' is used in Britain to refer to all shorthaired varieties other than the British Shorthairs. These cats differ in type from the British Shorthairs, having long, slim bodies, wedge-shaped heads and long, tapering tails. In Britain, therefore, Russian Blues, Abyssinians, Burmese, Havanas, Cornish Rex, Devon Rex, Korats, Oriental Spotted are referred to collectively as Foreign. In addition, certain varieties that have foreign type and are self-coloured – that is,

they are the same colour all over – have been recognized with 'Foreign' as part of their official variety name: Foreign Black, Foreign White, Foreign Lilac.

In North America, however, these cats are divided into specific categories, such as Colourpoint Shorthairs, Exotic Shorthairs and Oriental Shorthairs. In Britain the title 'Oriental' is used only for cats with foreign type that have a patterned coat, such as the Oriental Spotted Tabby (see page 100).

OFFICIAL STANDARD
Governing Council of the Cat Fancy

FOREIGN LILAC: VARIETY 29c

The same standard and scale of points applies to the Foreign Lilac, except for coat colour. Coat colour should be a frosty-grey with a distinct pinkish tone. Nose leather and pads should be pinkish. Coat colour too blue or fawn is a fault. Otherwise the same faults apply to the Foreign Lilac as to the Havana.

FOREIGN WHITE: VARIETY 35

The body of the Foreign White cat should be lightly built, long and lissom and the cat should have a well proportioned and graceful appearance. The overall type should be similar to that of Siamese cats. The head should be long and wedge-shaped in profile, and the face should narrow in straight lines to a fine muzzle. The eyes should be clear, brilliant blue and oriental in set; the ears wide at base, large and pricked. The coat should be completely white, and the paw and nose leather pink. Coloured hairs and spotting on paw and nose leather shall be disqualifying faults.

Coat
Pure white, short, silky, even and close-lying.

Head
Face narrowing in straight lines to a fine muzzle, in profile wedge-shaped with a strong chin; even teeth and bite; head set well on a graceful neck.

Ears
Large and pricked with a good width between.

Eyes
Almond-shaped and slanting, clear brilliant blue.

Body
Long and slender, the rump carried higher than the shoulders. Well muscled and elegant.

Legs
Long and proportionately slender; paws neat and oval.

Tail
Long and tapering, whiplike, without kink.

SCALE OF POINTS

Coat		
	Texture	10
	Colour	5
Head		20
Eyes		
	Shape	10
	Colour	10
Body		15
Legs and paws		10
Tail		10
Condition		10
	Total	100

Foreign White kittens

Foreign White

PROVISIONAL STANDARD
Governing Council of the Cat Fancy

FOREIGN BLACK: VARIETY 37

Shape
Body and tail
Medium in size, body long and svelte, legs proportionately slim, hind legs slightly higher than the front ones, feet small and oval, tail long and tapering and free from any kink. A visible kink shall disqualify. The body, legs, feet, head and tail all in proportion, giving the whole a well-balanced appearance.

Head and ears
Head long and well-proportioned with width between the eyes, narrowing in perfectly straight lines to a fine muzzle, with straight profile, strong chin and level bite. Ears rather large and pricked, wide at the base.

Foreign Black

Notes and definitions
Definition of a squint: when the eyes are so placed that they appear to look permanently at the nose.

The Foreign Black cat should be a beautifully balanced animal with head, ears and neck carried on a long svelte body, supported on fine legs and feet with a tail in proportion. The head and profile should be wedge shaped, neither round nor pointed. Expression alert and intelligent. Scattered white hairs and rusty or other shadings in the coat are often present during kittenhood and should not be too severely penalized in an otherwise good kitten. Scattered white hairs are undesirable in adults. White locket, white chin or white belly spots are serious faults.

Body: long and svelte

Eyes
Green. Shape oriental and slanting towards the nose. No tendency to squint.

Body colour
Jet black to the roots. No rusty tinge.

Nose leather
Black.

Paw pads
Black or brown.

Coat
Very short and fine in texture, glossy and close-lying.

SCALE OF POINTS

Type and shape		
Head		15
Ears		5
Eyes		5
Body		15
Legs and paws		5
Tail		5
	Total	50
Colour		
Eyes		5
Body colour		30
Texture of coat		10
Condition		5
	Total	50

OFFICIAL STANDARD
Cat Fanciers' Association, Inc.

ORIENTAL SHORTHAIR

POINT SCORE

Head (25)	
Long, flat profile	7
Wedge, fine muzzle, size	6
Ears	5
Chin	4
Width between eyes	3
Eyes (10)	
Shape, size, slant, and placement	10
Body (25)	
Structure and size, including neck	12
Muscle tone	5
Legs and feet	5
Tail	3
Coat (10)	10
Color (30)	
Body color, uniform density of coloring, proper foot pads, and nose leather	20
Eye color	10

General
The ideal Oriental Shorthair is a svelte cat with long, tapering lines, very lithe but muscular. Excellent physical condition. Eyes clear. Strong and lithe. Neither bony nor flabby. Not fat.

Lavender Oriental Shorthair

Head
Long tapering wedge, in good proportion to body. The total wedge starts at the nose and flares out in straight lines to the tips of the ears forming a triangle, with no break at the whiskers. No less than a width of an eye between the eyes. When the whiskers are smoothed back, the underlying bone structure is apparent. Allowance must be made for jowls in the stud cat.

Head: long, tapering wedge

Skull
Flat. In profile, a long straight line is seen from the top of the head to the tip of the nose. No bulge over eyes. No dip in nose.

Nose
Long and straight. A continuation of the forehead with no break.

Muzzle
Fine, wedge-shaped.

Chin and jaw
Medium size. Tip of chin lines up with tip of nose in the same vertical plane. Neither receding nor excessively massive.

Ears
Strikingly large, pointed, wide at the base, continuing the lines of the wedge.

Eyes
Almond shaped, medium size. Neither protruding nor recessed. Slanted towards the nose in harmony with lines of wedge and ears. Uncrossed.

Body
Long and svelte. A distinctive combination of fine bones and firm muscles. Shoulders and hips continue the same sleek lines of tubular body. Hips never wider than shoulders. Abdomen tight. Males may be somewhat larger than females.

CFA OFFICIAL STANDARD continued –

Neck
Long and slender.

Legs
Long and slim. Hind legs higher than front. In good proportion to body.

Paws
Dainty, small and oval. Toes, five in front and four behind.

Paws: dainty, small and oval

Smoke Oriental Shorthair

Tail
Long, thin at the base and tapered to a fine point.

Coat
Short, fine textured, glossy, lying close to body.

Penalize
Crossed eyes.

Disqualify
Any evidence of illness or poor health. Weak hind legs. Mouth breathing due to nasal obstruction or poor occlusion. Emaciation. Visible kink. Miniaturization. Lockets and buttons.

Eye color
Green preferred, amber permitted. In white cats, bright blue- or green-eyed preferred, amber permitted, but not odd-eyed.

ORIENTAL SHORTHAIR COLORS

SOLID COLORS CLASS

WHITE
Pure glistening white.

Nose leather and paw pads
Pink.

EBONY
Dense coal black, sound from roots to tip of fur. Free from any tinge of rust on tips or smoke undercoat.

Nose leather
Black.

Paw pads
Black or brown.

BLUE
Blue, lighter shade preferred, one level tone from nose to tip of tail. Sound to the roots. A sound darker shade is more acceptable than an unsound lighter shade.

Nose leather
Blue.

Paw pads
Blue.

CHESTNUT
Rich chestnut brown, sound throughout. Whiskers and nose leather same color as coat.

Paw pads
Cinnamon.

LAVENDER
Frost-gray with a pinkish tone, sound and even throughout.

Nose leather and paw pads
Lavender-pink.

RED
Deep, rich, clear, brilliant red; without shading, markings or ticking. Lips and chin the same color as coat.

Nose leather
Brick red.

Paw pads
Brick red.

CREAM
One level shade of buff cream, without markings. Sound to the roots. Lighter shades preferred.

Nose leather
Pink.

Paw pads
Pink.

SHADED COLORS CLASS

SILVER
Undercoat white. Coat on back, flanks, head and tail sufficiently tipped with black to give the characteristic sparkling silver appearance. Face and legs may be shaded with tipping. Rims of eyes, lips and nose outlined with black.

Nose leather
Brick red.

Paw pads
Black.

CAMEO
Undercoat white, the coat on the back, flanks, head and tail to be sufficiently tipped with red to give the characteristic sparkling appearance. Face and legs may be shaded with tipping.

Nose leather and paw pads
Rose.

SMOKE COLORS CLASS

EBONY SMOKE
White undercoat, deeply tipped with black. Cat in repose appears black. In motion the white undercoat is clearly apparent.

Points and mask
Black with narrow band of white at base of hairs next to skin which may be seen only when the fur is parted.

Nose leather
Black.

Paw pads
Black.

BLUE SMOKE
White undercoat, deeply tipped with blue. Cat in repose appears blue. In motion the white undercoat is clearly apparent.

Points and mask
Blue with narrow band of white at base of hairs next to skin which may be seen only when fur is parted.

Nose leather
Blue.

Paw pads
Blue.

CHESTNUT SMOKE
White undercoat, deeply tipped with chestnut brown. Cat in repose appears chestnut brown. In motion the white undercoat is clearly apparent.

Points and mask
Chestnut brown, with narrow band of white at base of hairs next to skin which may be seen only when fur is parted.

Nose leather
Chestnut.

Paw pads
Cinnamon.

LAVENDER SMOKE
White undercoat, deeply tipped with lavender. Cat in repose appears lavender. In motion the white undercoat is clearly apparent.

Points and mask
Lavender with narrow band of white at base of hairs next to skin which may be seen only when fur is parted.

Nose leather and paw pads
Lavender pink.

CAMEO SMOKE (Red Smoke)
White undercoat, deeply tipped with red. Cat in repose appears red. In motion the white undercoat is clearly apparent.

Points and mask
Red with narrow band of white at base of hairs next to skin, which may be seen only when fur is parted.

Nose leather and paw pads
Rose.

Rims of eyes
Rose.

Ebony Oriental Shorthair

CFA OFFICIAL STANDARD continued –

TABBY COLORS CLASS

CLASSIC TABBY PATTERN

Markings dense, clearly defined and broad. Legs evenly barred with bracelets coming up to meet the body markings. Tail evenly ringed. Several unbroken necklaces on neck and upper chest, the more the better. Frown marks on forehead form intricate letter "M". Unbroken line runs back from outer corner of eye. Swirls on cheeks. Vertical lines over back of head extend to shoulder markings which are in the shape of a butterfly with both upper and lower wings distinctly outlined and marked with dots inside outline. Back markings consist of a vertical line down the spine from butterfly to tail with a vertical stripe paralleling it on each side, the three stripes well separated by stripes of the ground color. Large solid blotch on each side to be encircled by one or more unbroken rings. Side markings should be the same on both sides. Double vertical row of buttons on chest and stomach.

MACKEREL TABBY PATTERN

Markings dense, clearly defined, and all narrow pencillings. Legs evenly barred with narrow bracelets coming up to meet the body markings. Tail barred. Necklaces on neck and chest distinct, like so many chains. Head barred with an "M" on the forehead. Unbroken lines running back from the eyes. Lines running down the head to meet the shoulders. Spine lines run together to form a narrow saddle. Narrow pencillings run around body.

SPOTTED TABBY PATTERN

Markings on the body to be spotted. May vary in size and shape with preference given to round evenly distributed spots. Spots should not run together in a broken Mackerel pattern. A dorsal stripe runs the length of the body to the tip of the tail. The stripe is ideally composed of spots. The markings of the face and forehead shall be typically tabby markings, underside of the body to have 'vest buttons". Legs and tail are barred.

TICKED TABBY PATTERN

Body hairs to be ticked with various shades of marking color and ground color. Body when viewed from top to be free from noticeable spots, stripes, or blotches, except for darker dorsal shading. Lighter underside may show tabby markings. Face, legs, and tail must show distinct tabby striping. Cat must have at least one distinct necklace.

EBONY TABBY

Ground color brilliant coppery brown. Markings dense black. Lips and chin the same shade as the rings round the eyes. Back of leg black from paw to heel.

Nose leather
Black, or brick red rimmed with black.

Paw pads
Black or brown.

BLUE TABBY

Ground color, including lips and chin, pale bluish ivory. Markings a very deep blue affording a good contrast with ground color. Warm fawn overtones or patina over the whole.

Nose leather
Blue, or old rose rimmed with blue.

Paw pads
Rose.

CHESTNUT TABBY

Ground color is warm fawn, markings are bright chestnut.

Nose leather
Chestnut, or pink rimmed with chestnut.

Paw pads
Cinnamon.

LAVENDER TABBY

Ground colour is pale lavender. Markings are rich lavender affording a good contrast with the ground color.

Nose leather
Lavender, or pink rimmed with lavender.

Paw pads
Lavender-pink.

RED TABBY

Ground color red. Markings deep, rich red. Lips and chin red.

Nose leather
Brick red.

Paw pads
Brick red.

CREAM TABBY

Ground color, including lips and chin, very pale cream Markings of buff or cream sufficiently darker than the ground color to afford good contrast, but remaining within the dilute color range.

Nose leather
Pink.

Paw pads
Pink.

SILVER TABBY

Ground color, including lips and chin, pale, clear silver. Markings dense black.

Nose leather
Black, or brick red rimmed with black.

Paw pads
Black.

CFA OFFICIAL STANDARD continued –

CAMEO TABBY
Ground color off-white. Markings red.

Nose leather
Rose.

Paw pads
Rose.

PARTI-COLORS COLOR CLASS

TORTOISESHELL
Black with unbrindled patches of red and cream. Patches clearly defined and well broken on both body and extremities. Blaze of red or cream on face is desirable.

BLUE-CREAM
Blue with patches of solid cream. Patches clearly defined and well broken on both the body and extremities.

CHESTNUT-TORTIE
Chestnut brown with unbrindled patches of red and cream. Patches clearly defined and well broken on both body and extremities. Blaze of red or cream on face is desirable.

LAVENDER-CREAM
Lavender with patches of solid cream. Patches clearly defined and well-broken on both the body and extremities.

A pair of Tortoiseshell Oriental Shorthairs

EGYPTIAN MAU

Egyptian Mau kittens

The first Mau, a natural breed, were introduced into the United States in 1957 by Princess Troubetskoy. In the first place she had brought them from Egypt to Italy. They are said to have typical Egyptian type, and are not so foreign in appearance as the Siamese. The heads are slightly rounded, with moderately-pointed large ears; the almond-shaped eyes are gooseberry green. Their muscular bodies are medium in length, and the tails are of medium length also. Too oriental a body or a whip-like tail would be penalized by a judge. The silky, fine fur is of medium length, showing at least two bands of ticking. The coat is a transition between spots and stripes, appearing not only in the fur, but also showing in the skin pigmentation. The pattern is complex, and is given in full in the American standard. One broken necklace, at least, under the chin is a must.

Quiet, friendly cats, they love the attention they attract at the shows.

They are recognized by the Cat Fanciers' Association of America in three colours: Silver, which has a light silver ground colour, with charcoal markings; Bronze, which has a honey-coloured background, with dark brown markings; and Smoke, which has a luminous black ground colour, a light undercoat, and charcoal spots.

OFFICIAL STANDARD
Cat Fanciers' Association, Inc.

EGYPTIAN MAU

POINT SCORE

Head (20)	
Muzzle	5
Skull	5
Ears	5
Eye shape	5
Body (25)	
Torso	10
Legs and feet	10
Tail	5
Coat (10)	
Texture and length	10
Pattern	25
Color (20)	
Eye color	5
Coat color	15

General

The Egyptian Mau is the only natural domesticated breed of spotted cat. The Mau conformation strikes a balance between the heftiness of the cobby and sveltness of the Oriental types. Its overall impression should be one of an active, colorful cat of medium size, with well developed muscles. Perfect physical condition with an alert appearance. Well balanced physically and temperamentally.

Head

A modified, slightly rounded wedge without flat planes; the brow, cheek and profile all showing a gentle contour. A slight rise from the bridge of the nose to the forehead, which then flows into the arched neck without a break. Allowance to be made for broad heads in adult males.

Muzzle

Not pointed. Allowance to be made for jowls in adult males.

Ears

Alert, large, and moderately pointed; broad at base and upstanding, with ample width between ears. Hair on ears short and close lying. Inner ear a delicate, almost transparent, shell pink, and may be tufted.

Eyes

Large and alert, almond shaped, with slight slant towards the ears. Skull apertures neither round nor Oriental.

Body

Medium long and graceful, showing well developed muscular strength. General balance is more to be desired than size alone. Allowance to be made for very muscular necks and shoulders in adult males.

Legs and feet

In proportion to body. Hind legs proportionately longer, giving the appearance of being on tip-toe when standing upright. Feet small and dainty slightly oval, almost round in shape. Toes: five in front and four behind.

Tail

Medium long, thick at base, with slight taper.

Coat

Silky and fine in texture but dense and resilient to the touch with a lustrous sheen. Hair medium in length but long enough to accommodate two or more bands of ticking, separated by lighter bands.

Penalize

Short or round head. Pointed muzzle. Small ears. Small, round or Oriental eyes. Cobby or Oriental body. Short or whip tail. Spots on body which run together. Poor condition.

Disqualify

Lack of spots. Wrong eye color.

MAU PATTERN
(Common to all colors)

Pattern

Good contrast between pale ground color and deeper markings. Forehead barred with characteristic "M" and frown marks, forming lines between the ears which continue down the back of the neck, ideally breaking into elongated spots, along the spine. As the spinal lines reach

Head: modified, slightly rounded wedge

the rear haunches they meld together to form a dorsal stripe which continues along the top of the tail to its tip. The tail is heavily banded and has a dark tip. The cheeks are barred with "mascara" lines; the first starts at the outer corner of the eye and continues along the contour of the cheek, with a second line, which starts at the center of the cheek and curves upwards, almost meeting below the base of the ear. On the upper chest there are one or more necklaces, preferably broken in the center. The shoulder markings are a transition between stripes and spots. The upper front legs are heavily barred but do not necessarily match. Markings on the body are to be randomly spotted with variance in size and shape; round, evenly distributed spots are preferred. Spotting pattern on each side of the body may not match, but spots should not run together in a broken, mackerel pattern. Haunches and upper hind legs to be a transition of spots and stripes, breaking into bars on the thighs and back to elongated spots on the lower leg. Underside of body to have "Vest Button" spots; dark in color against the correspondingly pale ground color.

COLORS

(All colors compete within one color class)

Eye color
Light green. "Gooseberry green" preferred, amber cast acceptable. Allowance to be made for slow eye color development in young adults.

SILVER
Pale silver ground color across the head, shoulders, outer legs, back, and tail. Underside fades to a brilliant pale silver. All markings charcoal color, showing good contrast against lighter ground colors. Back of ears grayish-pink and tipped in black. Nose, lips and eyes outlined in black. Upper throat area, chin and around nostrils pale clear silver, appearing white.

Nose leather
Brick red.

Paw pads
Black, with black between the toes and extending beyond the paws of the hind legs.

BRONZE
Light bronze ground color across head, shoulders, outer legs, back and tail, being darkest on the saddle and lightening to a tawny-buff on the sides. Underside fades to a creamy ivory. All markings dark brown, showing good contrast against the lighter ground color. Back of ears tawny-pink and tipped in dark brown. Nose, lips, and eyes outlined in dark brown, with bridge of nose ocherous. Upper throat area, chin, and around nostrils pale creamy white.

Nose leather
Brick red.

Paw pads
Black or dark brown, with same color between toes and extending beyond the paws of the hind legs.

SMOKE
Charcoal gray color with silver undercoat across head, shoulders, legs, tail and underside. All markings jet black, with sufficient contrast against ground color for pattern to be plainly visible. Nose, lips, and eyes outlined in jet black. Upper throat area, chin, and around nostrils lightest in color.

Nose leather
Black.

Paw pads
Black with black between the toes and extending beyond the paws of the hind legs.

ORIENTAL SPOTTED TABBY

Brown Oriental Spotted Tabby

In Britain the cats once referred to as Egyptian Mau, although not quite the same as those in America, have now been named Oriental Spotted Tabbies. Their history is very different from the Mau, as they are not a naturally occurring variety but have been produced by crossbreeding. Their type and shape is definitely Siamese; the bodies and the tails long. The markings are most distinctive: the heads have a clear scarab marking, and the spots are quite clear; the tail should be ringed. The following colours are now recognized: Brown, which has black spotting on a sable brown ground colour; Blue, which has blue spotting on a beige ground colour; Chocolate, which has chocolate brown spotting on a bronze ground colour; Lilac, which has lilac spotting on a beige colour; Red, which has rich red spotting on an apricot ground colour; and Cream, which has rich cream spotting on paler cream ground colour. The eye colour should be green, except in the cases of the Red and Cream, in which all shades of copper to green are allowed.

It is also possible to breed Oriental Tabbies with similar colourings, but with the classical or mackerel tabby pattern of markings. All the Oriental Tabbies are real personalities, usually very friendly, but most demanding, loving attention, refusing to be ignored, and certainly most decorative.

PROVISIONAL STANDARD
Governing Council of the Cat Fancy

ORIENTAL SPOTTED TABBY: VARIETY 38

Shape
Body and tail
Medium in size, body long and svelte, legs proportionately slim, hind legs slightly higher than the front ones, feet small and oval, tail long and tapering, and free from any kink. A visible kink shall disqualify. The body, legs, feet, head and tail all in proportion, giving the whole a well balanced appearance.

Head and ears
Head long and well proportioned with width between the eyes, narrowing in perfectly straight lines to a fine muzzle, with straight profile, strong chin and level bite. Ears rather large and pricked, wide at base.

Eyes
Shape oriental and slanting towards the nose. No tendency to squint.

Colour and pattern
On the head there should be a clear scarab marking. There should be unbroken lines running back from the outer corners of the eyes and there should be pencillings on the cheeks. Thumbprints on the ears are desirable. Good clear spotting is essential on the body. Legs should be barred and/or spotted. A broken spine line is desirable. The tail should be ringed.
Brown: dense black spotting on a sable brown agouti ground. Nose leather black or pink rimmed with black. Paw pads black or brown. Eye rims black. Eye colour green.
Blue: blue spotting on a beige agouti ground. Nose leather blue or pink rimmed with blue. Paw pads and eye rims blue. Eye colour green.
Chocolate: rich chocolate brown spotting on a bronze agouti ground. Nose leather chocolate or pink rimmed with chocolate. Eye rims chocolate. Paw pads chocolate. Eye colour green.
Lilac: lilac spotting on a beige agouti ground. Nose leather faded lilac or pink rimmed with faded lilac. Paw pads and eye rims faded lilac. Eye colour green.
Red: rich red spotting on an apricot ground. Nose leather pink or pink rimmed with red. Paw pads pink. Eye rims pink or red. Eye colour all shades of copper to green.
Cream: rich cream spotting on a paler cream ground. Nose leather pink or pink rimmed with cream. Paw pads pink. Eye rims pink or cream. Eye colour all shades of copper to green.

Coat
Very short and fine in texture, glossy and close lying.

Notes and definitions
Definition of a squint: when the eyes are so placed that they appear to look permanently at the nose.

The Oriental Spotted Tabby should be a beautifully balanced animal with head, ears and neck carried on a long svelte body, supported on fine legs and feet with a tail in proportion. The head and profile should be wedge shaped, neither round nor pointed. Expression alert and intelligent. The term 'clear spotting' defines spots that are not elongated to become broken stripes, and exhibits should not be penalized for lack of colour contrast between the spotting and ground colours. This note particularly applies to Blue, Lilac and Cream Spotted Tabbies.

SCALE OF POINTS

Type and shape	
Head	15
Ears	5
Eyes	5
Body	15
Legs and paws	5
Tail	5
Total	50

Colour and markings	
Eyes	5
Body colour and spotting	30
Texture of coat	10
Condition	5
Total	50

Oriental Spotted Tabby

KORAT

Korat

The Korat is a shorthair cat recognized by the Cat Fanciers' Association of America and granted the breed number 34 by the Governing Council of the Cat Fancy in Britain but without championship status. It is a rare cat, even in Thailand, where it originated.

The head of the Korat is heart-shaped and the single coat is glossy and fine, lying close to the body. Unlike most other shorthairs, the eyes are large for the size of the head and possess an extraordinary depth and brilliance. The eye colour is a luminous green. Kittens' eyes are yellow or amber and take one or often two years to attain their adult colour. The Korat is a truly delightful cat and possesses a very sweet and loving nature.

OFFICIAL STANDARD

Cat Fanciers' Association, Inc.

KORAT

POINT SCORE

Head (23)	
Broad head	5
Profile	5
Breadth between eyes	5
Ear set and placement	5
Chin and jaw	3
Eyes (15)	
Size	5
Shape	5
Placement	5
Body (25)	
Body	15
Legs and feet	5
Tail	5
Coat (12)	
Short	4
Texture	4
Close lying	4
Color (25)	
Body color	20
Eye color	5

A pair of Korats

General
The Korat is a rare cat even in Thailand, its country of origin, and because of its unusually fine disposition, is greatly loved by the Thai people who regard it as a "good luck" cat. Its general appearance is of a silver blue cat with a heavy silver sheen, medium sized, hard-bodied, and muscular. All smooth curves with huge, prominent eyes, brilliant, alert, and expressive. Perfect physical condition, alert appearance.

Head
When viewed from the front, or looking down from just back of the head, the head is heartshaped with breadth between and across the eyes. The eyebrow ridges forming the upper curves of the heart, and the sides of the face gently curving down to the chin to complete the heart-shape. Undesirable: any pinch or narrowness, especially between or across the eyes.

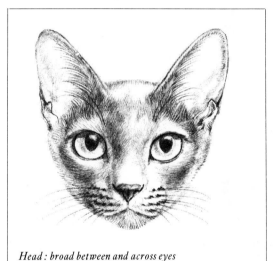

Head : broad between and across eyes

Nose
In profile there is a slight stop between nose and forehead, and tip of nose just above leather has a lion-like downward curve. Undesirable: nose that appears long in proportion to head, or nose that appears short enough to give the head a squashed down look.

Chin and jaw
Strong and well-developed, making a balancing line for the profile and properly completing the heartshape. Neither overly squared nor sharply pointed, nor a weak chin that gives the head a pointed look.

Ears
Large, with a rounded tip and large flare at base, set high on head, giving an alert expression. Inside ears sparsely furnished. Hairs on outside of ears extremely short and close.

Body
Semi-cobby (that is neither short coupled like the Manx nor long like the Siamese), muscular, supple, with a

CFA OFFICIAL STANDARD continued –

feeling of hard-coiled "spring" power and unexpected weight. Back carried in a curve. Males, renowned in Thailand for their prowess as fighters, must look the part —powerful and fit. Females should be smaller and dainty, medium and curved describe the body size and shape.

Legs
Well proportioned to body. Distance along back from nape of neck to base of tail appears to be equal to distance from base of tail to floor. Front legs slightly shorter than back legs.

Paws
Oval. Toes, five in front and four behind.

Tail
Medium in length, heavier at the base, tapering to a rounded tip. Non-visible kink permitted.

Eyes
Large and luminous. Particularly prominent with an extraordinary depth and brilliance. Wide open and over-sized for the face. Eye aperture, which shows as well-rounded when fully open, has an Asian slant when closed or partially closed. Undesirable: Small or dull looking eyes.

Korat

Coat
Single. Hair is short to medium in length, glossy and fine, lying close to the body. The coat over the spine is inclined to break as the cat moves.

Color
Silver blue all over, tipped with silver, the more silver tipping the better. Without shading or tabby markings. Where coat is short, the sheen of the silver is intensified. Undesirable: coats with silver tipping on only the head, legs, and feet.

Nose leather
Dark blue or lavender.

Lips
Dark blue or lavender.

Paw pads
Dark blue ranging to lavender with a pinkish tinge.

Eye color
Luminous green preferred, amber cast acceptable. Kittens and adolescents have yellow or amber to amber-green eyes. Color is not usually true until the cat is mature, usually two to four years of age.

Disqualify
Visible kink. Incorrect number of toes. White spot or locket. Any colour but silver blue.

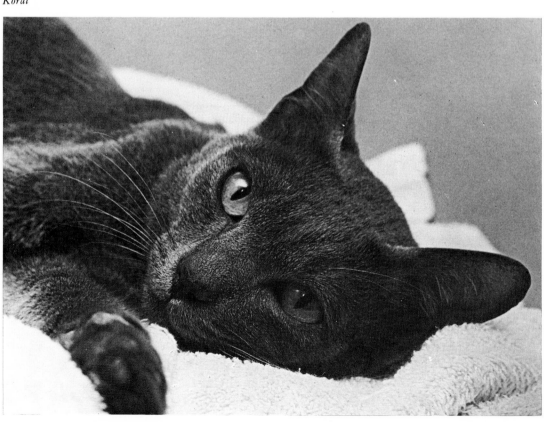

OFFICIAL STANDARD
Governing Council of the Cat Fancy

KORAT CATS: VARIETY 34
This variety does not carry challenge certificate status

Head and ears
When viewed from the front the head is heart-shaped, with breadth between and across the eyes, gently curving to a well-developed but neither sharply pointed nor squared muzzle. Forehead large, flat.

Ears are large and with a rounded tip and large flare at base, set high on head, giving an alert expression. Inside ears sparsely furnished.

Eyes, colour and shape
Large and luminous, particularly prominent. Wide open and oversized for the face. Eye aperture, which appears as well-rounded when fully open, has Asian slant when closed or partially closed.

Colour, brilliant green, but amber cast acceptable. Kittens and adolescents up to 2 years have yellow or amber to amber-green eyes.

Nose
Short and with slight downward curve. In profile there is a slight stop between forehead and nose.

Korat

Chin and jaw
Strong.

Body and tail
Medium sized body, strong, muscular and semi-cobby. Medium bone structure. Back carried in a curve. Tail medium in length, heavier at the base, tapering to a rounded tip. Non-visible kink at extremity permissible.

Body colour
Silver-blue all over, tipped with silver, the more silver tipping the better. Without shading or tabby markings. When the coat is short the silver sheen is intensified. Silver tipping develops through kittenhood and adolescence to full intensity at about 2 years old.

Nose leather and lips
Dark blue or lavender.

Pads
Dark blue ranging to lavender with pinkish tinge.

Coat
Single. Hair is short to medium in length, glossy and fine and lying close to body. The coat over the spine is inclined to break as the cat moves.

Legs and paws
Legs should be well-proportioned to body and paws oval, 5 toes in front, 4 behind.

Condition
Perfect physical condition, muscular, alert appearance.

Faults
White hair or white spots. Incorrect eye colour.

SCALE OF POINTS

Head (20)	
Broad head	5
Profile	6
Breadth between eyes	4
Ear set and placement	5
Eyes (15)	
Shape and placement	15
Body (25)	
Body	15
Legs and feet	5
Tail	5
Coat (10)	
Short	4
Texture	4
Close-lying	2
Condition	5
Colour (25)	
Body colour	20
Eye colour	5
Total	100

BOMBAY

Bombay

This is a comparatively new variety of shorthaired cat, and not very many are seen at the shows at present. The variety was first produced by the crossing of Burmese to black American Shorthairs. The fur is similar to that of the Burmese, but should be black, fine and short, with a wonderful sheen. The head should be round, not angular, with medium-sized ears that are slightly rounded at the tips. The eye colour is important, and should be gold to deep copper; green eyes are considered a bad fault.

OFFICIAL STANDARD

Cat Fanciers' Association, Inc.

BOMBAY

POINT SCORE

Head and ears (25)	
Round of head	9
Full face and proper profile	9
Ears	7
Eyes (5)	
Placement and shape	5
Body (15)	
Body	10
Tail	5
Coat (20)	
Shortness	10
Texture	5
Close lying	5
Color (35)	
Body color	20
Eye color	15

Bombay

Head

The head should be pleasingly round without flat planes, whether viewed from front or side. The face should be full with considerable breadth between the eyes, tapering slightly to a short, well-developed muzzle. In profile there should be a visible nose break.

Face: full, tapering to a well-developed muzzle

Ears

The ears should be medium in size and set well apart on a rounded skull, alert, tilting slightly forward, broad at the base and with slightly rounded tips.

Eyes

Set far apart with rounded aperture.

Body

Medium in size, muscular in development, neither compact nor rangy. Allowance is to be made for larger size in males.

Legs

In proportion to body and tail.

Tail

Straight, medium in length.

Coat

Fine, short, satin-like texture; very close-lying with a shimmering patent leather sheen no other black cat possesses.

Color

The mature specimen should be black to the roots. Kitten coats should darken and become more sleek with age.

Nose leather

Black.

Paw pads

Black.

Eye color

Ranging from gold to deep copper, the greater the depth and brilliance the better.

Disqualify

Kinked or abnormal tail. Lockets or spots. Incorrect number of toes. Nose leather or paw pads other than black. Green eyes.

REX

Cornish Rex

In 1950 a curly-coated kitten appeared in a litter on a farm in Cornwall, England. Mrs Ennismore, the owner, realized that it was an unusual kitten, and took veterinary advice. When the kitten, named Kallibunker, matured, he was mated back to his mother, a straight-haired Tortoiseshell and White. Several curly-coated kittens resulted from this mating, and a new variety of cat was established and soon became popular in many countries. The variety was given the name Rex, after the well-known curly-coated rabbit variety.

When Kallibunker died, Poldhu, one of his curly sons, was used to continue the line by mating him to other members of the growing family. Mrs Ennismore realized that this in-breeding could reduce the vigour of the line and therefore outcrossed Poldhu to ordinary shorthaired females. The resulting progeny, all of whom were plain-coated, were either mated back to Poldhu or among themselves. From the former

cross Rex kittens were born in a succession of litters in the ratio of one Rex to one plain-coated kitten. From the latter type of mating the proportion of Rex born was 1:3; that is, one Rex to three plain-coated kittens.

At about this time a litter-sister of Poldhu, in kitten by her brother, was registered in the name Lamorna Cove and exported to the United States, where a different strain of Rex also had occurred in much the same way as the Cornish strain.

In 1960 another curly cat was discovered in England, this time in the County of Devon. It was naturally assumed that the Devon and the Cornish Rex were of the same breed. But, surprisingly, when a Devon Rex named Kirlee was mated to one of Kallibunker's descendants, all the resulting kittens were plain-coated. After the cross had been repeated several times, and exclusively plain-coated kittens continued to be born, it was realized that the Cornish and Devon varieties possessed different genes for curly coats. Both are recessive mutations and will produce curly-coated offspring only if both parents carry the same type of gene. Kirlee was then outcrossed to a plain-coated female and the offspring from this union were mated back to their father. These matings produced Rex kittens in the ratio of 1:1; that is, one Rex to one plain-coated kitten.

The Cornish and Devon strains were named Gene 1 Rex and Gene 2 Rex respectively, and it was noted that the Cornish Rex had a denser but slightly less curly coat than the Devon Rex. At about the same time a Rex kitten was born in Germany. Specimens of each variety of Rex – American, Cornish, Devon and German – were mated to each of the other varieties. In every case the mating produced plain-coated kittens in the first

Devon Rex

generation. This proved that the four Rex varieties possessed different recessive genes for curly coats.

As any of the four fundamental Rex genes can be bred into any plain-coated cat, there is virtually no variety of cat that cannot be rexed. However, only shorthaired Rex cats are recognized, and the cat fancies disapprove and discourage the breeding of longhaired Rexes because the grooming of such cats would be extremely difficult. The type of cats chosen by breeders to represent the different spontaneous varieties of Rex were chosen by consensus, as more or less any type could have been selected.

In Britain the cat fancy recognizes two varieties of Rex: Cornish and Devon. In America the cat fancy used to recognize only one variety of Rex – that descended from the British-exported Lamorna Cove. However, the Cornish and Devon Rex genes were investigated by the Cat Fanciers' Association Breed Council and the CFA Board, and in 1979 they decided to recognize the Rex in these two varieties. Although Rex cats have been found occurring naturally in Oregon, Ohio, California, and in Italy and Germany, all apparently carrying different rexing genes, none of them has been granted official recognition.

Rex cats are remarkably affectionate animals. Unlike most cats, many of them tend to wag their tails when pleased. This, coupled with their curly coats, has earned them the nickname 'poodle cats'.

Rex

Cornish Rex

OFFICIAL STANDARD
Cat Fanciers' Association, Inc.

REX

POINT SCORE

Head (25)	
Size and shape	5
Muzzle and nose	5
Eyes	5
Ears	5
Profile	5
Body (30)	
Size	3
Torso	10
Legs and paws	5
Tail	5
Bone	5
Neck	2
Coat (40)	
Texture	10
Length	5
Wave, extent of wave	20
Close lying	5
Colour (5)	5

General
The Rex cat, a spontaneous mutation of the domestic cat, has accentuated the characteristic features of the breed to create a longer, slighter and more agile creature than its ancestors. Its arched back and muscular hind legs develop the flexibility for high jumps, quick starts and amazing speed. At ease its relaxed appearance is contradictory to its capacity for sudden and fast movements. When handled it feels firm and because of its short coat, warm to the touch.

Head
Comparatively small and narrow; length about one-third greater than the width. A definite whisker break.

Muzzle
Narrowing slightly to a rounded end.

Ears
Large, wide at base and come to a modified point at the top. Placed high on the head and erect.

Eyes
Medium to large in size, oval in shape and slanting slightly upward. A full eye's width apart. Color should be clear, intense and appropriate to coat color.

Nose
Roman. Length is one-third length of head. In profile a straight line from end of nose to chin with considerable depth and squarish effect.

Cheeks
Lean and muscular.

Chin
Strong, well-developed.

Body
Small to medium, males proportionally larger. Torso long and slender. Back is arched with lower line of the body following the upward curve.

Cream Cornish Rex

Shoulders
Well knit.

Rump
Rounded, well muscled.

Legs
Very long and slender. Hips well muscled, somewhat heavy in proportion to the rest of the body. The Rex stands high on its legs.

Paws
Dainty, slightly oval. Toes, five in front and four behind.

Tail
Long and slender, tapering toward the end and extremely flexible.

Neck
Long and slender.

Bone
Fine and delicate.

Coat
Short, extremely soft, silky, and completely free of guard hairs. Relatively dense. A tight, uniform marcel wave, lying close to the body and extending from the top of the head across the back, sides, and hips continuing to the tip of the tail. The fur on the underside of the chin and on chest and abdomen is short and noticeably wavy.

CFA OFFICIAL STANDARD continued –

Condition
Firm and muscular.

Disqualify
Kinked or abnormal tail. Incorrect number of toes. Any coarse or guard hairs. Evidence of hybridization resulting in the colors chocolate, lavender, the Himalayan pattern or these combinations with white.

REX COLORS

WHITE
Pure glistening white.

Nose leather
Pink.

Paw pads
Pink.

Eye color
Deep blue or brilliant gold. Odd-eyed whites shall have one blue and one gold eye with equal color depth.

BLACK
Dense coal black, sound from roots to tip of fur. Free from any tinge of rust on tips.

Nose leather
Black.

Paw pads
Black or brown.

Eye color
Gold.

BLUE
Blue, lighter shade preferred, one level tone from nose to tip of tail. Sound to the roots. A sound darker shade is more acceptable than an unsound lighter shade.

Nose leather
Blue.

Paw pads
Blue.

Eye color
Gold.

RED
Deep, rich, clear, brilliant red; without shading, markings or ticking. Lips and chin the same color as the coat.

Nose leather
Brick red.

White Cornish Rex, showing curly whiskers

Paw pads
Brick red.

Eye color
Gold.

CREAM
One level shade of buff cream, without markings. Sound to the roots. Lighter shades preferred.

Nose leather and paw pads
Pink.

Eye color
Gold.

CHINCHILLA
Undercoat pure white. Coat on back, flanks, head and tail sufficiently tipped with black to give the characteristic sparkling silver appearance. Legs may be slightly shaded with tipping. Chin, stomach and chest, pure white. Rims of eyes, lips and nose outlined with black.

Nose leather
Brick red.

Paw pads
Black.

Eye color
Green or blue-green.

SHADED SILVER
Undercoat white with a mantle of black tipping shading down from sides, face, and tail from dark on the ridge to white on the chin, chest, stomach, and under the tail. Legs to be the same tone as the face. The general effect to be much darker than a chinchilla. Rims of eyes, lips and nose outlined with black.

Nose leather
Brick red.

Paw pads
Black.

Eye color
Green or blue-green.

BLACK SMOKE
White undercoat, deeply tipped with black. Cat in repose appears black. In motion the white undercoat is clearly apparent.

Points and mask
Black with narrow band of white at base of hairs next to skin which may be seen only when the fur is parted.

Nose leather
Black.

Paw pads
Black.

Eye color
Gold.

BLUE SMOKE
White undercoat, deeply tipped with blue. Cat in repose appears blue. In motion the white undercoat is clearly apparent.

Points and mask
Blue with narrow band of white at base of hairs next to skin which may be seen only when fur is parted.

Nose leather and paw pads
Blue.

Eye color
Gold.

CLASSIC TABBY PATTERN
Markings dense, clearly defined and broad. Legs evenly barred with bracelets coming up to meet the body markings. Tail evenly ringed. Several unbroken necklaces on neck and upper chest, the more the better. Frown marks on forehead form intricate letter "M". Unbroken line runs back from outer corner of eye. Swirls on cheeks. Vertical lines over back of head extend to shoulder markings which are in the shape of a butterfly with both upper and lower wings distinctly outlined and marked with dots inside outline. Back markings consist of a vertical line down the spine from butterfly to tail with a vertical stripe paralleling it on each side, the three stripes well separated by stripes of the ground color. Large solid blotch on each side to be encircled by one or more unbroken rings. Side markings should be the same on both sides. Double vertical row of buttons on chest and stomach.

MACKEREL TABBY PATTERN
Markings dense, clearly defined, and all narrow pencillings. Legs evely barred with narrow bracelets coming up to meet the body markings. Tail barred. Necklaces on neck and chest distinct, like so many chains. Head barred with an "M" on the forehead. Unbroken lines running back from the eyes. Lines running down the head to meet the shoulders. Spine lines run together to form a narrow saddle. Narrow pencillings run around body.

PATCHED TABBY PATTERN
A Patched Tabby (Torbie) is an established silver, brown, or blue tabby with patches of red and/or cream.

BROWN PATCHED TABBY
Ground color brilliant coppery brown with classic or mackerel tabby markings of dense black with patches of red and/or cream clearly defined on both body and extremities; a blaze of red and/or cream on the face is desirable. Lips and chin the same shade as the rings around the eyes.

CFA OFFICIAL STANDARD continued –

Eye color
Brilliant gold.

SILVER TABBY
Ground color, including lips and chin, pale, clear silver. Markings dense black.

Nose leather
Brick red.

Paw pads
Black.

Eye color
Green or hazel.

RED TABBY
Ground color red. Markings deep, rich red. Lips and chin red.

Nose leather
Brick red.

Paw pads
Brick red.

Eye color
Gold.

BROWN TABBY
Ground color brilliant coppery brown. Markings dense black. Lips and chin the same shade as the rings around the eyes. Back of leg black from paw to heel.

Nose leather
Brick red.

Paw pads
Black or brown.

Eye color
Gold.

BLUE TABBY
Ground color, including lips and chin, pale, bluish ivory. Markings a very deep blue affording a good contrast with ground color. Warm fawn overtones or patina over the whole.

Nose leather
Old rose.

Paw pads
Rose.

Eye color
Gold.

CREAM TABBY
Ground color, including lips and chin, very pale cream. Markings buff or cream sufficiently darker than the ground color to afford good contrast, but remaining within the dilute color range.

Nose leather
Pink.

Paw pads
Pink.

Eye color
Gold.

TORTOISESHELL
Black with unbrindled patches of red and cream. Patches clearly defined and well broken on both body and extremities. Blaze of red or cream on face is desirable.

Eye color
Gold.

CALICO
White with unbrindled patches of black and red. White predominant on underparts.

Eye color
Gold.

DILUTE CALICO
White with unbrindled patches of blue and cream, white predominant on underparts.

Eye color
Gold.

BLUE-CREAM
Blue with patches of solid cream. Patches clearly defined and well broken on both body and extremities.

Eye color
Gold.

BI-COLOR
White with unbrindled patches of black, or white with unbrindled patches of blue, or white with unbrindled patches of red, or white with unbrindled patches of cream. Cats with no more white than a locket and/or button do not qualify for this color class. Such cats shall be judged in the color class of their basic color with no penalty for such locket and/or button.

Eye color
Gold.

ORC (Other Rex Colors)
Any other color or pattern with the exception of those showing evidence of hybridization resulting in the colors chocolate, lavender, the himalayan pattern, or these combinations with white, etc.

Eye color
Appropriate to the predominant color of the cat.

BLUE PATCHED TABBY
Ground color, including lips and chin, pale bluish ivory with classic or mackerel tabby markings of very deep blue affording a good contrast with ground color. Patches of cream clearly defined on both body and extremities; a blaze of cream on the face is desirable. Warm fawn overtones or patina over the whole.

Eye color
Brilliant gold.

SILVER PATCHED TABBY
Ground color, including lips and chin, pale silver with classic or mackerel tabby markings of dense black with patches of red and/or cream clearly defined on both body and extremities. A blaze of red and/or cream on the face is desirable.

Eye color
Brilliant gold or hazel.

Silver Tabby Rex

Calico Rex

The Cornish Rex cats in Britain today were developed from, among others, an American descendant of Lamorna Cove that carried many Siamese characteristics, and therefore they are distinctly 'foreign' in type.

The Devon Rex is a more delicately sculptured cat. It was deliberately bred to have a type based on a statue of the Cat Goddess Bast at the Metropolitan Museum of Art in New York. One of the problems associated with this variety is that its hair, although beautifully curled, tends to be somewhat sparse in several breed-lines, particularly on the underparts. To correct this tendency, any suggestion of relative hair-lessness has been deemed a serious fault. This policy is producing good results, for breeders naturally do not want to breed cats that are doomed to failure on the show bench.

One very popular sub-variety of Devon Rex in Britain is known unofficially as the Si Rex. It has been evolved by rexing the Siamese cat, and carries the Siamese genes responsible for limiting coat colour mainly to the points. It combines the charm of the Rex with the joyous independence and vivacity of the Siamese and is very popular on the showbench.

Devon Rex kitten

OFFICIAL STANDARD
Governing Council of the Cat Fancy

CORNISH REX: VARIETY 33

Coat
Short and plushy, without guard hairs, and should curl, wave or ripple particularly on back and tail. Whiskers and eyebrows crinkled and of good length. All coat colours acceptable, but any white markings must be symmetrical, except in Tortoiseshell and white.

Head
Medium wedge. Head length about one-third greater than the maximum width, narrowing to a strong chin. The skull to be flat. In profile a straight line to be seen from the centre of forehead to end of nose.

Top: Cornish Rex head; bottom: Devon Rex head

Eyes
Oval shaped, medium in size, colour in keeping with coat colour.

Ears
Large, set rather high on head, wide at base, tapering to rounded tips and well covered with fine fur.

Body and legs
Body hard and muscular, slender and of medium length. Legs long and straight, giving an overall appearance of being high on the legs. Paws small and oval.

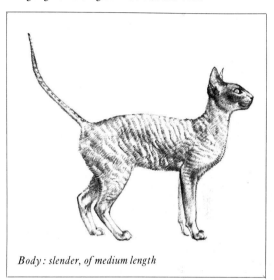

Body: slender, of medium length

Tail
Long, fine and tapering, well covered with curly fur.

Faults
1. Asymmetrical white markings, except in Tortoiseshell and white.
2. Shaggy or too short a coat.
3. Bare patches to be considered a fault in kittens and a serious fault in cats.
4. Shorthair type head, or too long a wedge.
5. Small ears.
6. Cobby body.
7. Lack of firm muscles.
8. Short or bare tail.
9. Kinks in the tail shall be considered a fault.

SCALE OF POINTS

Coat	35
Whiskers and eyebrows	5
Head shape	15
Eyes	10
Ears	10
Body and legs	20
Tail	5
Total	100

OFFICIAL STANDARD
Governing Council of the Cat Fancy

DEVON REX: VARIETY 33a

Coat
Very short and fine, wavy and soft, without guard hairs. Whiskers and eyebrows crinkled, rather coarse and of medium length. All coat colours, except bi-colours acceptable. Any white markings other than in Tortoiseshell and white will be considered a fault.

Head
Wedge-shaped with face full cheeked. Short muzzle with strong chin and whisker break. Nose with a strongly marked stop. Forehead curving back to a flat skull.

Eyes
Wide set, large, oval shaped and sloping towards outer edges of ears. Colour in keeping with coat colour, or, except in Si-Rex, chartreuse, green or yellow.

Ears
Large, set rather low, very wide at base, tapering to rounded tops and well covered with fine fur. With or without ear muffs.

White Devon Rex

Body, legs and neck
Body hard and muscular, slender and of medium length, broad in chest, carried high on long slim legs, with length hind legs emphasized. Paws small and oval. Neck slender.

Tail
Long, fine and tapering, well covered with short fur.

Faults
1. Straight of shaggy coat.
2. Any white markings, other than Tortoiseshell and white.
3. Bare patches to be considered a fault in kittens and a serious fault in cats.
4. Narrow, long or shorthair head.
5. Cobby body.
6. Lack of firm muscles.
7. Small or high set ears.
8. Short, bare or bushy tail.
9. Kinks in the tail shall be considered a fault.

Note
Many Devon Rex cats have down on the underparts. This should not be misinterpreted as bareness. Si-Rex, mentioned above, is not a variety and means simply a Rex cat showing Siamese colour restriction.

SCALE OF POINTS

Coat	40
Head	15
Eyes	5
Ears	10
Body, legs and neck	25
Tail	5
Total	100

Devon Rex kitten

BRITISH SHORTHAIR

Brown Tabby British Shorthair

In her great classic *The Book of the Cat*, published in 1903, Frances Simpson recounts that in 1895 the shows held at the Crystal Palace offered numerous classes for the Shorthaired cat; and that it was not until 1896, when the National Cat Club took over the shows, that the Longhair, or Persian, cat came into its own. From that time the British Shorthair suffered a steady decline in popularity and it was not until the 1930s that the devoted work of a small number of breeders, outstanding among whom was Miss Kit Wilson, began a general resurgence of this beautiful breed.

The British Shorthair was the native cat of Britain and was to be seen in every street. Without much doubt the first champions were alley cats, picked up here and there and selectively bred together in the hope of producing specimens of beauty. It was probably Mr Harrison Weir, the man whose unique devotion to cats entitles him to be called 'The Father of the Cat Fancy', who did most in those early days to popularize the breeding of the British cat. 'The ordinary garden cat', he wrote, 'has survived every kind of hardship and persecution. That he exists at all, is tribute to his strength of character and endurance.' Weir's devotion to the common British cat was supported by that of Mr Jung, one of the new fancy's first Shorthair judges. He made the point that if the British cat could be taken up and thoughtfully bred there would grow up a race of cats bearing aristocratic pedigrees, as a result of which they would become popular and wanted, for such is the nature of man that he tends to see not inherent quality and goodness but that reflection of these virtues to be found on a piece of paper – a pedigree supplied by an official body.

Weir's and Jung's version of 'high-level salesmanship' encouraged many cat lovers to breed British varieties. Today the British cat fancy recognizes seven-teen distinct colours. These cats are strong, sturdy and very beautiful, and as a bonus, are less susceptible than any other breed to the illnesses that plague the domestic cat. Many of the varieties of British Shorthair seen on the showbench today were produced by mating the original Shorthairs with longcoated cats. This practice resulted in the production of a race of cats that combined the round head and beautiful orange or copper eye colour of the longcoated cats with the sturdiness of the Shorthairs. The occasional outcross to a Longhair/ Persian is still used to strengthen type, maintaining or improving the shape of the head and the large, round eyes, in a breed-line.

Pedigree British Shorthairs were exported to America fairly early in their history and became popular because, unlike many varieties of cat, they seem to possess an avid love for killing mice and other small mammals even when they are well-fed. In addition, they make the most affectionate pets and are particularly good with children and with dogs. In America these cats were bred somewhat differently from the way in which they are usually bred in Britain, and a different variety of cat, the American Shorthair,

Silver Tabby British Shorthair

Blue British Shorthair male

came into being (see page 135). For some time the American Shorthair virtually replaced the British Shorthair in America, but recently the original British type has been revived.

It seems natural that the show variety of the natural domestic cat should have evolved slightly differently in different countries. The European Shorthair, for example, although its standard of points is based on the British standard, tends to differ very slightly from the latter. This is particularly to be seen in the Shorthaired Blue, a version of which, called the Chartreuse, is popular in Europe. This has given rise to some confusion among both breeders and judges, each of whom tends to view the desired characteristics of the cat in the light of an individual interpretation of the official standard.

In all parts of the world and by whatever name it is called, the domestic Shorthair is popularly regarded as being a charming, strongly-built, working cat well-deserving of a place both on the showbench and in front of the domestic fire. Moreover, this variety of cat has shown itself to possess a remarkable resistance to every kind of disease. No wonder it has survived a couple of thousand years of hard living and several periods of the cruellest persecution.

Black British Shorthair

PROVISIONAL STANDARD

Cat Fanciers' Association, Inc.

BRITISH SHORTHAIR

POINT SCORE

Head (30)	
Muzzle	5
Skull	5
Ears	5
Neck	5
Eye shape	10
Body (10)	
Torso	20
Legs and feet	5
Tail	5
Coat (20)	
Length	10
Texture	10
Colour (20)	20

General

The British Shorthair is hard and muscular with no indication of fat, giving a general appearance of activity. The type required is the same for all British Shorthair cats. The males are more massive in all characteristics.

Head

Very broad with well rounded contours when viewed from any angle. Cheeks are well developed. Good muzzle.

Nose

Short and broad.

Ears

Ear set is important. Medium in size and set far enough apart that the base of the inner ear is perpendicular to the outer corner of the eye. Broad at the base and rounded at the tips.

Neck

Short and bull-like, particularly in the males.

Eyes

Large, round, and well opened. Set to show breadth of nose. Eye color to conform to the requirements listed in coat color.

Body

Medium to large. Shoulders broad and flat. Hips same width as shoulders. Chest broad and rounded. Body well knit and powerful especially in males.

Legs and feet

Legs strong and well proportioned. Feet and toes are well rounded.

Tail

In proportion to the body. Thick at base with a slight taper.

Color

As described in color standard. For cats with special markings—10 for color and 10 for markings. Shadow tabby markings in solid colored kittens are not a fault.

Coat

Coat should be short, well bodied; resilient and firm to the touch. Not double coated or woolly. Dense with a natural protective appearance.

Penalize

Open coat, light undercoat. Wrong eye color.

BRITISH SHORTHAIR COLORS

BLUE EYED WHITE

White to be pure, untinged with yellow.

Eye color
Very deep sapphire blue.

ORANGE EYED WHITE

White to be pure, untinged with yellow.

Eye color
Golden, orange, or copper.

ODD EYED WHITE

White to be pure, untinged with yellow.

Eye color
Sapphire blue and golden, orange, or copper.

BLACK

Jet black to roots, no rusty tinge, no white hair anywhere.

Eye Color
Copper, orange, or yellow with no trace of green.

BLUE

Light to medium blue, very level in color. No tabby markings or shadings of white.

Eye colour
Copper, orange, or yellow.

CREAM

Rich cream, level in color, free from bars, no sign of white.

Eye color
Copper or orange.

Red Tabby British Shorthair

Smoke British Shorthair kitten

Blue British Shorthair

Cream British Shorthair

CFA OFFICIAL STANDARD Continued –

BLUE-CREAM
Colors to be softly mingled, **not** patched.

Eye color
Copper, orange, or yellow.

SILVER TABBY
Dense black, not mixed with the ground color and quite distinct from it. Ground color pure, clear silver, uniform throughout, no white anywhere.

Eye color
Green or hazel.

RED TABBY
Very dense and dark red, not mixed with the ground color and quite distinct from it. Ground color and markings to be as rich as possible.

Eye color
Orange or hazel.

BROWN TABBY
Very dense and black and not mixed with the ground color, quite distinct from it. Ground color rich sable or brown, uniform throughout, no white anywhere.

Eye color
Orange, hazel, deep yellow, or green.

BLACK SMOKE
No standard available.

SPOTTED
Good and clear spotting is the first essential. The spots can be round, oblong, or rosette-shaped. Any of these markings may be of equal merit but the spots, however shaped or placed, shall be distinct and not running into each other. They may be of any color suitable to the ground coloration. Color of eyes to conform to the coat color.

Faults
Stripes and bars (except on face and head), brindling.

TORTOISESHELL
Black and red (light and dark), equally balanced, and each color to be as brilliant as possible, no white. Patches to be clear and defined, no blurring and no tabby or brindle markings. Legs, feet, tail and ears to be as well patched as body and head. Red blaze desirable.

Eye color
Orange, copper, or hazel.

TORTOISESHELL AND WHITE
Black and red (dark and light) on white, equally balanced. Colors to be brilliant and absolutely free from brindling or tabby markings. The tri-color patching should cover the top of the head, ears and cheeks, back and tail and part of the flanks. Patches to be clear and defined. White blaze desirable.

Eye color
Orange, copper, or hazel.

BI-COLORS
Black and white, blue and white, orange and white, cream and white. No tabby markings in the self-colored portion. *Markings:* The self color, i.e. black, blue, orange or cream to start immediately behind the shoulders round the barrel of the body and include tail and hind legs, leaving the hind feet white. Ears and mask of face also self-colored. White shoulders, neck, forelegs and feet, chin, lips and blaze up face and over top of head joining or running into the white at back of skull, thus dividing the mask exactly in half.

Eye color
Copper, orange, or yellow.

OFFICIAL STANDARD
Governing Council of the Cat Fancy

BRITISH SHORTHAIRS

The British cat is compact, well balanced and powerful showing good depth of body, a full broad chest, short strong legs, rounded paws, tail thick at base with a rounded tip. The head is round with good width between the ears, round cheeks, firm chin, small ears, large round and well opened eyes with a short straight nose. The coat is short and dense.

Head
Round and massive, with good breadth of skull. Round face with round underlying bone structure, well set on a short thick neck.

Head: round and massive

Nose
Short, broad and straight.

Chin
Firm and well-developed.

Ears
Small, rounded at tips, with good width between and well furnished.

Eyes
Large, round, well opened, set wide apart and level.

Body
Well knit and powerful. Level back and a deep broad chest.

Legs
Short, well boned and strong. Straight forelegs.

Paws
Round and firm.

Tail
Short and thick but in proportion to body length with a rounded tip.

Body: compact, hard and muscular

Coat
Short and dense.

Condition
Hard and muscular.

Faults
Tail defects. Definite nose stops. Overlong or fluffy coat.

SCALE OF POINTS

Head	20
Eyes	10
Body	20
Legs and paws	10
Tail	10
Coat, colour and condition	30
Total	100

WHITE BLUE-EYED: VARIETY 14

Colour
White to be pure, untinged with yellow. Dark mark on head permissible in kittens.

Eyes
Very deep sapphire blue. No green rims or flecks.

Nose leather and pads
Pink.

Withhold certificates
Incorrect eye colour. Green rims.

GCCF OFFICIAL STANDARD continued –

WHITE ORANGE-EYED: VARIETY 14a

Colour
White to be pure, untinged with yellow.

Eyes
Gold, orange or copper. No green rims or flecks.

Nose leather and Pads
Pink.

Withhold certificates
Incorrect eye colour. Green rims.

WHITE ODD-EYED: VARIETY 14b

Colour
White to be pure, untingued with yellow.

Eyes
One gold, orange or copper. One blue. No green rims or flecks.

Nose leather and pads
Pink.

Withhold certificates
Incorrect eye colour. Green rims.

BLACK: VARIETY 15

Colour
Jet black to roots, no rusty tinge. No white hairs anywhere. Rusty tinge permissible in kittens.

Eyes
Deep copper or orange with no trace of green.

Nose leather
Black.

Pads
Brown or black.

Withhold certificates
Incorrect eye colour. Green rims.

BLUE: VARIETY 16

Colour
Light to medium blue. Even colour and no tabby markings or white anywhere.

Eyes
Copper or orange.

Nose leather and pads
Blue.

Faults
Unsound coats. Silver tipping to coats.

Withhold certificates
Incorrect eye colour. Green rims.

CREAM: VARIETY 17

Colour
Lighter shades preferred. Level in colour and free from markings. No sign of white anywhere.

Eyes
Copper or orange.

Nose leather and pads
Pink.

Withhold certificates
Incorrect eye colour. Green rims. Heavy tabby markings.

Blue British Shorthair kitten

Cream British Shorthair kittens

Orange-eyed White British Shorthair

Blue British Shorthair

Black British Shorthair

Cream British Shorthair

Black British Shorthair

GCCF OFFICIAL STANDARD continued –

CLASSIC TABBY PATTERN

All markings to be clearly defined and dense. Legs barred evenly with bracelets going down from the body markings to the toes. Ground colour and markings should be equally balanced. Evenly ringed tail. On the neck and upper chest there should be unbroken necklaces, the more the better. On the forehead there should be a letter 'M' made by frown marks. There should be an unbroken line running back from the outer corner of the eye. There should be pencillings on the cheeks. There should be a vertical line which runs over the back of the head and extends to the shoulder markings, which should be shaped like a butterfly. Both the upper and the lower wings should be defined clearly in outline with dots inside this outline.

On the back there should be a line running down the spine from the butterfly to the tail, and there should be a stripe on each side of this running parallel to it. These stripes should be separated from each other by stripes of the ground colour. On each flank there should be a large solid oyster or blotch which should be surrounded by one or more unbroken rings. The markings on each side should be identical. All Tabby cats should be spotted in the abdominal region. In all Tabby cats the tails should be evenly ringed.

SILVER TABBY: VARIETY 18

Colour
Clear silver ground colour which should include chin and lips. Markings dense black.

Eyes
Green or hazel.

Nose leather
Brick red for preference, although black is permissible.

Pads
Black.

Faults
Brown on nose or paws. Brindling.

Withhold certificates
Incorrect eye colour. White anywhere. Incorrect Tabby pattern.

RED TABBY: VARIETY 19

Colour
Red ground colour and markings of deep rich red. Lips and chin red. Sides of feet dark red.

Eyes
Brilliant copper.

Nose leather
Brick red.

Pads
Deep red.

Faults
Brindling.

Withhold certificates
Incorrect eye colour. White anywhere. Incorrect Tabby pattern.

BROWN TABBY: VARIETY 20

Brilliant coppery brown ground with dense black markings. Back of legs from paw to heel should be black.

Eyes
Orange, hazel or deep yellow.

Nose leather
Brick red.

Pads
Black or brown.

Faults
Brindling.

Withhold certificates
Incorrect eye colour. White anywhere. Incorrect Tabby pattern.

MACKEREL TABBY PATTERN

Head, legs and tail as for Classic Tabby. There should be a narrow unbroken line running from the back of the head to the base of the tail. The rest of the body to be covered with narrow lines running vertically down from the spine line and to be unbroken. These lines should be as narrow and as numerous as possible.

Type faults
As for Classic Tabby.

Pattern faults
Solid back, broken tail rings, solid sides, white tip to tail and white anywhere. Spotting on back. Brindling.

Withhold certificates
Incorrect eye colour. White anywhere. Incorrect Mackerel pattern.

TORTOISESHELL: VARIETY 21

Colour
Black with brilliant patches of cream and red. All these patches should be clearly defined and well broken on the legs and body. A red or cream blaze on the head is desirable.

Red Tabby British Shorthair kitten

Red Tabby British Shorthair adult

Tortoiseshell British Shorthair

GCCF OFFICIAL STANDARD *Continued –*

Nose leather
Pink and/or black.

Pads
Pink and/or black.

Eyes
Brilliant copper or orange.

Faults
Tabby markings. Brindling. White anywhere. Colour unbroken on paws. Unequal balance of colour.

Withhold certificates
Incorrect eye colour. White anywhere. Green rims.

TORTOISESHELL AND WHITE: VARIETY 22

Colour
Black, cream and red on white, equally balanced. Colours to be brilliant. The tri-colour patchings should cover the top of the head, ears and cheeks, back, tail and part of the flanks. Patches to be clear and defined. White blaze desirable.

Eyes
Copper or orange.

Nose leather and pads
As for Tortoiseshell.

Faults

Tabby markings. Brindling. Colour unbroken on paws. Unequal balance of colour. White must **never** predominate; the reverse is preferable.

Withhold certificates
Incorrect eye colour. White predominating. Green rims.

Tortoiseshell and White British Shorthair kitten

Tortoiseshell and White British Shorthair adult

Bicolour British Shorthair

Blue-Cream British Shorthair

GCCF OFFICIAL STANDARD continued –

BLUE CREAM: VARIETY 28

Colour
Blue and cream to be softly intermingled. No blaze.

Eyes
Copper or orange.

Nose leather
Blue.

Pads
Blue and/or pink.

Faults
Tabby markings. White anywhere. Colour unbroken on paws. Unequal balance of colour.

Withhold certificates
Incorrect eye colour. Green rims. Solid patches of colour.

SPOTTED: VARIETY 30

Head markings
As Classic Tabby. Body and legs good, clear spotting essential. Spots as numerous and distinct as possible.

Tail
Spots or broken rings desirable.

Colour
Silver with black spots. Brown with black spots. Red with deep rich red spots. Any other recognized ground colours acceptable with appropriate spotting.

Eyes
Silver spotted: green or hazel.
Brown spotted: orange, hazel or deep yellow.
Red spotted: brilliant copper.

Nose leather and paws
As for Classic Tabby.

Faults
Solid spine.

Pattern faults
Brindling (e.g. linked spots). White tip to tail. White anywhere.

Withhold certificates
Incorrect eye colour. Incorrect pattern. White anywhere.

Spotted British Shorthair newborn kitten

Spotted British Shorthair kitten

BI-COLOUR: VARIETY 31

Colour
Any accepted colour and white. The patches of colour to be clear and evenly distributed. Not more than two-thirds of the cat's coat to be coloured and not more than one-half white. Face to be patched with colour. White blaze desirable. Symmetry in design is desirable.

Eyes
Brilliant copper or orange.

Faults
Brindling, or Tabby markings.

Withhold certificates
White patching on solid colours. Incorrect eye colour. Green rims.

SMOKES: VARIETY 36

Colour
Black or blue. Undercoat pale silver.

Eyes
Yellow or orange.

Nose leather and pads
Blue or black to correspond with coat colour. (Kittens should not be penalized for ghost markings.)

Faults
White guard hairs. Overlong coat.

Withhold certificates
Incorrect eye colour. Tabby markings in adults. Overlong coat.

GCCF OFFICIAL STANDARD continued –

BRITISH TIPPED: VARIETY 39

SCALE OF POINTS

Head	20
Eyes	10
Body	20
Legs and paws	10
Tail	10
Coat and condition	30
Total	100

The general conformation to adhere strictly to that laid down for other British Shorthaired breeds.

The following points to be specific:

Colours
Tipping can be of any colour accepted in the recognized British breeds, with the addition of chocolate and lilac.

Coat
The undercoat to be as white as possible, coat on the back, flanks, head, ears, and tail tipped with colour. This tipping should be evenly distributed to give a sparkling effect.

The legs may be very slightly shaded with tipping, but the chin, stomach, chest and undertail to be as white as possible.

Nose leather and pads
In all colours, nose leather and pads corresponding to colour of tipping.

Eyes
Cats with black tipping should have green eye colour, otherwise eye colour to be from orange to copper.

British Tipped Shorthair

Faults
(i) Any tendency towards foreign type cannot be too strongly deprecated.
(ii) An orange rim in a green-eyed cat, or a green rim in the eye of an orange-eyed cat.
(iii) Tabby markings or spots in the coat colouring, with the exception of vestigial tail rings, which should not penalize an otherwise good exhibit.

Chartreuse

In France for very many years there has been a variety of shorthaired cat known as the Chartreuse. They were said to have been bred originally a long time ago by the Carthusian monks in their monastery, La Grand Chartreuse. There is even a legend that the many visitors to the monastery greatly admired the kittens and were always anxious to buy them. The wily monks, anxious to keep the variety exclusively their own, always neutered any animals before they went to their new homes. Some people insisted that these large solid cats with good broad chests, big round heads, and greyish-blue fur were the same as the British Blues. There may have been some difference between the British Blue and the Chartreuse in the early days, but it is now generally accepted in Europe that the two varieties are really the same, although some judges claim that they can still differentiate between them.

Chartreuse

AMERICAN SHORTHAIR

Smoke American Shorthair

The American Shorthair has a similar, but shorter, history than that of the British and European Shorthairs. There were no indigenous domestic cats in North America, and it is thought that the first ones arrived with the Pilgrim Fathers and with early missionaries. Over the years more settlers brought more cats, many of them from Britain. All these immigrant cats intermated freely for generations, producing strong healthy animals, with varying coat colourings and patterns. Many of these cats accompanied the pioneers across the continent, thus establishing themselves throughout the country. Much appreciated for decades for their prowess in dealing with vermin and

for their companionship, these cats were more or less taken for granted until the beginning of the twentieth century.

According to the Cat Fanciers' Association's records the first Shorthair to be registered in the United States was a cat from Britain, bred by Mr Kuhnel, and imported by Miss J. Cathcart. Although an Orange (now Red) tabby male, it was called Champion Belle of Bradford, and was born on 1 June, 1900. Miss Cathcart imported at least one other Shorthair from Britain. By crossbreeding these cats with resident Shorthairs, she was one of the first people to be instrumental in establishing the Domestic (now American) cats as a variety, although without standards or championships.

It should be appreciated that these were the early days of the American cat fancy, and far more interest was shown in producing more unusual varieties that could be shown and possibly become champions, than in breeding an 'ordinary' variety. The American Shorthairs did appear later in Household Pet classes; powerful looking cats, with great appeal. Eventually, it was realized that by selective breeding a great number of coat patterns and colourings could be produced. Breeders became interested in specializing in particular colours, but it was a slow process in many cases. Over the years imported cats were mated to the resident cats, which helped to establish varying coat patterns. In recent years the American Shorthairs have become well and truly established, many taking their place among the top cats at a number of shows.

They in no way resemble the Exotics, which have been produced by crossing Persian/Longhairs with Shorthairs. The Shorthairs have short fur, never fluffy, hard rather than soft to the touch, and their bodies are of medium length, not cobby as are the Longhairs. In fact, cobbiness would be penalized at the show.

The Cat Fanciers' Association's standard for the American Shorthair is most explicit and does give a very clear picture of what a really outstanding cat is like. It is interesting that, although this variety got off to a very slow start in the American cat fancy, there are now nearly thirty colour variations possible, while the British varieties number only about sixteen, not including the Manx, but it does not enumerate the possible colour variations, such as the different coloured Spotties or Smokes. These colours are mentioned in the different standards given.

It is difficult to differentiate between the American and British Shorthairs. In fact, in some cases there appears to be very little difference, although, on the whole, the American variety is a slightly larger animal, its head not quite as round, and its nose slightly longer than the British variety. Both varieties are delightful animals and adaptable pets. They are very companionable, highly intelligent, and truly worthy of their long, if not always pedigree, ancestry.

Silver Tabby American Shorthair

OFFICIAL STANDARD
Cat Fanciers' Association, Inc.

AMERICAN SHORTHAIR

POINT SCORE

Head (including size and shape of eyes, ear shape, and set and structure of nose)	30
Type (including shape, size, bone and length of tail)	25
Coat	15
Color	20
Eye color	10

General
The American Shorthair is believed by some naturalists to be the original breed of domestic cat. It has for many, many centuries adapted itself willingly and cheerfully to the needs of man, but without allowing itself to become effete or its natural intelligence to diminish. Its disposition and habits are exemplary as a house pet, a pet and companion for children, but the feral instinct lies not too far beneath the surface and this breed of cat remains capable of self-sufficiency when the need arises. Its hunting instinct is so strong that it exercises the skill even when well provided with food. This is our only breed of true "working cat." The conformation of the breed is well adapted for this and reflects its refusal to surrender its natural functions. This is a cat lithe enough to stalk its prey, but powerful enough to make the kill easily. Its reflexes are under perfect control. Its legs are long enough to cope with any terrain and heavy and muscular enough for high leaps. The face is long enough to permit easy grasping by the teeth with jaws so powerful they can close against resistance. Its coat is dense enough to protect from moisture, cold and superficial skin injuries, but short enough and of sufficiently hard texture to resist matting or entanglement when slipping through heavy vegetation. No part of the anatomy is so exaggerated as to foster weakness. The general effect is that of the trained athlete, with all muscles rippling easily beneath the skin, the flesh lean and hard, and with great latent power held in reserve.

Head
Large, with full-cheeked face giving the impression of an oblong just slightly longer than wide.

Neck
Medium in length, muscular and strong.

Nose
Medium in length, same width for entire length, with a gentle curve.

Muzzle
Squared. Definite jowls in studs.

Chin
Firm and well-developed, forming perpendicular line with upper lip.

Ears
Medium, slightly rounded at tips, set wide and not unduly open at base.

Eyes
Round and wide with slight slant to outer aperture. Set well apart. Bright, clear and alert.

Body
Medium to large, well-knit, powerful and hard with well-developed chest and heavy shoulders. No sacrifice of quality for the sake of mere size.

Legs
Medium in length, firm-boned and heavily muscled, showing capability for easy jumping.

Head: full-cheeked face

Body: well-knit, powerful

CFA OFFICIAL STANDARD continued –

Paws
Firm, full and rounded, with heavy pads. Toes: five in front, four behind.

Tail
Medium long, heavy at base, tapering to an abrupt blunt end in appearance, but with normal tapering final vertebrae.

Coat
Short, thick, even and hard in texture. Somewhat heavier and thicker during the winter months.

Penalize
Excessive cobbiness and ranginess. Very short tail. Obesity or boniness.

Disqualify
Deep nose break. Long or fluffy fur. Kinked or abnormal tail. Locket or button. Any appearance of hybridization with any other breed. Incorrect number of toes.

AMERICAN SHORTHAIR COLORS

WHITE
Pure glistening white.

Nose leather
Pink.

Paw pads
Pink.

Eye color
Deep blue or brilliant gold. Odd-eyed whites shall have one blue and one gold eye with equal color depth.

BLACK
Dense coal black, sound from roots to tip of fur. Free from any tinge of rust on tips or smoke undercoat.

Nose leather
Black.

Paw pads
Black or brown.

Eye color
Brilliant gold.

BLUE
Blue, lighter shade preferred, one level tone from nose to tip of tail. Sound to the roots. A sound darker shade is more acceptable than an unsound lighter shade.

Nose leather
Blue.

Paw pads
Blue.

Eye color
Brilliant gold.

RED
Deep, rich, clear, brilliant red; without shading, markings, or ticking. Lips and chin the same color as coat.

Shaded Silver American Shorthair

Nose leather
Brick red.

Paw pads
Brick red.

Eye color
Brilliant gold.

CREAM
One level shade of buff cream, without markings. Sound to the roots. Lighter shades preferred.

Nose leather
Pink.

Paw pads
Pink.

Eye color
Brilliant gold.

CHINCHILLA
Undercoat pure white. Coat on back, flanks, head and tail sufficiently tipped with black to give the characteristic sparkling silver appearance. Legs may be slightly shaded with tipping. Chin and ear tufts, stomach and chest pure white. Rims of eyes, lips and nose outlined with black.

Nose leather
Brick red.

Paw pads
Black.

Eye color
Green or blue-green.

SHADED SILVER
Undercoat white with a mantle of black tipping shading down from sides, face and tail from dark on the ridge to white on the chin, chest, stomach and under the tail. Legs to be the same tone as the face. The general effect to be much darker than a chinchilla. Rims of eyes, lips and nose outlined with black.

Nose leather
Brick red.

Paw pads
Black.

Eye color
Green or blue-green.

SHELL CAMEO (Red Chinchilla)
Undercoat white, the coat on the back, flanks, head and tail to be sufficiently tipped with red to give the characteristic sparkling appearance. Face and legs may be very slightly shaded with tipping. Chin, ear tufts, stomach and chest white.

Nose leather
Rose.

Rims of eyes
Rose.

Paw pads
Rose.

Shaded Cameo American Shorthair

CFA OFFICIAL STANDARD continued –

Eye color
Brilliant gold.

SHADED CAMEO (Red Shaded)
Undercoat white with a mantle of red tipping shading down the sides, face, and tail from dark on the ridge to white on the chin, chest, stomach, and under the tail. Legs to be the same tone as face. The general effect to be much redder than the Shell Cameo.

Nose leather
Rose.

Rims of eyes
Rose.

Paw pads
Black.

Eye color
Brilliant gold.

BLACK SMOKE
White undercoat, deeply tipped with black. Cat in repose appears black. In motion the white undercoat is clearly apparent. Points and mask black with narrow band of white at base of hairs next to skin which may be seen only when the fur is parted.

Nose leather
Black.

Paw pads
Black.

Eye color
Brilliant gold.

BLUE SMOKE
White undercoat, deeply tipped with blue. Cat in repose appears blue. In motion the white undercoat is clearly apparent. Points and mask blue, with narrow band of white at base of hairs next to skin which may be seen only when fur is parted.

Nose leather
Blue.

Paw pads
Blue.

Eye color
Brilliant gold.

CAMEO SMOKE (Red Smoke)
White undercoat, deeply tipped with red. Cat in repose appears red. In motion the white undercoat is clearly apparent. Points and mask red with narrow band of white at base of hairs next to skin, which may be seen only when fur is parted.

Nose leather
Rose.

Rims of eyes
Rose.

Paw pads
Rose.

Eye color
Brilliant gold.

CLASSIC TABBY PATTERN
Markings dense, clearly defined and broad. Legs evenly barred with bracelets coming up to meet the body markings. Tail evenly ringed. Several unbroken necklaces on neck and upper chest, the more the better. Frown marks on forehead form intricate letter "M". Unbroken line runs back from outer corner of eye. Swirls on cheeks. Veritcal lines over back of head extend to shoulder markings which are in the shape of a butterfly with both upper and lower wings distinctly outlined and marked with dots inside outline. Back markings consist of a vertical line down the spine from butterfly to tail with a vertical strip paralleling it on each side, the three stripes well separated by stripes of the ground color. Large solid blotch on each side to be encircled by one or more unbroken rings. Side markings should be the same on both sides. Double vertical row of buttons on chest and stomach.

MACKEREL TABBY PATTERN
Markings dense, clearly defined, and all narrow pencillings. Legs evenly barred with narrow bracelets coming up to meet the body markings. Tail barred. Necklaces on neck and chest distinct, like so many chains. Head barred with an "M" on the forehead. Unbroken lines running back from the eyes. Lines running down the head to meet the shoulders. Spine lines run together to form a narrow saddle. Narrow pencillings run around body.

PATCHED TABBY PATTERN
A Patched Tabby (Torbie) is an established silver, brown, or blue tabby with patches of red and/or cream.

BROWN PATCHED TABBY
Ground color brilliant coppery brown with classic or mackerel tabby markings of dense black with patches of red and/or cream clearly defined on both body and extremities; a blaze of red and/or cream on the face is desirable. Lips and chin the same shade as the rings around the eyes.

Eye color
Brilliant gold.

BLUE PATCHED TABBY

Ground color, including lips and chin, pale bluish ivory with classic or mackerel tabby markings of very deep blue affording a good contrast with ground color. Patches of cream clearly defined on both body and extremities; a blaze of cream on the face is desirable. Warm fawn overtones of patina over the whole.

Eye color
Brilliant gold.

SILVER PATCHED TABBY

Ground color, including lips and chin, pale silver with classic or mackerel tabby markings of dense black with patches of red and/or cream clearly defined on both body and extremities. A blaze of red and/or cream on the face is desirable.

Eye color
Brilliant gold or hazel.

SILVER TABBY

Ground color, including lips and chin, pale, clear silver. Markings dense black.

Nose leather
Brick red.

Paw pads
Black.

Eye color
Green or hazel.

RED TABBY

Ground color red. Markings deep rich red. Lips and chin red.

Nose leather
Brick red.

Paw pads
Brick red.

Eye color
Brilliant gold.

BROWN TABBY

Ground color brilliant coppery brown. Markings dense black. Lips and chin the same shade as the rings around the eyes. Back of leg black from paw to heel.

Nose leather
Brick red.

Paw pads
Black or brown.

Eye color
Brilliant gold.

BLUE TABBY

Ground color, including lips and chin, pale bluish ivory. Markings a very deep blue affording a good contrast with ground color. Warm fawn overtones or patina over the whole.

Nose leather
Old rose.

Paw pads
Rose.

Eye color
Brilliant gold.

CREAM TABBY

Ground color, including lips and chin, very pale cream. Markings of buff or cream sufficiently darker than the ground color to afford good contrast, but remaining within the dilute color range.

Nose leather
Pink.

Paw pads
Pink.

Eye color
Brilliant gold.

CAMEO TABBY

Ground color off-white. Markings red.

Nose leather
Rose.

Paw pads
Rose.

Eye color
Brilliant gold.

TORTOISESHELL

Black with unbrindled patches of red and cream. Patches clearly defined and well broken on both body and extremities. Blaze of red or cream on face is desirable.

Eye color
Brilliant gold.

CALICO

White with unbrindled patches of black and red. White predominant on underparts.

Eye color
Brilliant gold.

DILUTE CALICO

White with unbrindled patches of blue and cream. White predominant on underparts.

CFA OFFICIAL STANDARD continued –

Eye color
Brilliant gold.

BLUE-CREAM
Blue with patches of solid cream. Patches clearly defined and well broken on both body and extremities.

Eye color
Brilliant gold.

BI-COLOR
White with unbrindled patches of black, or white with unbrindled patches of blue, or white with unbrindled patches of red, or white with unbrindled patches of cream.

Eye color
Gold, the more brilliant the better.

Blue Tabby American Shorthair

Black and White Bicolour American Shorthair

AMERICAN WIREHAIR

Silver Tabby American Wirehair

From the distance at first glance the American Wirehair looks much the same as many other shorthairs, as it has similar type. As one gets nearer, the difference in coat can be clearly seen, and when handled the texture is very different to the touch. Very dense and harsh to feel, the hairs spring up again when pressed down with the hand. Looked at individually through a magnifying glass, each hair looks as if it has been crimped with minute curling tongs.

The Wirehair started as a spontaneous mutation in the mid-1970s, and selective breeding has proved that it is possible to produce the coat in all colours.

Strangely enough, prior to this cats with similar coats had been found on derelict bomb sites in London. Since the Second World War these sites had harboured many colonies of homeless and unwanted cats that

intermated among themselves. They produced generations of animals with very unusual colourings in some cases, and a few with coats exactly the same as the American Wirehair cats. Two of these cats were exhibited in the pet section at the National Cat Club Show in Britain two years before they were seen in the United States. Although they were very similar to the American Wirehair in appearance, the heads were more British in type. They had no pedigrees, and possibly did not breed true.

It is fascinating to realize that coats so similar could be produced by spontaneous mutation at places separated by such great distances. Of course, Rex cats also appeared by mutation in different parts of the world at approximately the same time. All this certainly makes cats seem more mysterious than ever.

OFFICIAL STANDARD
Cat Fanciers' Association, Inc.

AMERICAN WIREHAIR

POINT SCORE

Head (including size and shape of eyes, ear shape and set)	25
Type (including shape, size, bone and length of tail)	20
Coat	45
Color and eye color	10

General
The American Wirehair is a spontaneous mutation. The coat, which is not only springy, dense, and resilient, but also coarse and hard to the touch, distinguishes the American Wirehair from all other breeds. Characteristic is activity, agility, and keen interest in its surroundings.

Head
In proportion to the body. Underlying bone structure is round with prominent cheek bones and well developed muzzle and chin. There is a slight whisker break.

Nose
In profile the nose shows a gentle concave curve.

Muzzle
Well-developed. Allowance for jowls in adult males.

Chin
Firm and well developed with no apparent malocclusion.

Ears
Medium, slightly rounded at tips, set wide and not unduly open at the base.

Eyes
Large, round, bright and clear. Set well apart. Aperture has slight upward tilt.

Body
Medium to large. Back level, shoulders and hips same width, torso well rounded and in proportion. Males larger than females.

Legs
Medium in length and bone, well muscled and proportionate to body.

Paws
Oval and compact.

Tail
In proportion to body, tapering from the well rounded rump to a rounded tip, neither blunt nor pointed.

Coat
Springy, tight, medium in length. Individual hairs are crimped, hooked, or bent, including hair within the ears. The overall appearance of wiring and the coarseness and resilience of the coat is more important than the crimping of each hair. The density of the wired coat leads to ringlet formation rather than waves. That coat, which is very dense, resilient, crimped, and coarse, is most desirable, as are curly whiskers.

Penalize
Deep nose break. Long or fluffy fur.

Disqualify
Incorrect coat. Kinked or abnormal tail.

AMERICAN WIREHAIR COLORS

WHITE
Pure glistening white.

Nose leather
Pink.

Paw pads
Pink.

Eye color
Deep blue or brilliant gold. Odd-eyed whites shall have one blue and one gold eye with equal color depth.

BLACK
Dense coal black, sound from roots to tip of fur. Free from any tinge of rust on tips or smoke undercoat.

Nose leather
Black.

Paw pads
Black or brown.

Eye color
Brilliant gold.

BLUE
Blue, lighter shade preferred, one level tone from nose to tip of tail. Sound to the roots. A sound darker shade is more acceptable than an unsound lighter shade.

Nose leather
Blue.

Paw pads
Blue.

Eye color
Brilliant gold.

RED
Deep, rich, clear, brilliant red, without shading, markings or ticking. Lips and chin the same color as coat.

Tail: a rounded tip

Head: nose shows slight concave curve

Nose leather
Brick red.

Paw pads
Brick red.

Eye color
Brilliant gold.

CREAM
One level shade of buff cream, without markings. Sound to the roots. Lighter shades preferred.

Nose leather
Pink.

Paw pads
Pink.

Eye color
Brilliant gold.

CHINCHILLA
Undercoat pure white. Coat on back, flanks, head and tail sufficiently tipped with black to give the characteristic sparkling silver appearance. Legs may be slightly shaded with tipping. Chin and ear tufts, stomach and chest, pure white. Rims of eyes, lips and nose outlined with black.

Nose leather
Brick red.

Paw pads
Black.

Eye color
Green or blue-green.

SHADED SILVER
Undercoat white with a mantle of black tipping shading

down from sides, face and tail from dark on the ridge to white on the chin, chest, stomach and under the tail. Legs to be the same tone as the face. The general effect to be much darker than a chinchilla. Rims of eyes, lips and nose outlined with black.

Nose leather
Brick red.

Paw pads
Black.

Eye color
Green or blue-green.

SHELL CAMEO (Red Chinchilla)
Undercoat white, the coat on the back, flanks, head and tail to be sufficiently tipped with red to give the characteristic sparkling appearance. Face and legs may be very slightly shaded with tipping. Chin, ear tufts, stomach and chest white.

Nose leather
Rose.

Rims of eyes
Rose.

Paw pads
Rose.

Eye color
Brilliant gold.

SHADED CAMEO (Red Shaded)
Undercoat white with a mantle of red tipping shading down the sides, face, and tail from dark on the ridge to white on the chin, chest, stomach, and under the tail. Legs to be the same tone as face. The general effect to be much redder than the Shell Cameo.

145

CFA OFFICIAL STANDARD continued –

Nose leather
Rose.

Rims of eyes
Rose.

Paw pads
Rose.

Eye color
Brilliant gold.

BLACK SMOKE
White undercoat, deeply tipped with black. Cat in repose appears black. In motion the white undercoat is clearly apparent. Points and mask black with narrow band of white at base of hairs next to skin which may be seen only when the fur is parted.

Nose leather
Black.

Paw pads
Black.

Tabby American Wirehair

Eye color
Brilliant gold.

BLUE SMOKE
White undercoat, deeply tipped with blue. Cat in repose appears blue. In motion the white undercoat is clearly apparent. Points and mask blue, with narrow band of white at base of hairs next to skin which may be seen only when fur is parted.

Nose leather
Blue.

Paw pads
Blue.

Eye color
Brilliant gold.

CAMEO SMOKE (Red Smoke)
White undercoat, deeply tipped with red. Cat in repose appears red. In motion the white undercoat is clearly apparent. Points and mask red with narrow band of white at base of hairs next to skin, which may be seen only when fur is parted.

Nose leather
Rose.

Rims of eyes
Rose.

Paw pads
Rose.

Eye color
Brilliant gold.

CLASSIC TABBY PATTERN
Markings dense, clearly defined and broad. Legs evenly barred with bracelets coming up to meet the body markings. Tail evenly ringed. Several unbroken necklaces on neck and upper chest, the more the better. Frown marks on forehead form intricate letter "M". Unbroken line runs back from outer corner of eye. Swirls on cheeks. Vertical lines over back of head extend to shoulder markings which are in the shape of a butterfly with both upper and lower wings distinctly outlined and marked with dots inside outline. Back markings consist of a vertical line down the spine from butterfly to tail with a vertical strip paralleling it on each side, the three stripes well separated by stripes of the ground colour. Large solid blotch on each side to be encircled by one or more unbroken rings. Side markings should be the same on both sides. Double vertical row of buttons on chest and stomach.

MACKEREL TABBY PATTERN
Markings dense, clearly defined, and all narrow pencillings. Legs evenly barred with narrow bracelets coming up to meet the body markings. Tail barred. Necklaces on neck and chest distinct, like so many chains. Head barred with an "M" on the forehead. Unbroken lines running back from the eyes. Lines running down the head to meet the shoulders. Spine lines run together to form a narrow saddle. Narrow pencillings run around body.

SILVER TABBY
Ground color, including lips and chin, pale, clear silver. Markings dense black.

Nose leather
Brick red.

Paw pads
Black.

Eye color
Green or hazel.

RED TABBY
Ground colour red. Markings deep, rich red. Lips and chin red.

Nose leather
Brick red.

Paw pads
Brick red.

Eye color
Brilliant gold.

BROWN TABBY
Ground color brilliant coppery brown. Markings dense black. Lips and chine the same shade as the rings around the eyes. Back of leg black from paw to heel.

Nose leather
Brick red.

Paw pads
Black or brown.

Eye color
Brilliant gold.

BLUE TABBY
Ground color, including lips and chin, pale bluish ivory. Markings a very deep blue affording a good contrast with ground color. Warm fawn overtones or patina over the whole.

Nose leather
Old rose.

Paw pads
Rose.

Eye color
Brilliant gold.

CREAM TABBY
Ground colour, including lips and chin, very pale cream. Markings of buff or cream sufficiently darker than the ground color to afford good contrast, but remaining within the dilute color range.

Nose leather
Pink.

Paw pads
Pink.

Eye color
Brilliant gold.

CAMEO TABBY
Ground color off-white. Markings red.

Nose leather
Rose.

Paw pads
Rose.

Eye color
Brilliant gold.

TORTOISESHELL
Black with unbrindled patches of red and cream. Patches clearly defined and well broken on both body and extremities. Blaze of red or cream on face is desirable.

CFA OFFICIAL STANDARD continued –

Eye color
Brilliant gold.

CALICO
White with unbrindled patches of black and red. White predominant on underparts.

Eye color
Brilliant gold.

DILUTE CALICO
White with unbrindled patches of blue and cream. White predominant on underparts.

Eye color
Brilliant gold.

BLUE-CREAM
Blue with patches of solid cream. Patches clearly defined and well broken on both body and extremities.

Eye color
Brilliant gold.

BI-COLOR
White with unbrindled patches of black, or white with unbrindled patches of blue, or white with unbrindled patches of red, or white with unbrindled patches of cream.

Eye color
Gold, the more brilliant the better.

OWC (Other Wirehair Colors)
White with smoke, any tabby pattern, tortie or blue-cream. Cats with no more white than a locket and/or button shall be judged in the color class of their basic color with no penalty for such locket and/or button.

Eye color
Brilliant gold.

Odd-eyed White American Wirehair

SCOTTISH FOLD

White Scottish Fold

The Scottish Fold, a cat in which the ears fold over through an angle of about 180°, appeared as a natural mutation in Scotland and was shown several times in Any Other Variety classes in Britain. The overturned ear flap covers the ear opening, and as it cartilaginous and unyielding, British judges and several veterinary surgeons arrived at the view that it would prevent the cat hearing well and would make it difficult, if not impossible, to clean the ears. After careful discussion, in the course of which the veterinary profession was fully consulted, the Governing Council of the Cat Fancy decided to disallow the registration of this variety and therefore forbade its exhibition at all shows licensed by the GCCF in Britain.

Nevertheless, the discoverers of the variety decided to continue breeding it, and to export it to America and to some European countries. Deformities soon appeared in the tail and back legs, but it proved possible with careful breeding, using heterozygous Fold crosses, to produce healthy kittens. The Scottish Fold has been recognized in the United States by the Cat Fanciers' Association. The cat is now never seen on the European showbench, but has been seen in Australia. In Europe neither the Fédération Internationale Féline d'Europe nor the independent cat bodies, such as the Cercle Feline, recognizes it.

Red Tabby Scottish Fold

OFFICIAL STANDARD
Cat Fanciers' Association, Inc.

SCOTTISH FOLD

POINT SCORE

Ears	30
Head	20
Eyes	15
Body and tail	25
Color	10

General
The Scottish Fold cat occurred as a spontaneous mutation in farm cats in Scotland. The breed has been established by crosses to British Shorthair and Domestic cats in Scotland and England. In America the outcross is the American and British Shorthair. All bona fide Scottish Fold cats trace their pedigree to Susie, the first fold-ear cat discovered by the founders of the breed: William and Mary Ross.

Head
Well rounded with a firm chin and jaw. Nose to be short with a gentle curve. Muzzle to have well rounded whisker pads. Head should blend into a short neck. Prominent cheeks with a jowly appearance in males.

Head : ears folded forward and downward

Eyes
Wide open with a sweet expression. Large, well rounded and separated by a broad nose. Eye color to correspond with coat color.

Ears
Fold forward and downward. Small, the smaller, tightly folded ear preferred over a loose fold and larger ear. The ears should be set in a caplike fashion to expose a rounded cranium. Eartips to be rounded. No matter how dramatically folded the ear, if the whole cat presents an overall appearance contrary to the standard for the whole cat, **type** must prevail.

Body
Short, rounded and even from shoulder to pelvic girdle. The cat should stand firm on a well padded body. Legs medium in length and in proportion to the body. There must be no hint of thickness or lack of mobility in the cat due to short, coarse legs. Toes to be neat and well rounded with five in front and four behind. Overall appearance is that of a well rounded cat with medium bone. Females may be slightly smaller.

Body : short, well-rounded

Tail
Tail should be medium to long but in proportion to the body. Tail should be flexible and tapering.

Coat
Short, dense and resilient.

Disqualify
Kinked, broad, thick or foreshortened tail.

SCOTTISH FOLD COLORS

WHITE
Pure glistening white.

Nose leather
Pink.

Paw pads
Pink.

Eye color
Deep blue or brilliant gold. Odd-eyed whites shall have one blue and one gold eye with equal color depth.

CFA OFFICIAL STANDARD continued –

BLACK
Dense coal black, sound from roots to tip of fur. Free from any tinge of rust on tips or smoke undercoat.

Nose leather
Black.

Paw pads
Black or brown.

Eye color
Brilliant gold.

BLUE
Blue, lighter shade preferred, one level tone from nose to tip of tail. Sound to roots. A sound darker shade is more acceptable than an unsound lighter shade.

Nose leather
Blue.

Paw pads
Blue.

Eye color
Brilliant gold.

RED
Deep, rich, clear, brilliant red; without shading, markings or ticking. Lips and chin the same color as coat.

Nose leather
Brick red.

Paw pads
Brick red.

Eye color
Brilliant gold.

CREAM
One level shade of buff cream, without markings. Sound to the roots. Lighter shades preferred.

Nose leather
Pink.

Paw pads
Pink.

Eye color
Brilliant gold.

CHINCHILLA
Undercoat pure white. Coat on back, flanks, head and tail sufficiently tipped with black to give the characteristic sparkling silver appearance. Legs may be slightly shaded with tipping. Chin and ear tufts, stomach and chest, pure white. Rims of eyes, lips and nose, outlined with black.

Nose leather
Brick red.

Paw pads
Black.

Eye color
Green or blue-green.

SHADED SILVER
Undercoat white with a mantle of black tipping shading down from sides, face and tail from dark on the ridge to white on the chin, chest, stomach and under the tail. Legs to be the same tone as the face. The general effect to be much darker than a chinchilla. Rims of eyes, lips and nose outlined with black.

Nose leather
Brick red.

Paw pads
Black.

Eye color
Green or blue-green.

SHELL CAMEO (Red Chinchilla)
Undercoat white, the coat on the back, flanks, head and tail to be sufficiently tipped with red to give the characteristic sparkling appearance. Face and legs may be very slightly shaded with tipping. Chin, ear tufts, stomach and chest white.

Nose leather
Rose.

Rims of eyes
Rose.

Paw pads
Rose.

Eye color
Brilliant gold.

SHADED CAMEO (Red Shaded)
Undercoat white with a mantle of red tipping shading down the sides, face, and tail from dark on the ridge to white on the chin, chest, stomach, and under the tail. Legs to be the same tone as face. The general effect to be much redder than the Shell Cameo.

Nose leather
Rose.

Rims of eyes
Rose.

Paw pads
Rose.

Eye color
Brilliant gold.

BLACK SMOKE

White undercoat, deeply tipped with black. Cat in repose appears black. In motion the white undercoat is clearly apparent.

Points and mask
Black with narrow band of white at base of hairs next to skin which may be seen only when the fur is parted.

Nose leather
Black.

Paw pads
Black.

Eye color
Brilliant gold.

BLUE SMOKE

White undercoat, deeply tipped with blue. Cat in repose appears blue. In motion the white undercoat is clearly apparent.

Points and mask
Blue, with narrow band of white at base of hairs next to skin which may be seen only when fur is parted.

Nose leather
Blue.

Paw pads
Blue.

Eye color
Brilliant gold.

CAMEO SMOKE (Red Smoke)

White undercoat, deeply tipped with red. Cat in repose appears red. In motion the white undercoat is clearly apparent.

Points and mask
Red with narrow band of white at base of hairs next to skin, which may be seen only when fur is parted.

Nose leather
Rose.

Rims of eyes
Rose.

Paw pads
Rose.

Eye color
Brilliant gold.

CLASSIC TABBY PATTERN

Markings dense, clearly defined and broad. Legs evenly barred with bracelets coming up to meet the body markings. Tail evenly ringed. Several unbroken necklaces on neck and upper chest, the more the better. Frown marks on forehead form intricate letter "M". Unbroken line runs back from outer corner of eye. Swirls on cheeks. Vertical lines over back of head extend to shoulder markings which are in the shape of a butterfly with both upper and lower wings distinctly outlined and marked with dots inside outline. Back markings consist of a vertical line down the spine from butterfly to tail with a vertical stripe paralleling it on each side, the three stripes well separated by stripes of the ground color. Large solid blotch on each side to be encircled by one or more unbroken rings. Side markings should be the same on both sides. Double vertical row of buttons on chest and stomach.

MACKEREL TABBY PATTERN

Markings dense, clearly defined, and all narrow pencillings. Legs evenly barred with narrow bracelets coming up to meet the body markings. Tail barred. Necklaces on neck and chest distinct, like so many chains. Head barred with an "M" on the forehead. Unbroken lines running back from the eyes. Lines running down the head to meet the shoulders. Spine lines run together to form a narrow saddle. Narrow pencillings run around body.

SILVER TABBY

Ground color, including lips and chin, pale, clear silver. Markings dense black.

Nose leather
Brick red.

Paw pads
Black.

Eye color
Green or hazel.

RED TABBY

Ground color red. Markings deep, rich red. Lips and chin red.

Nose leather
Brick red.

Paw pads
Brick red.

Eye color
Brilliant gold.

BROWN TABBY

Ground color brilliant coppery brown. Markings dense black. Lips and chin the same shade as the rings around the eyes. Back of leg black from paw to heel.

Nose leather
Brick red.

Paw pads
Black or brown.

CFA OFFICIAL STANDARD continued –

Eye color
Brilliant gold.

BLUE TABBY
Ground color, including lips and chin, pale bluish ivory. Markings a very deep blue affording a good contrast with ground color. Warm fawn overtones or patina over the whole.

Nose leather
Old rose.

Paw pads
Rose.

Eye color
Brilliant gold.

CREAM TABBY
Ground color, including lips and chin, very pale cream. Markings of buff or cream sufficiently darker than the ground color to afford good contrast, but remaining within the dilute color range.

Nose leather
Pink.

Paw pads
Pink.

Eye color
Brilliant gold.

CAMEO TABBY
Ground color off-white. Markings red.

Nose leather
Rose.

Paw pads
Rose.

Eye color
Brilliant gold.

TORTOISESHELL
Black with unbrindled patches of red and cream. Patches clearly defined and well broken on both body and extremities. Blaze of red or cream on face is desirable.

Scottish Fold adult and kitten

Eye color
Brilliant gold.

CALICO
White with unbrindled patches of black and red. White predominant on underparts.

Eye color
Brilliant gold.

DILUTE CALICO
White with unbrindled patches of blue and cream. White predominant on underparts.

Eye color
Brilliant gold.

BLUE-CREAM
Blue with patches of solid cream. Patches clearly defined and well broken on both body and extremities.

Eye color
Brilliant gold.

BI-COLOR
White with unbrindled patches of black, or white with unbrindled patches of blue, or white with unbrindled patches of red, or white with unbrindled patches of cream.

Eye color
Gold, the more brilliant the better.

MANX

American Bicolour Manx

The Manx cat possesses the special peculiarity of being tailless and having a rabbit-like gait. In fact, on their home ground, Manx are found both tailless and with tails ranging from a small protuberance to several inches in length.

It is extremely unlikely that the Manx cat originated as its name indicates, on the Isle of Man. In the late 1800s Mr Gambier Bolton wrote that it was believed that in 1558 one of the vessels of the Spanish Armada foundered on Spanish Rock, which stands close to the Manx shore. On it were several tailless cats, which had been procured by the captain during one of the ship's voyages to the Middle East. The cats first swam to the rock and then to the island at low tide. From these, it is alleged, sprang all the so-called Manx cats that are now to be found in Britain, Europe and America.

In *The Book of the Cat* Frances Simpson adds that 'Any traveller in the Far East, Japan, China, Siam and the Malay Peninsula, who is a lover of animals, must have noticed how rarely one meets with really, long-tailed cats. Instead, one meets with the kink-tailed, the short kink-tailed, and finally the tailless cats; and the naturalist Kaempfer states definitely that the specimens of this general variety, and particularly the tailless specimens now so common in parts of Russia, all came originally from Japan.'

Frances Simpson goes on to describe six distinct varieties of the Manx exhibited at the English cat shows at the turn of the century: the long straight-backed cat, the long roach-backed cat, the long straight-backed cat with high hind-quarters, the short straight-backed cat, the short roach-backed cat, the short-backed cat with high hindquarters. The last type is one given recognition by the cat fancies.

The Manx cat may be of any colour recognized in shorthaired varieties. Its essential characteristics are complete taillessness and the possession of a very short back, with the hind legs considerably longer than the front. The coat must be double, the soft topcoat lying over a thick undercoat. The standard of the Cat Fanciers' Association of America requires the head to be somewhat rounder than that specified by the British standard.

The cats are totally 'at home' with dogs. In the years 1893–5 a Mr H. C. Brook exhibited a Manx in the same pen as a bulldog and was often seen with his two exhibits, which were inseparable, at the South London Bulldog Show.

The issue of *Our Cats* for 1 March 1900 included the following translation of a paragraph from the German weekly paper *Mutter Erde*: 'A cat brought from the Isle of Man *(felis catus anura)* to St Germain en Laye and of which the pedigree is unknown, was mated with ordinary, long-tailed cats; and among the kittens born, of which there were twenty-four in all, were found kittens with ordinary tails, kittens with short and stump tails, kittens without tails (like the mother) and finally, kittens without the least sign of a tail having a hollow where the tail normally issues.' Kittens with very short tails or stumps are called 'stumpies'. Kittens without tails are called 'rumpies'.

The taillessness of the Manx has been scientifically investigated in recent years. It appears that the gene responsible for this phenomenon is a dominant one, to which the symbol M has been given (see page 25). The gene M affects not only the external tail but also the vertebrae, which nearly always show a range of skeletal defects and abnormalities. For example, in the front of the spinal column the individual vertebrae often appear to be shorter in length than is normal; and in the lower region the number and length appear to be decreased and show a marked tendency to fuse. Various degrees of spinal bifida occur and occasional or recurrent bowel stoppages sometimes occur because of a narrowing of the anal opening.

The best show specimens are born from matings between Manx and normal cats having the desired bodily configuration, or between 'stumpies'. The standard of the Cat Fanciers' Association of America allows the end of the spine to have an invisible rise. The judge

'Stumpy' Manx kitten

can assess the roundness of the rump by running a hand down the back and over the rump, rather than probing a very sensitive area of the spine, which might harm the Manx or cause it to be unmanageable at shows. If the rise stops the judge's hand, it is too great and will be penalized.

The top winning Manx in the United States was a copper-eyed white, Grand Champion Wila-Blite Pola of Silva-Wyte. At the remarkable age of 13 years, she won Best in Show.

The Manx gene is recognized to be a highly undesirable one, and many cat breeders, particularly in Sweden and Britain, have expressed the view that the Manx cat should not be encouraged or, indeed, perpetuated. Conversely, it is argued, with some justice, that a variety that has bred successfully and without aid since at least 1500 cannot be said to be all that undesirable. This, together with the undeniable charm of the Manx, is likely to ensure its continuance.

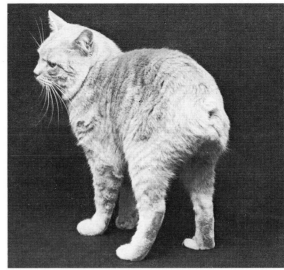

Rearview of 'rumpy' Manx

Sideview of a 'rumpy' Manx

OFFICIAL STANDARD
Cat Fanciers' Association, Inc.

MANX

POINT SCORE

Head and ears	25
Eyes	5
Body	25
Taillessness	15
Legs and feet	15
Coat	10
Color and markings	5

General
The overall impression of the Manx cat is that of roundness: round head with firm, round muzzle and prominent cheeks, broad chest, substantial short front legs, short back which arches from shoulders to a round rump, great depth of flank, and rounded, muscular thighs. The heavy, glossy double coat accentuates the round appearance. The constant repetition of curves and circles gives the Manx the appearance of great substance and durability, a cat that is powerful without the slightest hint of coarseness. With regard to condition, the Manx presented in the show ring should evidence a healthy physical appearance, feeling firm and muscular, neither too fat nor too lean. The Manx should be alert, clear of eye, with a glistening, clean coat.

Head and ears
Round head with prominent cheeks and a jowly appearance. Head is slightly longer than it is broad. Moderately rounded forehead, pronounced cheekbones and jowliness

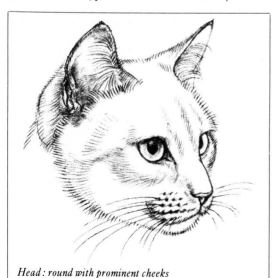

Head: round with prominent cheeks

(jowliness more evident in adult males) enhance the round appearance. Definite whisker break, with large, round whisker pads. In profile there is a gentle nose dip. Well-developed muzzle, slightly longer than broad, with a strong chin. Short, thick neck. Ears wide at the base, tapering gradually to a rounded tip, with sparse interior furnishings. Medium in size in proportion to the head, widely spaced and set slightly outward.

Eyes
Large, round and full, set at a slight angle toward the nose (outer corners slightly higher than inner corners). Ideal eye color conforms to requirements of coat color.

Body
Solidly muscled, compact and well-balanced, medium in size with sturdy bone structure. The Manx is stout in appearance, with broad chest and well-sprung ribs; surprisingly heavy when lifted. Males may be somewhat larger than females.

Flank (fleshy area of the side between the ribs and hip) has greater depth than in any other breed, causing considerable depth to the body when viewed from the side.

The short back forms a smooth, continuous arch from shoulders to rump, curving at the rump to form the desirable round look. Shortness of back is unique to the Manx, but is in proportion to the entire cat and may be somewhat longer in the male.

Body: hind legs longer than forelegs

Taillessness
Absolute in the perfect specimen, with a decided hollow at the end of the backbone where, in the tailed cat, a tail would begin. A rise of the bone at the end of the spine is allowed and should not be penalized unless it is such that it stops the judge's hand, thereby spoiling the tailless appearance of the cat. The rump is extremely broad and round.

Legs and feet
Heavily boned, forelegs short and set well apart to emphasize the broad, deep chest. Hindlegs much longer

than forelegs, with heavy, muscular thighs and substantial lower legs. Longer hindlegs cause the rump to be considerably higher than the shoulders. Hindlegs are straight when viewed from behind. Paws are neat and round, with five toes in front and four behind.

Coat

Double coat is short and dense, with a well-padded quality due to the longer, open outer coat and the close, cottony undercoat. Texture of outer guard hairs is somewhat hard; appearance is glossy. Coat may be thicker during cooler months of the year.

Transfer to AOV

Definite, visible tail joint; long, silky coat.

Disqualify

Evidence of poor physical condition; incorrect number of toes; evidence of hybridization; weak hind quarters causing inability to stand or walk properly.

MANX COLORS

WHITE
Pure glistening white.

Nose leather
Pink.

Paw pads
Pink.

Eye color
Deep blue or brilliant copper. Odd-eyed whites shall have one blue and one copper eye with equal color depth.

BLACK
Dense coal black, sound from roots to tip of fur. Free from any tinge of rust on tips.

Nose leather
Black.

Paw pads
Black or brown.

Eye color
Brilliant copper.

BLUE
Blue, lighter shade preferred, one level tone. Sound to the roots. A sound darker shade is more acceptable than an unsound light shade.

Nose leather
Blue.

Paw pads
Blue.

Eye color
Brilliant copper.

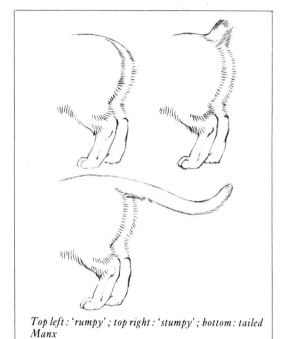

Top left: 'rumpy'; top right: 'stumpy'; bottom: tailed Manx

RED
Deep rich, clear, brilliant red; without shading, markings or ticking. Lips and chin the same color as coat.

Nose leather
Brick red.

Paw pads
Brick red.

Eye color
Brilliant copper.

CREAM
One level shade of buff cream, without markings. Sound to the roots. Lighter shades preferred.

Nose leather
Pink.

Paw pads
Pink.

Eye color
Brilliant copper.

CHINCHILLA
Undercoat pure white. Coat on back, flanks, and head sufficiently tipped with black to give the characteristic sparkling silver appearance. Legs may be slightly shaded with tipping. Chin, stomach and chest, pure white. Rims of eyes, lips and nose outlined with black.

Nose leather
Brick red.

Paw pads
Black.

Eye color
Green or blue-green.

SHADED SILVER
Undercoat white with a mantle of black tipping shading down from sides, and face, from dark on the ridge to white on the chin, chest, stomach. Legs to be of the same tone as the face. The general effect to be much darker than a chinchilla. Rims of eyes, lips and nose outlined with black.

Nose leather
Brick red.

Paw pads
Black.

Eye color
Green or blue-green.

BLACK SMOKE
White undercoat, deeply tipped with black. Cat in repose appears black. In motion the white undercoat is clearly apparent. Points and mask black with narrow band of white at base of hairs next to skin which may be seen only when the fur is parted.

Nose leather
Black.

Paw pads
Black.

Eye color
Brilliant copper.

BLUE SMOKE
White undercoat, deeply tipped with blue. Cat in repose appears blue. In motion the white undercoat is clearly apparent. Points and mask blue with narrow band of white at base of hairs next to skin which may be seen only when fur is parted.

Nose leather
Blue.

Paw pads
Blue.

Eye color
Brilliant copper.

CLASSIC TABBY PATTERN
Markings dense, clearly defined and broad. Legs evenly barred with bracelets coming up to meet the body markings. Several unbroken necklaces on neck and upper chest, the more the better. Frown marks on forehead form intricate letter "M". Unbroken line runs back from outer corner of eye. Swirls on cheeks. Vertical lines over back of head extend to shoulder markings which are in the shape of a butterfly with both upper and lower wings distinctly outlined and marked with dots inside outline. Back markings consist of a vertical line from butterfly down the entire spine with a vertical stripe paralleling it on each side, the three stripes well separated by stripes of the ground color. Large solid blotch on each side to be encircled by one or more unbroken rings. Side markings should be the same on both sides. Double vertical row of buttons on chest and stomach.

MACKEREL TABBY PATTERN
Markings dense, clearly defined, and all narrow pencillings. Legs evenly barred with narrow bracelets coming up to meet the body markings. Necklaces on neck and chest distinct, like so many chains. Head barred with an "M" on the forehead. Unbroken lines running back from the eyes. Lines running down the head to meet the shoulders. Spine lines run together to form a narrow saddle. Narrow pencillings run around body.

PATCHED TABBY PATTERN
A Patched Tabby (Torbie) is an established silver, brown, or blue tabby with patches of red and/or cream.

BROWN PATCHED TABBY
Ground color brilliant coppery brown with classic or mackerel tabby markings of dense black with patches of red and/or cream clearly defined on both body and extremities; a blaze of red and/or cream on the face is desirable. Lips and chin the same shade as the rings around the eyes.

Eye color
Brilliant copper.

BLUE PATCHED TABBY
Ground color, including lips and chin, pale bluish ivory with classic or mackerel tabby markings of very deep blue affording a good contrast with ground color. Patches of cream clearly defined on both body and extremities; a blaze of cream on the face is desirable. Warm fawn overtones or patina over the whole.

Eye color
Brilliant copper.

SILVER PATCHED TABBY
Ground color, including lips and chin, pale silver with classic or mackerel tabby markings of dense black with patches of red and/or cream clearly defined on both body and extremities. A blaze of red and/or cream on the face is desirable.

Eye color
Brilliant copper or hazel.

SILVER TABBY
Ground color, including lips and chin, pale, clear silver.

Markings dense black.

Nose leather
Brick red.

Paw pads
Black.

Eye color
Green or hazel.

RED TABBY
Ground color red. Markings deep, rich red. Lips and chin red.

Nose leather
Brick red.

Paw pads
Brick red.

Eye color
Brilliant copper.

BROWN TABBY
Ground color brilliant coppery brown. Markings dense black. Lips and chin the same shade as the rings around the eyes. Back of leg black from paw to heel.

Nose leather
Brick red.

Paw pads
Black or brown.

Eye color
Brilliant copper.

BLUE TABBY
Ground color, including lips and chin, pale bluish ivory. Markings a very deep blue affording a good contrast with ground color. Warm fawn overtones or patina over the whole.

Nose leather
Old rose.

Paw pads
Rose.

Eye color
Brilliant copper.

CREAM TABBY
Ground color, including lips and chin, very pale cream. Markings buff or cream sufficiently darker than the ground color to afford good contrast, but remaining within the dilute color range.

Nose leather
Pink.

Paw pads
Pink.

Eye color
Brilliant copper.

TORTOISESHELL
Black with unbrindled patches of red and cream. Patches clearly defined and well broken on both body and extremities. Blaze of red or cream on face is desirable.

Eye color
Brilliant copper.

CALICO
White with unbrindled patches of black and red. White predominant on underparts.

Eye color
Brilliant copper.

DILUTE CALICO
White with unbrindled patches of blue and cream. White predominant on underparts.

Eye color
Brilliant copper.

BLUE-CREAM
Blue with patches of solid cream. Patches clearly defined and well broken on both body and extremities.

Eye color
Brilliant copper.

BI-COLOR
White with unbrindled patches of black, or white with unbrindled patches of blue, or white with unbrindled patches of red, or white with unbrindled patches of cream. Cats with no more white than a locket and/or button do not qualify for this color class. Such cats shall be judged in the color class of their basic color with no penalty for such locket and/or button.

Eye color
Brilliant copper.

OMC (Other Manx Colors)
Any other color or pattern with the exception of those showing hybridization resulting in the colors chocolate, lavender, the himalayan pattern, or these combinations with white, etc.

Eye color
Appropriate to the predominant color of the cat.

OFFICIAL STANDARD
Governing Council of the Cat Fancy

MANX: VARIETY 25

Head
As near to British as possible. Fairly round and large with prominent cheeks. Appearance, rather jowled. Nose longish without a definite nose break but with no appearance of 'snipeyness'.

Ears
Wide at base, tapering slightly to a point. Taller than standard British and set more on top of head.

Eyes
Wide at base, tapering slightly to a point. Taller than standard British and set more on top of head.

Body
Solid, compact, cannot be too short and ending on a definite round rump. Back legs higher than front making an incline from back to front. Flanks of great depth.

Legs
Of good substance with front legs short and well set apart to show good depth of chest. Back legs longer with a heavy muscular thigh.

'Rumpy' Manx

Coat
Short, good texture. Double coated showing a well padded quality arising from the longer outer coat and the thicker undercoat. Coat colour and markings only taken into account when other points are equal.

Tail
Absolute taillessness is essential in a show specimen and there should be a decided hollow at the end of the backbone where, ordinarily the tail would begin.

Faults
A rise of bone at the end of the spine. A non-visible joint or cartilage.

Withhold certificates
Definite visible tail joint. Incorrect number of toes.

SCALE OF POINTS

Taillessness	25
Coat texture	15
Head and ears	15
Body shape	25
Eyes	5
Shortness of back	10
Condition	5
Total	100

JAPANESE BOBTAIL

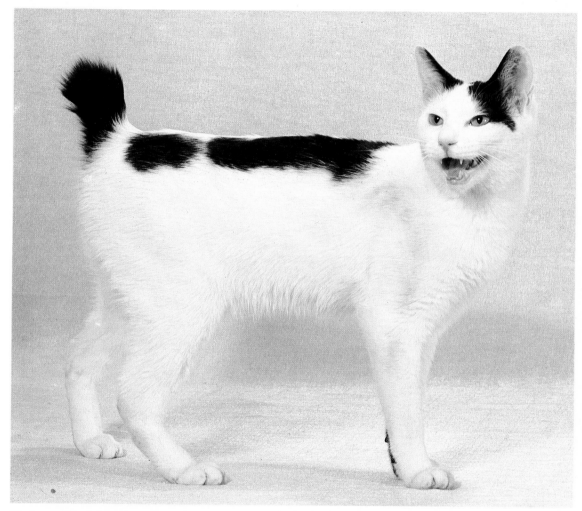

Black and White Japanese Bobtail

The Japanese Bobtail may be a comparatively new variety in the United States, but the original Bobtail, with colourful coat of black, red and white, known as Mi-Ke, has been seen in Japan for centuries, and has been portrayed by artists many times. It is not bred in Britain, but until 1977 there was a genuine Mi-Ke which had been brought to England by her owner, who had lived in Japan for many years. It has since died of old age.

The unique feature of the Bobtail is the tail, of course. Unlike the tails of any other variety, it is as much as four or five inches (10 or 12.5 centimetres) long, when pulled out to its full length, but usually looks only about two or three inches (5 or 7.5 centi-

metres) when it is held close to the body or upright. The way the hair grows really makes it look, from the distance, more like the tail of a rabbit.

The coat is longish, very soft to the touch, and although many colours are now recognized, the favourite is still the all-female tri-colour. The coats are very easy to groom, having very little undercoat and rarely knotting up, given the minimum of attention.

Every owner of a Bobtail is enthusiastic about this cat, its personality and character, and most of all its intelligence. The shortness of the tail does not appear to affect the cat's balance in jumping and playing. In fact, is is said to be more agile than usual.

OFFICIAL STANDARD
Cat Fanciers' Association, Inc.

JAPANESE BOBTAIL

POINT SCORE

Head	20
Type	30
Tail	20
Color and markings	20
Coat	10

Body: long, lean, well-muscled

General
The Japanese Bobtail should present the overall impression of a medium sized cat with long clean lines and bone structure, well-muscled but straight and slender rather than massive in build. The unique set of its eyes, combined with high cheek bones and a long parallel nose, lend a distinctive Japanese cast to the face, especially in profile, quite different from the other Oriental breeds. Its short tail should resemble a bunny tail with the hair fanning out in all directions to create a pom-pom appearance which effectively camouflages the underlying bone structure of the tail.

Head
Although the head appears long and finely chiselled, it forms almost a perfect equilateral triangle with gentle curving lines, high cheek bones, and a noticeable whisker break, the nose long and well-defined by two parallel lines from tip to brow with a gentle dip at, or just below, eye level.

Tail: opening out

Ears
Large, upright and expressive, set wide apart but at right angles to the head rather than flaring outward, and giving the impression of being tilted forward in repose.

Muzzle
Fairly broad and rounding into the whisker break; neither pointed nor blunt.

Eyes
Large, oval rather than round, but wide and alert; set into the skull at rather pronounced slant when viewed in profile. The eyeball shows a shallow curvature and should not bulge out beyond the cheekbone or the forehead.

Body
Medium in size, long and lean but shapely and well-muscled.

Legs
In keeping with the body, long, slender and high, but not dainty or fragile in appearance, the hind legs notice-

Tail: resembles a bunny tail

ably longer than the forelegs, but deeply angulated or bent when the cat is standing relaxed so that the torso remains nearly level rather than rising toward the rear. When standing, the cat's forelegs and shoulders form two continuous straight lines, close together.

Paws
Oval. Toes, five in front and four behind.

Coat
Medium length, soft and silky but without a noticeable undercoat. Relatively non-shedding.

Tail
The furthest extension of the tail bone from the body should be approximately two to three inches, even though the tail bone, if straightened out to its full length, might be four or five inches long. The tail is usually carried upright when the cat is relaxed. Hair on tail somewhat longer and thicker than body hair, growing outward in all directions to create a pom-pom or bunny-tail effect which appears to commence at the base of the spine and which camouflages the underlying bone structure of the tail. The tail bone is usually strong and rigid rather than jointed (except at the base), and may be either straight or composed of one or several curves and angles.

Color
In keeping with Japan's traditional mi-ke (mee-kay) cats, which are tri-colored (black, red and white), the preferred breeding colors are those that tend to produce tricolored females. In bi-colors and tri-colors, any color may predominate with preference given to bold, dramatic markings and vividly contrasting colors. Nose leather, paw pads, and eye color should harmonize generally with coat color.

Penalize
Short round head, cobby build.

Disqualify
Tail bone absent or extending too far beyond body; tail lacking in pom-pom or fluffy appearance; delayed bobtail effect (i.e. the pom-pom being preceded by an inch or two of normal tail with close-lying hair rather than appearing to commence at the base of the spine).

Japanese Bobtail kittens

CFA OFFICIAL STANDARD continued –

JAPANESE BOBTAIL COLORS

WHITE
Pure glistening white.

BLACK
Dense, coal black, sound from roots to tip of fur. Shiny and free from any tinge of rust on tips.

RED
Deep, rich, clear, brilliant red, the deeper and more glowing in tone the better.

BLACK AND WHITE

RED AND WHITE

MI-KE (Tri-Color)
Black, red, and white, or tortoiseshell with white.

TORTOISESHELL
Black, red, and cream.

OTHER JAPANESE BOBTAIL COLORS (OJBC)
Include the following categories and any other color or pattern or combination thereof except coloring that is point-restricted (i.e. Siamese markings) or un-patterned agouti (i.e. Abyssinian coloring). "Patterned" categories denote and include any variety of tabby striping or spotting with or without areas of solid (unmarked) color, with preference given to bold, dramatic markings and rich, vivid colouring.

Other Solid Colors: Blue or cream, Patterned Self-Colors: Red, black, blue, cream, silver, or brown. Other Bi-Colors: Blue and white or cream and white. Patterned Bi-Colors: Red, black, blue, cream, silver, or brown combined with white. Patterned Tortoiseshell. Blue-Cream. Patterned Blue-Cream. Dilute Tri-Colors: Blue, cream, and white. Patterned Dilute Tri-Colors. Patterned Mi-Ke (Tri-Color).

Black and White, and Tortoiseshell Japanese Bobtail kittens

EXOTIC SHORTHAIR

Mackerel Tabby Exotic Shorthair

The Exotic Shorthair is essentially an American variety produced by careful selective breeding using outstanding American shorthairs and the best Persian or Longhair cats. The breeding programme was designed to produce a cat with the type of the much-admired Persian, but having fur of medium length, which would be comparatively easy to groom, and would not matt or tangle. It has resulted in a very popular variety of beautiful cats, in various colours, with broad heads, short snub noses, medium length fur, and beautiful eyes. The standard of the Cat Fanciers' Association is very explicit as to the characteristics required. Possibly because of the crossbreeding, the Exotic Shorthairs are very strong and healthy, most affectionate and a joy to handle. Grooming is easy, but it is important to ensure that the medium length fur does not lie too close to the body as it would detract from the appearance.

The Exotics have been used for occasional matings to British and American Shorthairs to improve a particular line. There is no similar variety in Britain, as some breeders do not favour a cross between a Longhair and a Shorthair. However, British breeders do very occasionally crossbreed these cats with the object of improving a strain that shows signs of losing type. The first cross does tend to have a coat very similar to that of the Exotic, and, unless care is taken, it can prove difficult to breed out the long fur.

OFFICIAL STANDARD
Cat Fanciers' Association, Inc.

EXOTIC SHORTHAIR

POINT SCORE

Head (including size and shape of eyes, ear shape and set)	30
Type (including shape, size, bone and length of tail)	20
Coat	20
Color	20
Eye color	10

Head
Round and massive, with great breadth of skull. Round face with round underlying bone structure. Well set on a short, thick neck.

Head: round and massive

Nose
Short, snub, and broad. With "break".

Cheeks
Full.

Jaws
Broad and powerful.

Chin
Full and well developed.

Ears
Small, round tipped, tilted forward, and not unduly open at the base. Set far apart, and low on the head, fitting into (without distorting) the rounded contour of the head.

Eyes
Large, round and full. Set far apart and brilliant, giving a sweet expression to the face.

Body
Of cobby type, low on the legs, deep in the chest, equally massive across shoulders and rump, with a short, well-rounded middle piece. Large or medium in size. Quality the determining consideration rather than size.

Back
Level.

Legs
Short, thick and strong. Forelegs straight.

Paws
Large, round and firm. Toes carried close, five in front and four behind.

Tail
Short, but in proportion to body length. Carried without a curve and at an angle lower than the back.

Coat
Dense, plush, soft in texture, full of life. Stands out from body due to density, not flat or close-lying. Medium in length, slightly longer than other shorthairs but not long enough to flow.

Disqualify
Locket or button. Kinked or abnormal tail. Incorrect number of toes.

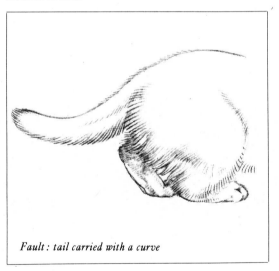

Fault: tail carried with a curve

EXOTIC SHORTHAIR COLORS

WHITE
Pure glistening white.

Nose leather
Pink.

Paw pads
Pink.

Eye color
Deep blue or brilliant copper. Odd-eyed whites shall have one blue and one copper eye with equal color depth.

BLACK
Dense coal black, sound from roots to tip of fur. Free from any tinge of rust on tips, or smoke undercoat.

Nose leather
Black.

Paw pads
Black or brown.

Eye color
Brilliant copper.

BLUE
Blue, lighter shade preferred, one level tone from nose to tip of tail. Sound to the roots. A sound darker shade is more acceptable than an unsound lighter shade.

Nose leather
Blue.

Paw pads
Blue.

Eye color
Brilliant copper.

RED
Deep, rich, clear, brilliant red; without shading, markings or ticking. Lips and chin the same color as coat.

Nose leather
Brick red.

Paw pads
Brick red.

Eye color
Brilliant copper.

CREAM
One level shade of buff cream, without markings. Sound to the roots. Lighter shades preferred.

Nose leather
Pink.

Paw pads
Pink.

Eye color
Brilliant copper.

CHINCHILLA
Undercoat pure white. Coat on back, flanks, head and tail sufficiently tipped with black to give the characteristic sparkling silver appearance. Legs may be slightly shaded with tipping. Chin and ear tufts, stomach and chest, pure white.

Rims of eyes, lips and nose
Outlined with black.

Nose leather
Brick red.

Red Tabby Exotic Shorthair

CFA OFFICIAL STANDARD continued –

Paw pads
Black.

Eye color
Green or blue-green.

SHADED SILVER
Undercoat white with a mantle of black tipping shading down from sides, face, and tail from dark on the ridge to white on the chin, chest, stomach, and under the tail. Legs to be the same tone as the face. The general effect to be much darker than a chinchilla.

Rims of eyes, lips and nose
Outlined with black.

Nose leather
Brick red.

Paw pads
Black.

Eye color
Green or blue-green.

SHELL CAMEO (Red Chinchilla)
Undercoat white, the coat on the back, flanks, head and tail to be sufficiently tipped with red to give the characteristic sparkling appearance. Face and legs may be very slightly shaded with tipping. Chin, ear tufts, stomach and chest white.

Nose leather
Rose.

Rims of eyes
Rose.

Paw pads
Rose.

Eye color
Brilliant copper.

SHADED CAMEO (Red Shaded)
Undercoat white with a mantle of red tipping shading down the sides, face, and tail from dark on the ridge to white on the chin, chest, stomach, and under the tail. Legs to be the same tone as face. The general effect to be much redder than the Shell Cameo.

Nose leather
Rose.

Rims of eyes
Rose.

Paw pads
Rose.

Eye color
Brilliant copper.

BLACK SMOKE
White undercoat, deeply tipped with black. Cat in repose appears black. In motion the white undercoat is clearly apparent. Points and mask black with narrow band of white at base of hairs next to skin which may be seen only when the fur is parted.

Nose leather
Black.

Paw pads
Black.

Eye color
Brilliant copper.

BLUE SMOKE
White undercoat, deeply tipped with blue. Cat in repose appears blue. In motion the white undercoat is clearly apparent. Points and mask blue, with narrow band of white at base of hairs next to skin which may be seen only when fur is parted.

Nose leather
Blue.

Paw pads
Blue.

Eye color
Brilliant copper.

CAMEO SMOKE (Red Smoke)
White undercoat, deeply tipped with red. Cat in repose appears red. In motion the white undercoat is clearly apparent. Points and mask red with narrow band of white at base of hairs next to skin which may be seen only when fur is parted.

Nose leather
Rose.

Rims of eyes
Rose.

Paw pads
Rose.

Eye color
Brilliant copper.

CLASSIC TABBY PATTERN
Markings dense, clearly defined, and broad. Legs evenly barred with bracelets coming up to meet the body markings. Tail evenly ringed. Several unbroken necklaces on neck and upper chest, the more the better. Frown marks on the forehead form an intricate letter "M". An unbroken line runs back from the outer corner of the eye. Swirls on cheeks. Vertical lines over back of head extend

to shoulder markings which are in the shape of a butterfly with both upper and lower rings distinctly outlined and marked with dots inside outline. Back markings consist of a vertical line down the spine from butterfly to tail with a vertical stripe paralleling it on each side, the three stripes well separated by stripes of the ground color. Large solid blotch on each side to be encircled by one or more unbroken rings. Side markings should be the same on both sides. Double vertical row of buttons on chest and stomach.

MACKEREL TABBY PATTERN
Markings dense, clearly defined, and all narrow pencillings. Legs evenly barred with narrow bracelets coming up to meet the body markings. Tail barred. Necklaces on neck and chest distinct, like so many chains. Head barred with an "M" on the forehead. Unbroken lines running back from the eyes. Lines running down the head to meet the shoulders. Spine lines run together to form a narrow saddle. Narrow pencillings run around body.

PATCHED TABBY PATTERN
A Patched Tabby (Torbie) is an established silver, brown, or blue tabby with patches of red and/or cream.

BROWN PATCHED TABBY
Ground color brilliant coppery brown with classic or mackerel tabby markings of dense black with patches of red and/or cream clearly defined on both body and extremities; a blaze of red and/or cream on the face is desirable. Lips and chin the same shade as the rings around the eyes.

Eye color
Brilliant copper.

BLUE PATCHED TABBY
Ground color, including lips and chin, pale bluish ivory with classic or mackerel tabby markings of very deep blue affording a good contrast with ground color. Patches of cream clearly defined on both body and extremities; a blaze of cream on the face is desirable. Warm fawn overtones or patina over the whole.

Eye color
Brilliant copper.

SILVER PATCHED TABBY
Ground color, including lips and chin, pale silver with classic or mackerel tabby markings of dense black with patches of red and/or cream clearly defined on both body and extremities. A blaze of red and/or cream on the face is desirable.

Eye color
Brilliant copper or hazel.

SILVER TABBY
Ground color, including lips and chin, pale, clear silver. Markings dense black.

Nose leather
Brick red.

Paw pads
Black.

Eye color
Green or hazel.

RED TABBY
Ground color red. Markings deep, rich red. Lips and chin red.

Nose leather
Brick red.

Paw pads
Brick red.

Eye color
Brilliant copper.

BROWN TABBY
Ground color brilliant coppery brown. Markings dense black. Lips and chin the same shade as the rings round the eyes. Back of leg black from paw to heel.

Nose leather
Brick red.

Paw pads
Black or brown.

Eye color
Brilliant copper.

BLUE TABBY
Ground color, including lips and chin, pale bluish ivory. Markings a very deep blue affording a good contrast with ground color. Warm fawn overtones or patina over the whole.

Nose leather
Old rose.

Paw pads
Rose.

Eye color
Brilliant copper.

CREAM TABBY
Ground color, including lips and chin, very pale cream. Markings of buff or cream sufficiently darker than the ground color to afford good contrast, but remaining within the dilute color range.

Nose leather
Pink.

Paw pads
Pink.

CFA OFFICAL STANDARD continued –

Eye color
Brilliant copper.

CAMEO TABBY
Ground color off-white. Markings red.

Nose leather
Rose.

Paw pads
Rose.

Eye color
Brilliant copper.

TORTOISESHELL
Black with unbrindled patches of red and cream. Patches clearly defined and well broken on both body and extremities. Blaze of red or cream on face is desirable.

Eye color
Brilliant copper.

CALICO
White with unbrindled patches of black and red. White predominant on underparts.

Eye color
Brilliant copper.

DILUTE CALICO
White with unbrindled patches of blue and cream. White predominant on underparts.

Eye color
Brilliant copper.

BLUE-CREAM
Blue with patches of solid cream. Patches clearly defined and well broken on both body and extremities.

Eye color
Brilliant copper.

BI-COLOR
White with unbrindled patches of black, or white with unbrindled patches of blue, or white with unbrindled patches of red, or white with unbrindled patches of cream.

Eye color
Brilliant copper.

Black Exotic Shorthair

SOMALI

Red Somali

This is a very new variety, having been given championship status by the Cat Fanciers' Association in October 1978. At one time it was thought that the Somali was a spontaneous mutation of the Abyssinian, with kittens with longish fur begin born in some Abyssinian litters. However, investigation into the genetic history of the Somali shows that the gene for longhair may have been introduced by the crossbreeding of Abyssinians to longhaired cats in Britain about the turn of the century. In time British Abyssinians were exported to cat fancies in Europe, North America, New Zealand and Australia. Some of these cats carried the recessive gene for longhair, with the result that Somalis are now bred in all these areas.

The coat colourings are typically Abyssinian, but the appropriate ticking may take some months to be seen in its true beauty, and the official standard makes allowance for this.

Ruddy Somali

PROVISIONAL STANDARD

Cat Fanciers' Association, Inc.

SOMALI

POINT SCORE

Head (25)	
Skull	6
Muzzle	6
Ears	7
Eye shape	6
Body (25)	
Torso	10
Legs and feet	10
Tail	5
Coat (25)	
Texture	10
Length	15
Color (25)	
Color	10
Ticking	10
Eye color	5

General

The overall impression of the Somali is that of a well-proportioned medium to large cat, firm muscular development, lithe, showing an alert, lively interest in all surroundings, with an even disposition and easy to handle. The cat is to give the appearance of activity, sound health and general vigor.

Head

A modified, slightly rounded wedge without flat planes; the brow, cheek, and profile lines all showing a gentle contour. A slight rise from the bridge of the nose to the forehead, which should be of good size with width between the ears flowing into the arched neck without a break.

Muzzle

Shall follow gentle contours in conformity with the skull, as viewed from the front profile. Chin shall be full, neither undershot nor overshot, having a rounded appearance. The muzzle shall not be sharply pointed and there shall be no evidence of snipiness, foxiness, or whisker pinch.

Ears

Large, alert, moderately pointed, broad and cupped at the base. Ear set on a line towards the rear of the skull. The inner ear shall have horizontal tufts that reach nearly to the other side of the ear; tufts desirable.

Eyes

Almond shaped, large brilliant and expressive. Skull aperture neither round or oriental. Eyes accented by dark lidskin, encircled by light-colored area. Above each a short dark vertical pencil stroke with a dark pencil line continuing from the upper lid towards the ear.

Body

Torso medium long, lithe and graceful, showing well-developed muscular strength. Rib cage is rounded; back is slightly arched, giving the appearance of a cat about to spring; flank level with no tuck up. Conformation strikes a medium between the extremes of cobby and svelte lengthy types.

Somali kittens

CFA OFFICIAL STANDARD continued –

Head: modified, slightly rounded wedge

Legs and feet
Legs in proportion to torso; feet oval and compact. When standing, the Somali gives the impression of being nimble and quick. Toes: Five in front and four in back.

Tail
Having a full brush, thick at the base and slightly tapering. Length in balance with torso.

Coat
Texture very soft to the touch, extremely fine and double coated. The more dense the coat, the better. Length: A medium-length coat, except over shoulders, where a slightly shorter length is permitted. Preference is to be given to a cat with ruff and breeches, giving a full-coated appearance to the cat.

Penalize
Color faults: Cold gray or sandy tone to coat color; mottling or speckling on unticked areas. *Pattern faults:* Necklaces, leg bars, tabby stripes or bars on body, lack of desired markings on head and tail. Black roots on body.

Disqualify
White locket or groin spot or white anywhere on body other than on the upper throat, chin and nostrils; any skeletal abnormality; wrong color paw pads or nose leather; unbroken necklace, incorrect number of toes, kinks in tail.

SOMALI COLORS

RUDDY
Overall impression of an orange-brown or ruddy tipped with black. Color has radiant or glowing quality. Darker shading along the spine allowed. Underside of body and inside of legs and chest to be an even ruddy tone, harmonizing with the top coat; without ticking, barring, necklaces or belly marks. Tail continuing the dark spine line ending at the black at the tip. Complete absence of rings on tail. Preference given to unmarked ruddy color. Ears tipped with black or dark brown.

Nose leather
Tile red.

Paw pads
Black or brown with black between toes and extending upward on rear legs. Toe tufts on front and rear feet black or dark brown. White or off-white on upper throat, lips and nostrils only.

Eye color
Gold or green—the more richness and depth of color the better.

RED
Warm glowing red ticked with chocolate-brown. Deeper shades of red preferred. Ears and tail tipped with chocolate brown.

Paw pads
Pink with chocolate-brown between toes, extending slightly beyond paws.

Nose leather
Rosy pink.

Eye color
Gold or green—the more richness and depth of color the better.

Please note: The Somali is extremely slow in showing mature ticking and allowances should be made for kittens and young cats.

Ruddy Somali kitten

Longhair Cats

It is impossible to say with any certainty exactly the origin of the domestic cat, but it is generally accepted that the Caffre or African wild cat and other similar species must have been the forebears. The Caffre is an animal slightly larger than the domestic cat, not unlike the pedigree Abyssinian in type, and has buffish-coloured short fur, with some stripes and rings but without the definite tabby pattern seen in some cats. The correct tabby markings should include clear pencil markings on the face, with swirls on the cheeks, marks resembling spectacles around the eyes and an 'M' mark on the forehead. There should be two 'mayoral' chains on the chest, three dark bars down the spine with other bars and swirls along the flanks. On looking down at the shoulders a distinct 'butterfly' marking may be seen. The tail should be ringed with bracelets around the length of each leg. The stripes should be clear and distinct, not smudged or brindled. This classic pattern is the same for all pedigree tabbies, whether long or shorthaired.

The Caffre may well account for the shorthairs, but how did cats with the long coats come into being? For some time this honour was given to the wild cat, still found in Scotland and

Tortie and White Persian/Longhair

Chinchilla kittens

Tortoiseshell Persian/Longhair kittens

Bicolour Turkish Angora kitten

some parts of Europe. This cat has a full, longish coat, a broad head, a short bushy tail, and, given the opportunity, is known to mate with the domestic cat. However, zoologists consider that the differences between the two animals are such that the wild cat would not be the ancestor of the longhaired domestic cat.

The *manul*, or Pallas's cat, so called after the explorer who saw it first in Asia, was also thought to be responsible. This animal has a thick and longish coat, a broad head, small ears, and high-placed large eyes, but this theory has also proved to be unacceptable.

According to De Buffon (1707–1788), the French naturalist, in his *Natural History* published between 1749 and 1804, the cats with the longer fur came from Asia Minor. They were seen in Europe about the middle of the sixteenth century, with credit for their introduction to Italy, probably from Asia, being given to the Italian traveller, Pietro della Valle (1586–1652). At the end of the same century Nicholas Claude Fabri de Peirese, an eminent scientist and traveller, is said to have introduced them into France. It is an interesting fact that the first longhairs known in Britain were referred to as French cats, although in his book De Buffon does refer to the early longhairs as Angoras. This name was given to them as they were believed to come from Angora, now Ankara, in Turkey.

The long fur probably arose in the first place through a spontaneous mutation that could have been perpetuated through interbreeding in confined mountainous areas, as found in Turkey and Persia. This would certainly seem to be true of the Turkish cats brought to Britain in 1956. These cats, which are similar in type to the original Angoras, were found in the area around Lake Van, until recently a fairly inaccessible area, and were found to breed true; that is, the kittens born to these Turkish cats were always like the parents in appearance.

The original Angoras had small heads, tallish ears, rangy bodies, and long, pointed tails. Their fur was longish rather than luxurious. The cats that were reputed to come from Persia had longer fur, rounder heads, sturdier bodies and fluffier tails, and in time they came to be preferred by both the cat fanciers and would-be owners. Dr Gordon Stables writing on the Longhairs in England in 1876 referred to them as the 'Asiatics', while Mr Harrison Weir a few years later bemoaned the fact that these 'foreign' cats were ousting the residents (the shorthairs) in popularity. Gradually, the Angoras seemed to disappear, and all the Longhairs were referred to as Persians. As there was no understanding of breeding procedures at that time, any longhaired cat was mated to another regardless of type and fur length. Eventually, the strong features of the Persian/Longhair predominated, which resulted in cats with broader heads, smaller ears, longer coats and shorter tails than the original Angoras. In 1903 the eminent breeder, cat judge and writer Miss Frances Simpson, said that she had never been able to distinguish between the Angoras and Persians and considered all longhaired cats Persians and all shorthairs as either English or foreign cats. Much later the Governing Council of the Cat Fancy in Britain decided that the cats with long fur should be known simply as Longhairs, but the name Persian is still used by many people, and in North America and other parts of the world it is still the official name.

It is difficult to trace the early history of the Longhairs that appeared at the first shows. There was no pure breeding as such, and the parentage in the catalogues in most cases was 'Unknown'. The majority of exhibits were shorthaired, but there were classes for Angoras and Persians of various colours and coat patterns. By the early 1900s the situation had changed completely, and the proportion of longhair to shorthair cats at the shows was four to one.

The Siamese soon began to appear at the shows in large numbers. They quickly became the most popular variety, and caused the swing to a higher proportion of shorthairs to longhairs at the cat shows for many years. In recent years, however, the longhairs have re-established their popularity, and the numbers at the cat shows have increased. At many of the shows, such as the National Cat Club show held in London, approximately half the pedigree exhibits are now longhair cats.

PERSIAN/LONGHAIR

Orange-eyed White Persian/Longhair

The white cats with long fur are thought to be the oldest longhaired variety known in Europe. Harrison Weir writing on these cats, then known as Angoras, said that he had been told that they were great favourites with the Turks and the Armenians and 'the best are of high value, a pure White with blue eyes, being thought the perfection of all cats, all other points being good and its hearing by no means defective.'

They first arrived in Britain from Paris and were referred to as French cats for several years. To quote Harrison Weir again: 'The pure White, with long, silky hair, bedecked with blue or rose-coloured ribbon, with a silver collar with its name inscribed thereon or one of scarlet leather studded with brass, might often be seen stretching its full lazy length on luxurious woollen rugs – the valued pampered pets of "West End" life.' This still holds good in some cases today.

Whites with long fur were introduced from Persia, but their appearance was not quite the same; the fur was of different texture, and often the eyes were yellow. Gordon Stables, writing in 1876, on the Asiatic or Eastern cats, called also Persian or Angora, remarked on the 'difference in the texture of the coat, it being exceedingly fine, soft and satiny in the Angora and not so much so in the Persian'. He went on to say that of the 'Asiatic cats, those of the blue [coat] and the pure white are usually of the smallest dimensions'. The early Angoras had narrower heads and bigger ears than the Persians, but by 1903 apparently most of the Angoras had gradually disappeared, and all the Longhairs were referred to as Persians.

The fact that there were so few Whites with Angora type could probably be traced back to the fact that many of them having blue eyes were frequently deaf

Odd-eyed White Persian/Longhair

Blue-eyed White Persian/Longhair

and fanciers were loathe to use them for breeding. This fact was not always appreciated and so they were thought to be dull of intellect and slow in thinking. Some strains of the Whites with blue eyes still do suffer from deafness. These animals are not albinos, lacking the pink eyes seen in albino humans and rabbits, although there may be some connection.

Not all Blue-eyed Whites are deaf, and some breeders say that a kitten born with some black hairs in the white fur, often on the forehead, will have good hearing. The Whites with orange eyes usually are not deaf, and the Odd-eyed (having one blue eye and one orange) may be deaf on the blue side and have hearing on the orange, while others have perfect hearing.

At the first shows there was only one class for the Whites irrespective of eye colouring, but it frequently happened that those with orange eyes had Persian type, (rather than Angora), which was by now preferred, and they won. The owners of blue-eyed Whites complained bitterly, and eventually, in 1930, the Governing Council of the Cat Fancy in Britain recognized the Blue-eyed and the Orange-eyed as two separate varieties. However, it still did not recognize the Odd-eyed. The consequence was that the Odd-eyed Whites had to be shown in Any Other Variety classes, which again brought complaints from the breeders. Eventually, the Odd-eyed Whites were given full recognition too, and there are now three classes for these varieties at the shows.

The show reports on the early cat shows were not very explicit, so it is not possible to know what colour eyes many of the Whites had. In 1910 one judge's report read 'A beautiful White in full bloom – very deep eyes'. This must refer to colour, as deep-set eyes would be a fault, but there is no clue as to what the colour was. The Whites at the shows at the beginning of the century were almost equally divided between make and female, but today in Britain there are far more females and few males.

At the turn of the century the Whites were a great favourite among members of the aristocracy, many of whom began breeding them on a large scale. Lady Decies, for example, bred numerous cats, all bearing the prefix 'Fulmer', and they appeared at shows all over Britain. The Honorable Mrs McLaren Morrison had a number of Whites in her cattery. Many of these were of unknown parentage, but one cat, Crystal, was the dam of several. Mrs McLaren Morrison wrote that Crystal was certainly a good investment, as, up to the time of writing in 1902, she had had sixteen white kittens, ten with blue eyes.

There are several mentions of imported Whites being exhibited in Britain in the early 1900s, but nothing is said about the country of origin. They may have come from Turkey and Persia, as they were said 'to be of rather savage disposition and extremely fiery with their fellows'.

Whites were also fashionable at about this time in the United States, with so many being exhibited at the Beresford Cat Club Show that the classification was divided into Blue-eyed and Golden-eyed, and then again into male and female. A male called Jungfrau must have been a good stud, as his name appears as sire and grandsire of a number of the winners. Mrs Clinton Locle showed a number of Whites, which she had imported from time to time. She wrote that the first White she had owned was brought to her from Persia by a traveller. This cat had amber eyes, which 'showed that white cats brought from their native land have not always blue eyes'. Apparently, the descendants of this particular cat mated both to amber and blue-eyed cats produced blue-eyed kittens.

The popularity of Whites increased over the years in the United States, but seemed to be almost at a standstill in Britain. The 1960s saw a sudden surge of interest in the Whites in Britain, possibly due to the appearance of White cats and kittens in television advertisements. Many more breeders became interested in the variety, but the majority of kittens produced were Orange-eyed. This was due to the continuing difficulty of improving the type of the Blue-eyed without losing the eye colour, as any outcross to improve the type meant mating to say a Blue or a Black, and thus introducing orange eyes again.

When first born, the kittens are pink rather than white, but in a very short time the fur grows, and they soon become fascinating bundles of white fluff. As the eyes do not open until the kittens are two to twelve days old, and as they all have blue eyes when tiny, it is exceedingly difficult, particularly for a novice breeder, to know for certain for some weeks whether the kitten will be blue-eyed orange-eyed, or even odd-eyed. If the eyes are still a pale blue when the kitten is two months or older, it is unlikely that the colour will ever deepen. If the eyes are orange, changes in the colouring may be noticed after about five to six weeks, with the colour becoming denser with age. The Odd-eyed are easier to distinguish, as there will be the beginnings of a colour change in one eye. When buying a kitten in the hope of breeding Blue-eyed Whites, choose one with as deep a blue eye colouring as possible, although it must be borne in mind that even if the female has beautiful blue eyes, there is no guarantee that she will have kittens with similar eye colour.

When buying a White kitten the possibility of it being deaf should not be overlooked, as a kitten may be deaf without the breeder even realizing it. Kittens are so quick to notice any movement that it may be difficult to carry out any tests. The deafness appears to affect the Blue-eyed more than the Orange (although very occasionally these too may be deaf), but it must be stressed that not all Blue-eyed cats are deaf. Deaf cats can feel vibrations and usually are very intelligent, quickly learning to respond to signals. It is, however, a handicap if the cat is kept in a house near busy roads, and has complete freedom. A wired-in garden or large run is the answer in such cases, or keeping the cat in the house all the time. Deaf cats are usually very intelligent and love to be handled.

Some would-be owners would like to have a White, but are apprehensive about grooming and keeping the fur looking immaculate. It is not such a problem really, as most Whites appear to be proud of their appearance, and do keep themselves looking immaculate. The fur does not become shady, as does that of the other self colours. If kept as a pet, rather than as a show cat, daily grooming with the use of talcum powder, good brushing and combing, wiping the feet and the tail when the cat has been out, and wiping the corners of the eyes to prevent staining of the face should suffice.

Many breeders believe in bathing their cats prior to the show (see page 256), as there must be no yellow staining on the fur, and the exhibit must look whiter than white on the show bench.

The Whites of today, particularly the Orange-eyed and Odd-eyed, have really outstanding type, with the Blue-eyed rapidly improving. The long, flowing coats may be as much as six inches (15 centimetres) long, the heads are broad, with neat ears, large, round eyes, and short broad noses. Such Whites may be mated to other Whites, with an occasional outcross to keep the type. They may also be mated to Tortoiseshells to breed Tortoiseshell and Whites, and to Bicolours to breed Bicolours. Mated to Black, they may produce both White and Black kittens, often outstanding, in the same litter. Although the cats look so aristocratic, they are in no way delicate, and certainly make the most ornamental pets.

OFFICIAL STANDARD

Cat Fanciers' Association, Inc.

PERSIAN

POINT SCORE

Head (including size and shape of eyes, ear shape and set)	30
Type (including shape, size, bone and length of tail)	20
Coat	10
Balance	5
Refinement	5
Color	20
Eye color	10

In all tabby varieties, the 20 points for color are to be divided 10 for markings and 10 for color.

Head
Round and massive, with great breadth of skull. Round face with round underlying bone structure. Well set on a short, thick neck.

Head : round and massive

Ears
Small, round tipped, tilted forward, and not unduly open at the base. Set far apart, and low on the head, fitting into (without distorting) the rounded contour of the head.

Eyes
Large, round and full. Set far apart and brilliant, giving a sweet expression to the face.

Nose
Short, snub, and broad. With "break".

Cheeks
Full.

Jaws
Broad and powerful.

Chin
Full and well-developed.

Body
Of cobby type, low on the legs, deep in the chest, equally massive across shoulders and rump, with a short, well-rounded middle piece. Large or medium in size. Quality the determining consideration, rather than size.

Body : cobby type, low on the legs

Back
Level.

Legs
Short, thick and strong. Forelegs straight.

Paws
Large, round and firm. Toes carried close, five in front and four behind.

Tail
Short, but in proportion to body length. Carried without a curve and at an angle lower than the back.

Coat
Long and thick, standing off from the body. Of fine texture, glossy and full of life. Long all over the body, including the shoulders. The ruff immense and continuing in a deep frill between the front legs. Ear and toe tufts long. Brush very full.

Disqualify
Locket or button. Kinked or abnormal tail. Incorrect number of toes.

CFA OFFICIAL STANDARD continued –

PERSIAN COLORS

WHITE
Pure glistening white.

Nose leather
Pink.

Paw pads
Pink.

Eye color
Deep blue or brilliant copper. Odd-eyed whites shall have one blue and one copper eye with equal color depth.

BLACK
Dense coal black, sound from roots to tip of fur. Free from any tinge of rust on tips, or smoke undercoat.

Nose leather
Black.

Paw pads
Black or brown.

Eye color
Brilliant copper.

BLUE
Blue, lighter shade preferred, one level tone from nose to tip of tail. Sound to the roots. A sound darker shade is more acceptable than an unsound lighter shade.

Nose leather
Blue.

Paw pads
Blue.

Eye color
Brilliant copper.

RED
Deep, rich, clear, brilliant red; without shading, markings or ticking. Lips and chin the same color as coat.

Nose leather
Brick red.

Paw pads
Brick red.

Eye color
Brilliant copper.

CREAM
One level shade of buff cream, without markings. Sound to the roots. Lighter shades preferred.

Nose leather
Pink.

Paw pads
Pink.

Eye color
Brilliant copper.

CHINCHILLA
Undercoat pure white. Coat on back, flanks, head, and tail sufficiently tipped with black to give the characteristic sparkling silver appearance. Legs may be slightly shaded with tipping. Chin and ear tufts, stomach and chest, pure white. Rims of eyes, lips and nose outlined with black.

Nose leather
Brick red.

Paw pads
Black.

Eye color
Green or blue-green.

SHADED SILVER
Undercoat white with a mantle of black tipping shading down from sides, face, and tail from dark on the ridge to white on the chin, chest, stomach and under the tail. Legs to be the same tone as the face. The general effect to be much darker than a chinchilla. Rims of eyes, lips and nose outlined with black.

Nose leather
Brick red.

Paw pads
Black.

Eye color
Green or blue-green.

CHINCHILLA GOLDEN
Undercoat rich warm cream. Coat on back, flanks, head and tail sufficiently tipped with seal brown to give golden appearance. Legs may be slightly shaded with tipping. Chin and ear tufts, stomach and chest, cream. Rims of eyes, lips and nose outlined with seal brown.

Nose leather
Deep rose.

Paw pads
Seal brown.

Eye color
Green or blue-green.

SHADED GOLDEN
Undercoat rich warm cream with a mantle of seal brown tipping shading down from sides, face, and tail from dark on the ridge to cream on the chin, chest, stomach, and

Shaded Silver Persian/Longhair

under the tail. Legs to be the same tone as the face. The general effect to be much darker than a chinchilla. Rims of eyes, lips and nose outlined with seal brown.

Nose leather
Deep rose.

Paw pads
Seal brown.

Eye color
Green or blue-green.

SHELL CAMEO (Red Chinchilla)
Undercoat white, the coat on the back, flanks, head, and tail to be sufficiently tipped with red to give the characteristic sparkling appearance. Face and legs may be very slightly shaded with tipping. Chin, ear tufts, stomach, and chest white.

Nose leather
Rose.

Rims of eyes
Rose.

Paw pads
Rose.

Eye color
Brilliant copper.

SHADED CAMEO (Red Shaded)
Undercoat white with a mantle of red tipping shading down the sides, face, and tail from dark on the ridge to white on the chin, chest, stomach, and under the tail. Legs to be the same tone as face. The general effect to be much redder than the Shell Cameo.

Nose leather
Rose.

Rims of eyes
Rose.

Paw pads
Rose.

Eye color
Brilliant copper.

SHELL TORTOISESHELL
Undercoat white. Coat on the back, flanks, head, and tail to be delicately tipped in black with well defined patches of red and cream tipped hairs as in the pattern of the Tortoiseshell. Face and legs may be slightly shaded with tipping. Chin, ear tufts, stomach, and chest white to very

CFA OFFICIAL STANDARD continued –

slightly tipped. Blaze of red or cream tipping on face is desirable.

Eye color
Brilliant copper.

SHADED TORTOISESHELL
Undercoat white. Mantle of black tipping and clearly defined patches of red and cream tipped hairs as in the pattern of the Tortoiseshell. Shading down the sides, face, and tail from dark on the ridge to slightly tipped or white on the chin, chest, stomach, legs, and under the tail. The general effect is to be much darker than the Shell Tortoiseshell. Blaze of red or cream tipping on the face is desirable.

Eye color
Brilliant copper.

BLACK SMOKE
White undercoat, deeply tipped with black. Cat in repose appears black. In motion the white undercoat is clearly apparent. Points and mask black with narrow band of white at base of hairs next to skin which may be seen only when the fur is parted. Light silver frill and ear tufts.

Nose leather
Black.

Paw pads
Black.

Eye color
Brilliant copper.

BLUE SMOKE
White undercoat, deeply tipped with blue. Cat in repose appears blue. In motion the white undercoat is clearly apparent. Points and mask blue with narrow band of white at base of hairs next to skin which may be seen only when fur is parted. White frill and ear tufts.

Nose leather
Blue.

Paw pads
Blue.

Eye color
Brilliant copper.

CAMEO RED (Red Smoke)
White undercoat, deeply tipped with red. Cat in repose appears red. In motion the white undercoat is clearly apparent. Points and mask red with narrow band of white at base of hairs next to skin which may be seen only when fur is parted. White frill and ear tufts.

Nose leather
Rose.

Rims of eyes
Rose.

Paw pads
Rose.

Eye color
Brilliant copper.

SMOKE TORTOISESHELL
White undercoat deeply tipped with black with clearly defined, unbrindled patches of red and cream tipped hairs as in the pattern of the Tortoiseshell. Cat in repose appears Tortoiseshell. In motion, the white undercoat is clearly apparent. Face and ears Tortoiseshell pattern with narrow band of white at the base of the hairs next to the skin that may be seen only when hair is parted. White ruff and ear tufts. Blaze of red or cream tipping on face is desirable.

Eye color
Brilliant copper.

CLASSIC TABBY PATTERN
Markings dense, clearly defined and broad. Legs evenly barred with bracelets coming up to meet the body markings. Tail evenly ringed. Several unbroken necklaces on neck and upper chest the more the better. Frown marks on forehead form intricate letter "M". Unbroken line runs back from outer corner of eye. Swirls on cheeks. Vertical lines over back of head extend to shoulder markings which are in the shape of a butterfly with both upper and lower wings distinctly outlined and marked with dots inside outline. Back markings consist of a vertical line down the spine from butterfly to tail with a vertical stripe paralleling it on each side, the three stripes well separated by stripes of the ground color. Large solid blotch on each side to be encircled by one or more unbroken rings. Side markings should be the same on both sides. Double vertical row of buttons on chest and stomach.

MACKEREL TABBY PATTERN
Markings dense, clearly defined, and all narrow pencillings. Legs evenly barred with narrow bracelets coming up to meet the body markings. Tail barred. Necklaces on neck and chest distinct, like so many chains. Head barred with an "M" on the forehead. Unbroken lines running back from the eyes. Lines running down the head to meet the shoulders. Spine lines run together to form a narrow saddle. Narrow pencillings run around body.

PATCHED TABBY PATTERN
A Patched Tabby (Torbie) is an established silver, brown, or blue tabby with patches of red and/or cream.

BROWN PATCHED TABBY
Ground color brilliant coppery brown with classic or mackerel tabby markings of dense black with patches of

Black Smoke Persian/Longhair kittens

Brown Tabby Persian/Longhair

CFA OFFICIAL STANDARD continued –

red and/or cream clearly defined on both body and extremities; a blaze of red and/or cream on the face is desirable. Lips and chin the same shade as the rings around the eyes.

Eye color
Brilliant copper.

BLUE PATCHED TABBY
Ground color, including lips and chin, pale bluish ivory with classic or mackerel tabby markings of very deep blue affording a good contrast with ground color. Patches of cream clearly defined on both body and extremities; a blaze of cream on the face is desirable. Warm fawn overtones or patina over the whole.

Eye color
Brilliant copper.

SILVER PATCHED TABBY
Ground color, including lips and chin, pale silver with classic or mackerel tabby markings of dense black with patches of red and/or cream clearly defined on both body and extremities. A blaze of red and/or cream on the face is desirable.

Eye color
Brilliant copper or hazel.

SILVER TABBY
Ground color, including lips and chin, pale, clear silver. Markings dense black.

Nose leather
Brick red.

Paw pads
Black.

Eye color
Green or hazel.

RED TABBY
Ground color red. Markings deep, rich red. Lips and chin red.

Nose leather
Brick red.

Paw pads
Pink.

Eye color
Brilliant copper.

BROWN TABBY
Ground color brilliant coppery brown. Markings dense black. Lips and chin the same shade as the rings around the eyes. Back of leg black from paw to heel.

Nose leather
Brick red.

Paw pads
Black or brown.

Eye color
Brilliant copper.

BLUE TABBY
Ground color, including lips and chin, pale bluish ivory. Markings a very deep blue affording a good contrast with ground color. Warm fawn overtones or patina over the whole.

Nose leather
Old rose.

Paw pads
Rose.

Eye color
Brilliant copper.

CREAM TABBY
Ground color, including lips and chin, very pale cream. Markings of buff or cream sufficiently darker than the ground color to afford good contrast, but remaining within the dilute color range.

Nose leather
Pink.

Paw pads
Pink.

Eye color
Brilliant copper.

CAMEO TABBY
Ground color off-white. Markings red.

Nose leather
Rose.

Paw pads
Rose.

Eye color
Brilliant copper.

TORTOISESHELL
Black with unbrindled patches of red and cream. Patches clearly defined and well broken on both body and extremities. Blaze of red or cream on face is desirable.

Eye color
Brilliant copper.

CALICO
White with unbrindled patches of black and red. White predominant on underparts.

Peke-Face Red Tabby Persian/Longhair

Eye color
Brilliant copper.

DILUTE CALICO
White with unbrindled patches of blue and cream white predominant on underparts.

Eye color
Brilliant copper.

BLUE-CREAM
Blue with patches of solid cream. Patches clearly defined and well broken on both body and extremities.

Eye color
Brilliant copper.

BI-COLOR
Black and white, blue and white, red and white, or cream and white. White feet, legs, undersides, chest and muzzle. Inverted "V" blaze on face desirable. White under tail and white collar allowable.

Eye color
Brilliant copper.

PERSIAN VAN BI-COLOR
Black and white, red and white, blue and white, cream and white. White cat with color confined to the extremities; head, tail, and legs. One or two small colored patches on body allowable.

Peke-Face head: nose very short, indented between eyes

PEKE-FACE RED AND PEKE-FACE RED TABBY
The Peke-Face cat should conform in color, markings and general type to the standards set forth for the red and red tabby Persian cat. The head should resemble as much as possible that of the Pekinese dog from which it gets its name. Nose should be very short and depressed, or indented between the eyes. There should be a decidedly wrinkled muzzle. Eyes round, large, and full, set wide apart, prominent and brilliant.

OFFICIAL STANDARD
Governing Council of the Cat Fancy

BLACK: VARIETY 1

Colour
Lustrous raven black to the roots and free from rustiness, shading, white hairs or markings of any kind.

Coat
Long and flowing on body, full frill, and brush, which should be short and broad.

Body
Cobby and massive, without being coarse, with plenty of bone and substance, and low on the leg.

Head
Round and broad, with plenty of space between the ears, which should be small, neat, and well covered; short nose, full cheeks and broad muzzle. An undershot jaw shall be considered a defect.

other respects, as these kittens frequently turn into the densest Blacks.

Poor type: eyes should be round, wide open

Head: round and broad

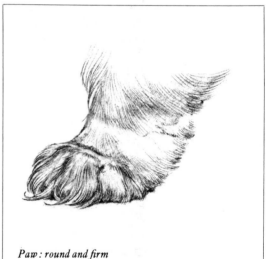

Paw: round and firm

Eyes
Large, round and wide open, copper or deep orange in colour, with no green rim.

Note
Black Longhair kittens are often a very bad colour up to five or six months, their coats being grey or rusty in parts, and sometimes freely speckled with white hairs. Fanciers should not condemn them on this account if good in

SCALE OF POINTS

Colour	25
Coat	20
Body	20
Head	20
Eyes	15
Total	100

Although the first cats with long fur seen in Europe were said to be white, the Blacks were the first to be given a recognized standard in Britain, hence the number 1 in the British standards. Black Longhairs, or Persians, certainly appeared at the first official cat show in Britain in 1871, which was organized by Harrison Weir, who also acted as one of the judges. In *Our Cats*, published in 1889, Weir mentions the Blacks among the various colours, saying that they should have orange eyes, which was unusual, as most cats had green eyes at that time. He also said that 'for a long time, not now, the Black was the most sought after and the most difficult to obtain. A good rich, deep black, with orange-coloured eyes and long flowing hair, grand in mane, large and with

graceful carriage, with a mild expression, is truly a beautiful object and one very rare.' The Points of Excellence Mr Weir provided in his book were the original British standards, the majority of which are very close to those of today. Even when, in the early days, a distinction was made between the Angoras and the Persians, and apparently there were Blacks in both varieties, with differences in fur textures and tail length, the class at the shows was just 'Blacks'.

Although such an old variety, the entries at shows were few, and no males were entered at the Crystal Palace show in 1886. Twenty-four Blacks were listed in the stud book for 1900 to 1905; by 1910, when the Governing Council of the Cat Fancy came into being, (having taken over from the original registering body,

Black Persian/Longhair

the National Cat Club), the number had fallen to seventeen, with very few of the original strains left.

The greatest Black of all time was said to have been Dirty Dick. Born in 1911, he won fourteen championships and sired many outstanding kittens. From the judges' reports of that time it is difficult to compare him with modern cats. One judge gave him a challenge certificate and contented herself with saying in her report that 'he was looking well', while another said 'beautiful head and altogether very shapely – jet black and with deep eyes'.

Blacks have always been popular in the United States, and King Max, a large male, won first prize at the Boston Cat Show in 1897, 1898 and 1899. Owned by Mrs E. R. Taylor, he was valued at one thousand dollars, and was said to have a beautiful, dense, shiny, black coat, with no sign of white hairs.

The years between the two World Wars saw a revived interest in Blacks in Britain, thanks to a number of dedicated breeders, including Mr Cyril Yeates, who became Chairman of the Governing Council of the Cat Fancy and was an outstanding judge. Unfortunately, the Second World War brought cat-breeding practically to a standstill in Britain. There were hardly any cat shows and little breeding, and the Cat Fancy took many years to recover. Many fine specimens were bred in the United States during this period, with Grand Champion Pied Piper of Barbe Bleue, owned and bred by Bess H. Moore, being Cat of the Year in 1951 and one of the most outstanding Blacks of the early 1950s. It was the great-grandsire of the Cat of the Year of 1959, Mr Richard Gebhardt's Grand Champion Vel-vene Voo Doo of Silva-Wyte. Voo Doo is said to have been one of the best Blacks ever seen, and the greatest sire of all time.

In the past many of the champions resulted from Blue to Black breeding and few from Black to Black matings. This was because at first the Blacks had poor type, which was improved by cross-breeding to Blues. Some were produced from Orange-eyed White and Black crosses, others from mating Black to Tortoiseshells.

Blacks have long been associated in the minds of some people with the supernatural, witchcraft and superstition. Many people believe that black cats are lucky and yet others swear that they bring misfortune. In 1893 John Jennings, in his book *Domestic and Fancy Cats*, said, 'It will be remembered that as recently as 1867 a woman in Pennsylvania was publicly accused of witchcraft (which she denied) for administering three drops of a black cat's blood to a child as a remedy for croup, from which it speedily recovered, as was proved by a large number of witnesses.' Nothing is said as to what happened to the woman or the cat. In Germany it was once thought that to dream about a black cat and Christmas was to foretell some alarming illness during the year.

Usually it is black cats with short, shining coats and narrow slit eyes that are depicted riding on witches' broomsticks. Some of the mystery surrounding black cats may have arisen from the fact that the Longhair Black seems to have more static electricity in his coat than many other varieties, so much so that when one is combed and brushed in a dark room the sparks may be seen, and it is quite possible to get a slight electric shock when stroking the fur. Harrison Weir noticed this too and wrote, 'In frosty weather it is the more noticeable, the coldness of the weather apparently giving intensity and brilliancy, which to the ignorant would certainly be attributed to the interference of the spiritual or superhuman.'

Black kittens are lively and full of fun, but rarely show signs of the dense black fur so much admired. The newly-born kittens are black, but the coat changes with growth. Would-be purchasers going to choose a kitten are frequently disappointed when a greyish-brown one is offered, not the black 'chocolate box' beauty they had in mind. The rustiest-looking kitten may be a future champion, but often, despite having wonderful type, a small kitten has been neutered because of this colouring. It may, eventually become an outstanding neuter when exhibited, but, of course, it can no longer be used to breed. Even experienced breeders have made mistakes when a litter has been produced by crossbreeding, not being sure whether a particular kitten is a Black or a Smoke. They are very alike in appearance when tiny, except immediately at birth, when Smoke kittens appear to have grey ashes on their faces and feet. Several have been registered in the wrong category and entered in the wrong class at a show.

A Black cat that is to be shown should not be allowed out for a long period in strong sunlight, as the fur quickly becomes sunburnt. Dampness, too, gives it a brownish, lifeless appearance. Grooming is all important if the cat is to be seen at its best, with particular attention being paid to the paws, which may take on a rusty shade just by walking through wet grass.

Faults are white hairs in the coat, and green rims to the eyes. The type should be as for other Longhairs/Persians, and is frequently outstanding, as are the eyes for colour and shape.

Black Persian/Longhair

OFFICIAL STANDARD
Governing Council of the Cat Fancy

BLUE-EYED WHITE: VARIETY 2

Colour
Pure white, without mark or shade of any kind.

Coat
Long and flowing on body, full frill, and brush which should be short and broad; the coat should be close and soft and silky, not woolly in texture.

Body
Cobby and massive, without being coarse, with plenty of bone and substance, and low on the leg.

Head
Round and broad, with plenty of space between the ears, which should be small, neat and well covered; short nose, full cheeks and broad muzzle. An undershot jaw shall be considered a defect.

Eyes
Large, round and wide open, deep blue in colour.

ORANGE-EYED WHITE: VARIETY 2a

Description as for Blue-Eyed White except for eye-colour, which should be orange or copper.

ODD-EYED WHITE: VARIETY 2b

Description as for Blue-Eyed White except for eye-colour, which should be one eye deep blue and one eye orange or copper.

Note
Whites are very liable to get yellow stains on their tails from accumulated dust, etc. This very damaging peculiarity should be carefully attended to and stains removed before showing.

SCALE OF POINTS FOR VARIETIES 2, 2a AND 2b

Colour	25
Coat	20
Body	20
Head	20
Eyes	15
Total	100

White Persian/Longhair kitten

American Orange-eyed White Persian/Longhair

OFFICIAL STANDARD
Governing Council of the Cat Fancy

BLUE: VARIETY 3

Coat
Any shade of blue allowable, sound and even in colour; free from markings, shadings, or any white hairs. Fur long, thick and soft in texture. Frill full.

Head
Broad and round, with width between the ears. Face and nose short. Ears small and tufted. Cheeks well developed.

Eyes
Deep orange or copper; large, round and full, without a trace of green.

Body
Cobby, and low on the legs.

Tail
Short and full, not tapering (a kink shall be considered a defect).

SCALE OF POINTS

Coat	20
Condition	10
Head	25
Eyes	20
Body	15
Tail	10
Total	100

Blue Persian/Longhair kitten

British Blue Persian/Longhair

The Blues arose by accident by crossbreeding between Blacks and Whites, blue being a diluted or weakened black. It proved possible to establish the colour and to produce the Blues in hues varying from light to very dark. At the first show the Blues had tabby markings, white lockets and patches, and were entered as 'Any Other Variety'. By 1889 they had a class of their own: 'Self-coloured, without white'. These early Blues had narrow skulls, long noses and dark colouring. Their eyes were orange-yellow, but many of them had green rims, a fault sometimes still seen. By the next year the numbers had increased so greatly that the adult classes were divided into male and female, and the kittens were shown in a class with the Blacks and Whites. Within a short time, however, the kittens too had their own classes. Queen Victoria and many members of 'society' owned Blues and this may have been the reason for their popularity and great increase in numbers, as they were more or less status symbols. At one show that the Queen attended with the Prince of Wales, later King Edward VII, he awarded a special prize to the Best Blue.

In 1901 the Blue Persian Society was founded 'to promote the breeding and exhibiting of Blue Persian cats and to urge the adoption . . . (of) the only recognized and unvarying standard by which the Blue Persian cats should be judged.' The Society drew up the first standard of points, which is almost that used today, ran the first specialist show, advised on breeding, and did much to make the Blues the most popular longhaired variety. At first it was found that the darkest Blues invariably had the best eye colour, and it took many years of careful breeding to produce them with the pale blue coats and the deep copper or orange eye colouring that is so much liked, although any shade of blue coat is permitted.

For many years the Blues were considered the closest to the recognized standard, that is, the nearest to perfection among the Persians/Longhairs. Their introduction through judicious crossbreeding improved the type and eye colour of other varieties, notably the Blacks, and they were used to produce the early Himalayans/Colourpoint Longhairs. Blues mated to Creams may produce Blue-Creams, the all-female variety. When a Blue female is mated to a Cream male, Blue male and Blue-Cream female kitens may result. When a Blue male is mated to a Blue-Cream, the kittens could be Blue males, Cream males, Blue females and Blue-Cream females.

At birth pure-bred Blue kittens may have shadow tabby markings, which disappear with growth. The most marked kitten in a litter often becomes the best coated adult.

The males, in particular, are massive cats when fully grown, with the prize-winning cats having luxurious full flowing coats. An outstanding Blue should have a broad head with small ears set wide apart, a broad, short nose, a strong chin, with well-developed cheeks; the whole giving the appearance of a well-balanced head. The big round eyes, deep orange or copper, must have no sign of a green rim, and should be bold.

The cobby body on the short sturdy legs should give the impression of strength. The tail should be short and full, not ending in a point. A kink in the tail is a defect, which could be passed on to future kittens. The tail fur should be brushed out until it is nearly as wide as the body.

The coat should be fine in texture, long and flowing and never woolly. The fur around the head should be brushed up, forming a frame around the face. Any shade of blue fur is permitted, as long as it is even in colour right down to the roots. The paler shades are preferred by most breeders. White hairs in the fur are a bad fault.

Blue Persian/Longhair

OFFICIAL STANDARD
Governing Council of the Cat Fancy

RED-SELF: VARIETY 4

Colour
Deep rich red, without markings.

Coat
Long, dense and silky, tail short and flowing.

Body
Cobby and solid, short thick legs.

British Red Self Persian/Longhair

Head
Broad and round, small ears well set and well tufted, short broad nose, full round cheeks.

Eyes
Large and round, deep copper colour.

SCALE OF POINTS

Coat	50
Body	15
Head	20
Eyes	15
Total	100

Perfect specimens of this variety are few and far between. The coat should be a deep, rich red with no markings, and therein lies the difficulty, as it is still almost impossible to produce such a cat with no tabby markings anywhere, particularly on the head.

Red Selfs were included in Harrison Weir's Points of Excellence, the early standards, but the colour was given as 'a brilliant, sandy, or yellowish-red colour'. Writing on Angoras, he included deep red as one of the colours, but Miss Frances Simpson in her *Book of the Cat*, gave the colour as 'orange', making no mention of red, and said that in this Persian variety 'the markings are gradually but surely vanishing.' Until 1894 the classes at the Crystal Palace shows were for 'Brown or Red Tabby, with or without white', but by 1895 there was also a class for 'Orange and Cream' cats. When the Orange, Cream, Fawn and Tortoiseshell Society was founded in Britain, it revised the standard for the Oranges and said the 'colour to be as bright as possible and either self, or markings to be as distinct as can be got.'

As the Oranges could be with or without markings, judges had no need to take this into consideration, and could judge on the colour and other points. The numbers must have been on the increase, as later there were two classes at the shows, one for Orange or Red Tabbies, and one for Orange or Red Self or Shaded.

It was not realized that pure orange or red breeding was necessary to produce orange male and female kittens in a litter, and the orange females, probably bred through correct breeding quite by chance, changed hands for high prices. There are a number of Oranges, some male, in the National Cat Club Stud Book and Register for 1900 to 1905, but many are of unknown parentage; some from Tortoiseshell mothers, while others surprisingly have Blue breeding on both sides. It would be most interesting to know what kittens the male Oranges produced; they were probably of varying colours.

Mrs Vidal, a well-known breeder at that time, wrote in 1902 that 'An orange stud cat is a very useful animal to have in a cattery, for crossing with him will improve many colours, *viz.* tortoiseshell, brown, grey, and sable tabbies; while if he is mated to a blue queen, the kittens, if orange, are beautiful in colour – brighter, I think, than if two orange cats are mated together.' She was one of the first to realize that to produce all orange kittens it is necessary to use an orange male, and mated her stud Torrington Sunnysides, a well-known male in his day, to an orange queen to get all orange kittens, both male and female.

The early fanciers tried many crosses to produce cats without markings. Several suggested Cream and Orange crossbreeding, but found that, although there were often few markings, the colour tended to be a pale sand rather than a deep orange.

By 1912 there were over twenty Red or Orange longhairs entered in the Stud Book and Register, apart from the Red or Orange Tabbies. Mr Western, a well-known judge in his day, wrote about his class at the

Red Self Persian/Longhair kittens

Richmond Show in 1912, 'The Oranges were poor in number; a mistake I think, to divide them into Tabbies and Selfs; the competition is thereby too limited to give satisfaction, even to the winners.'

Although the colour for these Selfs was first given as Orange, presumably the deeper, richer red was much preferred, and soon they were referred to as Reds. It seems to have proved difficult to find suitable studs to use to produce this colour and the numbers became less and less. The Second World War almost sounded the death knell of Red Selfs in Britain, and there were none entered in the Stud Book and Register for the years 1939–48.

Recently, interest has revived in this variety, although it still remains one of the rarest of all pedigree Longhairs. One that did appear at the shows, Champion Pathfinders Golden Dawn, was one of the best seen for years, winning a number of championships. Others have been entered at the shows, but very few have been completely free of markings, although the type and colour is frequently outstanding. The males are useful in breeding the elusive Tortoiseshells and the Tortoiseshell-and-Whites. It is possible to have Red Selfs and Red Tabbies in the same litter.

Two other Red varieties recognized in the United States but not in Britain are the Peke-Faced Red and Peke-Faced Red Tabby. These cats can appear in litters of the normal Reds. The body colourings and general characteristics are the same as for the Red Self and Red Tabbies. The faces resemble those of Pekinese dogs, with very short, indented noses and wrinkles, which in Britain is considered over-typed. The eyes are very large and bold. They are much liked in the United States and have quite frequently won top awards.

Mating a Peke-Faced Red to another Peke does not ensure that there will be Pekes in the resultant litter. They do appear in matings between Red Tabbies and Peke-Faced, but they also appear spontaneously in litters. Careful selective breeding is very necessary to make sure that the kittens produced do not have faulty teeth and noses so short that the animals have difficulty in breathing.

American Red Self Persian/Longhair

OFFICIAL STANDARD
Governing Council of the Cat Fancy

CREAM: VARIETY 5

Colour
To be pure and sound throughout without shading, or markings, pale to medium.

Coat
Long, dense and silky, tail short and flowing.

Body
Cobby and solid, short thick legs.

Head
Broad and round, small ears well set and tufted, short broad nose, broad round cheeks.

Eyes
Large and round, deep copper colour.

SCALE OF POINTS

Colour	30
Coat and condition	20
Body	15
Head	20
Eyes	15
Total	100

At first glance is seems that the Creams have a short history in the Cat Fancy compared with some of the other Longhair varieties, but this is not so, although it is difficult to trace the ancestry of any particular cat. Harrison Weir said of the original Angora cats 'the light fawns, deep reds, and mottled greys are shades that blend well with the Eastern furniture and other surroundings.' He mentioned light fawn, but there are no early records of cats of that colour. Either there were very few about or they were considered to be unimportant. In fact, the Fawns were the early Creams, although the colouring was different to the beautiful Cream of today, which is a dilute of the Red.

The Fawns appeared by chance, probably in litters of Tortoiseshell females mated to Red Tabby males, as they were said to have tabby markings and bars. Nothing was known of breeding for certain colours at this time, and at first these Fawn cats were 'few and far between', and usually were sold as pets. Many were also sent to the United States, where they were highly valued, and, as now, much liked.

Most of the kittens produced were males. The females that were born proved to be bad breeders, possibly because of the inbreeding, as there was little choice of suitable studs, so fanciers lost interest. The first recorded Cream was Cupid Bassanio, born in 1890, and bred by a Mrs Kinchant. A big full-coated male, with tabby markings and bars, he changed hands several times, but nowhere in any records is he down as the sire of kittens.

At the beginning of this century, Miss Frances Simpson wrote that the Creams were the latest variety and looked like becoming fashionable. She went on to say that the first cats of this colour were looked on as 'freak or flukes' and were shown as 'Any variety', but as fanciers were beginning to become systematic in choosing matings, 'there is now a breed of cats established which until late years were not recognized or classified.' A Miss W. Beal, writing at about the same time, said 'the cream and fawn kittens were a few years ago looked upon as a "Sport" and when cream kittens appeared in an orange strain [as a Red was called then], they were considered spoilt oranges, and were usually given away, sold for a few shillings or destroyed as useless.' She considered that the crossing of a Blue queen with a Cream or Orange sire was not successful from a Cream breeder's point of view. Modern breeders would not now agree, bearing in mind the beautiful Creams that have been, and are being, bred from Blue and Cream matings. Miss Beal went on to say that when breeding for colour people are apt to get surprises, with some cats producing all cream kittens in their litters, while others had creams and orange-and-creams. It is only fair to say that going through old records, few cats had pure colour breeding and that any resultant kittens in litters were probably of mixed colours. It would be interesting to know what the orange-and-creams she referred to were like, but there is no description anywhere, and one wonders whether they could have been a possible first step towards the first cameos or had patched coats, the latter being more likely.

The first classes for these cats were for 'Creams and Fawns', with the standard then reading 'All shades from palest fawn to be allowable'. No wonder it took many years to produce cats with coats that really were the colour of Devonshire cream, as the later standard required. In Britain the standard has been altered so that 'the shade may be pale to medium'. In the United States the standard says 'one level shade of buff cream'.

Mrs Clinton Locke introduced a number of Creams into the United States from Britain and her male Kew Laddie proved to be a very successful stud, siring a number of outstanding kittens. Kew Laddie was given to a Miss Johnstone, the Honorary Secretary of the

Beresford Club, who exhibited him at the Chicago Cat Show, where he did very well. An existing picture of him does show that he had tall ears and a long nose, but a beautiful coat; the type being very different to the short-nosed, small-eared outstanding Creams seen in the United States today.

As the Creams increased in number and popularity, many crosses were tried to improve both colour and type. Red Tabbies were used and proved not to be a good choice, as stripes and tabby markings were frequently introduced. These and the reddish tinge in the fur proved difficult to eradicate. Years later, Miss Kathleen Yorke, Chairman of the Governing Council of the Cat Fancy in Britain until her death, wrote in P. M. Soderberg's *Cat Breeding and General Management* that 'after breeding Cream to Cream for several generations one frequently notices that type begins to disappear, and the hot tinge along the backbone returns. The ears also tend to get larger. . . . when these faults are noticed the time has come to reintroduce Blue blood again.' Crossbreeding between Blues and Creams has resulted in not only outstanding Creams, but also the beautiful Blue-Creams.

There are faults, of course. For example, the fur may be 'hot', that is, the colour is reddish, rather than cream, particularly along the spine, and some cats have a whitish undercoat and white tips to the tail, rather than being of even colouring throughout. On the other hand, there are some very good cats to be seen on the show bench: massive cats, with full coats and short full tails, cobby bodies on short sturdy legs, and good broad heads, with neat small ears, and big round deep orange or copper eyes, really worthy champions.

At birth, the kittens may show some signs of barring, but these should disappear with growth. Any kittens with very definite markings at about eight to ten weeks should be sold as pets. Even in very tiny kittens the width of the head is important, as is the position of the ears, and the shape of the body. It is difficult to foretell the eye colour in young kittens, as all are born with blue eyes, and some take longer than others to develop the full colouring required.

A Cream is a useful cross for Tortoiseshells, Tortoiseshell and Whites (Calicos), Bicolours and Blacks. Creams mated to Blue or Blue-Creams may produce the following:

A Cream male mated to a Blue female: Blue-Cream females and Blue males.

A Cream female mated to a Blue male: Blue-Cream females and Cream males.

A Cream male mated to a Blue-Cream female: Blue-Cream females, Cream females, Blue males, Cream males.

Cream Persian/Longhair

OFFICIAL STANDARD
Governing Council of the Cat Fancy

SMOKE: VARIETY 6

A Smoke is a cat of contrasts, the undercolour being as ash-white as possible, with the tips shading to black, the dark points being most defined on the back, head and feet, and the light points on frill, flanks and ear-tufts.

Colour
Body: black shading to silver on the sides and flanks. *Mask and feet:* black with no markings. *Frill and ear-tufts:* silver. *Undercolour:* as nearly white as possible.

Coat
Silky texture, long and dense, extra long frill.

Head
Broad and round with width between the ears, which should be small and tufted; snub nose.

Body
Cobby, not coarse but massive; short legs.

Eyes
Orange or copper in colour, large and round in shape, pleasing expression.

Tail
Short and bushy.

Note
An obvious under, or over-short jaw shall be considered a defect.

SCALE OF POINTS

Colour: body, mask and feet, frill and ear-tufts and undercolour	40
Coat texture and condition	10
Head (including ears)	20
Body	15
Eyes	10
Tail	5
Total	100

American Smoke Persian/Longhair

GCCF OFFICIAL STANDARD continued –

BLUE SMOKE: VARIETY 6a

A Smoke cat is a cat of contrasts, the undercolour being as ash-white as possible, with the tips shading to blue, the dark points being most defined on the back, head and feet, and the light points on frill, flanks and ear-tufts.

Colour
Body: blue shading to silver on the sides and flanks. *Mask and feet:* blue with no markings. *Frill and ear-tufts:* silver. *Undercolour:* as nearly white as possible.

Coat
Silky texture, long and dense, extra long frill.

Head
Broad and round with width between the ears, which should be small and tufted; snub nose.

Body
Cobby, not coarse but massive; short legs.

Eyes
Orange or copper in colour, large and round in shape, pleasing expression.

Tail
Short and bushy.

Note
An obvious under, or over-short jaw shall be considered a defect.

SCALE OF POINTS

Colour: body, mask and feet, frill and ear-tufts and undercolour	40
Coat texture and condition	10
Head (including ears)	20
Body	15
Eyes	10
Tail	5
Total	100

Blue Smoke Persian/Longhair

Black Smoke Persian/Longhair

'The Smoke is a cat of great beauty but unfortunately is very rare.' This has been said quite truthfully ever since 1893 when the Smoke was given an open class at the shows and no longer had to compete in Any Other Variety classes.

According to Frances Simpson, the first Smokes were produced by crossbreeding three varieties: the Black, the White and the Blue. She realized that their rarity was due to the difficulty of choosing the right males as studs, and wrote, 'above all things shun, as you would Sin, Tabbies of any colour, and let your choice fall on a heavily-coated sire.'

Despite Miss Simpson's remarks about scarcity, there were relatively far more Smokes at the end of the nineteenth and the beginning of the twentieth century in Britain than there are now. It is difficult to assess the quality of these Smokes and to compare them with those of today, as often all that is known about them is that they were constant winners. The most successful breeder of her day was Mrs H. V. James, who wrote about Smokes in 1903 and supplied notes for a book published in 1948, evidence that she certainly was dedicated to this variety for a very long time. She started breeding them more or less by accident when a

Blue Persian she had bought died and the breeder sent her a replacement. This kitten was, to her disappointment, very dark in colour on arrival and grew a coat of 'deep cinder colour', certainly not blue. Mrs James thought he looked something like a Smoke, so entered him under that heading in a show, where to her great surprise he won all his classes. He grew up and sired a number of kittens. One of these became the famous Champion Backwell Jogram, and another of his kittens was exported to the United States to found new breeding lines there.

Mrs James advocated pure breeding, but said that to improve Smokes an outcross was sometimes necessary. Her advice is still well worth taking to heart by any would-be breeder:

'If two females were taken, and one was mated to a Black and the other to a Blue, the cross-mating of the young from these two families might produce a Smoke with the type of the Blue and the ebony blackness of the Black. It must nevertheless be remembered that few kittens produced by such a mating would be useful for the future breeding of Smokes. The great mistake made in experimental breeding is that usually breeders are not sufficiently ruthless in discarding crossbred animals and confining their breeding operations to the select few. [Modern breeders of all varieties please take note.] Experimental work is bound to produce far more disappointments than successes and it will need much perseverence to restore the Smoke to its eminence among show cats.'

There were thirty Smokes in the National Cat Club Stud Book and Register for the years 1900 to 1905, but when the newly-formed Governing Council of the Cat Fancy published its first Stud Book in 1912, there were only eighteen Smokes. By the end of the Second World War in 1945, the Smokes were practically non-existent. They have made a comeback in recent years in Britain, and have always been popular in the United States, with some outstanding specimens appearing at the shows.

One of the most striking of the Longhair varieties, frequently referred to as 'the cat of contrasts', a Black Smoke should have a full silver ruff framing the jet-black face, a broad head with neat black ears having silver tufts, and a white undercoat. On the face and paws the hair should be black to the roots. The top black body coat should shade to silver on the sides and flanks, and it is really only in walking that the true beauty of the coat is appreciated, as it is the movement that causes the silver gleams to appear through the black fur.

When first born the kittens show very little promise of their future beauty or show potentialities, and it takes a very experienced breeder to distinguish a baby Smoke from a baby Black. Immediately at birth a close examination may show tiny white smudges of white around the eyes and possibly, a slightly greyish hue on the stomach, but it will be many months before the contrasts are seen. Many kittens have been incorrectly registered as Smokes only to become beautiful Blacks when adult, and sometimes just the opposite is the case.

Smokes may be mated to Smoke, but should there be a deterioration in type and eye colour, an occasional outcross with an outstanding Black, Blue, or White could be tried.

In Britain and the United States Smokes are recognized in two varieties, the Black and the Blue, another attractive variety in which the blue colour replaces the black. At first glance the Blue Smoke may look like a Blue, but when it walks the white undercoat gleams through. The mask should be blue and the frill and ear tufts white.

In the United States there also are Smoke Tortoise-shells, a female-only variety, in which the white undercoat is tipped with black, and the cat also has well-defined patching of red and cream. Cameo or Red Smokes are recognized in the United States and some other countries.

In Britain they are being shown only in the Assessment classes. In time, no doubt, they will also be given recognition. The Cameo looks like a red cat until it moves, when the contrasting white undercoat may be seen. It is a pretty cat, with red replacing the black of the original Smoke. It takes a long time to produce a perfect Cameo Smoke, but one close to the required standard with the correct colouring, good type, deep copper eyes and wealth of coat attracts a great deal of attention at the shows.

All varieties should have long dense coats, short full tails, and extra long frills around the faces.

More so even than the other Longhair varieties, grooming is essential if a Smoke is to be seen in its true beauty. Until maturity the coat is not seen at its best, with full contrasts. According to some breeders, there is a period of only two months in the year when the coat is in peak condition. Unfortunately, the fur is quickly affected by damp and strong sunlight, so that a cat that is to be exhibited should not be allowed to spend long hours basking in the sun. Preparing a Smoke for a show is said to be a true art, needing many hours spent in careful grooming and combing, so that the undercoat is well brushed up to show through the top coat, without pulling it out and spoiling the effect.

Blue Smoke Persian/Longhair

OFFICIAL STANDARD
Governing Council of the Cat Fancy

SILVER TABBY: VARIETY 7

Colour
Ground colour pure pale silver, with decided jet black markings; any brown tinge a drawback.

Head
Broad and round, with breadth between ears and wide at muzzle, short nose, small well tufted ears.

Shape
Cobby body, short thick legs.

Eyes
Colour: green or hazel.

Coat and condition
Silky in texture, long and dense, extra long on frill.

Tail
Short and bushy.

SCALE OF POINTS

Colour	40
Head	20
Shape	10
Tail	5
Eyes (green or hazel)	10
Coat and condition	15
Total	100

Silver Tabby Persian/Longhair

When cat shows started, the Silver Tabby classes were well-filled, although judging by modern standards, few of those entered could now be called good specimens. These Tabbies had narrow heads and long, upright noses, but, as old photographs show, they did have definite tabby markings. The difficulty experienced in finding suitable males to improve the type, and the subsequent cross-matings with Blues and Blacks, caused deterioration in the markings rather than improvement, and one judge wrote 'Silver Tabby classes at our shows are full of nondescript cats with shaded silver bodies and markings only on legs and head.'

Eventually, classes were put on for Chinchillas and Shaded Silver, and the numbers in the Silver Tabby classes declined rapidly. Arguments arose among the breeders as to the correct eye colour, with many preferring green, and the Reverend T. Maynard, a Silver Tabby breeder, even wrote to the newspapers to complain: 'In former days we never had anything to do with a cat that had green eyes, and now that so much is being done to improve the feline race, why should we try to think the green eye right and even dsirable?' Frances Simpson and others favoured the green eyes, and so were accused of being responsible for the decline in popularity of the Silver Tabbies, as the breeders, in trying to produce cats with green eyes, frequently bred them with few markings. Another breeder, Miss Leake, joined in the controversy, saying that she considered 'the correct colour for the eyes of a Silver Tabby is neither green, orange, nor yellow, but hazel – deep nut-brown.' The arguments went on and on, and Louis Wain, the artist, cat judge and show manager, wrote, 'Everyone, judges and exhibitors alike, is bitten by the craze for the "Correct coloured eyes".' Until fairly recently there were arguments about the eye colouring; the standard now says 'green or hazel'.

Over the years various crossings were tried to improve type and markings. Blues and Blacks were used, which did improve the type, but not the markings. One breeder writing in tye early 1930s said 'this is one of the very lonely breeds which have fallen on evil days. Frequently their classes have only two or three entries and sometimes are cancelled.'

Brown Tabbies were tried as crosses to improve the pattern of markings, but this was inclined to introduce brownish tinges into the fur. Mr Cyril Yeates, cat judge, breeder, and Chairman of the Governing Council of the Cat Fancy advocated the use of Blacks to deepen the markings, but unfortunately this often resulted in orange eyes.

The Silver Tabbies are still few in number, which is a pity, as a cat with the correct silver background fur and good jet-black pattern of markings can be one of the most striking of the Longhairs. Frequently, the coats are brindled, the markings smudged and there are yellow or brown marks in the fur.

The kittens are born dark, and the darkest kitten often proves to be the best, with the pale silver colouring appearing as the fur grows. Careful grooming is essential to make the silver undercoat stand up to show the tabby pattern of markings to the best advantage.

Silver Tabby, showing well-tufted ears

OFFICIAL STANDARD
Governing Council of the Cat Fancy

BROWN TABBY: VARIETY 8

Colour and markings
Rich tawny sable, with delicate black pencillings running down face. The cheeks crossed with two or three distinct swirls, the chest crossed by two unbroken narrow lines, butterfly markings on shoulders. Front of legs striped regularly from toes upwards. The saddle and sides to have deep bands running down, and the tail to be regularly ringed.

Coat
Long and flowing, tail short and full.

Body
Cobby and massive; short legs.

Head
Round and broad, small well-placed and well-tufted ears, short broad nose, full round cheeks.

Eyes
Large and round, hazel or copper colour.

SCALE OF POINTS

Coat	50
Body	15
Head	20
Eyes	15
Total	100

Brown Tabby Persian/Longhair

From the end of the last century up to the Frist World War, Brown Tabbies were very popular, but since that time the numbers bred and exhibited have been very small. It is possible that the early Tabbies did not have the explicit pattern of markings required, although Rajah, belonging to Frances Simpson, won many prizes. He looks very good in his photographs and became the best known stud of his day, producing a number of outstanding kittens.

The ground colouring should be a rich sable, difficult to get even today; in the last century a Miss Southam's Birkdale Ruffie was said to have beautiful sable colouring and dense black markings. For some years, however, this was not appreciated by the judges,

as, according to his owner, he was deliberately passed over at his first shows for 'other and more inferior cats'! She did not show him for some time, determined that he should not be further 'insulted by such flagrant injustice'. She must have changed her mind, for records show that the injustice was rectified in 1896 at the famous Crystal Palace show, when Birkdale Ruffie swept the board, winning many prizes including an autographed photograph of the Prince of Wales (later King Edward VII), which the Prince presented personally for the best 'rough-coated cat in show'.

Brown Tabbies were also proving popular in the United States at this time, many being exported from Britain to gain honours at the shows. One, Lord

Humbert, arrived in the United States in 1885 and apparently caused a sensation. His owner, Mr E. Barker, an American cat judge, later refused an offer of one thousand dollars from an American millionaire for him. This was a vast sum in those days to pay for a cat, when fifty dollars was considered a high price.

The next thirty years show very few registrations for Brown Tabbies in Britain, although various imports from the United States were introduced; one female failed to breed, and perhaps the others, through mixed breeding, did not produce kittens of show standard. The problem with the 'Brownies', as they are often referred to, is the difficulty in finding suitable outcrosses, as mating Brown to Brown indefinitely invariably means loss of type. A Red Tabby is not a suitable cross because it will not intensify the markings, Blues and Blacks have been used with some success, and a Tortoiseshell or a Blue-Cream mated to a Brown Tabby male has proved successful. A Silver Tabby would probably cause more problems than pro-

vide improvement because it would not help the colour in any way and might introduce green eyes into the strain. From time to time, Brown Tabbies appear quite unexpectedly in crossbred litters from Blues mated to a Chinchilla, or a Red Tabby mated to a Blue.

At birth the kittens may be quite dark, with very little sign of a pattern of markings. As the coat grows, the background colour may be seen, with the stripes and bars gradually emerging. It may be several months before the markings appear distinctly, so that sometimes the kitten with the heaviest markings turns out to be a beautifully marked cat with a coat of rich tawny sable and the deep black markings required. Brown kittens are delightful, sturdy, full of life and sell so readily as pets that this could be one of the reasons why so few are exhibited. A full-grown Brown Tabby, particularly a neuter, can be a large cat, with a beautiful full coat, very striking in appearance, generally very good tempered, highly intelligent, making a quiet, companionable and affectionate pet.

OFFICIAL STANDARD
Governing Council of the Cat Fancy

RED TABBY: VARIETY 9

Colour and markings
Deep rich red colour, markings to be clearly and boldly defined, continuing on down the chest, legs and tail.

Coat
Long, dense and silky; tail short and flowing, no white tip.

Body
Cobby and solid, short thick legs.

Head
Broad and round, small ears, well set and well tufted, short broad nose, full round cheeks.

Eyes
Large and round, deep copper colour.

SCALE OF POINTS

Coat	50
Body	15
Head	20
Eyes	15
Total	100

The Red Tabby has always fascinated many breeders. A good specimen with the deep, rich red colour with the deeper red pattern of tabby markings is most striking and could never be confused with the many sandy or marmalade pet cats seen around.

At the first cat shows the Brown and Red Tabbies, with or without white, were entered in the same classes. Often these cats were spotted and striped, but had no definite pattern of markings, and the colour was anything but red. The formation of the Orange, Cream, Fawn and Tortoiseshell Society in 1900 was responsible for better classifications at the shows for the Tabbies and for establishing the standard for the 'Orange Self or Tabby'. This said the colour was to be 'as bright as possible, and either self, or markings to be as distinct as can be got'. The term Orange was preferred in those days to Red because the colour was nearest to 'that of a ripe orange when in perfection'. It was thought, since the standard said 'self, or markings', that, as had happened in the case of the early Blue Persians, with suitable matings, the markings would

go, the Tabbies would vanish, and the Selfs take over. This has not happened, although there are quite a number of Self Reds around. However, they have proved exceedingly difficult to produce without some tabby markings, usually on the heads.

The original standard stated that the eyes would be bright orange or hazel, but, as with the Silver Tabbies, there were arguments as to which was the correct eye colouring, some breeders preferring 'golden bronze' and others endeavouring to breed Oranges with bright blue eyes. The latter proved impossible, but as all kittens are born with blue eyes, some unscrupulous breeders sold them as 'unique Oranges with blue eyes'. The buyers were greatly disappointed when the eye colour changed as the kittens grew older.

More attention was paid in these early days to breeding Oranges without the white lips and chins, a fault that still does occur, than to producing cats with the correct tabby markings. Various crosses were tried, and Oranges mated to Cream were said to have kittens with the best unmarked coats. Matings with Tortoise-

Red Tabby Persian/Longhair

shells gave kittens various colours, but few were orange. Some breeders gave up in despair, turning to other varieties when they found that the Oranges they bred were always males. It was some years before it was realized that to have both male and female orange kittens in a litter, there must be pure red (orange) parents on both sides, and that a red and tortoiseshell mating may produce red males, but not red females.

The early stud books simply gave the heading as 'Orange, Longhaired', so it is impossible to know whether the cats were self or tabbies. As many were of unknown parentage, they would have been useless for pedigree breeding and probably produced very mixed litters. By the time the Governing Council of the Cat Fancy published its first stud book in 1912, things had been sorted out and there were two headings 'Red or Orange, Longhaired' and 'Red or Orange Tabby, Longhaired'. However, as has already been pointed out (see page 203) Mr Western believed it was a mistake to divide the Tabbies and Selfs into separate classes in 1912 because the numbers were so limited.

Many good Reds have been produced from Black to Tortoiseshell breeding, Black to Red breeding, and of course, Red to Red. Through careful breeding the present-day Reds, both in Britain and in the United States, frequently excel in type, having good round heads and short broad noses, and magnificent big, deep, copper coloured eyes in Britain, and brilliant gold in the United States. The first Red Tabby declared a grand champion by the Cat Fanciers' Association of America – Grand Champion Eastbury Trigo – was imported from England.

It is still difficult to breed the correct pattern in a deep rich red, so that the markings stand out quite distinctly from the rich brilliant red background fur. The face markings are usually good, but often those on the back are too solid, and it may be difficult to distinguish the butterfly shape on the shoulders in the long fur. The colour nowadays is usually very good, but faults are still the occasional white chins, white tips to the tails, and paler fur colouring on the stomach.

A litter of red kittens is a joy to see, and, if good, the coat pattern may be detected very soon after birth. If the markings are barely distinguishable when the kitten is young, it is unlikely that they will improve to any great extent with age.

OFFICIAL STANDARD
Governing Council of the Cat Fancy

CHINCHILLA: VARIETY 10

Colour
The undercoat pure white, the coat on back, flanks, head, ears and tail being tipped with black; this tipping to be evenly distributed, thus giving the characteristic sparkling silver appearance: the legs may be very slightly shaded with the tipping, but the chin, ear tufts, stomach and chest must be pure white; any tabby markings or brown or cream tinge is a defect. The tip of the nose brick-red, and the visible skin on eyelids and the pads black or dark brown.

Head
Broad and round, with breadth between ears, which should be small and well tufted; wide at the muzzle; snub nose.

Shape
Cobby body; short thick legs.

Eyes
Large, round and most expressive; emerald or blue-green in colour.

Coat and condition
Silky and fine in texture, long and dense, extra long on frill.

Tail
Short and bushy.

Note
An obvious under- or over-shot jaw shall be considered a defect.

SCALE OF POINTS

Colour	25
Head	20
Shape	15
Eyes	15
Coat and condition	15
Tail	10
Total	100

Chinchilla Persian/Longhair

Considered by many to be the most glamorous of the Longhair cats, the Chinchillas are constantly referred to as ethereal in appearance. A prize-winning specimen certainly lives up to this description. This was not always so; the modern Chinchillas differ greatly from the first examples of this variety, as the early fanciers all had their own ideas about the cat's appearance.

In 1893 John Jennings wrote that 'the Chinchilla is a peculiar but beautiful variety; the fur at the roots is silver, and shades to the tips to a decided slate hue, giving a most pleasing and attractive appearance.' It is strange that he gives the name Chinchilla because they were not classified as such until the Crystal Palace shows. Until then the class was for 'Silver Tabbies, including Blue Tabbies with or without white', and so any exhibit with white and silver in the coat was entered in this class with the tabbies. The owners' descriptions of their cats were various, including 'Silver Grey', 'Silver Chinchilla', 'Chinchilla Tabby', and 'Blue or Silver Striped'. There were very many arguments as to the name by which they should be called officially before Chinchilla was decided on, and then not to everyone's satisfaction.

The chinchilla is a small rodent found in South America and bred for its fur. Frances Simpson protested that 'it is really a most misleading title, as the cats are quite unlike the fur which we know as chinchilla, this being dark at the roots and lighter towards the tips. Now, cats of this variety ought to be just the reverse.' She suggested that they should be referred to as Silver, which would be more in keeping with their appearance. In the United States the Chinchillas and the Shaded Silvers sometimes are referred to collectively as Silvers.

There are several stories about the origin of the Chinchillas, but one thing is sure: they were a 'man-made' variety, before it was even realized that it was possible to produce variations in cats' colourings and coat patterns through various cross-matings. One story is that a Chinchilla appeared in a litter produced by a mating between a Tortoiseshell and a Silver Tabby or a Blue, while another is that a Silver Tabby gave birth to a kitten with no tabby markings. However, a Mrs Vallence definitely owned the first, called Chinnie, (obviously short for Chinchilla), which came to be known as the 'Mother of the Chinchillas'. The kitten was apparently bred by a Miss Grace Hurt from a cat she had bought, and which she mated to a part-pedigree male she owned. Chinnie was a light lavender in colour and was mated to a male known as Fluffy I, said to have quality of coat and a cherub face. The kitten they produced was named Beauty. She eventually was mated to a light Smoke, Champion Perso and produced a male kitten, Silver Lambkin, known as 'the pillar of the Chinchilla stud book'. Silver Lambkin was said to be remarkable for his size, length of fur, and enormous frill. He lived to be 17 years old, and achieved fame by being stuffed and put on show at the Natural History Museum in London, England.

The early Chinchillas were much darker than those of today, some being a lavender colour, the coats heavily ticked, and having barrings on the legs and tabby markings on the face. Some kittens in the same litter were dark, others light. The lighter ones came to be preferred, and eventually a class was put on for the darker ones, which became known as Shaded Silvers.

Yet once again, the correct eye colouring proved a vexed question; some cats had amber eyes, others yellow, and yet others bright green. According to one writer, the first silver cat with green eyes exhibited in Britain was disqualified, but later one with blue-green eyes aroused so much admiration that that colour eyes became the vogue. These early Chinchillas had a long way to go to turn into today's beauties, as the standard in 1903 was for 'palest Silver, lavender tint preferred, nearly white at the roots. No dark stripes, blotches or brown tint', and still some were light and some were dark. Although there were now separate classes for them, the situation was so very confused that cats were being disqualified for being entered in the wrong class. No one seemed to be sure when a darkish Chinchilla became a Shaded Silver, but matters came to a head when at one show somehow a cat was entered in both the Chinchilla and Shaded Silver classes, and won special prizes in each. In 1902, by general agreement, the Shaded Silver standard was dropped in Britain, and although these cats are still recognized in many other countries, they have not yet been re-recognized in Britain. Some have been exhibited in Assessment classes, and doubtless it is only a matter of time before they again have a Shaded Silver standard. There should be no mistakes this time, as the general appearance of the Shaded Silver is so different (see page oo).

As the lighter tipped cats become more popular, more breeders endeavoured to produce them, but, unfortunately, this resulted in lighter boned animals with little stamina. The modern Chinchillas are hardy cats, belying their fairylike appearance.

The end of the nineteenth and the beginning of the twentieth century was the time of the large catteries, which frequently were owned by the wealthy members of society; members of the nobility and the royal family were interested in breeding and showing. Domestic labour was plentiful and cheap, and the cats were groomed and fed by cattery maids especially employed to look after them. Rivalry was fierce and frequently a winning cat was purchased for a large sum, never to be seen at the shows again, so that a particular breeder would not have her cat beaten. This applied not only to Chinchillas, but also to most other pedigree varieties.

Many cats were exported to the United States, and any outstanding cat that had proved too dark for the Chinchilla class in Britain did well in the Shaded Silver classes in America. It should be remembered that there was no quarantine in those days, and sometimes cats returned to Britain when their owners returned home after living in the United States for some years.

By 1911 the Chinchillas were well-established in Britain and the United States, with brilliant deep green eyes being approved by all. The tabby markings were gradually being bred out, and more well-known breeders took up Chinchilla breeding seriously and by careful matings were able to produce kittens very close to the required standard.

Today's cats have pure white fur lightly ticked with black on the back, sides, ears and tails, giving the effect of shining silver coats with delicate pencil shadings. Too-heavy ticking is considered a fault, as are dark patchings, tabby markings and brown or yellow tinges in the coat. The type is as for other Longhairs, although they are inclined to be finer in bone; their dainty colouring is misleading, and, brought up correctly, they are as healthy and sturdy as other cats. Show preparation must be very thorough to ensure that every hair stands away from the body and the ruff is brushed up to form a soft frame to the expressive face.

The kittens are born dark, often with tabby markings, which vanish as the fur grows. Frequently the darkest kitten becomes the best adult.

Shaded Silver

This is an old variety, once recognized in Britain, which at the moment is still appearing in the Assessment classes. However, in North America and other parts of the world the Shaded Silver is very popular in both the longhaired and shorthaired varieties. The Shaded Silvers were dropped in Britain in 1902 because of the difficulty breeders had in deciding which were Chinchillas and which were Shaded Silvers, as both varieties could appear in the same litters.

The American standard calls for a white uncoat with the black tippings forming a mantle shading down from the sides. When the Chinchilla and Shaded Silver stand side by side, there is now no mistaking which is which; the eye colouring of both is the same, but the Chinchilla tippings give the characteristic sparkling appearance, while the Shaded Silver definitely looks much darker.

Both varieties do appear in the same litter, and it may be difficult at first to differentiate between them, as both are born dark with tabby markings, but as the fur grows, the difference soon becomes evident. It is far more difficult to produce Shaded Silvers with the correct shadings than with the delicate tippings of the Chinchillas. The fur is long and fine, and correct grooming is vital so that the true mantle effect is clearly seen. Many breeders give the cats a bath a few days prior to the show, which allows the natural grease to return while still giving the coat an immaculate appearance. Other breeders prefer bathing the cats the night before a show, and fluff-drying them.

Chinchilla Golden and Shaded Golden

In the United States it has been found possible to produce cats with the chinchilla and shaded appearances in varying colours, with the newest being the Chinchilla Golden and the Shaded Golden. The undercoats are rich cream, rather than white, with the tippings and shadings of seal brown, rather than silver. The eye colour, the same as for the Chinchillas and Shaded Silvers, is green or blue-green, which is very unusual for such coat colourings. The type is the same as that of other Longhairs.

OFFICIAL STANDARD
Governing Council of the Cat Fancy

TORTOISESHELL: VARIETY 11

Colour
Three colours, black, red and cream, well broken into patches; colours to be bright and rich and well broken on face.

Coat
Long and flowing, extra long on frill and brush.

Body
Cobby and massive; short legs.

Head
Round and broad; ears small, well-placed and well tufted; short broad nose, full round cheeks.

Eyes
Large and round, deep orange or copper.

SCALE OF POINTS

Coat	50
Body	15
Head	20
Eyes	15
Total	100

TORTOISESHELL AND WHITE: VARIETY 12

Colour
Three colours, black, red and cream, or their dilutions to be well distributed and broken and interspersed with white.

Coat
Long and flowing, extra long on brush and frill.

Body
Cobby and massive; short legs.

Head
Round and broad; ears small, well-placed and tufted; short broad nose, full round cheeks.

Eyes
Large and round, deep orange or copper.

SCALE OF POINTS	
Coat	50
Body	15
Head	20
Eyes	15
Total	100

Tortoiseshell and White Persian/Longhair

These fascinating varieties have been spoken of as the cats with no history. This is more or less true of the Longhair, or Persian, varieties, but the short-coated cats with the same colourings have been known for centuries on farms in Britain. They have no recorded pedigrees, but many such kittens appear in litters dating back for some generations. As for the Longhairs, Harrison Weir's opinion was that the Tortoiseshell was not one of the early varieties that came to Britain via Europe from Asia, but probably resulted from matings with long-coated blacks and the short-coated farm tortoiseshells. Darwin thought that the orange tomcat and the tortoiseshell were originally the male and female of the same variety. This was before it was known that pure red (orange) breeding can produce orange kittens of both sexes in one litter.

Frances Simpson spoke of the Tortoiseshells as having no past and said there were no celebrities in feline history of that colour except a cat called Queen Elizabeth. Apparently she was not only a fine example of her kind but was well-known too for her dislike of being exhibited, showing her resentment by biting anyone who handled her. Even today, although cats of all varieties usually behave very well at the shows, there is the occasional one that resents being judged, showing her resentment accordingly. Judges and stewards are now supposed to report any such incidents, and any animal that really inflicts bad injuries is banned from future showing.

At the end of the last century, a Mrs Bignell owned a Tortie, Topsy by name, 'a Noted Prizewinner', and judging by her photograph, even by modern standards, she appeared to have good type. In an endeavour to breed this variety, the owner tried a number of different matings. Mated to a Blue, Topsy produced two Creams and two Smokes. One of the latter was sent to the United States and was said to have been one of the best ever seen there. Topsy mated to a Black had only Black kittens. The next time a Blue was used, and the result was a litter of two Orange males and one Tortoiseshell, but a repeat of this mating resulted in one Black and two Orange males and no Torties.

Tortoiseshell breeding was, and still is, unpredictable. At the beginning of the century a Miss Beal appears to have been successful in breeding Tortoiseshells by mating her own Torties to prizewinning Creams; an outstanding specimen, called Snapdragon, was exported to the United States.

Breeders became intrigued with this female-only variety – the occasional male born invariably proving sterile – that could produce so many different-coloured kittens. A number of crosses were tried, resulting in Blacks, Oranges (Reds), Creams, Blue-Creams and the occasional Tortoiseshell. Even today using one of the self colours, the breeding is still very much a matter of chance. Red Tabbies are not recommended because they introduce tabby markings, which are very difficult to breed out.

Whatever their origin, Tortoiseshells have always been popular. The coats should be well-patched with black, red and cream, as bright as possible. This is very difficult to produce in the long fur, and more often than not there is too much black in the coat. Ideally, the colours should be evenly distributed all over the body, with lesser patching on the legs, head and even on the ears. The standard of the Cat Fanciers' Association states that a blaze – that is, a strip of colour, frequently cream, running from the top of the head to the nose – is desirable. The British standard does not specify a blaze, but it is liked by the breeders and definitely does add character to the face.

The Tortoiseshell and Whites have a very similar history to that of the Tortoiseshells. They were once known as the Chintz cats in Britain and are referred to as Calico cats in the United States.

Another female-only variety, with no males available for mating, the same more or less hit-or-miss breeding procedure was used as for the Torties, and very few Tortoiseshell and Whites were produced. From these matings, some kittens in the litters had coats of two colours, which were eventually recognized as Bicolours, and one enterprising British breeder worked out a breeding programme that could, and did, quite frequently produce the much-longed-for Tortie and Whites. By mating with self-coloured Red, Black, White and Blue males, and using the resultant male Red and White, and Black and White cats as studs, Tortoiseshell and Whites did appear in some litters. Once such a line has been established, self-coloured males should no longer be used, as this may result in the loss of white from the coats. Planned breeding is absolutely essential for any would-be producer of this variety. On the other hand, the Tortoiseshell and White mated to a self-coloured male will give a wonderful variety of kittens, which are usually very much liked.

The colourings are as for the Torties with the addition of white. The British standard calls for a well-patched coat of black, red and cream, interspersed with white, while the standard of the Cat Fanciers' Association of America calls for a white cat with black and red patching. Too much white is considered undesirable in Britain. In both countries brindling – that is, white hairs in the colour patches – is faulted when being judged. Tabby markings of any kind are a fault too. As in the Tortoiseshell, a blaze of red or cream is liked. The American Cat Fanciers' Association, referred to as the ACFA, (the next largest registering body in the United States after the Cat Fanciers' Association, referred to as the CFA) describes the Tortoiseshell and White 'as if a white cat had been daubed with a paintbrush'.

It is also possible to have a Tricolour, akin to the Tortie and White, and often appearing in the same litter. They may be shown in the same class at the shows. They are referred to as the Dilute Calico in the United States, and should have clear patching of blue and cream. A very attractive variety, they are much liked as pets.

The type of all three varieties is usually very good, and the bodies are cobby, with short, full tails. The coat texture makes for easy grooming, and appears to matt up less than many of the other Longhair cats. They are all very intelligent animals, make good mothers, and are a delight to see with their multi-coloured litters.

OFFICIAL STANDARD
Governing Council of the Cat Fancy

BI-COLOUR: VARIETY 12a

Colour and distribution
Any solid colour and white, the patches of colour to be clear, even and well distributed. Not more than two-thirds of the cat's coat to be coloured and not more than a half to be white. Face to be patched with colour and white.

Coat
Silky texture. Long and flowing, extra long on frill and tail.

Head
Round and broad with width between the ears, which should be small, well placed and tufted. Short broad nose, full cheeks, wide muzzle and firm chin (level bite).

Body and legs
Body cobby and massive, short thick legs.

Eyes
Large and round, set well apart, deep orange or copper in colour.

Tail
Short and full.

Serious faults
Tabby markings. A long tail. Yellow or green eyes.

SCALE OF POINTS

Colour	25
Coat	15
Body	15
Tail	5
Head	25
Eyes	15
Total	100

Blue and White Bicolour Persian/Longhair

In 1889 Harrison Weir gave details of cats with two-coloured coats, the Black and White, White and Black, and Brown, Red, Yellow, or Blue Tabbies all with white. These were shorthaired, and the pattern of markings required was for the feet, chest, nose and pads, to be white. He made no mention of Angoras or Persians with coats of two colours, although they had appeared in the Any Other Colour classes at the early shows. These cats had resulted from the crossbreeding of self-colour varieties, and although very striking in appearance, appeared then to be of little use for breeding, and so were neglected by the early fanciers. In the United States they were far more popular, and there were even special classifications at the early shows for the Orange and White, and the Blue and White.

In Britain Lady Alexander, a well-known breeder of her day, with a very large cattery, endeavoured to popularize them by guaranteeing special classes at the Crystal Palace shows, but the entries were few. Mr Cyril Yeates, one-time Chairman of the Governing Council of the Cat Fancy, cat judge and breeder, was also very interested in the 'Magpies', as he called them. He considered the cats should be black, with white chests and feet, with a white blaze on the heads, and that a perfect specimen should have a white necklace completely encircling the neck.

For many years cats with two-coloured coats continued to be exhibited in the Any Other Colour classes. Eventually they were given a standard, but this proved far too exacting to reproduce, as the markings were as for a Dutch rabbit, with even the face being divided exactly in half by the two colours. Very rarely were the cats anywhere near the required standard, and invariably the judges withheld the challenge certificates, and the breeders lost heart.

Breeders met to discuss the characteristics required for a Bicolour and decided that it was quite impossible to continue breeding unless a new standard could be drawn up that was simpler to produce. In 1971 a revised standard was approved, and the numbers at the shows increased rapidly, and a number of Bicolours eventually became champions. Any solid colour with white is permitted, but the white must not predominate.

There are many delightful specimens seen nowadays; several have achieved Best in Show. The Blue and White, the Black and White, and the Red and

White have proved to be the most popular, although one or two Cream and Whites have been shown. They have been most successfully used in the breeding of Tortoiseshell and White (see page 219).

The crossbreeding involved produces strong healthy cats. The males are quite massive, with a wealth of coat, broad heads with small ears, and big round eyes. Usually excellent breeders, the females make good mothers, and, depending on the pedigree, the kitten colourings are various.

OFFICIAL STANDARD
Governing Council of the Cat Fancy

BLUE-CREAM: VARIETY 13

Colour markings
To consist of blue and cream, softly intermingled; pastel shades.

Coat
To be dense and very soft and silky.

Body
Short, cobby and massive; short thick legs.

Head
Broad and round, tiny ears, well placed and well tufted, short broad nose, colour intermingled on face.

Eyes
Deep copper or orange.

SCALE OF POINTS

Colour	30
Coat and condition	20
Body	15
Head	20
Eyes	15
Total	100

Blue-Creams are said to be a modern variety, as they were not recognized in Britain until 1930. However, as far back as the end of the nineteenth century, they were appearing in litters from Blue and Fawn (now Cream) matings. They were thought of little use and few breeders recognized their importance. A Mrs D'Arcy Hildyard must have done so, however, for when she wrote about breeding creams in 1901 she said that she began by mating her mixed Blue and Cream queen, Sanga, to a Cream male, D'Arcy, the result being four kittens, all female, two Creams and two 'marked Blues'. She mentions that she kept the Cream kittens and that they won at the shows, but says nothing further about the mixed Blue and Cream or the 'marked Blue' ones.

Miss H. Cochran, a well-known breeder of the same period, not realizing that Creams could come from Blue and Cream matings, said that she found it almost impossible to breed females. She had tried several crossings to do so, but invariably the Creams were males. She believed that in breeding Creams, the natural males were the Fawns (Creams) and the Oranges (Reds), and that their complementary queens were the Blue Tortoiseshells and the ordinary Tortoiseshells. The term 'Creams' and 'Fawns' appeared to be used indiscriminately, but there may have been a slight difference in the colourings.

Miss Beal's Creams (see page 205) again come into the picture. She wrote that 'Nearly all the best-known Creams are bred in the first place from orange and blue strains, but I believe the present strains sprang from crossing blue and orange.' She went on to say that if one wanted to start breeding Creams and could not

Blue-Cream Persian/Longhair kitten

afford a Cream female, it was a good ploy to buy a well-bred nondescript female, either Blue and Cream, Tabby or Tortoiseshell. There are constant references to Blue and Cream, but only in connection with the breeding for Creams, and they were never thought of as a variety on their own. Blues were mated to Creams to improve the type of the Creams or to produce paler Blues.

These early Blue-Creams were frequently patched, and more often than not were sold as pets. Gradually, it began to be appreciated that their type was generally very good, and that further cross-matings of the progeny to Blues or Creams could produce outstanding Blue, Cream and Blue-Cream kittens. After long discussions, the Governing Council of the Cat Fancy eventually agreed to give the Blue-Creams recognition.

It was still some years before it was definitely realized that there was a sex-linkage involved and that the Blue-Creams were invariably female, while the sex of the Blues and Creams depended on the colour of the male used.

Mrs E. Soame writing on Blue-Creams in 1939 remarked, 'caused by interbreeding Blues with Creams or Reds in the past, it is hoped to breed Blue-Cream to Blue-Cream in the future. That is, providing we produce some males.' Time has proved this impossible, as it soon became definitely established that Blue-Creams are a female-only variety, and any males that are produced prove to be sterile.

After recognition, many of the first Blue-Creams had a distinct reddish tinge in the coat, and, much to the annoyance of their owners, were referred to as Blue Tortoiseshells. This was the name that was first used in the United States for this variety, but by 1931 the name Blue-Cream came into general use.

The mating of Blues and Creams has proved to be one of the most successful crossbreedings known, resulting in cats with excellent round heads, neat ears and big round copper or orange eyes. Their bodies are cobby on short thick legs, and the tails short and flowing. In the fur the two pastel shades of blue and cream should be softly intermingled, giving a shot-silk effect, which is quite difficult to achieve. Often there are solid blue or cream patches, particularly on the paws and face, which are considered faults in Britain, but would not be penalized in the United States. The American standard calls for the colour of the cat to be blue with patches of solid cream, and the patches to be clearly defined and well-broken. Indeed, a winning cat in one country would be penalized in the other. It happened that when Blue-Creams were first recognized, those with distinct patching were sent from Britain to the United States and quite frequently became Champions, which they would not have been in their country of origin. A cream blaze – that is, a mark from the forehead to the nose – is not mentioned in the British standard but is liked by most breeders. There should be no reddish tinge in the coat, and when choosing a Cream male as a stud, it is important to find one with pale cream fur.

The kittens from a Blue-Cream vary according to the stud used, and this varied breeding appeals to a number of fanciers. It is difficult, referring to the British standard, to know if there are any Blue-Creams in the litter at birth, because if exceptionally well-intermingled, a kitten may appear as pale Blue, only to become an outstanding Blue-Cream as the fur grows. Blue-Creams may appear occasionally in litters from Tortoiseshells.

In Blue-Cream breeding the following variations are possible.

A Blue-Cream female mated to a Blue male may produce Cream males, Blue males, Blue females, and Blue-Cream females.

A Blue-Cream female mated to a Cream male may produce Cream females, Cream males, Blue males and Blue-Cream females.

A Cream male mated to a Blue female may have Blue-Cream females and Blue males, but a Cream female mated to a Blue male may produce Blue-Cream females and Cream males.

Blue-Cream Persian/Longhair adult

PROVISIONAL STANDARD
Governing Council of the Cat Fancy

PEWTER

Colour
White evenly shaded with black giving an overall effect of a Pewter mantle. White undercoat, legs shaded; chin, ear-tufts and stomach white. Nose leather brick-red outlined with black, visible skin on eyelids and on pads of feet to be black or dark brown.

Coat and condition
Coat long and dense, silky and fine in texture, with extra long frill.

Head
Broad and round with broad snub nose; good width between the well-tufted ears. Firm chin and level bite.

Body and legs
Cobby, not coarse but massive, well coupled with short firm legs.

Eyes
Orange or copper with black rim. Large and round with a pleasing expression. A green rim to the eye is considered to be a fault.

Tail
Short with full brush.

Faults
Heavy tabby markings, brown or cream tarnishing, kink in the tail.

SCALE OF POINTS

Colour	30
Coat and condition	10
Head	25
Body and legs	15
Eyes (shape and colour)	10
Tail	10
Total	100

At present the Pewters are appearing in the Assessment classes in Britain. These cats are similar in appearance to the Shaded Silver seen in the United States. They have a white undercoat and even black shading, giving the appearance of a pewter mantle. The eye colour should be golden/orange, orange or copper. These cats were once referred to as Blue Chinchillas because they were produced in the first instance by the mating of Chinchillas to Blue and, later, to Black Longhairs. However, as the eye colour is so different, it was thought best to give them a name not associated with Chinchillas or Shaded Silvers, which have sea-green eyes. The type is as for other Longhairs/Persians.

Pewter Persian/Longhair

PROVISIONAL STANDARD

Governing Council of the Cat Fancy

CAMEO

A Cameo is a cat of contrasts, the undercoat being as white as possible, with the tips shading to red, tortie or blue-cream. The deepest intensity of colour being most defined on mask, along the spine from head to tip of tail, and on legs and feet. The light points on frill, flanks, and under-surfaces, and ear tufts.

Coat and condition
Coat long and dense, silky and fine in texture, extra long frill.

Head
Broad and round with snub nose, good width between small, well-tufted ears. Firm chin and level bite.

Eyes
Deep orange or copper, large and round with a pleasing expression. A green rim to the eye considered a fault.

Body and legs
Cobby, not coarse but massive, well coupled with short firm legs.

Colours
(i) Shell: Characteristic sparkling silver appearance, lightly dusted with rose-pink. Nose leather and pads pink.

(ii) Shaded: White evenly shaded with red giving the over-all effect of a red mantle. Nose leather and pads pink. Tabby markings undesirable.

(iii) Red Smoke: Body red shading to white on the sides and flanks. Mask and feet, red with no markings. Frill and ear tufts, white. Undercoat, as nearly white as possible. Tabby markings not allowed.

N.B. Cream Cameo: The above standards also apply to the cream dilution, and where the word red is used, cream should be substituted.

(iv) Tortie Cream: Tipping to comprise black, red and cream, well broken into patches, colours to be rich and bright and well broken on face. Tipping of any intensity acceptable. Solid colour on legs or feet undesirable. Nose leather black, pink or a combination of the two.

(v) Blue Cream Cameo: Tipping to consist of blue and cream softly intermingled. Tipping of any intensity acceptable. Nose leather blue, pink or combination of the two.

SCALE OF POINTS

Colour	30
Coat and condition	10
Head	25
Body and legs	15
Eyes (shape and colour)	10
Tail	10
Total	100

Cameo Persian/Longhair

Cameos are now being bred in many countries, and are seen in the Assessment classes in Britain. They were first bred in the United States in 1954, having been developed by Dr Rachel Salisbury from Smoke and Tortoiseshell matings. Various other matings were tried, including the Silvers and Reds in the early stages. Chinchilla crosses presented problems in that the sea-green eye colouring was introduced, which proved exceedingly difficult to breed out. A great deal of time and money was spent in developing Cameos, and now many of those seen at the American shows are really outstanding.

There are five main colour variations possible, the Shell Cameo or Red Chinchilla, the latter name giving a clear indication as to the appearance; the Shaded Cameo or Red Shaded, which is equivalent to the Shaded Silver; the Smoke Cameo or Red Smoke, which has similar contrasts to the Black counterpart, and the Cameo Tabby, with red markings. In addition there are Shell and Shaded Tortoiseshells, female-only varieties. It is also possible to have Cameos with cream tippings, but the American standards state red, as do the British provisional standards.

The type required is the same for most other Longhairs and, possibly because the Cameos arise from crossbreeding, it is usually very good, with the heads being broad, the ears small and the big round eyes deep copper in colour.

The Cameo kittens are born almost white, and it as they grow that the colouring becomes apparent; the

Cameo Persian/Longhair

Shell is lighter than the Shaded, and the Smokes are even darker.

Attractive, decorative and affectionate, the Cameos have become very popular in the United States. Their numbers are steadily increasing in the Assessment classes in Britain, and it is only a matter of time before they are granted recognized standards, and ultimately championship status.

PROVISIONAL STANDARD
Governing Council of the Cat Fancy

CHOCOLATE

Coat
Medium to dark chocolate brown, sound and even in colour; free from markings, shading, or any white hairs.

Chocolate Persian/Longhair

Head
Broad and round with width between the ears. Face and nose short. Ears small and tufted. Cheeks well developed.

Eyes
Deep orange or copper; large, round and full, without a trace of green.

Body
Cobby and low on the legs.

Tail
Short and full, not tapering (a kink shall be a fault).

SCALE OF POINTS

Coat	20
Condition	10
Head	25
Eyes	20
Body	15
Tail	10
Total	100

CHOCOLATE TORTOISESHELL

Coat
Three colours, chocolate, red and cream, well broken into patches; colours bright and rich and well broken on the face. Fur long, thick and soft in texture. Frill full.

Head
Broad and round with width between the ears. Face and nose short. Ears small and tufted. Cheeks well developed. An undershot jaw shall be a fault.

Eyes
Deep orange or copper; large round and full, without a trace of green.

Body
Cobby and low on the legs.

Tail
Short and full, not tapering (a kink shall be a fault).

SCALE OF POINTS

Coat	20
Condition	10
Head	25
Eyes	20
Body	15
Tail	10
Total	100

LILAC

Coat
Pinkish dove grey, sound and even in colour; free from markings, shadings, or any white hairs. Fur long, thick and soft in texture. Frill full.

Head
Broad and round with width between the ears. Face and nose short. Ears small and tufted. Cheeks well developed.

Lilac Persian/Longhair

Eyes
Pale orange; large, round and full, without a trace of green.

Body
Cobby and low on the legs.

Tail
Short and full, not tapering (a kink shall be a fault).

SCALE OF POINTS

Coat	20
Condition	10
Head	25
Eyes	20
Body	15
Tail	10
Total	100

GCCF PROVISIONAL STANDARD continued –

LILAC-CREAM

Coat

Shades of lilac and cream, softly intermingled, sound and free from white hairs or other markings. Fur long and thick and soft in texture. Frill full.

Head

Broad and round with width between the ears. Face and nose short. Ears small and tufted. Cheeks well developed. An undershot jaw shall be a fault.

Eyes

Pale orange or copper; large, round and full without a trace of green.

Body

Cobby and low on the legs.

Tail

Short and full, not tapering (a kink shall be a fault).

SCALE OF POINTS

Coat	20
Condition	10
Head	25
Eyes	20
Body	15
Tail	10
Total	100

Still appearing in the Assessment classes in Britain, but in the Himalayan classes in the United States, are the Chocolate and Lilac Longhairs, or Persians. These cats have been bred in Britain for many years. One, exhibited at the National Cat Club show in Britain in 1961, was produced by selective breeding starting with the mating of a Blue Longhair and a Havana to a programme worked out genetically by the late Mr Brian Stirling-Webb, who was responsible for the first Colourpoint/Himalayan.

It has taken many years to improve the type and to achieve the correct eye colouring, which should be deep orange or copper. The Lilac is a dilute form of the Brown. The necessary introduction of shorthairs into the breeding to get the correct colours invariably meant loss of type, hence the slow progress.

Those now seen in the Assessment classes are much improved in colour and type, and a number have been sent abroad to breeders, who are carefully carrying out a breeding programme on similar lines to that in Britain.

The mixing of the colours and breeding have also produced cats with chocolate tortoiseshell colouring and lilac-cream colouring, both of which are female-only varieties.

The characteristics for all four colours are as for other Longhairs, with the colour descriptions as given in the preliminary standards of points.

HIMALAYAN/COLOURPOINT LONGHAIR

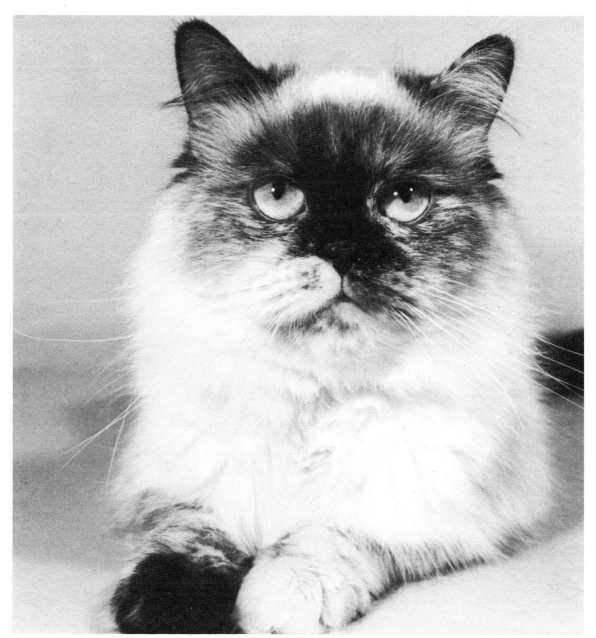

Tortie-Point Himalayan/Colourpoint Longhair

Over the years many breeders have thought of the possibilities of producing coats with long flowing coats combined with the coat pattern of the Siamese.

As long ago as 1922 a Swedish doctor, Dr K. Tjebbes, made a start by crossing White Longhairs with Siamese, but he appears to have been unsuccessful, as there are no records of the resulting colours. In 1924 cats with such colouring were seen in the United States and were called Malayan Persians, but these too vanished. In the 1930s in the United States, Mrs Virginia Cobb and Dr Clyde Keeler crossed Siamese and Longhairs/Persians, but again they faded out. Mrs Cobb tried

Blue-Cream Point Himalayan/Colourpoint Longhair

Seal Point Himalayan/Colourpoint Longhair

further matings, but the Second World War put an end to her breeding programme. In 1935, Mrs Barton-Wright founded the Experimental Breeders Club in Britain in an endeavour to produce cats following the same programme of breeding begun by Mrs Cobb. A kitten from such breeding, the result of a mating between a Blue Longhair and a Siamese, went to Miss Collins. This cat was known as Kala Dawn, and one of her kittens, Kala Sabu, went to Mr Brian Stirling Webb, who was already working on a breeding programme for longcoated colourpoints. Previously, a woman who had found a stray cat with Siamese coat pattern, a long coat, and quite good type had brought the cat to Mr Sterling Webb's stud. Her owner had hoped that the resultant kittens would be like the mother. She was told that as the shorthair was dominant, it was unlikely. This made Mr Stirling Webb think quite seriously about breeding a perfect cat with full coat, Persian type and Siamese colouring. Having a thorough knowledge of genetics, he realized that this would take a long time and much money. He experimented with various cross-matings and, by using out-

standing Black and Blue Persians as outcrosses, managed to improve the type. Many kittens were discarded, neutered and given away as pets. From these matings Mr Stirling Webb chose the best kittens that were not too nearly realated and, by careful selective breeding managed to produce Seal Colourpoint kittens for the necessary three generations of pure breeding. In 1955 the Colourpoint Longhair was given a breed number and an approved standard by the Governing Council of the Cat Fancy in Britain.

At the same time in the United States Mrs Goforth was working on similar lines, producing similar cats. They were given the name Himalayans, as their coat patterns were similar to that of the rabbits with the same name, and the Cat Faciers' Association refused to recognize them as Persians since they resulted from crossing two established breeds. Recognition was given by the CFA in 1957, and Mrs Goforth's La Chiquita became the first champion. By the 1960s all the cat fancy associations in the United States had accepted them, and now they are one of the most popular varieties.

The Seal and Blue Colourpoints steadily improved in type over the years, and Mrs Harding, famed for her cats bred under the prefix 'Mingchiu', who had been associated with Mr Stirling Webb in producing the Colourpoints, took over a number of his cats on his death, and continued breeding on the same lines. She realized too that by using Chocolate-point Siamese and Havanas it would be possible to produce Colourpoints with chocolate and lilac points. The re-introduction of shorthaired cats meant loss of type and body shape, which took many years to breed out. Some really beautiful specimens of Tortoiseshell and Red-points with outstanding type have also been produced and it is also possible to breed Colourpoints with Cream, Blue-Cream, Chocolate-Cream, and Lilac-Cream points, as the necessary genes are already in several varieties.

The general standard is the same for each variety, and the type has improved greatly over the years. The body shape is cobby on low sturdy legs, the coat is long and thick, and the tail is short and full. In many individuals the blue eye colouring is very good, but sometimes it does tend to be too pale. The difficulty is that any outcross used to improve the type invariably means the loss of the correct eye colour.

The kittens are cream-coloured at birth, with pink noses, foot pads and ears. The masks and points darken with growth, and it may be eighteen months or more before the points reach their true colour. The coats of kittens with the darker points may darken slightly with age, but the coats of the Colourpoints with lighter points, such as the Lilacs, usually remain pale all their lives.

In the United States there are separate open classes for the various points colouring. This may soon be the practice in Britain too, as the number of Colourpoint Longhairs is increasing rapidly.

OFFICIAL STANDARD
Cat Fanciers' Association, Inc.

HIMALAYAN

POINT SCORE

Head (including size and shape of eyes, ear shape and set)	30
Type (including shape, size, bone, and length of tail)	20
Coat	10
Body color	10
Point color	10
Eye color	10
Balance	5
Refinement	5

Head
Round and massive, with great breadth of skull. Round face with underlying bone structure. Well set on a short, thick neck.

Head: broad, cheeks full

Nose
Short, snub and broad. With "break".

Cheeks
Full.

Jaws
Broad and powerful.

Chin
Full and well-developed.

Ears
Small, round tipped, tilted forward, and not unduly open at the base. Set far apart, and low on the head fitting into (without distorting) the rounded contour of the head.

Eyes
Large, round and full. Set far apart and brilliant, giving a sweet expression to the face.

Body
Of cobby type—low on the legs, deep in the chest, equally massive across shoulders and rump, with a short well-rounded middle piece. Large or medium in size. Quality the determining consideration rather than size.

Body: cobby, deep in the chest

Back
Level.

Legs
Short, thick and strong. Forelegs straight.

Paws
Large, round and firm. Toes carried close, five in front and four behind.

Tail
Short, but in proportion to body length. Carried without a curve and at an angle lower than the back.

Coat
Long and thick, standing off from the body. Of fine texture, glossy and full of life. Long all over the body, including the shoulders. The ruff immense and continuing in a deep frill between the front legs. Ear and toe tufts long. Brush very full.

Color
Body: Even, free of barring, with subtle shading when allowed. Allowance to be made for darker coloring on older cats. Shading should be subtle with definite contrast between points. *Points:* Mask, ears, legs, feet, tail, dense and clearly defined. All of the same shade, and free of barring. Mask covers entire face including whisker pads and is connected to ears by tracings. Mask should

CFA OFFICIAL STANDARD continued

not extend over top of head. No ticking or white hairs in points.

Penalize
Lack of pigment in nose leather and/or paw pads in part or in total. Any resemblance to Peke-Face.

Disqualify
Locket or button. Any tail abnormality. Crossed eyes. Incorrect number of toes. White toes. Eyes other than blue except for solid chocolate and solid lilac. Apparent weakness in hind quarters. Deformity of skull and/or mouth.

HIMALAYAN COLORS

SEAL POINT
Body even pale fawn to cream, warm in tone, shading gradually into lighter color on the stomach and chest.

Points
Deep seal brown.

Nose leather and paw pads
Same color as points.

Eye color
Deep vivid blue.

CHOCOLATE POINT
Body ivory with no shading.

Points
Milk-chocolate color, warm in tone.

Nose leather and paw pads
Cinnamon-pink.

Eye color
Deep vivid blue.

BLUE POINT
Body bluish white, cold in tone, shading gradually to white on stomach and chest.

Points
Blue.

Nose leather and paw pads
Slate colored.

Eye color
Deep vivid blue.

LILAC POINT
Body glacial white with no shading.

Points
Frosty gray with pinkish tone.

Nose leather and paw pads
Lavender-pink.

Eye color
Deep vivid blue.

FLAME POINT
Body creamy white.

Points
Delicate orange flame.

Nose leather
Flesh or coral pink.

Paw pads
Flesh or coral pink.

Eye color
Deep vivid blue.

TORTIE POINT
Body creamy white or pale fawn.

Points
Seal with unbrindled patches of red and cream. Blaze of red or cream on face is desirable.

Nose leather and paw pads
Seal brown with flesh and/or coral pink mottling to conform with colors of points.

Eye color
Deep vivid blue.

BLUE-CREAM POINT
Body bluish white or creamy white, shading gradually to white on the stomach and chest.

Blue-Point Himalayan

Points
Blue with patches of cream.

Nose leather
Slate blue, pink, or a combination of slate blue and pink.

Paw pads
Slate blue, pink, or a combination of slate blue and pink.

Eye color
Deep vivid blue.

CHOCOLATE SOLID COLOR
Rich, warm chocolate brown, sound from roots to tip of fur.

Nose leather
Brown.

Paw pads
Brown.

Eye color
Brilliant copper.

LILAC SOLID COLOR
Rich, warm lavender with a pinkish tone, sound and even throughout.

Nose leather
Pink.

Paw pads
Pink.

Eye color
Brilliant copper.

Flame-Point Himalayan

OFFICIAL STANDARD
Governing Council of the Cat Fancy

COLOURPOINT: VARIETY 13b

Coat
Fur long, thick and soft in texture, frill full.

Colour
(i) Seal points with cream body colour
(ii) Blue points with glacial white body colour
(iii) Chocolate points with ivory body colour
(iv) Lilac points with magnolia body colour
(v) Red points with off white body colour
(vi) Tortie points with cream body colour
(vii) Cream
(viii) Blue Cream
(ix) Chocolate Cream
(x) Lilac Cream

Colours i–v inclusive: Points to be of a solid colour and body colour shading, if any, to tone with the points.
Colour vi: Points colour of Tortie Points to be restricted to the basic Seal colour, body shading, if any, to tone with points.

Head
Broad and round with width between the ears. Short face and short nose with distinct break or stop. Ears small and tufted and cheeks well developed.

Eyes
Large, round and full. Clear, bright and decidedly blue.

Body
Cobby and low on leg.

Tail
Short and full, not tapering. A kink shall be considered a defect.

Note
Any similarity in TYPE to Siamese, in particular a long straight nose to be considered most undesirable and incorrect.

SCALE OF POINTS

Coat	15
Points and body colour	10
Head	30
Shape of eye	10
Colour of eye	10
Body	15
Tail	10
Total	100

Seal-Point Himalayan

BIRMAN (SACRED CAT OF BURMA)

Seal-Point Birman

There are many strange stories concerning the early foreign varieties; some were said to have been found in the palaces of kings and others in temples. There is such a legend regarding the Birmans. It is said of them that centuries ago in Burma white cats were guardians of the Temple of Lao-Tsun, which housed a golden goddess with deep blue eyes, Tsun-Kyan-Kse. One beautiful cat, Sinh, was the close companion of the head priest, Mun-Ha. As the priest and his cat sat in front of the goddess, the temple was attacked by raiders and Mun-Ha was killed while praying. Sinh placed his paws on his dying master and faced the golden goddess. As he did this, his white fur took on the golden hue. His yellow eyes became a deep blue, and his face, tail and legs turned to the colour of the earth, but the part of his paws that touched the dead priest, remained white, the symbol of purity. The other priests watched in amazement. Then inspired by this sacred transformation, they attacked the raiders, who fled from the temple. For the next seven days Sinh refused all food,

and finally died, taking his master's soul into paradise. When the priests met to choose Mun-Ha's successor, the temple's hundred cats came into the holy chamber, but they were no longer white: their coats had turned the same golden colour as Sinh's, and their eyes had become just as blue. They encircled a young priest, Lioa, who became the new head priest.

Thus ran the legend until the beginning of this century. Then apparently the temple was raided again, but this time it was saved by the help given by Major Gordon Russell and Monsieur Auguste Pavie. A year or two later, the two men, who were now living in France, were sent two of the sacred cats from the temple as a gift. The male died en route, but the female survived and proved to be in kitten. The litter lived and became the first Birmans seen in Europe, or so the story goes. Presumably the kittens were used for breeding, and it was in 1925 that this variety was recognized in France. It was in danger of becoming extinct during the Second World War, but it survived

Blue-Point Birman

due to the efforts of one or two breeders, and by the 1960s the breed was again well-established. British visitors to French cat shows were fascinated by the Birmans, with their so-different little white gloves, and two British breeders imported some from France.

In 1960 a pair of Tibetan temple kittens was sent to Mrs G. Griswold in the United States. Their colouring and coat pattern were the same as those of the Birmans, and their history was similar too, and it was realized that long, long ago they must have had the same origin. Letters and kittens were eventually exchanged by the French and American breeders and before long Birmans were seen in the experimental classes in the United States.

They were recognized in Britain in 1966 and in the United States in 1967. They are now well-established in both countries, as well as in France, and have proved exceedingly popular. The three standards are very similar, but that of the Cat Fanciers' Association goes into greater detail, saying, for example, that the nose should be Roman in shape, and is more explicit about the gloves and gauntlets. In Britain the point colourings are Seal and Blue, but others are being produced. In the United States, four points colours are recog-nized: Seal, Blue, Chocolate and Lilac.

The coat of this enchanting cat is long, but not so full as that of the Persian, and very silky in texture. It is easy to keep in order and if groomed daily, it does not matt. The head shape is not as round and broad as that of the Longhairs, but should in no way resemble that of the Siamese. The body is long, with the tail bushy and in proportion to the body length. Affectionate and intelligent, the kittens are in great demand.

Faults are incorrectly-shaped gloves and gauntlets, but it is difficult to produce a cat with the two front paws exactly matching and with both gauntlets on the back legs coming to exactly the same height.

Despite the legend and tales regarding the origin of the Birmans, some people consider that the variety really started as a mutation, or resulted, as did the Colourpoint/Himalayan from crossbreeding Siamese and Longhair cats, following carefully selected matings. It is, however, interesting to note that the origins of a number of varieties are said to have begun with gifts of cats that either lived in temples or were the pets of kings and princes long ago. There may be a grain of truth in that any unusual cat would be much prized, protected, and given as gifts to monarchs in the Orient.

OFFICIAL STANDARD
Cat Fanciers' Association, Inc.

BIRMAN (Sacred Cat of Burma)

POINT SCORE

Head (including size and shape of eyes, ear shape and set)	30
Type (including shape, size, bone and length of tail)	25
Coat	10
Color	25
Eye color	10

Head
Skull strong, broad, and rounded. Forehead slopes back and is slightly convex. There is a slight flat spot just in front of the ears.

Nose
Roman in shape, nostrils set low. Length in proportion to size of head.

Cheeks
Full. The fur is short in appearance about the face, but to the extreme outer area of the cheek, the fur is longer.

Jaws
Heavy.

Chin
Full and well-developed. Lower lip is strong, forming perpendicular lines with upper lip.

Ears
Medium in length. Almost as wide at the base as tall. Modified to a rounded point at the tip; set as much to the side as into the top of the head.

Eyes
Almost round.

Body
Long but stocky.

Legs
Medium in length and heavy.

Paws
Large, round and firm. Five toes in front, four behind.

Tail
Medium in length, in pleasing proportion to the body.

Coat
Long, silken in texture, with heavy ruff around the neck, slightly curly on stomach. This fur is of such a texture that it does not mat.

Color
Body: Even, with subtle shading when allowed. Strong contrast between body color and points. *Points except paws:* Mask, ears, legs and tail dense and clearly defined, all of the same shade. Mask covers entire face including whisker pads and is connected to ears by tracings. No ticking or white hair in points. *Front paws:* Front paws have white gloves ending in an even line across the paw at the third joint. *Back paws:* White glove covers the entire paw and must end in a point, called the laces, that goes up the back of the hock.

Paw pads
Pink preferred, but dark spot on toe/pad acceptable because of the two colors in pattern.

Eyes
Blue in color. The deeper blue the better. Almost round in shape.

Penalize
White that does not run across the front paws in an even line. Siamese type head. White shading on stomach and chest.

Disqualify
Lack of white gloves or any paw. Kinked or abnormal tail. Crossed eyes. Incoorect number of toes. Areas of pure white in the points, except paws.

BIRMAN COLORS

SEAL POINT
Body even pale fawn to cream, warm in tone, shading gradually to lighter color on the stomach and chest.

Points
Except for gloves, deep seal brown. Gloves pure white.

Nose leather
Same color as the points.

Paw pads
Pink.

Eye color
Blue, the deeper and more violet the better.

BLUE POINT
Body bluish white, cold in tone, shading gradually to almost white on stomach and chest.

Points
Except for gloves on paws, deep blue. Gloves pure white.

Nose leather
Slate color.

Paw pads
Pink.

CFA OFFICIAL STANDARD continued –

Eye color
Blue, the deeper and more violet the better.

CHOCOLATE POINT
Body ivory with no shading.

Points
Except for gloves on paws, milk-chocolate color, warm in tone. Gloves pure white.

Nose leather
Cinnamon-pink.

Paw pads
Pink.

Eye color
Blue, the deeper and more violet the better.

LILAC POINT
Body a cold, glacial tone verging on white with no shading.

Points
Except for gloves, frosty gray with pinkish tone. Gloves pure white.

Nose leather
Lavender-pink.

Paw pads
Pink.

Eye color
Blue, the deeper and more violet the better.

OFFICIAL STANDARD
Governing Council of the Cat Fancy

BIRMAN: VARIETY 13c

Body
Long but low on the legs. Short strong paws. Four white paws, the white on the rear paws to go up the back of the legs to a point like a gauntlet.

Head
Wide, round but strongly built, with full cheeks.

Fur
Long with good full ruff, bushy tail, silky texture, slightly curled on belly.

Eyes
Bright china blue.

Tail
Bushy (not short).

Colour and condition
The colouring is the same as Siamese, Seal and Blue but face (mask) tail and paws are dark brown, in the seals and blue/grey in the blues. However, the beige of the coat is slightly golden. The paws are white gloved, this being the characteristic of the Birman cat.

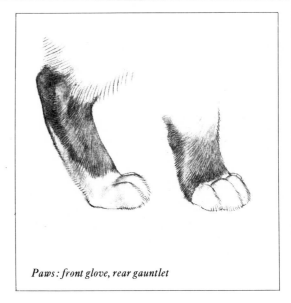

Paws: front glove, rear gauntlet

SCALE OF POINTS

Body	20
Head	20
Fur	25
Eyes	5
Tail	10
Colour and condition	20
Total	100

BALINESE

Lilac-Point Balinese

In the 1950s in the United States there appeared in several litters of pure-bred Siamese, kittens that were different. They had the typical Siamese type, but the fur was fluffy, rather than short, and silky. They were considered of little value, and in most cases were neutered and sold as pets, or destroyed as freaks. Further litters produced other fluffy kittens, which, when old enough, were mated together and bred true, that is, the kittens looked exactly like the parents: they had the Siamese coat pattern but fur of medium length, and very silky texture.

These cats were confused at first with the Himalayans, or Colourpoints, but comparison between the two varieties showed that the Balinese were most definitely Siamese in type and personality, whereas the Colourpoint/Himalayan had typical Longhair/

Persian characteristics – wealth of coat and broad heads, with neat ears and big round eyes. The Balinese are dainty cats, with wedge-shaped heads, large pointed ears, almond shaped eyes, long, lithe bodies, with long, thin tails, but well covered with fur. They are bred with Seal, Chocolate, Blue and Lilac points. It is also possible to have Frost Tortie, Blue Tortie, Chocolate Tortie, and Seal Tortie.

They are now being produced in Britain, with a standard very similar to that of the Cat Fanciers' Association of America. The Balinese are not a recognized variety in Britain, but are being shown in the Assessment classes. If, in due course, enough merit awards are given, and there are a number of breeders interested, they will be given championship status in Britain too.

OFFICIAL STANDARD

Cat Fanciers' Association, Inc.

BALINESE

POINT SCORE

Head (20)	
Long flat profile	6
Wedge, fine muzzle, size	5
Ears	4
Chin	3
Width between eyes	2
Eyes (5)	
Shape, size, slant, and placement	5
Body (30)	
Structure and size, including neck	12
Muscle tone	10
Legs and feet	5
Tail	3
Coat (20)	
Length	10
Texture	10
Color (25)	
Body color	10
Point color—matching points of dense color, proper foot pads and nose leather	10
Eye color	5

General

The ideal Balinese is a svelte, dainty cat with long, tapering lines, very lithe but muscular. Excellent physical condition. Eye clear. Strong and lithe. Neither flabby nor boney. Not fat.

Head

Long tapering wedge. Medium size in good proportion to body. The total wedge starts at the nose and flares out in straight lines to the tips of the ears forming a triangle, with no break at the whiskers. No less than the width of an eye between the eyes. When the whiskers and face-hair are smoothed back, the underlying bone structure is apparent. Allowance must be made for jowls in the stud cat.

Skull

Flat. In profile, a long straight line is seen from the top of the head to the tip of the nose. No bulge over the eyes. No dip in nose.

Nose

Long and straight. A continuation of the forehead with no break.

Muzzle

Fine, wedge-shaped.

Chin and jaw

Medium size. Tip of chin lines up with tip of nose in the same vertical plane. Neither receding nor excessively massive.

Ears

Strikingly large, pointed, wide at base, continuing the lines of the wedge.

Eyes

Almond shaped. Medium size. Neither protruding nor recessed. Slanted towards the nose in harmony with lines of wedge and ears. Uncrossed.

Body

Medium size. Dainty, long, and svelte. A distinctive combination of fine bones and firm muscles. Shoulders and hips continue same sleek lines of tubular body. Hips never wider than shoulders. Abdomen tight.

Neck

Long and slender.

Legs

Long and slim. Hind legs higher than front. In good proportion to body.

Paws

Dainty, small, and oval. Toes, five in front and four behind.

Tail

Bone structure long, thin, tapering to a fine point. Tail-hair spreads out like a plume.

Coat

Long, fine, and silky without downy undercoat.

Head: long, tapering wedge

Colour

Body: Even, with subtle shading when allowed. Allowance should be made for darker color in older cats as Balinese generally darken with age, but there must be definite contrast between body color and points. *Points:* Mask, ears, legs, feet, tail dense and clearly defined. All of the same shade. Mask covers entire face including whisker pads and is connected to ears by tracings. Mask should not extend over top of head. No ticking or white hairs in points.

Penalize

Lack of pigment in nose leather in part or in total; crossed eyes.

Disqualify

Any evidence of illness or poor health. Weak hind legs. Mouth breathing due to nasal obstruction or poor occlusion. Emaciation. Kink in tail. Eyes other than blue. White toes and/or feet. Incorrect number of toes. Definite double coat (i.e. downy undercoat).

Seal-Point Balinese

BALINESE COLORS

SEAL POINT

Body even pale fawn to cream, warm in tone, shading gradually into lighter color on the stomach and chest.

Points
Deep seal brown.

Nose leather
Same color as points.

Paw pads
Same color as points.

Eye color
Deep vivid blue.

CHOCOLATE POINT

Body ivory with no shading.

Points
Milk-chocolate color, warm in tone.

Nose leather
Cinnamon-pink.

Paw pads
Cinnamon-pink.

Eye color
Deep vivid blue.

BLUE POINT

Body bluish white, cold in tone, shading gradually to white on stomach and chest.

Points
Deep blue.

Nose leather
Slate colored.

Paw pads
Slate coloured.

Eye color
Deep vivid blue.

LILAC POINT

Body glacial white with no shading.

Points
Frosty gray with pinkish tone.

Nose leather
Lavender-pink.

Paw pads
Lavender-pink.

Eye color
Deep vivid blue.

TURKISH ANGORA

Odd-eyed White Turkish Angora

The first longhaired cats seen in Europe in the sixteenth century came from Angora, now Ankara, in Turkey. The heads were narrow, the ears tall, the bodies and tails were longish, the fur of medium length, without the wealth of coat seen in the Longhairs today, and they were said to be always white. Intermating with the later arrivals from Persia and Russia meant the disappearance of the Angora type. Travelling in Turkey in 1955, two cat lovers saw cats very similar to the old Angora type near Lake Van.

Although the fur was chalk-white, there were auburn markings on the face, and the tails too were auburn, ringed with darker auburn. Although most cats can swim if they have to, these cats differed in that they would quite voluntarily swim in shallow rivers and warm pools. Much intrigued, the two cat lovers made enquiries, and learned that these cats were mostly privately owned and greatly prized. They were given a pair and introduced them into Britain, where they attracted much attention.

This pair produced kittens exactly the same as themselves, and others brought over from Turkey also proved to breed true. Unfortunately, no records had been kept in Turkey, so it took quite a few years to produce the necessary three generations of pure breeding required before they could even be considered as a recognized variety. They were officially recognized in Britain in 1969, and a number of breeders became interested.

The kittens have a pinkish look when born, which disappears as the fur grows, but the auburn markings are apparent right from birth. Although the cats carry a full winter coat – but never as full as the majority of Longhairs – they lose most of it in the summer, appearing almost short coated. This may be due to the very extreme temperatures in their country of origin; there is snow in the Lake Van area in the winter and it is quite hot in the summer.

The number of Turkish Angoras in Britain is small. These cats are not prolific breeders, and many have been exported to other parts of the world, particularly to the United States.

Comparatively recently, Angoras have been introduced into the United States directly from Turkey. The original was pure white, but now a number of colours has also been bred and recognized. They are known as the Turkish Angoras, and the type is similar to that of the British Turkish cats.

Strong, hardy animals, their silky coats have no woolly undercoat, make grooming a relatively easy task. Some breeders give their stock a bath prior to a show, as the Turkish cats have no objection to water. This is usually done a few days before they are exhibited, otherwise the fur is inclined to have a fly-away look.

The first Turkish cats introduced into Britain were inclined to be nervous, but if the young kittens are handled right from birth and treated as pets, they are very lovable and most affectionate.

Calico Turkish Angora

White Turkish Angora

Blue-eyed White Turkish Angora kitten

OFFICIAL STANDARD
Cat Fanciers' Association, Inc.

TURKISH ANGORA

POINT SCORE

Head	35
Body	30
Color	20
Coat	15

General
Solid, firm, giving the impression of grace and flowing movement.

Head
Size, small to medium. Wedge-shaped. Wide at top. Definite taper toward chin. Allowance to be made for jowls in stud cat.

Ears
Wide at base, long, pointed, and tufted. Set high on the head.

Eyes
Large, almond shaped to round. Slanting upwards slightly.

Nose
Medium long, gentle slope. No break.

Neck
Slim and graceful, medium length.

Chin
Gently rounded. Tip to form a perpendicular line with the nose.

Jaw
Tapered.

Body
Small to medium size in female, slightly larger in male. Torso long, graceful and lithe. Chest, light framed. Rump slightly higher than front. Bone, fine.

Legs
Long. Hind legs longer than front.

Paws
Small and round, dainty. Tufts between toes.

Tail
Long and tapering, wide at base, narrow at end, full. Carried lower than body but not trailing. When moving relaxed tail is carried horizontally over the body, sometimes almost touching the head.

Above: Turkish Angora ; below : Turkish

Above : long, graceful torso ; below : long, full tail

Coat
Body coat medium-long, long at ruff. Full brush on tail. Silky with a wavy tendency. Wavier on stomach. Very fine and having a silk-like sheen.

Balance
Proportionate in all physical aspects with graceful lithe appearance.

Penalize
Kinked or abnormal tail.

Disqualify
Persian body type.

TURKISH ANGORA COLORS

WHITE
Pure white, no other coloring.

Paw pads
Pink.

Nose leather
Pink.

Lips
Pink.

Eye color
Odd-eyed, blue-eyed, amber-eyed.

BLACK
Dense coal black, sound from roots to tip of fur. Free from any tinge of rust on tips or smoke undercoat.

Nose leather
Black.

Paw pads
Black or brown.

Eye color
Amber.

BLUE
Blue, lighter shade preferred, one level tone from nose to tip of tail. Sound to the roots. A sound darker shade is more acceptable than an unsound lighter shade.

Nose leather
Blue.

Paw pads
Blue.

Eye color
Amber.

BLACK SMOKE
White undercoat, deeply tipped with black. Cat in repose appears black. In motion the white undercoat is clearly apparent.

Points and mask
Black with narrow band of white at base of hairs next to skin which may be seen only when the fur is parted.

Nose leather
Black.

Paw pads
Black.

BLUE SMOKE
White undercoat, deeply tipped with blue. Cat in repose appears blue. In motion the white undercoat is clearly apparent.

Points and mask
Blue, with narrow band of white at base of hairs next to skin which may be seen only when fur is parted.

Nose leather
Blue.

Paw pads
Blue.

Eye color
Amber.

CLASSIC TABBY PATTERN
Markings dense, clearly defined and broad. Legs evenly barred with bracelets coming up to meet the body markings. Tail evenly ringed. Several unbroken necklaces on neck and upper chest, the more the better. Frown marks on forehead form intricate letter "M". Unbroken line runs back from outer corner of eye. Swirls on cheeks. Vertical lines over back of head extend to shoulder markings which are in the shape of a butterfly with both upper and lower wings distinctly outlined and marked with dots inside outline. Back markings consist of a vertical line down the spine from butterfly to tail with a vertical strip paralleling it on each side, the three stripes well separated by stripes of the ground color. Large solid blotch on each side to be encircled by one or more unbroken rings. Side markings should be the same on both sides. Double vertical row of buttons on chest and stomach.

MACKEREL TABBY PATTERN
Markings dense, clearly defined, and all narrow pencillings. Legs evenly barred with narrow bracelets coming up to meet the body markings. Tail barred. Necklaces on neck and chest distinct, like so many chains. Head barred with an "M" on the forehead. Unbroken lines running back from the eyes. Lines running down the head to meet the shoulders. Spine lines run together to form a narrow saddle. Narrow pencillings run around body.

SILVER TABBY
Ground color, including lips and chin, pale clear silver. Markings dense black.

CFA OFFICAL STANDARD continued –

Nose leather
Brick red.

Paw pads
Black.

Eye color
Green or hazel.

RED TABBY
Ground color red. Markings deep rich red. Lips and chin red.

Paw pads
Pink.

Nose leather
Brick red.

Paw pads
Black or brown.

Eye color
Amber.

BROWN TABBY
Ground color brilliant coppery brown. Markings dense black. Lips and chin the same shade as the rings around the eyes. Back of leg black from paw to heel.

Nose leather
Brick red.

Paw pads
Black or brown.

Eye color
Amber.

BLUE TABBY
Ground color, including lips and chin, pale bluish ivory. Markings a very deep blue affording a good contrast with ground color. Warm fawn overtones or patina over the whole.

Nose leather
Old rose.

Paw pads
Rose.

Eye color
Amber.

CALICO
White with unbrindled patches of black and red. White predominant on underparts.

Eye color
Amber.

BI-COLOR
Black and white, blue and white, red and white, or cream and white. White feet, legs, undersides, chest and muzzle. Inverted "V" blaze on face desirable. White under tail and white collar allowable.

Eye color
Amber.

OFFICIAL STANDARD
Governing Council of the Cat Fancy

TURKISH: VARIETY 13d

Colour and coat
Chalk white with no trace of yellow. Auburn markings on face with white blaze. Ears white; nose tip, pads and inside ears a delicate shell pink. Fur long, soft and silky to the roots; no woolly undercoat.

Head
Short wedge; well feathered large ears upright and set fairly close together; long nose.

Eyes
Round, colour light amber, rims pink-skinned.

Body
Long but sturdy, legs medium in length; neat round feet with well tufted toes. Males should be particularly muscular on neck and shoulders.

Tail
Full, medium length, auburn in colour with faint auburn rings in cats, more distinct ring markings in kittens.

Note
This is the ideal; some cats may have small auburn markings irregularly placed, but this should not disqualify an otherwise good specimen.

SCALE OF POINTS

Colour and coat	35
Head	25
Eyes	10
Body	10
Brush	10
Condition	10
Total	100

MAINE COON

Blue-Cream Maine Coon

The history of the Maine Coon cats goes back to the 1850s, when long-coated cats were brought to the state of Maine from foreign ports by seafaring men and travellers. These cats mated with the resident domestic shorthairs, producing strong, healthy, massive animals, high on the legs. The longish fur of many resembled that of racoons, and local people thought that they must be the result of matings between racoons and cats, which is biologically impossible.

The random breeding produced cats with multi-coloured cats, some self and others tabby, often with white. These cats developed thick coats well able to withstand the rigours of the extreme winters in Maine.

There are very few records, but Mr F. Pierce wrote about a Maine Coon that he and his brother owned in 1861. It had the splendid name of Captain Jenks of the Horse Marines, and was a beautiful black with some white.

There were special shows for the Maine Coon as early as the 1860s, which was years before the first official shows. At first these cats were only known in New England, but visitors to that part of the country so much admired the kittens, that many were taken to homes elsewhere in the country. Unfortunately, many were neutered as pets, so this did little to increase the numbers. As interest grew in pedigree cats and shows were held for them, the Maine Coons lost their popularity, and for a number of years little was heard about them.

In 1953 the Maine Coons staged a comeback when the Central Maine Cat Club was formed, running an annual show to choose the Maine State Champion Cat of the Year. In 1968 the Maine Coon Breeders and Fanciers Association was formed to promote the advancement of the breed. These cats are now known throughout the United States, and have received recognition and championship status. They are not yet known in Britain, but cross-matings of varied coloured Longhairs and Shorthairs, sometimes mongrels, have produced very similar cats, which frequently have been seen in the pet sections of shows, but, of course, have no pedigrees.

In comparison with many other varieties, the Maine Coon cats are massive in size, with muscular, powerful, long bodies on substantial legs. The heads are not round and broad, but of medium length, with high cheek bones; the ears are large rather than small, and the noses longish rather than short. The eye colour may be green, gold or copper, or even blue, if the cats are white. The original Maine Coon appears to have been a tabby cat with a white chest, but the multi-crossbreeding has produced almost every coat pattern and colour imaginable. The silky texture of the fur makes it easy to groom but the coat length may vary with climatic conditions.

Quite an intelligent cat, the Maine Coon makes an excellent house pet, usually being very gentle, and easy to handle.

OFFICIAL STANDARD
Cat Fanciers' Association, Inc.

MAINE COON

POINT SCORE

Head (30)	
Shape	15
Ears	10
Eyes	5
Body (35)	
Shape	20
Neck	5
Legs and feet	5
Tail	5
Coat (20)	20
Color (15)	
Body color	10
Eye color	5

General
Solid, firm, muscular; presented well-groomed.

Head shape
Medium in width and medium long in length with a squareness to the muzzle. Allowance should be made for broadening in older studs. Cheek bones high. Chin firm and in line with nose and upper lip. Nose medium long in length.

Ears
Large, well-tufted, wide at base, tapering to appear pointed. Set high and well apart.

Eyes
Large, wide set. Slightly oblique setting.

Neck
Medium long.

Body shape
Muscular, broad-chested. Size medium to large. Females may be smaller than males. The body should be long with all parts in proportion to create a rectangular appearance.

Legs and feet
Legs substantial, wide set, of medium length and in proportion to the body. Paws large, round, well-tufted. Five toes in front; four at back.

Tail
Long, wide at base and tapering. Fur long and flowing.

Coat
Heavy and shaggy; shorter on the shoulders and longer on the stomach and britches. Frontal ruff desirable. Texture silky with coat falling smoothly.

Penalize
A coat that is short or overall even.

Disqualify
Delicate bone structure. Undershot chin, crossed eyes, kinked tail, incorrect number of toes, buttons, lockets, or spots.

Head : squareness to the muzzle

MAINE COON CAT COLORS

Eye color
Eye color should be shades of green, gold, or copper, though white cats may also be either blue or odd-eyed. There is no relationship between eye color and coat color.

SOLID COLOR CLASS

WHITE
Pure glistening white.

Nose leather
Pink.

Paw pads
Pink.

BLACK
Dense coal black, sound from roots to tip of fur. Free from any tinge of rust on tips or smoke undercoat.

Nose leather
Black.

Paw pads
Black or brown.

BLUE
One level tone from nose to tip of tail. Sound to the roots.

Nose leather
Blue.

Paw pads
Blue.

RED
Deep, rich, clear, brilliant red; without shading, markings or ticking. Lips and chin the same color as coat.

Nose leather
Brick red.

Paw pads
Brick red.

CREAM
One level shade of buff cream, without markings. Sound to the roots.

Nose leather
Pink.

Paw pads
Pink.

Black Bicolour Maine Coon

Red Tabby Maine Coon

TABBY COLOR CLASS

CLASSIC TABBY PATTERN
Markings dense, clearly defined and broad. Legs evenly barred with bracelets coming up to meet the body markings. Tail evenly ringed. Several unbroken necklaces on neck and upper chest, the more the better. Frown marks on forehead form intricate letter "M". Unbroken line runs back from outer corner of eye. Swirls on cheeks. Vertical lines over back of head extend to shoulder markings which are in the shape of a butterfly with both upper and lower wings distinctly outlined and marked with dots inside outline. Back markings consist of a vertical line down the spine from butterfly to tail with a vertical stripe paralleling it on each side, the three stripes well separated by stripes of the ground color. Large solid blotch on each side to be encircled by one or more un-broken rings. Side markings should be the same on both sides. Double vertical row of buttons on chest and stomach.

MACKEREL TABBY PATTERN
Markings dense, clearly defined and all narrow pencillings. Legs evenly barred with narrow bracelets coming up to meet the body markings. Tail barred. Necklaces on neck and chest distinct, like so many chains. Head barred with an "M" on the forehead. Unbroken lines running back from the eyes. Lines running down the head to meet the shoulders. Spine lines run together to form a narrow saddle. Narrow pencillings run around the body.

SILVER TABBY
Ground color pale, clear silver. Markings dense black. White trim around lip and chin allowed.

Nose leather
Brick red desirable.

Paw pads
Black desirable.

RED TABBY
Ground color red. Markings, deep, rich red. White trim around lip and chin allowed.

Nose leather
Brick red desirable.

Paw pads
Brick red desirable.

BROWN TABBY
Ground color brilliant coppery brown. Markings dense black. Back of leg black from paw to heel. White trim around lip and chin allowed.

Nose leather
Brick red desirable.

Paw pads
Black or brown desirable.

BLUE TABBY
Ground color pale, bluish ivory. Markings a very deep blue affording a good contrast with ground colour. Warm fawn overtones or patina over the whole. White trim around lip and chin allowed.

Nose leather
Old rose desirable.

Paw pads
Rose desirable.

CREAM TABBY
Ground color very pale cream. Markings of buff or cream sufficiently darker than the ground color to afford good contrast, but remaining within the dilute range. White trim around lip and chin allowed.

Nose leather
Pink desirable.

Paw pads
Pink desirable.

CAMEO TABBY
Ground color off-white. Markings red.

Nose leather
Rose.

Paw pads
Rose.

PARTI-COLOR CLASS

TORTOISESHELL
Black with unbridled patches of red and cream. Patches clearly defined and well broken on both bodies and extremities. Blaze of red or cream on face is desirable.

CALICO
White with unbridled patches of black and red. White predominant on underparts.

DILUTE CALICO
White with unbridled patches of blue and cream. White predominant on underparts.

BLUE-CREAM
Blue with patches of solid cream. Patches clearly defined and well broken on both body and extremities.

BI-COLOR
A combination of a solid color with white. The colored areas predominate with the white portions being located on the face, chest, belly, legs, and feet. Colors accepted are red, black, blue, or cream.

OTHER MAINE COON COLORS CLASS

TORTOISESHELL WITH WHITE
Color as defined for Tortoisehell with or without white on the face. Must have white on bib, belly, and all four paws. White on one-third of body is desirable.

TABBIES WITH WHITE
Color as defined for Tabby with or without white on the face. Must have white on bib, belly and all four paws. White on one-third of body is desirable. Colors accepted are silver, red, brown, blue, or cream.

CHINCHILLA
Undercoat pure white. Coat on back, flanks, head and tail sufficiently tipped with black to give the characteristic sparkling silver appearance. Legs may be slightly shaded with tipping. Chin and ear tufts, stomach and chest, pure white. Rims of eyes, lips and nose outlined with black.

Nose leather
Brick red.

Paw pads
Black.

SHADED SILVER
Undercoat white with a mantle of black tipping shading down from sides, face and tail from dark on the ridge to white on the chin, chest, stomach and under the tail. Legs to be the same tone as the face. The general effect to be much darker than a chinchilla. Rims of eyes, lips and nose outlined with black.

Nose leather
Brick red.

Paw pads
Black.

SHELL CAMEO (Red Chinchilla)
Undercoat white, the coat on the back, flanks, head and tail to be sufficiently tipped with red to give the characteristic sparkling appearance. Face and legs may be very slightly shaded with tipping. Chin, ear tufts, stomach and chest white.

Nose leather
Rose.

Rims of eyes
Rose.

Tabby and White Maine Coon

Blue-Cream Maine Coon

Paw pads
Rose.

SHADED CAMEO (Red Shaded)
Undercoat white with a mantle of red tipping shading down the sides, face, and tail from dark on the ridge to white on the chin, chest, stomach, and under the tail. Legs to be the same tone as face. The general effect to be much redder than the Shell Cameo.

Nose leather
Rose.

Rims of eyes
Rose.

Paw pads
Rose.

BLACK SMOKE
White undercoat, deeply tipped with black. Cat in repose appears black. In motion the white undercoat is clearly apparent. Points and mask black with narrow band of white at base of hairs next to skin which may be seen only when the fur is parted.

Nose leather
Black.

Paw pads
Black.

BLUE SMOKE
White undercoat, deeply tipped with blue. Cat in repose appears blue. In motion the white undercoat is clearly apparent. Points and mask blue, with narrow band of white at base of hairs next to skin which may be seen only when fur is parted.

Nose leather
Blue.

Paw pads
Blue.

CAMEO SMOKE (Red Smoke)
White undercoat, deeply tipped with red. Cat in repose appears red. In motion the white undercoat is clearly apparent. Points and mask red with narrow band of white at base of hairs next to skin, which may be seen only when fur is parted.

Nose leather
Rose.

Rims of eyes
Rose.

Paw pads
Rose.

Show Preparation

All cats, longhaired or shorthaired, pedigree or pet, need some form of grooming, although, as most cats wash themselves frequently, this is not always realized. Brushing and combing will remove dirt and fleas, and help to keep the fur clean and to prevent furball. The longer the coat, the more attention is necessary to keep a cat looking a picture of perfection. This should be borne in mind when getting a kitten. A nine- or ten-week-old kitten with an easily manageable fluffy coat may have fur 5 to 6 inches (12.5 to 15 centimetres) long by the time it has reached maturity.

Perfect grooming cannot be achieved unless the animal is in first-class condition. A cat in poor condition through incorrect feeding, worms, or illness will have lank, spiky-looking fur that tends to look messed up and clings to the body, refusing to stand away or fall in place, however good the brushing and combing.

Coat care is essential not only to improve the cat's appearance, but also to remove the loose hairs that otherwise may be licked off and eventually form a wad, known as a hairball or furball, in the intestines.

Grooming should start at an early age. This gets the kitten used to being handled, and encourages the fur to grow the way it should. If the kitten objects to its stomach being attended to, place it flat on its back on your lap with its legs sticking up and comb and brush it gently from under the chin towards the tail. Unfortunately, some cats prove difficult to groom, and the owner will need a great deal of patience if the cat tries to scratch and bite. In such cases, it is better to groom the cat when it is sitting quietly, and then for just a few minutes at a time, leaving off the moment it objects. It is hoped that in time the cat will accept the inevitable, and allow itself to be groomed.

Most cats wash themselves carefully

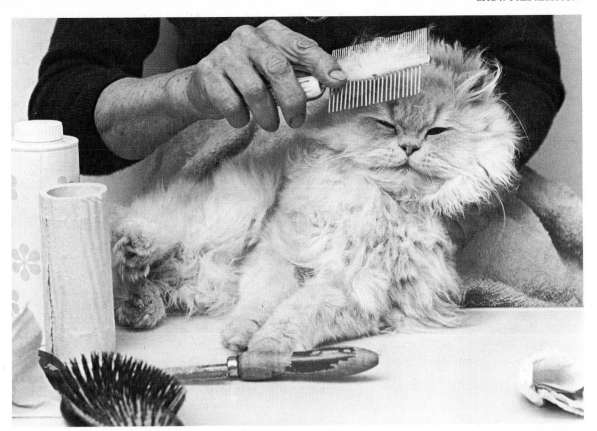

Combing a longhaired cat

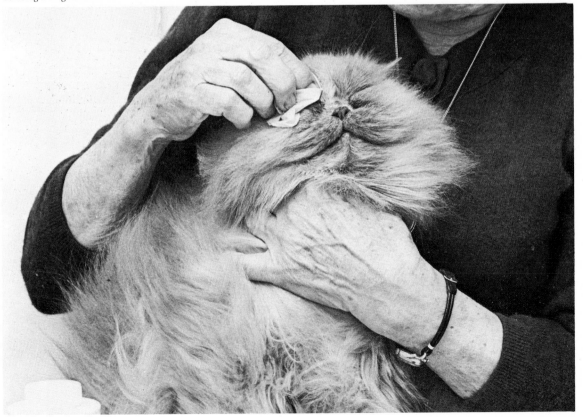

Cleaning the eye area

You can buy pet grooming equipment in most pet shops. A variety of grooming utensils is available for the different breeds and coat types. A brush with hair bristles is better than a wire or equally harsh brush, which can pull the fur out from the roots. You will need two combs, preferably made of steel: one with wide teeth for general grooming, and one with very close teeth for removing dirt and fleas.

Fleas, mites and other problems

Begin grooming any cat by inspecting the fur closely for fleas and flea-dirts, which look like tiny specks of coal-dust. Any animal can pick up an odd flea or two, and normal grooming will cope with this. But fleas can be a problem for cats living in the country where rabbits and hedgehogs, noted flea-carriers, abound. Some years are much worse than others, when almost a plague of fleas can prove

Brushing

very difficult to control. If, despite daily grooming, fleas keep appearing, inspect the cat's sleeping quarters or anywhere it is fond of sitting. Remember, fleas do not breed on the animal, but in the cracks of wooden floors, in the sides of armchairs and settees, and in dark corners in dust and dirt. A cat can pick them up from any of these places.

Any preparation used on a cat to get rid of fleas must be one that is particularly recommended by a vet or other authority as being suitable for cats. Insecticides used on dogs are not always suitable for cats. Having found a safe insecticide, stand the cat on a sheet of newspaper and rub or spray the preparation well down into the roots of the fur. Leave it in for a few minutes, and prevent the cat from licking it. Then brush and comb the fur until all traces of insecticide have been removed. Have a container of water and disinfectant ready to put the fleas in, and burn the newspaper after you have finished. Combing the fur daily with a comb dipped in a very mild solution of a non-toxic disinfectant may be all that is necessary to trap any flea remaining. Repeat the process in a week.

For a very severe infestation of fleas you should ask your vet to treat the cat or to recommend an appropriate course to follow. In Britain one practice is to apply the insecticide and put the cat in a pillowcase (which may require assistance), leaving only the head out. The cat is kept in the pillowcase for a short period until the fleas have dropped off, then brushed and combed to remove every trace of the insecticide.

It is important to keep the cat's ears clean too, and there are commercial preparations available for doing this. Usually the ears stay clean, and may need only to be gently wiped with a lightly dampened piece of cottonwool to remove any dust. If there are signs of brownish matter in the ears, the cause is probably ear mites. Ask a veterinary surgeon to prescribe the correct treatment.

Many longhaired cats have a blocked lachrymal duct between the eye and the nose, which can cause brownish matter to accumulate in the corner of the eye. This must be wiped away daily to prevent brown staining on the face and permanent ruts each side of the nose. If the haws, which are membranes in the corners of the eyes, are up, consult the veterinary surgeon, as this may be a sign of worms or the first sign of an illness.

Claws can grow too long and need clipping. If you do not know how to do this properly, ask your vet to show you. It takes only a few minutes to clip a cat's claws, but incorrect or too-deep clipping can cause pain and bleeding. If you still do not feel confident of doing it correctly, ask your vet or some other experienced person to help you. Given the opportunity, most cats keep their claws in good condition by scratching on trees, table legs and other similar objects. This is to clean the claws, not sharpen them, as often thought. Stop kittens from scratching on the furniture at their first attempt. Just a firm 'No' is usually most effective in preventing this. If the animal has no opportunity for outside exercise, provide a scratching post for it. A range of posts is available in most pet shops.

Should a cat get paint on its coat, clip it out, even if it means spoiling the appearance for a while. Do not remove it with solvent or paint remover, which can burn the skin, cause some form of dermatitis, and may be licked off by the cat.

Longhaired cats

The general daily grooming for all the longcoated cats should begin with a thorough inspection, followed by a brushing and combing, and finish with brushing the fur around the head and shoulders upwards to form a frame around the face. There are two major distinct types of fur: one very fine and silky, and the other fluffy and springy. The latter is more difficult to keep in good order and is quicker to matt, while the former frequently looks immaculate with comparatively little attention.

The late autumn and spring are the worst times for fur shedding; it is then that the fur of the longhairs may twist and snarl up, forming felt-like masses. The occasional tangle can be teased out gently with the fingers or a thick knitting needle. If the cat objects, try subterfuge when it is sleeping on your lap. Always avoid pulling the skin, which can be very painful.

If left unattended, these snarls can form into thick wads, impossible to comb through. These may have to be clipped away a little at a time with rounded surgical scissors, with great care being taken not to pull or clip the skin. If neglected, the felting-up can result in nasty sores, and may become so bad that veterinary attention may be necessary to strip the coat under anaesthetic. Daily grooming is therefore very important. Twice daily is even better when the cat is moulting.

In very hot climates, such as parts of North America in the summer, some breeders clip off the fur of the longhairs, giving the cats almost a poodle look. This certainly avoids any tangles in the coat, makes it easy to catch any fleas, and seems to promote growth. This cannot be done in Britain if the cat is to be exhibited, as cutting or clipping the fur is not permitted by the Governing Council

Keeping cool: a clipped coat for summer

of the Cat Fancy's regulations governing the shows (see pages 261–264).

Inspect the feet too and brush the long hair between the toes; if this is allowed to matt, it can cause painful sores.

Talcum or baby powder can be used on cats with light-coloured fur. Sprinkle the powder in lightly right down to the roots and brush it out completely. The tail will need special attention: part it down the middle and sprinkle it with the powder, then brush it out until the tail is almost as wide as the back of the cat, with the fur standing up well.

Talcum powder should not be used on the Blacks, as it may be difficult to remove completely, and will look like dandruff or scurf in the fur. Cologne sprinkled into the fur and rubbed dry removes the grease. Some breeders recommend wiping the fur all over with a cloth that has been dipped in warm water to which a few drops of ammonia have been added to remove grease and give the coat a wonderful sheen. Finish by polishing the fur with a piece of velvet or silk to give it a shining appearance. Smokes need careful grooming so that the contrast of black and silver is seen to the best advantage. Talcum powder may be used on the undercoat, but must be brushed out completely so that it does not appear on the black fur.

Talcum powder does not suit all cats, and can cause dribbling and running noses. If powder upsets the cat, try one of the various preparations on the market recommended for use on cats' coats. They are also suitable for the Silver Tabbies, Reds and the Tortoiseshells.

The buff-coloured fuller's earth is recommended by many breeders. It is used in exactly the same way as talcum powder and is suitable for the Brown Tabbies, Colourpoint Longhairs (Himalayans) and the Birmans.

Talcum or baby powder may be used with care, avoiding the coloured parts, on the Tortoiseshells and Whites, and on the Bi-Coloured and the Turkish cats.

Staining and scurf, or dandruff, seem to affect the tails of many male and some female cats. This condition is referred to as stud tail. The best way to treat it is by washing. Sit the cat on the draining board of the sink, with his back to the sink. Mix baby or poodle shampoo with warm, rather than hot, water in a jug or pitcher. Swish the tail in and out of the shampoo, rubbing it gently, and then rinse it thoroughly until all traces of the shampoo are gone. If the scurf is bad and difficult to remove by washing, put a little vaseline on the affected part to soften it. Leave it on for some hours and then wipe it off. The tail must not be rubbed too hard, as this can make it sore. Repeat this treatment several times, if necessary, until the scurf has gone, and then wash the tail as before.

Most cats go their whole lives without being bathed, but many exhibitors of Whites and Chinchillas in particular give their cats a bath several days before a show, giving the coat time for the natural grease to return. The kitchen sink is ideal for this, rather than the bath, as it is the right height and saves bending. Some cats prefer having their back legs only in the sink, with the front paws on the draining board, and this makes washing underneath much easier too. Prepare everything in advance, without the cat seeing, as it might be intelligent enough to realize what is about to happen and do a disappearing trick. Have ready in a small jug baby shampoo mixed with warm water, and have 3 or 4 inches (7.5 or 10 centimetres) of warm water in the sink. Plug the cat's ears with cottonwool to keep the water out, and moisten the coat all over. Rub in the shampoo, avoiding the cat's eyes, and rinse thoroughly. Repeat the process to ensure that the fur is quite clean. A hand spray attachment is useful to ensure that no shampoo is left in the coat. Rub the cat dry with a towel or, if the cat does not mind, use a hair dryer. Cats are very susceptible to chills, so keep the animal indoors until its fur is completely dry; then groom it in the usual way.

Preparation should never be left until the last minute for a cat that is to be exhibited, but should start several weeks in advance. You should not go to extremes, of course; it is possible to over-groom to such an extent that the fur around the head is pulled out instead of forming a frame for the face.

Trial and error will show very clearly which method of grooming is most suited to the different coat textures and colours, so that eventually it should be possible for any cat to appear a picture of perfection.

Kitten washing

Shorthaired cats

One of the easiest varieties to groom is the Siamese, with its short, fine-textured fur. Most Siamese seem to enjoy hard hand stroking, which may also cause any loose hairs to drop out. However, using a fine-toothed comb first will remove any dirt and fleas. Should the coat be very dirty, a little talcum powder or fuller's earth sprinkled into the fur and well brushed out, should soon clean it. Hard hand stroking, followed by polishing with a chamois leather, will restore the natural sheen. This method of grooming is also suitable for the Burmese, Russian Blues and other foreign varieties. If talcum powder is used, it must never be left in the coat, but brushed out immediately. The coats of Abyssinians respond well to a light sprinkling of Cologne and a rubdown, followed by hard hand stroking.

The Exotics, and the domestic shorthairs need much the same form of grooming. A fine comb should be used, never one with wide teeth, as this tends to leave track marks in the coat. Remove bad stains or grease with a little surgical spirit or cologne rubbed into the fur with a small pad of cottonwool, taking care to protect the eyes. Rub the fur dry and groom afterwards as for Siamese. Powder is unsuitable for dark-coated cats, but the special preparations for cats' and dogs' coats seem to suit them very well, as does hand stroking.

Powdering seems to be sufficient for most White shorthairs, but it may be necessary, especially if the cat is being exhibited, to give it a bath, and this procedure is the same as that described for the longcoated cats.

Pet cats

Grooming is just as important for pet cats as for show cats, and should be done in the same way, varying according to the colours and coat lengths. If the pet is allowed the run of the streets, it should be groomed for the sake of your health and comfort as well as its own. It would be most unpleasant and unhealthy to have a dirty, smelly, flea-infested animal living as one of the family.

Grooming a few minutes each day is better than once a week, and if time can be spared to play with the cat afterwards, it will look forward to being brushed and combed as a preparation for playtime.

Expectant queens

An expectant queen needs careful grooming. Avoid hard brushing and stroking, especially on the flanks, the week or two before the litter is due. In the longhairs the fur may be clipped away from the nipples and under the tail with rounded surgical scissors. This is not only for cleanliness, but also makes it easier for the kittens to feed when they arrive. The nipples may be prepared and softened by washing, with a mild antiseptic and applying a little vaseline. Even if the cat has picked up a flea or two, try to remove only by combing; avoid using an insecticide, which can prove fatal to the newly-born kittens.

Show Rules

Whatever the country, the way a judge appraises a cat and makes the decision whether or not to give it a prize is much the same, as all cats are judged according to an official standard.

Britain

In Britain the judge goes to each pen accompanied by a steward, who brings a wheeled table, or trolley. The steward takes the cat out of the pen, and places it on the trolley for the judge to handle and assess. The judge makes notes in a book, and when all the exhibits in a particular class have been seen, places them accordingly. The steward has to make sure that the judge has entered the correct results in triplicate in the book. Two slips are torn out – one goes on the award board and the other is kept as a record by the club running the show. The steward also has to check that there has been no cross-judging; that is, he must ensure that if the judge assesses some of the same cats in other classes he always places them in the same relative order.

Some clubs have a Best in Show award. The judges nominate their choices to be assessed by a panel of judges, who then choose the best cat, kitten and neuter in show in each section; that is, Longhair, Shorthair and Siamese. It is very rare now to have a top cat Best in Show, except at the Supreme Show organized by the Governing Council of the Cat Fancy. The exhibits accepted at this show have to qualify beforehand by wins at other shows throughout the country.

The majority of shows now have a Best in Breed category – that is, the best of each variety – and present rosettes to the winners. Many shows do not give prize monies for the open classes but give rosettes to the first, second and third prize winners. Most shows give special prizes and wins on club cups.

British judges do not have to take examinations. They are nominated by breed clubs and chosen by panels after years of stewarding and breeding various varieties. They are usually made probationers first, and have to judge kittens at least three

Richard Gebhardt, President of the CFA, judging in the United States

Judging in progress in the United States

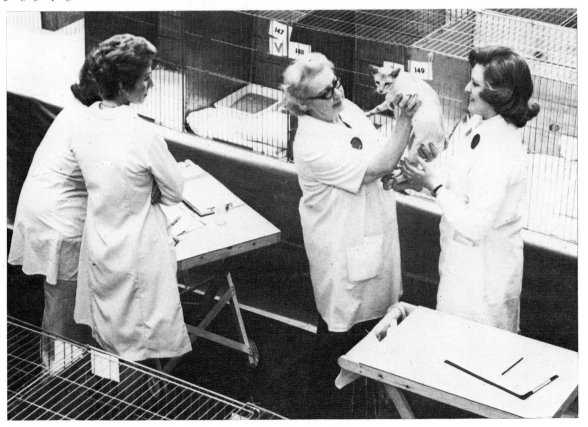

Judging at the pen in Britain

times and have their capabilities assessed, before they can become full judges. Judges are not paid for their services, but are reimbursed for travel and, if required, hotel expenses.

North America

In North America the judge does not go to the pens, as these are hung with curtains covered with the rosettes and ribbons previously won, and would therefore make the cat recognizable. The judge sits or stands behind a table, and in front of a row of pens. As the classes are relatively small, it usually is possible for a whole class to be penned behind the judge at once. The judge handles the cats, placing them in turn on the table, in front of which there are many rows of exhibitors eager to watch the judging. Once the judge has made up his or her mind as to the winners, he places the coloured ribbons on the pens, usually telling the audience why he likes particular cats.

The results are written down by a clerk. The winner of the novice class may move up into the Open class; if it wins that, it can move up to the next class, and, if really outstanding, could finish being chosen as the Best Cat. No prize money is given, but there are rosettes, special awards, and cups to be won. The five best cats are chosen to receive special honours. In America a would-be judge has to breed cats for many years, exhibit winning cats, attend judging schools, and take examinations before being considered as a judge. The judges are paid according to the number of cats they judge, and also receive hotel and travelling expenses.

Europe

In Europe the pens are decorated with curtains and ribbons, and stewards take the cats to the judges, who sometimes are in a separate room so that the public cannot see the judging. Prize money is not awarded, but there are many ribbons, rosettes and special prizes, and Best in Show is suitably awarded, sometimes by a cup or vase.

Would-be judges have to be examined by senior judges, orally and in writing, before being passed as qualified to judge.

Waiting for the judge

Show Rules of the Governing Council of the Cat Fancy

1. With the exception noted in Note 1 below, all cats and kittens exhibited for competition at a show held under licence of the GCCF must be registered with the GCCF and must be the **bona fide** property of the Exhibitor. Cats with unregistered parents but which are themselves registered (on 1 June, 1971) and which were eligible for challenge certificates on that date, shall continue to be so and so shall their suitable progeny for three generations from 20 October, 1971. Thereafter only cats with registered parents, grandparents and great grandparents shall be eligible.

Note 1: Show Managements are authorized to offer classes for 'Household Pets'.

Note 2: Household Pets are unregistered cats of unknown pedigree and no registered cat may be exhibited in classes offered for them.

Note 3: Household Pets are either 'Longhair' or 'Shorthair' and breed or varietal names and/or numbers allocated to registered cats must not be applied to them in Show classifications, schedules or catalogues.

2. The owner of a cat is the person so named in the GCCF Register and is not necessarily the legal owner named by right of gift or purchase. If the legal owner is not also the owner named in the Register, a transfer certificate must be obtained before the cat concerned can be exhibited at a show held under GCCF licence.

3. In order to exhibit in any show held under GCCF licence the exhibitor must complete the official entry form for the show and subscribe to the following declaration:

(a) I/We am/are the registered owner(s) of the cats and/or kittens named on this form and I/we agree to be bound by and submit to the Constitution and Rules of the Governing Council of the Cat Fancy presently in force and to any additional rules formulated specifically for this show, provided only that the latter do not conflict with the former.

(b) I/We declare that to the best of my/our knowledge and belief the exhibits named on this form or any other cats living in my/our household or cattery, are not suffering from any infectious or contagious disease and have not been exposed to such disease during the twenty-one days prior to the date of my/our signature(s) on this form. I/We further declare that if I/we or any cat owned by me/us should be exposed to such infection between the date of my/our signature(s) on this form and the date of the show, I/we and the cats and/or kittens from my/our household/cattery will not be present at the show.

(c) I/We declare that no cat or kitten from my/our household/cattery will be exhibited at any show or public exhibition within the fourteen days prior to the date of this show.

4. Exhibitors or others whose cats may be suffering from any infectious or contagious disease (including any form of nasal catarrh or conjunctivitis), and members of their households, are barred from attending or exhibiting at any show until a certificate of freedom from infection has been obtained from a veterinary surgeon.

Note 1: Evasion of this rule will render the offender liable to severe disciplinary action and ignorance will not be an acceptable excuse.

Note 2: Pregnant or lactating queens (even if they have lost their kittens or the kittens have been weaned) may not compete and must not be exhibited at any show or exhibition and veterinary surgeons in attendance are instructed to reject any queen in these conditions.

Note 3: Monorchid and cryptorchid adult males are not acceptable exhibits and veterinary surgeons in attendance are instructed to reject them.

Note 4: No kitten shall be exhibited under the age of three calendar months. This applies to litters for exhibition also.

Note 5: Any cat or kitten which in the opinion of the judge is very under-developed or in very poor condition shall be disqualified from competition.

Note 6: Any cat or kitten disqualified by a judge on grounds of condition must be reported by the Show Manager to the Cat Care Committee.

5. Registration and transfer applications must be received by the Registrar not less than twenty-one days prior to the show. The date of receipt by the Registrar of such applications shall be the relevant date. All applications must be accompanied by a stamped self-addressed envelope.

6. Exhibits must arrive at the show hall in a suitable container and must be accompanied by the owner or the owner's agent. The owner or his agent must be within call throughout the period of the show except for those times when the hall is cleared for judging. All cats must be removed from pens prior to dismantling, but must not be removed during the period of the show without the explicit permission of the Show Manager.

7. Exhibits must be presented on arrival at the show to a veterinary surgeon or veterinarian, for examination before entering the penning arena and must be so presented during the times stated in the show schedule. Late arrivals may be refused entry.

Note: Evasion or attempted evasion of this rule will lead to disciplinary action by the GCCF. The decision of the examining veterinary surgeon or veterinarian to reject an exhibit is final and no appeal can be entertained.

8. Every exhibit must be identified on the entry form exactly as recorded on the registration or transfer certificate relating to it.

Note: Errors in these details (except minor spelling

errors) will disqualify the entry, with forfeiture of all entry and penning fees. Show Managements, however, are permitted to accept corrections, at their own discretion, up to a date not later than seven days prior to the date of the show. Any such corrections must be incorporated in the marked catalogues sent to the GCCF, but need not be incorporated in any other catalogues.

9. Every exhibit must be provided with a sanitary tray and a clean plain white or near white blanket without distinctive marking or edging.
Note: Show Managements are empowered to apply this rule rigidly and to disqualify any exhibit appearing with a dirty, coloured or otherwise distinctive blanket. Cellular blankets are not allowed.

10. Except that when necessary or otherwise desirable a hot water bottle or other heating device may be concealed by the blanket, no articles or decorations may be placed in or on the pen until after judging has been completed. The only exception to this rule is that a container with water may be placed in the pen, towards the rear.
Note: Containers with food and drink may be placed in the pen after the time announced for the admission of the public. Food containers, if used earlier, must be removed before judging commences.

11. Apart from the current show award cards and a simple 'For Sale' card competitive pens must not carry any advertisement or other printed or manuscript matter except that a Judge or Show Manager may affix a note if a cat is found to be dangerous to handle or unwell.

12. Any exhibit which cannot be safely handled by a judge and/or judge's steward will be disqualified in those classes in which it could not be handled, with forfeiture of the relevant entry fees. A judge's decision in this matter is final.
Note: Any cat biting a judge or steward, shall be reported by the judge to the Show Manager. The Show Manager shall inform the owner of the cat in writing, and send a copy of the letter to the Secretary to the GCCF. If the cat bites at three shows, then it shall be disqualified from all future shows.

13. Exhibits may be groomed immediately before penning with a clean brush, comb or cloth, but the use of powder or other grooming aids in the show hall is prohibited on pain of disqualification and forfeiture of all penning and entry fees.
Note: Breaches of this rule may be notified to the Show Manager by any person present and the Show Manager will then take immediate action to investigate and to implement this rule.

14. Any exhibit prepared for show in any artificial manner calculated or liable to change its appearance relative to the standard of points shall be disqualified, and the exhibitor will become liable to disciplinary action.
Note 1: Such fraudulent preparation includes the uses of dyes, other colouring matter or whitening or darkening substances, or any oils or greasy preparations, or any other cleaning substances which remain in the exhibit's coat during the show; it includes also trimming, clipping, singeing or rasping down of the fast coat, any eye treatment causing a temporary or permanent change in normal relation to light, any drug treatment causing temporary or permanent change in the normal appearance or physical reactions of the exhibit, or any surgery (cosmetic or otherwise) leading to changed appearance or reactions.
Note 2: Exhibits which have been de-clawed will be at once disqualified and normally will be refused entry to the show hall by the officiating veterinary surgeon or veterinarian.

15. Disqualification under paragraph 14 above, must be certified by two judges, or by the Show Manager and one judge, or by a veterinary surgeon or veterinarian. The Show Manager shall at once inform the GCCF of all relevant details, in writing, and shall similarly inform the exhibitor concerned that this action has been taken and that disciplinary action may follow. The exhibitor may lodge an appeal against disqualification with the GCCF on grounds of fact only, provided that such an appeal is lodged within seven days of the date of the show.

16. Exhibitors must vacate the judging area when required to do so by the Show Management, and must not re-enter until the doors are opened to the public, unless requested to do so by the Show Management.

17. Exhibitors are forbidden to enter into conversation with any judge under whom he is exhibiting until after the judge's engagement is completed.

18. Exhibitors are reminded that the decisions of judges are final. Any overt or covert attempt to influence such decisions will render the offender liable to severe disciplinary action.

19. Except in so far as the conditions under which entry was made may be changed, exhibits may not be withdrawn from competition after entering the show hall unless such withdrawal is sanctioned by the Show Manager. In case of such sanctioned withdrawal entry and penning fees will be forfeited.

20. Exhibits may be withdrawn before judging starts from classes in which (a) the judge is changed from the judge named in the Schedule, (b) classes are amalgamated unless such amalgamation was announced as a possibility in the Schedule. In case of such withdrawal, the exhibitor shall be entitled to claim refund of entry fees for all classes from which the exhibit is withdrawn, but refund of penning fees is not permitted. Claims for refunds must be made within seven days of the date of the show.

21. Exhibitors or their agents must not remove any exhibit from its pen while judging of any class in which it is entered is in progress except by direction of the Show Manager or other official on pain of disqualification and forfeiture of entry fee.

22. Exhibits must not be removed from the exhibition

before the declared time for closure of the show, except that exhibitors may apply for earlier removal when making their entry. Such early removal may be made at the discretion of the Show Manager.

23. Exhibitors are requested to point out to the Show Manager any errors in regard to their own entries which may appear in the show catalogue, at the earliest possible moment.

Note: Errors on entry forms which are reproduced in the catalogue cannot be corrected, but exhibits which may be placed in wrong classes or wrongly identified as a result of them, will be disqualified. Errors which have occurred as typing, printing or other managerial mistakes must be corrected if pointed out at a reasonable time during the Show, and/or exhibitor compensated for any loss.

24. The registered owner of cats and/or kittens may not enter them in any show while under disciplinary disqualification imposed by the GCCF and any exhibits entered in contravention of this rule will be disqualified with forfeiture of all entry and penning fees. At the same time the owner will be subjected to further disciplinary action.

General notes for the guidance of Exhibitors

(a) If your exhibit is rejected by the examining veterinary surgeon or veterinarian before or during a show, the GCCF will require you to produce a veterinary certificate of freedom from infection as indicated in Rule 4 above before being permitted to attend or exhibit at any future show. This certificate must be dated not less than seven

days after the show at which the exhibit(s) was/were rejected and submitted to the GCCF with all relevant details.

(b) If you have any cats or kittens living at an address other than the one given on your entry form, or at an address other than your own, the relevant facts should be submitted to the GCCF. This is in order to safeguard you and others in case of apparent evasion of the fourteen day rule mentioned in Rule 3(c) above.

(c) Evasion or breech of any of the GCCF rules, or of the articles of its constitution may, and often will, lead to disciplinary action and you are advised to familiarize yourself with all sections of the Rules and with the Constitution. These are obtainable from the GCCF secretary.

(d) Except where the context demands otherwise, the word 'cat' in these rules includes kittens and neuters. A kitten is defined as a young cat under nine calendar months of age. Thus a kitten born on 12 January becomes a cat (adult) on the following 12 October.

CLASSES AT THE CHAMPIONSHIP SHOWS IN BRITAIN

Open Breed class: for each recognized variety, adult and kitten. A challenge certificate may be given to the winner of the adult Open class, if it is considered worthy.

CATS CLASS: for exhibits 9 months old and over on the day of the Show.

KITTENS CLASS: for exhibits 3 to 9 months old on the day of the Show.

NEUTERS CLASS: for neutered cats, male or female. Neuters may only enter Neuter Classes, and may not

Steward removing cat from pen for waiting judge

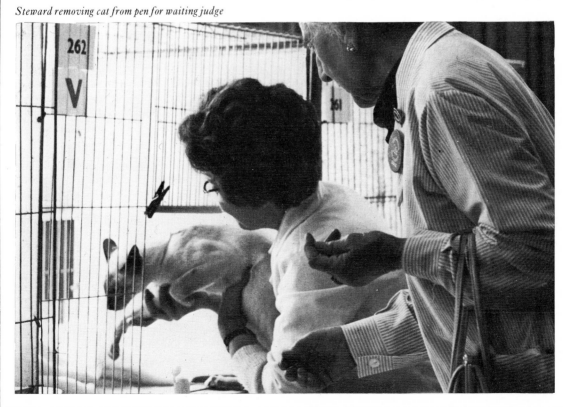

compete with entire cats or kittens. Neutered kittens may enter any class specified for Neuters, other than Open Classes.

NOVICE CLASS: for exhibits that have not won a First Prize under GCCF Rules.

LIMIT CLASS: for exhibits that have not won more than four First Prizes under GCCF Rules.

DEBUTANTE CLASS: for exhibits that have never been shown under GCCF Rules.

MAIDEN CLASS: for exhibits that have not won a First, Second or Third prize under GCCF Rules.

BREEDERS CLASS: for exhibits bred by exhibitor.

JUNIOR CLASS: for cats under two years old on the day of the Show.

SENIOR CLASS: for cats over two years old on the day of the Show.

RADIUS CLASS: for exhibits that live within certain distances of the Show hall.

Notes

Wins as kittens do not count when entering cat classes.

All wins previous to the midnight preceding the day specified in the schedule for close of entries shall be counted when entering any class.

No kitten may be entered into any Adult Class, unless specified for Cat or Kitten.

Cats and Kittens registered as Breeds 13a, 26 and 32x may only enter in Assessment Classes.

No exhibit is to be entered in more than 12 classes – GCCF recommendation – which is endorsed by the Committee.

CHAMPIONS AND PREMIERS

The title of Champion for Cats and Premier for Neuters
Winning neuter inspecting its rosette

shall be granted to exhibits winning three Challenge Certificates at three shows, under separate judges. A GCCF Challenge Certificate will be offered for each Cat/Neuter Open Class of recognized breed with Championship status.

CHAMPION OF CHAMPIONS – PREMIER OF PREMIERS

The title of Grand Champion shall be granted to a cat winning three Champion Challenge Certificates at three shows, under separate judges. To compete in a Champion of Champions Class a Cat must be a full Champion. A Champion Cat may be entered into its ordinary breed Open Class and in the Champion of Champions Class. Only one prize, with a Reserve, in case of disqualification, will be awarded.

The title of Grand Premier shall be granted to Neutered Cats under the same rules and conditions as those for Grand Champion.

In addition to the classes mentioned above, the various clubs throughout the country may put on classes for their members at each other's shows, so that altogether the classes in a schedule may number more than seven hundred and require eighty or more judges to judge them.

The majority of the British shows are divided into sections: Longhair, Shorthair, (British and Foreign), and Siamese. There is usually a pet section as well, with classes for unregistered mongrel cats and kittens.

In addition to the exhibits entered for competition there are also the assessment classes for exhibits that are of a new, unrecognized variety. The cats in these are judged individually by three judges, who may grant merit certificates if they consider that the cat meets its provisional standards.

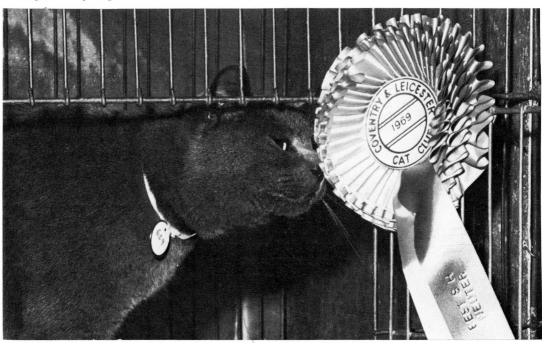

Show Rules of the The Cat Fanciers' Association, Inc.

ARTICLE I
DEFINITIONS

1. CAT is used in these rules to mean a domesticated feline of the age of 8 calendar months or more of either sex, neutered or spayed.

2. A KITTEN is a cat under the age of 8 calendar months.

3. BREED is used in these rules to mean, respectively, natural breeds (Abyssinian, American Shorthair, Egyptian Mau, Japanese Bobtail, Maine Coon, Manx, Persian, Russian Blue, Turkish Angora, and Siamese); established breeds (Balinese, Birman, British Shorthair, Burmese, Havana Brown, Korat, and Somali); mutations (American Wirehair, Rex, and Scottish Fold); and hybrids (Bombay, Colorpoint Shorthair, Exotic Shorthair, Himalayan, and Oriental Shorthair).

4. A REGISTERED CAT is a cat for which a CFA registration certificate has been received from the Central Office.

5. A BENCHED CAT is one that is present and qualified for competition. Such cat is presumed to be benched and present for competition throughout the entire show.

6. A NEUTER is a castrated male. A SPAY is an altered female.

7. A RING is a competition judged by one judge.

8. A SHOW is a concurrent series of rings.

9. For the purpose of these rules, a CONCURRENT ring is not a SUBSEQUENT SHOW.

10. COMPETITIVE CATEGORY refers to the three major competitive groups: Non-Championship, Championship, and Premiership (Alter).

11. CLASS refers to the competitive divisions within the Competitive Categories as follows: Kitten, AOV, Provisional Breed, Miscellaneous (Non-Competitive), and Household Pet Classes; Open, Champion, and Grand Champion Classes; Open, Premier, and Grand Premier Classes.

12. COLOR CLASS refers to the various color-pattern classifications recognized in Article XXIV.

13. To PENALIZE: a Judge deducts from an exhibit a portion, or all, of the points allotted to a specific part of the Standard for that exhibit.

14. To WITHHOLD AWARDS: a Judge withholds all awards from an otherwise eligible entry, with the exception of first, second, or third, when in his opinion an entry is not worthy of them. Causes for withholding awards are listed in Article XXVIII, Paragraph 238.

15. To DISQUALIFY: to remove from competition. The class is judged as if the entry were not present. Causes for disqualification are listed in Article III and in each Breed Standard. An entry may be disqualified by the Show Committee, the Veterinarian, the Judge, or the Central Office.

16. A Substitute Judge is the same as the advertised Judge in all situations.

17. *NON-CHAMPIONSHIP CLASSES*
   a) The KITTEN CLASS is for any kitten, male or female, not less than 4 months but under 8 calendar months old on the opening day of the show, which, if an adult, would be eligible to compete in a Championship Class. Kittens are not eligible for any "Bests" in show except Kitten awards.
   b) The AOV (Any Other Variety) CLASS is for any registered, adult, whole cat or registered kitten, the ancestry of which entitles it to Championship competition, but which does not (colorwise, coatwise, or, in the case of Manx, tailwise) conform to the accepted show standard. An AOV entry is eligible only for awards in the AOV class of its own breed.
   c) The PROVISIONAL BREED CLASS is for any registered cat or registered kitten of a breed not accepted for Championship competition when CFA has approved a provisional standard for that breed. Cats entered in the Provisional Breed Class are eligible only for awards in the Provisional Breed Class. Provisional Breeds shall compete separately as Kittens, Altered Cats, or Adult, whole cats.
   d) The MISCELLANEOUS (Non-Competitive) CLASS is for any registered cat or registered kitten of a breed not yet accepted for Provisional Breed competition.
   e) The HOUSEHOLD PET CLASS is for any domestic kitten or altered cat entry not otherwise eligible. Household Pets are eligible only for awards in the Household Pet Class. Household Pets are to be judged separately from all other cats, solely on beauty and condition. Feral cats or feral cat-domestic cat hybrid crosses are not eligible for entry.

18. *CHAMPIONSHIP CLASSES*
   a) The OPEN CLASS is for CFA registered cats of either sex, 8 months or over, except cats that have completed requirements for Championship confirmation. When a cat has completed requirements for confirmation, it is ineligible for the Open Class at any subsequent show.
   b) The CHAMPION CLASS is for cats that have com-

pleted Championships in this Association, and for which the required Championship claim has been mailed to the Central Office.

c) The GRAND CHAMPION CLASS is for cats that have completed Grand Championships in CFA.

19. *PREMIERSHIP CLASSES*

a) Premiership Classes are for CFA registered neutered or spayed cats, 8 months old or over, that would, as whole cats, be eligible to compete in the Championship classes.

b) The following classes will be recognized for neuters and spays of each Championship Color Class: Grand Premier, Premier, and Open. The eligibility for each class will be determined in the same manner as for the corresponding class in Championship competition.

20. Wins made in Championship competition may not be transferred to Premiership records. However, titles won in Championship competition are retained.

ARTICLE II
ELIGIBILITY FOR ENTRY

21. Any cat or kitten of sound health not less than 4 calendar months old on the opening day of a show is eligible (subject to the exceptions herein) for exhibition at shows sanctioned by CFA and may compete for and be entitled to win, under the rules herein, any ribbon or prize offered.

22. Any cat or kitten from a house or cattery where there has been fungus or any infectious or contagious illness within 21 days prior to the opening date of a show is ineligible for entry, and, should entry have been made prior to the onset of any such condition, such entry is ineligible for admission into the showroom.

23. Only cats registered with CFA are eligible for entry in the Championship and Premiership Competitive Categories and the Provisional Breed, Miscellaneous (Non-Competitive), or AOV Classes. The Show Management is expressly prohibited from accepting a Championship, Premiership, Provisional Breed Miscellaneous (Non-Competitive), or AOV entry unless the official Entry Blank contains a registration number. It is the responsibility of the owner to enter the cat with its proper registration number as shown on the registration certificate.

24. Each cat must be entered in the breed under which it is registered.

25. When an officiating Judge is the breeder of a cat or kitten, such cat or kitten is not eligible for competition in that Judge's ring. This rule shall not apply to shows in Hawaii and Japan.

26. A neutered or spayed kitten is not eligible for entry.

27. A cat that has completed requirements for Championship or Premiership confirmation is ineligible for further competition until claim has been filed for Championship or Premiership.

28. A cat that has won a Championship or Premiership in one color class is not eligible for entry in a different color class except that a cat that has been confirmed as a Champion or Premier in one color class and, after confirmation, changes color, may be shown in the correct color class by notifying the Central Office of the color change and payment of a fee of $5.00. The cat may then compete as an open in the proper color class. The Central Office must confirm the color class change prior to competition in a new color class. Only one change will be permitted.

29. A cat not having all its physical properties – eyes, ears, legs, tail (except Manx), claws, for example, is not eligible for entry subject to the following exceptions:

a) cats in Premiership classes have been altered; and

b) altered cats are eligible for adult Household Pet classes.

30. An adult male must have at least one descended testicle to be eligible for entry.

31. Male kittens are not required to have descended testicles.

32. The Show Committee may refuse to accept an entry received after midnight of the advertised date for the closing of entries, or after the advertised limit of entries has been reached.

33. The Show Committee may permit kittens 4 months old or older, or cats, to be entered for exhibition or sale.

34. No more than two kittens or one cat may be benched in a single cage whether entered for exhibition, for sale, or for competition.

35. No cat or kitten shall be benched at more than one show per week (Monday through Sunday inclusive).

ARTICLE III
CAUSES FOR DISQUALIFICATION

36. A cat shown in the wrong class or under incorrect name, ownership, or registration number will be disqualified by the Central Office and any wins voided.

37. The Veterinarian has the power to order the immediate removal of any sick cat. Such cat will be entitled to all prizes allotted to it prior to the decision of the Veterinarian.

38. A cat may be disqualified in all rings if removed from the showroom contrary to the provisions in these Rules.

39. A Judge must disqualify a cat for a defect listed in the "Disqualify" section of the Standard for that particular breed or color.

40. A Judge will disqualify and dismiss from his ring any cat that bites or that is in his judgment behaving in a recalcitrant or threatening manner. The Chief Clerk in that ring is responsible for notifying Chief Clerks in remaining rings of the action taken.

41. The excessive use of powder or chalk and any use of tints, color rinses, or other artificial coloring or concealment media on a cat entered in a CFA show is strictly forbidden. Any drug, i.e., tranquilizer, hormone, antihistamine, etc., that will alter the natural actions of a cat, is forbidden. Evidence of such use as determined by the personal opinion of the Judge will result in the immediate disqualification of the entry.

42. The plucking of lockets or buttons is forbidden. Evidence of such plucking as determined by the personal judgment and opinion of the Judge will result in the immediate disqualification of the entry.

43. Any entry that is entered contrary to these Rules will be disqualified in all rings by the Show Committee. The Judge will disqualify any entry (including declawed cats and adult, whole males that do not have one descended testicle) entered contrary to these Rules if such an entry has not previously been disqualified. The Central Office will disqualify in all rings and void any wins of any entry that is entered contrary to these Rules should such entry not have been previously disqualified.

44. Cats that are disqualified are not eligible for any award in the ring where such disqualification applies with the exception of cats removed by the Veterinarian under Paragraph 37 above.

ARTICLE IV
ENTRY PROCEDURES

45. Any person entering a cat or kitten in a show held under the Rules of CFA shall by such act agree to abide by, and this person and the entry of this person shall be subject to, these Rules.

46. It is the responsibility of the owner to enter a cat correctly under its exact registered name, registered ownership, and registration number.

47. It is the responsibility of the owner to show a cat in its correct competitive category, class, and color class.

48. There must be an official CFA Entry Blank or facsimile thereof for each entry. All information required on the Entry Blank, with the exception of the owner's signature, must be typed or printed.

49. Each entry must have a name.

50. Each entry must be accompanied by the stipulated entry fee. No entry fee will be returned because of failure to bench except as provided in Paragraph 54b.

51. An entry must be the property of the person who is shown on the Entry Blank as the owner. The records in the Central Office are conclusive where the ownership of the entry is concerned. If title is transferred between the date of entry and the date of the show, the transfer must be reported to the Show Secretary. It is essential that transfer of ownership papers be filed with the Central Office immediately upon transfer of title.

52. An exhibitor entering a cat or kitten is strongly advised to have such entry inoculated before entry by a licensed Veterinarian against feline enteritis, feline rhinotracheitis, and calici viruses.

53. The claws of each entry must be clipped prior to benching.

ARTICLE V
PROCEDURES PRIOR TO BENCHING

54. Procedures for shows with veterinarian inspection.

a) For a show with veterinarian inspection, a licensed practising veterinarian acting for the club must examine each cat or kitten, including household pets and entries for sale or exhibition, prior to benching and shall disqualify any cat that shows evidence of fungus, fleas, ear mites, or any infectious or contagious illness.

b) In the event that the Veterinarian is unable to officiate or does not appear at the designated time for benching inspection and a substitute Veterinarian cannot be engaged to perform the benching inspection, the show shall be declared a show without veterinarian inspection. Those exhibitors who so request shall be reimbursed for all entry fees for the entries present, and their entries shall be marked "absent".

c) Cats arriving at a show the night before the show opens must be examined by the Veterinarian that night or placed in a room separated from the showroom until the Veterinarian is in attendance.

d) The owner or the owner's agent of each cat considered by the Veterinarian to be in good health shall be issued a card to that effect and thereby benched.

55. Inspection subsequent to benching for shows with veterinarian inspection.

a) The Veterinarian has the power to order the immediate removal of any sick cat from the show. Such cat will be entitled to all prizes awarded to it prior to the decision of the Veterinarian.

b) Any exhibitor, Judge, or Show Committee member suspecting any cat of having contagious or infectious illness may report same to the Show Manager, and it will be the duty of the Show Manager to remove such cat to a room apart from the regular showroom until the Veterinarian can pass upon the health of the suspected animal. In the event that the Veterinarian confirms and/or diagnoses contagious or infectious illness, the entry shall be disqualified, but awards received prior to the decision shall stand. If the Veterinarian certifies the entry as free from contagious or infectious illness, it shall be returned to the showroom and to normal competition. It shall be the responsibility of the owner or agent of the suspected Entry to obtain a Veterinarian's services although Show Management shall provide as much assistance as possible.

56. Procedures for shows without veterinarian inspection.

a) Show Management shall reserve the right to hold a

show without the provision of veterinarian inspection prior to benching.

b) The Show Secretary shall mark all those entries present for competition. The owner or the owner's agent of each cat present for competition shall be issued a card to that effect and thereby benched.

c) The Show Announcement for a show held under the provisions of this paragraph must include the following statement: "No Veterinarian inspection prior to benching will be required."

d) Any exhibitor, Judge, or Show Committee member suspecting any cat of having contagious or infectious illness may report same to the Show Manager and it will be the duty of the Show Manager to remove such cat to an area apart from the regular showroom until a Veterinarian can pass upon the health of the suspected cat. In the event that a Veterinarian confirms and/or diagnoses contagious or infectious illness, the entry shall be disqualified, but awards received prior to the decision shall stand. If a Veterinarian certifies the entry as free from contagious or infectious illness, it shall be returned to the showroom and to normal competition. It shall be the responsibility of the owner or agent of the suspected Entry to obtain a Veterinarian's services although Show Management shall provide as much assistance as possible.

57. In the event of a disqualification by a Veterinarian, all other entries from the same house or cattery and all cats for whom such exhibitor is agent shall be automatically disqualified and removed from the showroom immediately but shall retain, under the provisions of this Article, awards already received. In the event an agented cat is disqualified, the agent's own cats shall be disqualified.

58. a) A Copy of Article V of these Show Rules must be given to the Veterinarian for his careful review prior to his inspection of entries.

b) The Show Committee is responsible for answering any questions that the Veterinarian may have regarding these Rules.

59. Any decision based on the judgment of a Veterinarian acting under these Rules shall not be questioned.

ARTICLE VI
BENCHING PROCEDURES

60. No entry may be benched prior to inspection by the designated Veterinarian or prior to presentation to the Show Secretary, whichever is applicable.

61. When an exhibitor does not accompany his cat, a designated agent must be in attendance.

62. Late Arrivals: an entry arriving at the showroom after the stipulated hour may be benched, at the option of the Show Management, after examination by the designated Veterinarian, if applicable, at the expense of the exhibitor. For any ring in which its class is judged prior to its benching, it shall be marked absent and no class will be reopened.

63. The owner or agent of a late arrival is responsible for checking in with the Show Secretary and notifying all ring clerks and the master clerk once the late arrival is benched.

64. A substitute cat or kitten will not be accepted in place of any entry.

65. Absentees and Transfers: before judging begins, an exhibitor is responsible for reporting to the Show Secretary any of his cats that are absent, or that require transfer to another competitive category, class, color class, or that have a transfer of ownership.

66. No stacking of benching cages will be permitted.

67. When the contract Judge does not officiate, an exhibitor may withdraw his entries from competition in that ring prior to commencement of any judging, but may not remove them from the showroom for this reason.

68. Show Management shall assign benching cages for all entries. All entries of a particular exhibitor or those entries for which that exhibitor is the designated agent shall be benched together. No change of benching assignments shall be made without the permission of the Show Manager. Non-benched shows are not permitted.

69. Exhibitors will be allowed to display ribbons in exhibition cages. No decorations or advertising shall extend above the top of the cage. Ribbons or rosettes not won at a current show, with the exception of CFA National or Regional Award Rosettes, must be confined to the inside of the exhibit's cage.

70. Stud service in the showroom is absolutely prohibited. Any owner whose entry participates in such action is subject to disciplinary action under Article XIV, Section 4, of the CFA Constitution.

71. The Show Management may make such special rules specifying the time when the Household Pets entries are required to be in the showroom as it may desire, subject to the provision of Paragraph 73b.

ARTICLE VII
REMOVAL PROCEDURES

72. Kittens may be removed from the showroom at the completion of all Kitten judging.

73. All benched entries must remain in the show hall until the advertised hours of the show and must be present for competition in all rings entered. Failure to be present for competition may cause all awards won in that show by that entry to be voided with the following exceptions:

a) entries absent from rings judged after the advertised closing time of the final day of the show shall retain awards previously won but shall not be eligible for any awards made after their removal provided the Show Manager is notified of the cat's absence; and

b) Household Pets may be removed at an earlier hour than the closing of the show as determined by the Show

Management.

ARTICLE VIII
CHAMPIONSHIPS AND PREMIERSHIPS

74. Of each color class recognized as entitled to Championship or Premiership, the winning Open male or neuter and the winning female or spay will be awarded the "Winners Ribbon."

75. Winners claimed must all be won in the same color class and must be won under the *exact name in which the cat is registered*. The cat's registration number must be printed in the catalog. Ownership shown in the show catalog must agree with the registered ownership, subject to the provisions of Article IV, Paragraph 51.

76. Six (6) winners ribbons won under at least four (4) different Judges are required for Championship or Premiership confirmation. In Hawaii or Japan, four (4) winners ribbons won under at least three (3) different Judges are required for Championship or Premiership confirmation. When the advertised Judge is unable to officiate, wins made under the substitute Judge will be considered as having been earned under a "different Judge" regardless of the identity of such substitute Judge.

77. Each claimant of a Championship or Premiership must mail to the Central Office on the official CFA Championship Claim Form, or facsimile thereof, *before the opening day of the next show in which the cat is benched*, a list of shows where Winners Ribbons have been won with dates, names of shows, and Judges. Fee for confirmation is $1.00; certificates for framing are $3.00 extra.

78. A cat that has completed requirements for Championship or Premiership confirmation is ineligible for further competition in any subsequent show until this claim has been mailed.

ARTICLE IX
GRAND CHAMPIONSHIPS AND
GRAND PREMIERSHIPS

79. a) A cat eligible for and shown in the Champion or Premier Class will compete for Best Champion or Best Premier in Show. Best Champion will receive one point for every benched Champion defeated. Best Premier will receive two points for every benched Premier defeated.

b) Second Best Champion will receive 90% of the points received by the Best Champion. The Second Best Premier will receive 90% of the points received by the Best Premier.

c) For shows held in Hawaii and Japan, any Champion or Premier deemed worthy by the officiating Judge may be awarded the CFA Grand Ribbon. Seven (7) Grand Ribbons won under at least five (5) different Judges are required for Grand Championship or Grand Premiership confirmation.

For cats in Hawaii or Japan that have Grand Championship or Grand Premiership points, the following method will be used to convert said points to equivalent Grand

Ribbons: Divide the number of points earned by twenty (20) and discard any leftover points. (For example, a cat that has earned 87 Grand Points will be credited with 4 Grand Ribbons. Eighty-seven (87) divided by 20 = 4 and 7/20 remainder. Drop the 7/20 remainder.)

80. Best Longhair Premier and Best Shorthair Premier in All Breed rings will receive 2 points for every benched Premier defeated in show except that Best and 2nd Best Premier are not eligible for these points.

81. Breed and Division Points.
a) The following will receive one Grand Championship point for every benched Champion defeated in the Breed or Division:
Best Longhair Champion
Best Solid Color Persian Champion
Best Shaded Persian Champion
Best Smoke Persian Champion
Best Tabby Persian Champion
Best Parti-Color Persian Champion
Best Balinese Champion
Best Birman Champion
Best Himalayan Champion
Best Maine Coon Champion
Best Turkish Angora Champion
Best Shorthair Champion
Best Abyssinian Champion
Best American Shorthair Champion
Best American Wirehair Champion
Best Bombay Champion
Best Burmese Champion
Best Colorpoint Shorthair Champion
Best Egyptian Mau Champion
Best Exotic Shorthair Champion
Best Havana Brown Champion
Best Japanese Bobtail Champion
Best Korat Champion
Best Manx Champion
Best Oriental Shorthair Champion
Best Rex Champion
Best Russian Blue Champion
Best Scottish Fold Champion
Best Siamese Champion
b) The Second Best Longhair Champion will receive 90% of the points received by the Best Longhair Champion, and the Second Best Shorthair Champion will receive 90% of the points received by the Best Shorthair Champion.
c) Best and Second Best Champion and Best and Second Best Longhair and Shorthair Champion in All Breed shows are not eligible for Divisional Points.

82. Two Hundred (200) points are required for Grand Championship; one hundred and fifty (150) points for Grand Premiership.

83. Points must be won under at least three (3) different Judges.

84. Cats that have completed requirements for Grand Championship or Grand Premiership will be automatically confirmed by the Central Office. Certificate of confirmation will be mailed as soon as possible after show records are received and wins have been recorded.

85. After certificate of confirmation has been mailed, a cat is ineligible to compete in the Champion or Premier Class and must be transferred and compete in the Grand Champion or Grand Premier Class at any subsequent show.

ARTICLE X
VIOLATIONS

86. A protest asserting an alleged violation of these rules by any show official, Judge, exhibitor, or member club may be made by an exhibitor or by a member of a member club and shall first be made to the Show Committee in writing at the show or within thirty (30) days following the show. The Show Committee shall endeavor to gather all pertinent facts concerning the alleged violation(s) and in the event the Show Committee deems the protest to be supported by substantial evidence, the written protest and all relevant matter gathered by the Show Committee shall be forthwith forwarded to the CFA Executive Board.

The Executive Board may at its option proceed to hear the protest after giving the party charged due notice and opportunity to be heard in accordance with Article XIV of the CFA Constitution. Upon a finding of guilty, the Board shall prescribe punishment in accordance with Article XIV of the CFA Constitution.

87. Whether or not a formal protest has been made, the CFA Executive Board shall have full power to inquire into any alleged violation(s) of these rules by any show official, Judge, exhibitor, or member club provided that notice and opportunity to be heard is first given to the party charged.

ARTICLE XI
SHOW DATES

88. Show dates and Judges are subject to approval of the Executive Board, and application for such dates must be made to the Central Office at least 91 days prior to the opening day of the show.

89. No show date shall be denied because the same date has been scheduled by one or more other clubs.

90. A Member Club requesting show dates must be good standing for the given year.

ARTICLE XII
SHOW LICENSES

91. A member club or Regional Director(s) holding any type of show where CFA awards are to be made must schedule a show date and secure a license. A member club or Regional Director(s) applying for a license shall by such act be deemed to have agreed to conduct the show in strict conformity with these Rules, and, if called upon by the Executive Board or Judging Program Chairman to do so, submit a report on the work and conduct of the officiating Judge(s).

92. Application for license must be made at least 90 days prior to the opening day of the show on the official form that may be obtained from the Central Office. The Show Secretary of the sponsoring club must submit to the Central Office for the approval of the Executive Board the following:
a) license applications for each ring (in triplicate); and
b) ONE executed copy of each judging contract.

These documents must be submitted as a package, and the Central Office will not issue the license for any show until all the papers have been received in proper order. The Office will return copies of the approved licenses to the sponsoring clubs.

Once a show license is approved by the Central Office, no change in club sponsorship for that show will be allowed.

93. Any club or Regional Director(s) may sponsor any type or number of rings to be held concurrently, provided that a cat may not be entered in more than four rings. When shows are held of a nature that would permit certain cats to be eligible for entry in more than four rings, the Show Committee may so state on the Show Announcement and Entry Blank in which shows such cats are to be entered.

94. Any club or Regional Director(s) may obtain licenses for as many All Breed and/or Specialty rings as required, all to be held concurrently. Any member club may request any other member club to sponsor one or more of its concurrent rings, but in such case the application for show license must be signed by the sponsoring club's secretary.

95. In a two (2) day eight (8) specialty ring show, a club may make application for a license to hold a Best of the Best competition. The only cats or kittens eligible for the Best of the Bests competition shall be those cats or kittens that have received an award of Best, Second Best, or Third Best Cat (Championship or Premiership) or Best, Second Best, or Third Best Kitten. The Judge for the Best of the Bests competition must be an Approved All Breed Judge who has not judged any of the concurrent rings. The Judge will select the five (5) Best Cats (Championship and Premiership) and five (5) Best Kittens. Participation in the Best of the Bests competition shall not be considered a violation of the provision in Paragraph 93 that a cat may not be entered in more than four rings.

96. A Best of the Bests Show will not be licensed for a one (1) day show or for a show holding All Breed rings.

ARTICLE XIII
RESPONSIBILITIES OF SHOW MANAGEMENT

97. *It is the policy of CFA to penalize member clubs by suspension or expulsion for shows that exhibit a flagrant disregard of these Show Rules.*

98. SHOW MANAGEMENT when used in these Rules refers to:

a) the club sponsoring the show or its Executive (governing) Board; or

b) the Regional Director(s) in the case of a Regional Show.

99. The Show Management must select a Show Committee consisting of a Show Manager, a Show Secretary, a Show Entry Clerk, and at least two (2) other persons who must be thoroughly familiar with these Show Rules and show procedures.

100. Assignment of any duty to one of these individuals does not exempt the Show Management (sponsoring club) from ultimate responsibility for proper observance of these Show Rules.

101. The Show Management must state the names of all Judges when soliciting prizes subject to the exception in Paragraph 108b.

102. When the contract Judge is unable to officiate, the Show Management should secure the services of a CFA Judge authorized to officiate at that type of show. A judging contract must be signed prior to the start of judging, a copy being sent to the Central Office as soon as possible.

103. a) Should a Judge become incapacitated while judging and be incapable of completing the assignment, the Show Management shall proceed as if the Judge had not appeared (see Paragraph 102), but awards made prior to that time shall stand. Once having left the ring in favor of the substitute Judge, the advertised Judge shall not return to that ring. If it is impractical for the club to bring in a substitute Judge to officiate who is qualified under these Rules, judging in the ring of the incapacitated Judge shall cease, awards made prior to that time stand; the club will refund $\frac{1}{4}$ of the entry fee involved, and CFA will reimburse the club for such refund.

b) In the event that a Judge is incapacitated because of a bite or injury received as a result of judging duties, such as a scratch, or a cut, and the officiating Judge is able to proceed if suitable assistance is provided, the Clerk for that Judge's ring, the Master Clerk, or a member of the Show Management may assist the Judge in handling.

104. The Show Management will take all reasonable care of cats, carriers, and other personal property of the exhibitors, but it is expressly stipulated that neither the Show Management, nor any other club member, nor any show official, nor the club sponsoring or conducting the show shall be liable for any loss or damage to such property.

105. Show Management must provide illumination (most closely simulating daylight as may be reasonably available) in each judging ring sufficient to allow thorough examination of each entry.

106. The Show Management should provide a watchman in the showroom during the hours when the show is not open to the public if entries are to remain in the showroom overnight. If for any reason under such circumstances it is not feasible to provide such a watchman, this fact must be stated in the Show Announcement.

107. The Show Management is responsible for providing the number of judging rings and judging cages required under these Rules. In the event that Household Pets are judged by a separate Judge, a ring must be provided for his use, and none of the regular officiating Judges shall be required to relinquish his ring for the use of the Household Pet Judge.

108. Number of entries permissible:

a) No club shall accept more than 400 entries to be judged by any one Judge over a full two-day period. For one-day shows, or where the Judge will not have a ring available for more than one day, no club shall accept more than 175 such entries. No allowance shall be made for absentees. (Note that if separate shows are held for non-championship and non-premiership classes in order to comply with this rule, additional judging rings must be provided.)

b) Where, after the Show Announcement has been printed and distributed, the sponsoring club desires to add an additional Judge or Judges to judge Kitten, AOV, Provisional Breed, or Household Pet Classes, such a change will not be considered a violation of Paragraph 101. Such a procedure is not recommended since the CFA Board is of the opinion that Judges should officiate as advertised, and the relaxation herein provided is effective because these Rules limit the number of entries to be judged by any one Judge. If an unadvertised Judge is used pursuant to this subsection, it is suggested that Kittens be the last classes to be dropped from the ring of the advertised Judge. In any event, the names of the various Judges under contract must be published in the show catalog.

109. The Show Management shall determine the amount of the entry fee, which must be at least $1.00 per ring.

110. Each Judge must be paid all moneys due him for expenses and judging fees in U.S. funds prior to the Judge's leaving the showroom at the completion of his judging.

111. Cats or kittens may not be given away at CFA shows by CFA clubs or individuals; however, cats or kittens may be placed by incorporated humane societies.

No animals other than domestic felines shall be allowed in the show halls.

112. Clubs are required to provide hotel accommodations for each Judge for the night before the beginning of that Judge's judging, the night after the completion of that Judge's judging, and for each night in between, if any.

113. In the event that a show is cancelled after licensing or after contracts have been signed for Judges, the Show Management must immediately notify all Judges and the Central Office by Western Union Telegram.

ARTICLE XIV
RESPONSIBILITIES OF SHOW COMMITTEE

114. The order of judging may be changed at the discretion of the Show Committee in an emergency. However, every possible effort should be made to adhere to the published show schedule.

115. Questions about the age or eligibility in Open or Kitten Classes or eligibility in competitive category, class, or color class must be referred to the Show Committee, which shall investigate the matter. In such cases the class must be judged as though the doubtful exhibit is eligible, and one additional award allotted so that the regular list of awards may be made if the doubtful exhibit is disqualified.

116. Any entry entered contrary to these Rules shall be disqualified by the Show Committee.

117. In all cases where an Apprentice or Approval Pending Judge is used, or when a Trainee is Judging Household Pets, a questionnaire supplied by the Chairman of the Judging Program *must* be filled out and signed by a majority of the Show Committee and forwarded to the Chairman of the Judging Program within 15 days of the close of the show.

118. The Show Committee shall receive and act upon any protests received concerning violations of these Rules under the provisions of Article X, Paragraph 86.

119. Acceptance of entries for exhibition or sale – see Article II, Paragraph 33.

120. Rejection of entries – see Article II, Paragraph 32.

121. The Show Committee may determine in which show rings exhibits may be entered – see Article XII, Paragraph 93.

ARTICLE XV
RESPONSIBILITIES OF SHOW MANAGER

122. The Show Manager is responsible for all aspects of conducting the show in accordance with these Rules with the exception of those duties specifically allotted to the Show Secretary or Show Entry Clerk. As a member of the Show Committee, he is jointly responsible for duties allotted to that Committee.

123. The Show Manager is responsible for making arrangements with exhibitors for removal of cats as provided in Article V, Paragraphs 55b and 56d, and Article VII.

124. It is the responsibility of the Show Manager that the judging begin at the advertised hour.

125. The Show Manager must provide suitable utensils and disinfectants for the use of the Veterinarians, Judges, and Stewards.

126. The Show Manager must provide an adequate First Aid Kit at an announced location in the show hall.

127. The Show Manager must provide litter sufficient for each entry.

128. a) Clerks must be engaged for each judging ring and a Master Clerk must be engaged to consolidate and check all of the judging records of the show.

b) The position of Master Clerk must be filled by a CFA Licensed Certified or Master Clerk (except in Hawaii and Japan). When possible, the positions of Chief Ring Clerks should be filled by CFA licensed clerks.

c) The CFA Licensed Certified or Master Clerk performing the function of Master Clerk shall be compensated at the rate of 15 cents per catalog entry. CFA Certified Clerks performing the Chief Ring Clerk function should negotiate terms for appropriate compensation with the sponsoring club. Such arrangements shall be made at the discretion of the club and the clerk. Contracts are recommended. Judges may act as Master Clerks, CF Rule 224.

129. Show Schedules.

a) The Show Manager must provide a Schedule of Judging for each ring in a form readily accessible to all exhibitors from which there should be no deviation with the exception of the provisions of Paragraph 114.

b) It is suggested that a larger number of entries be scheduled for each Judge on the first day of the show than on the second day.

c) It is recommended that the Burmese and the Abyssinians not be scheduled to be judged consecutively in any ring.

130. The Show Manager *must not* permit caging to be dismantled until all judging has been completed, including the finals.

131. The Show Manager should insofar as possible notify each clerk of any entries removed from the showroom prior to the start of the finals in his ring.

ARTICLE XVI
RESPONSIBILITIES OF SHOW SECRETARY

132. The Show Secretary must submit the show License Application to the Central Office as outlined in Article XII, Paragraph 92.

133. Judges Books, Entry Blanks, and copies of the Show Rules will be sent to the Show Secretary approximately four (4) months prior to the show date. Additional Supplies may be ordered at the usual fees.

134. The Show Secretary must file a copy of the Show Announcement and Entry Blank with the Central Office as soon as printed.

135. The Show Secretary must send a copy of the Show Announcement to the officiating Judge or Judges and the Regional Director.

136. The Show Secretary must advise the officiating Judges of the accommodations that have been made for them and the available ground transportation between airport, showroom, and hotel.

137. The Show Secretary is responsible for the preparing of the Judges' Books, including those for judging Best of the Bests competitions, which shall be in sequence by catalog numbers. A minimum of five (5) lines must be left between color classes. The color class number, age (indicated in years and months), and class for each entry must appear in the Judges' Books. At least two (2) spaces should be left between each class (Open, Champion, and Grand Champion) to allow for transfers. When a color class includes entries of more than one color, the exact color indicated on the Entry Blank must be entered in the Judges' books.

138. a) In a show without veterinarian inspection, the Show Secretary shall mark all those entries present for competition and therefore benched. The owner or the owner's agent of each cat benched shall be issued a card to that effect.

b) After benching, the Show Secretary must prepare and deliver to each ring a list of catalog numbers of entries that are absent, transferred, or withdrawn. Should an entry be withdrawn, the word "withdrawn" must appear opposite the catalog number in the Judges' Book.

139. The Show Secretary must fill all orders for marked catalogs. Should it become impracticable to fill any such order, the purchase price of such marked catalog must be promptly returned to the person ordering it.

140. The Show Secretary must send the following to the Central Office by PRIORITY MAIL within 12 hours of the close of the show:

a) one catalog completely marked for all rings and signed by the Master Clerk;

b) a complete set of Judging Slips, including Finals Sheets, for each ring;

c) a copy of the Transfer and Absentee List; and

d) a complete list of exhibitors' names and addresses and entry numbers if not included in the catalog.

This does not apply to Household Pet Exhibitors.

141. The Show Secretary must send a fully marked catalog to the Regional Director within one week after the close of the show.

142. The Show Secretary must retain in club records for one year the original entry blanks with the exception of official entry blanks sent to the Central Office for verification of a correction made by the Master Clerk because of a typographical error. See Paragraph 154. The Central Office may request that a blank or blanks be submitted as verification of a valid entry.

143. The Show Secretary must retain the posted Judges' Slips and Finals Sheets from each ring in club records for one calendar year.

ARTICLE XVII
RESPONSIBILITIES OF SHOW ENTRY CLERK

144. The Show Entry Clerk shall send to each prospective exhibitor a Show Announcement and official CFA Entry Blanks or facsimiles thereof.

145. The Show Entry Clerk must acknowledge receipt of all entries within a reasonable length of time.

146. The Show Entry Clerk must enter a cat in the breed and color class indicated on the Entry Blank regardless of the cat's registration number.

ARTICLE XVIII
RESPONSIBILITIES OF CLERKS

147. The Cheif Clerk of each ring shall function as the Executive Assistant of the officiating Judge.

148. Each Chief Clerk shall mark a catalog as the classes are judged and ribbons and rosettes are awarded, indicating 1st, 2nd, 3rd, winners, Best of Color, and 2nd Best of Color in all classes, as well as the final Bests. All absentees and transfers must be clearly marked.

149. When an award is withheld by the officiating Judge under the provisions of Article XXVIII, Paragraphs 237 and 238, the Chief Clerk shall clearly mark in the official catalog the reason: i.e., "Wrong Color Class," "No Award – Condition," or "NFA (No Further Award) IM (Insufficient Merit)."

150. The Chief Ring Clerk shall check the Judge's Slips against the marked catalog, shall advise the Judge as soon as prudently practical of any discrepancies, and shall initial completely checked slips.

151. Each Chief Clerk shall initial the Judge's Slips as each class is completed. The checked and initialled Judge's Slips shall then be turned over to the Master Clerk.

152. The Master Clerk shall consolidate all judging records into a master catalog. He shall check for completeness and mechanical correctness. Discrepancies shall be reported to the appropriate Chief Ring Clerk for resolution with the Judge. The Master Clerk is responsible for posting slips that have been fully checked.

153. The Master Clerk shall sign the cover of the official CFA catalog and note his current clerking status, his address, and telephone number.

154. The Master Clerk is authorized to make corrections in ink in the official catalog so that the entry information, if printed in error, corresponds to the entry information on the official entry blank. When such a correction is made, the official entry blank must be sent to the Central Office with the Master Catalog.

The Master Clerk is also authorized to make such corrections if the exhibitor has been notified by the Central Office that the cat has been incorrectly entered in a previous show.

155. The Chief Ring Clerk shall provide both the Judge and the Show Secretary with fully marked catalogs for his ring at the close of the show.

156. The Master Clerk will check each Judge's finals for mechanical correctness before the Judge leaves the show-hall and shall provide the Show Secretary with a fully marked catalog, including all rings, at the close of the show. (See Paragraph 221.)

157. The Chief Ring Clerk is responsible for notifying Chief Clerks in remaining rings when the Judge in that ring disqualifies any cat that bites or that in his judgment is behaving in a recalcitrant or threatening manner.

ARTICLE XIX
SHOW ANNOUNCEMENT

158. The Show Announcement must include the following:

a) the names of all Judges subject to the exception in Article XIII, Paragraph 108b;

b) advice to exhibitors who are showing cats or kittens that they be inoculated by a licensed Veterinarian against feline enteritis, feline rhinotracheitis, and calici viruses before entry;

c) the claws of each entry must be clipped prior to benching;

d) the notice "All Championship, Premiership, and *registered* Kitten entries will be scored for the CFA National Awards and Regional Awards; Registration numbers for cats must be printed in the catalog; registration numbers for kittens must be printed or written in ink in the catalog;

e) if wild animals or hybrid crosses between feral cats and domestic cats are to be on exhibition in conjunction with a show, their presence must be indicated in the Show Announcement;

f) when entries remain in the showroom overnight, if no watchman is to be provided during the hours the show is not open, this information must be indicated in the Show Announcement;

g) the hours of Veterinarian inspection or entry presentation to the Show Secretary, the hour judging will begin, and the advertised hour of closing;

h) a statement to the effect that the club reserves the right to add Judges not named in the Show Announcement to judge Non-Championship and Non-Premiership classes;

i) for shows without veterinarian inspection, the statement: "No veterinarian inspection prior to benching will be required."

j) the Show Announcement must state what climate control facilities will be provided at the show hall;

k) the size of benching cages;

l) if smoking will not be permitted in the showroom, this information must be indicated on the first page of the Show Announcement; and

m) if available, a phone number within the show hall be printed in the show announcement and/or confirmation of entry so that in case of an emergency an exhibitor can be reached.

159. No award requiring the decision of an officiating Judge other than the official CFA awards included in the Rules shall be offered.

ARTICLE XX
CATALOG

160. Show catalogs must not be smaller than $5\frac{1}{2} \times 8\frac{1}{2}$ inches.

161. An Official CFA Championship Claim Form or facsimile thereof must be printed or inserted in the show catalog.

162. Pages must be numbered.

163. The cover of the introductory (credit) page must contain the following information:

a) the full name of the club or clubs (including all Specialty Clubs) sponsoring the show;

b) the names and addresses of all officiating Judges;

c) the names of the Show Committee, indicating their positions as officials of the show; and

d) a notice that all Championship and Premiership entries and all *registered* Kittens (whose registration numbers are printed or written in ink in the catalog) will be scored for CFA National awards and Regional Awards.

164. All entries must appear in numerical order in the printed catalog that is required at shows held under these Rules. *No* addenda to the catalog will be permitted unless proof of an unintentional omission (including the original entry blank) be accepted by the Show Committee subject to the approval of the CFA Executive Board. Any cat or kitten included in an unauthorized addendum will be disqualified by the Central Office.

165. The name of each entry; its CFA registration number; date of birth, sire, dam, and breeder, if available; and the name and Region of residence of the owner – all must be PRINTED in the catalog. Each entry must have a name.

166. A list of exhibitors' and addresses with entry numbers should be printed in the catalog. In the event that this can not be done, a separate complete list of exhibitors' names and addresses with entry numbers *must* be forwarded to the Central Office with the completely marked catalog. This rule does not apply to Household Pet exhibitors.

167. CFA titles of Champion, Grand Champion, Premier, and Grand Premier must not appear in the catalog listing as a part of an entry's name.

168. If the Show Standard for any breed is printed in the catalog, it must be the exact CFA Standard for the breed.

169. When multiple rings are held concurrently, the catalog *must* be printed in the following manner:

a) a column for each ring must be headed with the name or initials of the Judge;

b) when a cat is not entered in a particular ring, "xxx" must be printed in the column for that ring;

c) the entry's cage number, its name (in capital letters with no title indicated), and spaces for its awards *must* appear on the same line;

d) all headings [Name of Breed, Color Class Number, Color Class Number, and the Competitive Class (if applicable)] should be centred on the page;

e) examples:

SIAMESE

Class 270 – Chocolate Point Male – OPEN

MAYPOLE MING'S SON. 270-1359. 175. — — — —
5/5/76. Maypole Ming ex Maypole
Lass. Br.-Own. Charles Smith. (6)

Alternate Catalog Format.

The Competitive Class is not included in the group headings, but is noted below each catalog entry number as in the following example. The following abbreviations should be used: "OPN" for Open, "CH" for Champion, and "GRC" for Grand Champion.

Class 270 – Chocolate Point Male

JAY'S JOHN BOY. 270-1067.   178. — — — —
3/4/75. Jay's Chocolate Lass ex Jay's   CH
Johnson. Br.-Own. Maggie Jones. (6)

f) if the entry is listed as being for sale on the Entry Blank, this information should be entered in the catalog following the owner's name;

g) entries in the catalog should appear in the following order:

Non-Championship: Kittens, Provisional Breeds, and Miscellaneous (non-competitive).

Championship: Longhair and Shorthair. AOV entries should appear at the end of the Championship entries for the particular breed.

Premiership: Longhair and Shorthair.

Non-Championship: Household Pets; and

h) the Best in Show pages, which must appear in the catalog, shall conform to the appropriate CFA format.

ARTICLE XXI
PRIZES AND TROPHIES

170. Prizes consistent with official CFA awards included in these Rules, where specified in the Show Announcement, must be given.

171. The only prizes allowed at shows held under these Rules are Ribbons, Cups, Trophies, CFA Stud Books, CFA Yearbooks, hardcover books on the subject of cats, magazine subscriptions, cash Specials, Savings Bonds, and class prize money. There is no limitation on the prizes that may be offered in the Household Pets Classes.

ARTICLE XXII
RIBBONS AND ROSETTES

172. Ribbons or rosettes must be awarded for First, Second, Third, Winners, Best of Color, and Second Best of Color.

173. Rosettes must carry the name of the club sponsoring the ring and the CFA insignia.

174. On all ribbons or rosettes designating prizes to be awarded in the various classes, the following words must appear: First, Second, Third, or Winners, and the CFA insignia. In the case of a standard Household Pet Show, the words "Household Pet Merit Award" and the CFA insignia must appear.

175. The colors for all ribbons or rosettes designating prizes must be as follows:

First Prize	Dark Blue
Second Prize	Red
Third Prize	Yellow
Championship Winners	Red, White, & Blue
Premiership Winners	Purple & White
Best of Breed or Division	Brown
Second Best of Breed or Division	Orange
Best Champion of Breed or Division	Purple
Best of Color	Black
Second Best of Color	White
Grand Ribbon (Hawaii and Japan)	Green
Household Pet Merit Award	Red & White

176. For ribbons and rosettes awarded for Best in Show, it is suggested that the Second Best ribbons and rosettes be of a lighter shade of the same color used for the Best ribbons and rosettes.

177. A ribbon or rosette *must* be awarded for the following Bests that carry Grand Championship or Grand Premiership points:

Best and 2nd Best Champion
Best Champion of Breed or Division
Best and 2nd Best Longhair Champion
Best and 2nd Best Shorthair Champion
Best and 2nd Best Premier
Best Longhair Premier
Best Shorthair Premier

178. It is suggested that clubs offer the following ribbons or rosettes:

Best Cat
2nd Best Cat
3rd Best Cat
4th Best Cat (where applicable)
5th Best Cat (where applicable)
Best and 2nd Best Grand Champion
Best and 2nd Best Champion
Best and 2nd Best Open
Best and 2nd Best of Breed or Division
Best Kitten
2nd Best Kitten
3rd Best Kitten
4th Best Kitten (where applicable)
5th Best Kitten (where applicable)
Best Cat in Premiership Classes
2nd Best Cat in Premiership Classes
3rd Best Cat in Premiership Classes
4th Best Cat in Premiership Classes (where applicable)
5th Best Cat in Premiership Classes (where applicable)

Best Household Pet

179. Ribbons or rosettes may be offered by CFA clubs and by non-affiliated clubs and by foreign cat associations, but they may not be offered by individuals.

180. Awards made by CFA Judges at CFA licensed shows may not be made the basis of any award other than those made by CFA, a CFA Region, or a CFA member club, provided that this provision shall not be construed to prevent donations of trophies or rosettes by CFA member clubs or non-affiliated clubs or foreign cat associations to the club sponsoring the show.

ARTICLE XXIII
SHOW RINGS

181. Judging cages in show rings may be placed in a straight row, in a U-shape, or in an L-shape.

182. All corners must be at an angle of at least 90 degrees.

183. In U-shaped rings there must be a minimum of six cages between the corners.

184. It is recommended that twelve (12) or more judging cages be provided in each ring. However, a minimum of nine (9) judging cages must be provided.

185. A buffer zone must be provided between judging cages and any walkway for spectators.

186. a) Judging cages must be provided with durable non-porous washable bottoms per unit.
b) Judging cages must be provided with solid, non-porous washable partitions between cages.

187. Judging cages must be provided with doors that "swing" open horizontally rather than doors that slide up and down.

188. Adult, whole males or neuters, including Household Pets, must not be placed in adjoining cages at any time. For the purposes of this rule, two corner cages at a 90 degree or greater angle to each other are considered to be adjoining cages.

189. Females may be placed in cages between males in any class at the option of the officiating Judge, who shall have the sole responsibility for determining in each class whether this shall be done.

190. Stacking of cages is not permitted.

191. Separate judging rings must be provided for each Judge officiating on a given day except for rings used only for non-championship.

192. Placement of booths using electrical devices such as engraving machines, drills, or saws, in either the benching area or the judging area is prohibited.

ARTICLE XXIV
COLOR CLASSES

193. Each Championship or Premiership Show must have classes available for each Breed and color in Championship or Premiership recognized for the show licensed, subject to the limitation in Article XII, Paragraph 93. In addition, classes may be provided for Kittens, AOVs, Household Pets, Provisional Breeds, Miscellaneous (non-competitive), and cats placed on exhibition.

194. An Entry Clerk must enter a cat in the Breed and Color Class indicated on the Entry Blank regardless of the cat's registration number. It is the responsibility of the exhibitor to enter a cat in the correct color class.

195. The following breeds and colors are recognized as entitled to win Championship or Premiership honors:

BALINESE	CLASS NUMBER	
	MALE	FEMALE
Chocolate Point	1270	1271
Seal Point	1272	1273
Lilac Point	1274	1275
Blue Point	1276	1277

BIRMAN (Sacred Cat of Burma)

Chocolate Point	180	181
Seal Point	182	183
Lilac Point	184	185
Blue Point	186	187

HIMALAYAN

Chocolate Point	170	171
Seal Point	172	173
Lilac Point	174	175
Blue Point	176	177
Flame Point	178	179
Tortie Point	—	193
Blue-Cream Point	—	189
Solid Color (Chocolate or Lilac)	194	195

MAINE COON CAT

Solid Color	1700	1701
Tabby	1736	1737
Parti-Color	1796	1797
OMMC (Other Maine Coon Colors)	1796	1797

PERSIAN

SOLID COLOR DIVISION

Blue-Eyed White	100	101

Copper-Eyed White	102	103
Odd-Eyed White	104	105
Blue	106	107
Black	108	109
Red	110	111
Peke-Face Red	112	113
Cream	114	115

SHADED DIVISION

Chinchilla Silver	130	131
Shaded Silver	132	133
Shell Cameo	160	161
Shaded Cameo	162	163
Chinchilla Golden	1170	1171
Shaded Golden	1172	1173
Shell Tortoiseshell	—	1175
Shaded Tortoiseshell	—	1177

SMOKE DIVISION

Black Smoke	134	135
Blue Smoke	138	139
Cameo (Red) Smoke	164	165
Tortoiseshell Smoke	—	125

TABBY DIVISION

Silver Tabby	136	137
Silver Mackerel Tabby	136M	137M
Silver Patched Tabby (Torbie)	136T	137T
Red Tabby	140	141
Red Mackerel Tabby	140M	141M
Peke-Face Red Tabby	142	143
Brown Tabby	144	145
Brown Mackerel Tabby	144M	145M
Brown Patched Tabby (Torbie)	144T	145T
Blue Tabby	152	153
Blue Mackerel Tabby	152M	153M
Blue Patched Tabby (Torbie)	152T	153T
Cream Tabby	154	155
Cream Mackerel Tabby	154M	155M
Cameo Tabby	166	167
Cameo Mackerel Tabby	166M	167M

PARTI-COLOR DIVISION

Tortoiseshell	—	147
Calico (White with Black and Red) or Dilute Calico (White with Blue and	—	149

Cream)

Blue-Cream	—	151
Bi-Color (Red & White, Blue & White, Cream & White, or Black & White or Persian Van (Red & White, Blue & White, Cream & White, Black & White, Calico & White, or Blue-Cream & White)	190	191

TURKISH ANGORA

SOLID COLOR CLASS	1800	1801
(Blue-Eyed White, Amber-Eyed White, Odd-Eyed White, Blue, or Black)		
TABBY COLOR CLASS	1836	1837
(Silver Tabby, Red Tabby, Brown Tabby, or Blue Tabby)		
PARTI-COLOR CLASS	—	1849
(Calico, Red & White, Blue & White, Cream & White, or Black & White)		
OTAC (Other Turkish Angora Colors)	1890	1891
(Black Smoke or Blue Smoke)		

ABYSSINIAN

Ruddy	380	381
Red	382	383

AMERICAN SHORTHAIR

SOLID COLOR CLASS	700	701
(Blue-Eyed White, Gold-Eyed White, Odd-Eyed White, Blue, Black, Red, or Cream)		
TABBY CLASS	736	737
[Silver Tabby (Classic, Mackerel, or Patched Pattern); Red Tabby (Classic or Mackerel Pattern); Blue Tabby (Classic, Mackerel, or Patched Pattern); Brown Tabby (Classic, Mackerel, or Patched Pattern); Cream Tabby (Classic or Mackerel Pattern; Cameo Tabby (Classic or Mackerel Pattern)]		
PARTI-COLOR CLASS	770	771
[Bi-Color (Red & White, Blue & White, Cream & White, or Black & White); Tortoiseshell; Calico (White with Black and Red) or Dilute Calico		

(White with Blue and Cream); or
Blue-Cream]

OASHC (Other American Shorthair Colors)	790	791

[Chinchilla Silver, Shaded Silver, Black Smoke, Blue Smoke, Shell Cameo, Shaded Cameo, or Smoke (Red) Cameo]

AMERICAN WIREHAIR

All Colors	9900	9901

BOMBAY

Black	410	411

BURMESE

Sable	400	401

COLORPOINT SHORTHAIR

Solid Color Point (Red or Cream Point)	2278	2279
Lynx Point (Seal, Chocolate, Blue, Lilac or Red Lynx Point)	2254	2255
Parti-Color Point (Seal-Tortie, Chocolate Cream, Blue-Cream, or Lilac Cream Point)	—	2249

EGYPTIAN MAU

All Colors	840	841

EXOTIC SHORTHAIR

SOLID COLOR CLASS	7700	7701

(Blue-Eyed White, Copper-Eyed White, Odd-Eyed White, Blue, Black, Red, or Cream)

TABBY CLASS	7736	7737

[Silver Tabby (Classic, Mackerel, or Patched Pattern); Red Tabby (Classic or Mackerel Pattern); Blue Tabby (Classic, Mackerel, or Patched Pattern); Brown Tabby (Classic Mackerel, or Patched Pattern); Cream Tabby (Classic or Mackerel Pattern); Cameo Tabby (Classic or Mackerel Pattern)]

PARTI-COLOR CLASS	7770	7771

[Bi-Color (Red & White, Blue & White, Cream & White, or Black & White); Tortoiseshell; Calico (White with Black and Red) or Dilute Calico (White with Blue and Cream); or Blue-Cream]

OESHC (Other Exotic Shorthair Colors)	7790	7791

[Chinchilla Silver, Shaded Silver, Black Smoke, Blue Smoke, Shell Cameo, Shaded Cameo, or Smoke (Red) Cameo]

HAVANA BROWN

Brown	408	409

JAPANESE BOBTAIL

White	6602	6603
Black	6608	6609
Red	6610	6611
Black and White	6660	6661
Red and White	6662	6663
Mi-Ke (Tri-Color)	—	6649
Tortoiseshell	—	6647
OJBC	6690	6691

KORAT

Silver Blue	504	505

MANX

SOLID COLOR CLASS	600	601

(Blue-Eyed White, Copper-Eyed White, Odd-Eyed White, Blue, Black, Red, or Cream)

TABBY CLASS	636	637

[Silver Tabby (Classic, Mackerel, or Patched Pattern); Red Tabby (Classic or Mackerel Pattern); Blue Tabby (Classic, Mackerel, or Patched Pattern); Brown Tabby (Classic, Mackerel, or Patched Pattern); Cream Tabby (Classic or Mackerel Pattern); Cameo Tabby (Classic or Mackerel Pattern)]

PARTI-COLOR CLASS	660	661
[Bi-Color (Red & White, Blue & White, Cream & White, or Black & White); Tortoiseshell; Calico (White with Black and Red) or Dilute Calico (White with Blue and Cream); or Blue-Cream]		

OMC (Other Manx Colors)	690	691
(Any other color or pattern with the exception of those showing evidence of hybridization resulting in the colors chocolate, lavender, the himalayan pattern, or these combinations with white, etc. Cats with no more white than a locket and/or button do not qualify for these color classes. Such cats shall be judged in the color class of their basic color with no penalty for such locket and/or button.)		

ORIENTAL SHORTHAIR

SOLID COLOR CLASS	2300	2301
(White, Ebony, Blue, Chestnut, Lavender, Red, or Cream)		

SHADED CLASS	2332	2333
(Silver or Cameo)		

SMOKE CLASS	2334	2335
(Ebony, Blue, Chestnut, Lavender, or Cameo Smoke)		

TABBY CLASS	2336	2337
(All-Patterns – Ebony, Blue, Chestnut Lavender, Red, Cream, Silver, or Cameo)		

PARTI-COLOR CLASS	—	2347
(Tortoiseshell, Blue-Cream, Chestnut-Tortie, or Lavender-Cream)		

REX

SOLID COLOR CLASS	900	901
(Blue-Eued White, Gold-Eyed White, Odd-Eyed White, Blue, Black, Red, or Cream)		

TABBY CLASS	936	937
[Silver Tabby (Classic, Mackerel, or Patched Pattern); Red Tabby (Classic or Mackerel Pattern); Blue Tabby (Classic, Mackerel, or Patched Pattern); Brown Tabby (Classic, Mackerel, or Patched Pattern); Cream Tabby (Classic or Mackerel Pattern); Cameo Tabby (Classic or Mackerel Pattern)]		

PARTI-COLOR CLASS	960	961
[Bi-Color (Red & White, Blue & White, Cream & White, or Black & White); Tortoiseshell; Calico (White with Black and Red) or Dilute Calico (White with Blue and Cream); or Blue-Cream]		

ORC (Other Rex Colors)	990	991
(Any other color or pattern with the exception of those showing evidence of hybridization resulting in the colors chocolate, lavender, the himalayan pattern, or these combinations with white, etc. Cats with no more white than a locket and/or button do not qualify for these color classes. Such cats shall be judged in the color class of their basic color with no penalty for such locket and/or button.)		

RUSSIAN BLUE

Blue	500	501

SCOTTISH FOLD

All Colors	8800	8801

SIAMESE

Chocolate Point	270	271
Seal Point	272	273
Lilac Point	274	275
Blue Point	276	277

196. For KITTEN CLASSES, the letter "K" should be added to the correct breed or color class number.

For PREMIERSHIP CLASSES, the letter "P" should be added to the correct breed or color class number.

197. *HOUSEHOLD PETS*

All Varieties	892	893

198. *PROVISIONAL BREEDS*

BRITISH SHORTHAIR

All Colors	2500	2501

SOMALI

Ruddy or Red	1380	1381

199. The AOV (Any Other Variety) Class is for an adult, whole cat or registered kitten, the ancestry of which entitles it to Championship competition, but which does not colorwise, coatwise, or, in the case of Manx, tailwise, conform to the accepted show standard. AOV cats must be CFA registered to be eligible for entry. The listings in the catalog should appear at the end of the championship listings for the Breed. The first three or four digits of the cat's registration number should be used as the Class number.

200. The MISCELLANEOUS (Non-Competitive) Class is for any breed recognized for registration that has not yet been recognized for Provisional Breed status. The first three or four digits of an entry's registration number should be used as the Class number.

ARTICLE XXV
INVITATIONS TO JUDGES AND ACCEPTANCES BY JUDGES

201. A member club must not call upon persons who are not on the CFA Judges List for judging engagements without first having secured approval from the Executive Board.

202. Invitations from clubs affiliated with Foreign Cat Associations are subject to the approval of the CFA Executive Board and may be considered only by approved All Breed Judges. Invitations from CFA clubs in Japan may be considered only by approved All Breed Judges.

203. An invitation from a club to a Judge must be answered, affirmatively or negatively, within 10 days.

204. If the Judge is willing to accept the invitation, he must send an offer in the form of a signed CFA Judge's Contract in triplicate, containing a provision that this contract is subject to the Judge's being an authorized CFA Judge on the day of the show. This offer must be dated on the date it is mailed and must include a listing of any judging assignments already accepted or that may be pending.

205. A Judge who has mailed an offer in the form of a signed contract to a club is bound to hold his offer to judge that show open for a period of 10 days from the date of the mailing. Unless a signed acceptance in the form of one copy of the contract executed by the club is received by the Judge within 10 days, the offer of the Judge will be considered to have expired.

206. A contract that has been signed by both the Judge and an officer of the club is binding on both Judge and club.

207. A binding contract may be abrogated or renegotiated by mutual agreement of the parties thereto.

208. When a Judge has asked to be released from his contract, he may not accept another judging assignment for another club that weekend.

209. One copy of the contract will be retained by the club for its files. The third copy will be sent to the Central Office with the Show License Applications. (See Article XII, Paragraph 92.)

210. A Judge may not accept two shows at different locations in any one weekend.

211. For Kitten and Premiership Classes, a CFA Judge (at least Apprentice) must be used. For Household Pet Classes it is permissible for a club to use a Trainee.

212. In the event that a show is cancelled, the Show Management must immediately notify all Judges and the Central Office by Western Union Telegram.

ARTICLE XXVI
JUDGING FEES AND EXPENSES

213. Judging Fees are as follows:
   a) Approved Judges will receive 60 cents per scheduled paid entry with no minimum;
   b) Approval Pending Judges will receive 40 cents per scheduled paid entry with no minimum;
   c) Apprentice Judges will receive 20 cents per scheduled paid entry with no minimum;
   d) A Judge who officiates at a Household Pet Show will be compensated at a rate commensurate with the highest status in either specialty.
   e) Trainee Judges shall receive no fee but shall be reimbursed for traveling expenses (Paragraph 214) when judging Household Pet Shows; and
   f) The fees for Best of the Bests judging are as follows: Kittens only – $20, Premiership only – $10, Championship only – $60. If finals judging of all categories is done in a one-day period, the total fee will be $60. If done over a two-day period, the total fee will be $90.
   g) All judging fees and expenses shall be paid in United States funds.

214. All Judges, regardless of status, and trainees used to judge Household Pet Classes will be reimbursed for traveling expenses (transportation, hotel, meals, taxis, and tips). Transportation costs will be paid as follows: if driving, mileage at 15 cents per mile or the equivalent of Coach Class air fare, whichever is less. If traveling by air, Coach Class air fare.

215. The above fees and expenses are applicable to any CFA licensed show including Kitten Matches, Premiership Shows, Household Pet Shows, or any combination thereof.

216. The applicable fee is determined by the status of the Judge at the time of the signing of his contract.

217. A Judge who has moved his place of residence subsequent to the signing of his contract, or who is traveling from a location other than his residence, will not be reimbursed any greater sum for his traveling expenses than would have been applicable at the time the contract was signed by the Judge.

ARTICLE XXVII
CONDUCT OF JUDGES

218. A Judge may not transport, supervise the transporting of, or in any way be cognizant by personal act of the entries made at a show at which he is to officiate.

219 a) A Judge may not make an entry at a show at which he officiates, but he may enter for exhibition only, provided that this limitation shall not apply to entries by a Judge who judges Household Pets only. A Judge may not judge and exhibit on the same weekend at the same location; similarly, a Judge may not judge and work color classes on the same weekend at the same location.

b) Anyone participating in the CFA Judging Program in any capacity may NOT agent cats; he may show only those cats that are registered in his name as owner.

c) Entries co-owned by a Judge and a member of his household, or owned by a member of the Judge's household, are not eligible for competition in any ring at a show at which that Judge is officiating, provided that this restriction shall not apply to a Judge who is judging Household Pets only.

220. A Judge *must not* permit exhibitors to talk to him before completing his duties.

221. A Judge may not have access to a catalog prior to the completion of all judging duties and the transfer of a completed set of Judge's Slips and Finals Sheet to the Show Secretary, and the checking of the Finals Sheet for mechanical accuracy by the Master Clerk or by a member of the Show Committee. The Judge MUST remain in the show hall until these requirements are met, at which time the Judge may receive a catalog and leave the show hall. The Show Committee will make certain that the Judge's Finals Sheet is checked for accuracy as soon as possible following the completion of the Judge's Finals so that no hardship is placed upon the Judge who must often meet the demands of a plane schedule.

222. No Judge or trainee shall solicit judging appointments. No promise or implied promise of securing entries shall be made by any person as an inducement for considering that person to judge a certain show. Having been sanctioned, no Judge shall solicit entries for any show at which he officiates.

223. A Judge may not officiate in any capacity in any ring other than his own, either prior to taking the stand or after leaving it.

224. A Judge shall not serve as Clerk for another Judge but may serve as Master Clerk, and a single specialty Judge may clerk for a ring in the category for which he is not licensed.

ARTICLE XXVIII
JUDGING PROCEDURES

225. The Judge is in complete charge of his ring. He will make every feasible effort to adhere strictly to the published show schedule. Judges are not encouraged to judge classes in advance of the schedule and must not do so except in an emergency as provided in Article XIV, Paragraph 114, with public announcement of any change made to the exhibitors well in advance.

226. Judges are not required to discuss entries with exhibitors.

227. Where a public address system is used, all numbers of all cats to be carried to each judging ring shall be announced over the system. This includes cats needed for finals.

228. An entry must be present and available for judging when the time for judging each entry is reached. An entry not so presented or available will be marked "absent", and the class will be judged as if such entry had not been benched. It is the responsibility of the exhibitor or the exhibitor's agent to see that the cat is presented for judging when the entry number is called.

229. No one other than the officiating Judge, a Trainee, or, as shown in Paragraph 230, the owner or his agent, may handle an entry in the judging ring, except as provided for in Rule 103b.

230. No one other than officials connected with the management of the show will be admitted to the judging ring except when the Clerk asks, upon the request of the Judge, that the owner or his agent hold an entry.

231. Exhibitors must not talk to the Judge or make any comments on exhibits within the Judge's hearing.

232. Exhibitors *must not* solicit the opinion of non-officiating Judges at any show.

233. Cats or kittens will not be judged with ribbons on their necks or with other identifying marks other than an optional identifying tattoo, such as the last digits of the CFA registration number placed on the left inside flank. The tattoo may not exceed $\frac{1}{2}$ inch in height nor exceed seven digits in length.

234. Handling.

a) A Judge must handle each cat in its respective class.

b) All cats must be judged in the judging ring.

c) A cat behaving in a recalcitrant or threatening manner must be disqualified and dismissed from the ring forthwith by the officiating Judge and shall not thereafter be recalled to that ring.

d) The decision of the Judge whether or not a cat is behaving in a recalcitrant or threatening manner is final and shall not be questioned.

e) In the event that a Judge is incapacitated because of a bite or injury received as a result of judging duties such as a scratch, or a cut, and the officiating Judge is able to proceed if suitable assistance is provided, The Clerk for that Judge's ring, the Master Clerk, or a member of the Show Management may assist the Judge in handling.

Note: Judges are instructed that it is the policy of CFA

not to take excessive risks or to delay unduly the oderly progression of the show in an effort to handle a cat that is behaving in a recalcitrant or threatening manner.

235. Questions about the age or eligibility of Open, Kitten, or Special Classes must be referred to the Show Committee, which shall investigate the matter. In such cases the class must be judged as though the doubtful exhibit is eligible, and one additional award allotted so that the regular list of awards may be made if the doubtful exhibit is disqualified.

236. Transfers.

A Judge may, with the consent of the exhibitor, transfer any exhibit wrongly entered, provided that the correct Color Class has not yet been judged.

237. Wrong Color Class.

When, in the opinion of the officiating Judge, an entry in the Kitten or Open classes has been entered in the wrong color class and it is mechanically impossible to transfer it to the correct color class because that color class has already been judged, the Judge may mark the entry "Wrong Color Class." When 1) the correct color class has not yet been judged and the owner refuses permission to transfer, or 2) the cat has completed a Championship or Premiership, such entry must be judged under the standard for the color class in which it is entered.

238. Withholding of Awards by the Judge:

a) A Judge must withhold all awards with the exception of first, second, and third when in his opinion ANY entry is not worthy of them.

b) Regardless of other considerations, an entry apparently suffering from emaciation or malnutrition, or showing evidence of neglect, shall receive no award.

Notwithstanding the above, a Judge remains free to disqualify under Paragraph 239.

c) When awards are withheld from an entry, the Judge shall record on the judging slips one of three reasons only: 1) "No Award – Condition," which shall include malnutrition, emaciation, evidence of neglect, or any lack of quality that is deemed by the Judge to be of a temporary nature; or

2) "NFA (No Further Award) – IM (Insufficient Merit)," which shall include overall lack of quality, deviation from the standard, congenital or acquired structural defects, or

3) "Wrong Color Class," cf. Rule 237.

239. Disqualification by the Judge:

a) a Judge must disqualify any cat showing powder, colored chalk or any other artificial coloring media; or by the plucking of buttons or lockets; or use of any drug that will alter the natural actions of a cat;

b) a Judge must disqualify any cat for a defect listed in the "Disqualify" section of the Show Standards for a particular breed or color;

c) a Judge must disqualify any cat that cannot be judged in the judging ring or that is behaving in a recalcitrant or threatening manner. This rule does not apply to cats after the completion of judging of color classes. [(see Article XXVIII, Paragraph 234(c) and (d)].

d) a Judge will disqualify any entry entered contrary to these Rules, including declawed cats and adult, whole males that do not have one descended testicle, if such entry has not therefore been disqualified; and

e) when an entry is disqualified, the Judge shall record on the judging slip "DISQ (Disqualified)."

240. Voiding of Wins by the Judge:

a) a Judge must void any win, including any win in the finals, when in his opinion there is no entry with sufficient merit to receive it; and

b) when an entry has been removed from the showroom and is not available for judging in the finals, in order that entries defeated by it may not thereby be deprived of their right to compete, the Judge may, if he so desires, void any win not yet awarded (including that of Best Cat), announce that had the absent cat been present it would have received that win, and thereafter award a lesser win or wins to an entry or entries previously defeated by the absent cat.

241. The following awards will be made by the Judge subject to the provisions of Paragraph 240.

a) CHAMPIONSHIP WINS	All Breed	LH Specialty	SH Specialty	Color or Breed Specialty – less than 20 Entries	Color or Breed Specialty – 20 or more Entries
Best Cat	x	x	x	x	x
2nd Best Cat	x	x	x	x	x
3rd Best Cat	x	x	x	x	x
4th Best Cat	x	x	x		
5th Best Cat	x	x	x		
Best Longhair	x				
2nd Best Longhair	x				
Best Shorthair	x				
2nd Best Shorthair	x				
Best Grand Champion	x	x	x		x
2nd Best Grand Champion	x	x	x		x
Best Champion	x	x	x	x	x
2nd Best Champion	x	x	x	x	x
Best Longhair Champion	x				
2nd Best Longhair Champion	x				

a) CHAMPIONSHIP WINS

a) CHAMPIONSHIP WINS	All Breed	LH Specialty	SH Specialty	Color or Breed Specialty – less than 20 Entries	Color or Breed Specialty – less or more Entries
Best Shorthair Champion	x				
2nd Best Shorthair Champion	x				
Best Open	x	x	x		x
2nd Best Open	x	x	x		x
Best of Each Persian Division	x	x		(1)	(1)
2nd Best of Each Persian Division	x	x		(2)	(2)
Best of Breed (except Persian)	x	x	x	(1)	(1)
2nd Best of Breed (except Persian)	x	x	x	′2)	(2)
Best Breed or Division Champion	x	x	x	(3)	(3)
Best of Color	x	x	x	x	x
2nd Best of Color	x	x	x	x	x
Championship Winners	x	x	x	x	x
First	x	x	x	x	x
Second	x	x	x	x	x
Third	x	x	x	x	x
AOV	(4)	(4)	(4)	(4)	(4)
Provisional Breed	(5)	(5)	(5)	(5)	(5)

b) PREMIERSHIP WINS

b) PREMIERSHIP WINS	All Breed	LH Specialty	SH Specialty	Color or Breed Specialty – less than 20 Entries	Color or Breed Specialty – 20 or more Entries
Best Cat	x	x	x	x	x
2nd Best Cat	x	x	x	x	x
3rd Best Cat	x	x	x	x	x
4th Best Cat	x				
5th Best Cat	x				
Best Premier	x	x	x	x	x
2nd Best Premier	x	x	x	x	x
Best Longhair Premier	x				
Best Shorthair Premier	x				
Best of Color	x	x	x	x	x
2nd Best of Color	x	x	x	x	x
Premiership Winners	x	x	x	x	x
First	x	x	x	x	x
Second	x	x	x	x	x
Third	x	x	x	x	x

c) KITTEN WINS

c) KITTEN WINS	All Breed	LH Specialty	SH Specialty	Color or Breed Specialty – less than 20 Entries	Color or Breed Specialty – 20 or more Entries
Best Kitten	x	x	x	x	x
2nd Best Kitten	x	x	x	x	x
3rd Best Kitten	x	x	x	x	x
4th Best Kitten	x	x	x		
5th Best Kitten	x	x	x		
Best Longhair Kitten	x				
2nd Best Longhair Kitten	x				
Best Shorthair Kitten	x				
2nd Best Shorthair Kitten	x				
Best of Color	x	x	x	x	x
2nd Best of Color	x	x	x	x	x
First	x	x	x	x	x
Second	x	x	x	x	x
Third	x	x	x	x	x

NOTES:

(1) Same as Best Cat.
(2) Same as 2nd Best Cat.
(3) Same as Best Champion.
(4) AOVs compete only within their Breed for First, Second, Third, Best of Color, and Second Best of Color.
(5) Provisional Breeds are eligible only for awards in the Provisional Breed Class.

d) HOUSEHOLD PETS

Awards made in the Household Pet Class shall be as follows:

Those individual entries deemed worthy shall receive the Household Pet Merit Award, which shall be red and white.

There shall be no distinction between Longhair and Shorthair entries in any Household Pet Show.

There shall be no distinction between Adult Neuters, Adult Spays, and Kittens.

The number of Household Pet judgings may be determined by the Show Management with a maximum of four (4) judgings. An additional "Best of the Bests" judging is permitted.

The awards for Household Pet Finals shall be Best, Second Best, Third Best, Fourth Best, and Fifth Best.

ALTERNATE HOUSEHOLD PET FORMAT
Stand Alone Household Pet shows may have such classes as Show Management specifies with the requirement that such classes must not detract from the beauty and dignity nor endanger the health of the exhibit. Judges must be advised of the proposed show format at the time of invitation. The Stand Alone Household Pet Judge, who is not judging a Championship ring, must be provided with a separate ring; however, a single specialty Judge may judge a single specialty on one day and a Stand Alone Household Pet show on the other day.

242. The Jdge shall make no cup list or trophy list awards not provided for in these Rules.

243. Any decision based on the judgment of a Judge acting under these Rules shall not be questioned.

ARTICLE XXIX
JUDGES RECORDS

244. All Judge's Slips must be signed as the color classes are judged and must immediately be posted in a manner readily accessible to exhibitors after checking and initialling by the Chief Clerk and the Master Clerk. Finals Sheets must be similarly completed, signed, checked, initialled, and posted. Awards as posted are final and may not be changed except by the CFA Executive Board. All questions or disputes regarding posted awards must be referred to the Executive Board.

245. The first complete set of signed Judge's Slips and Finals Sheets must be given by the Judge to the Show Secretary at the completion of judging for transmission to the Central Office.

246. The third complete set of signed Judge's Slips and Finals Sheets must be retained by the Judge for at least sixty days.

Design and Management of Stud Quarters

Many novice breeders decide to begin by purchasing an unrelated male and female. In fact, such a decision would be unlikely to produce the desired type of kittens, but could be guaranteed to involve the new breeder in countless tricky situations.

An entire male cat is a powerful animal, endowed with strong sexual urges that only a regular supply of queens will satisfy. If he is denied this natural satisfaction, he will be come frustrated, angry, difficult to handle, and even vicious. The 'foreign' breeds, in particular, need a sexual partner for every week of the year, and since no breeding queen should bear more than one litter every nine months, the stud owner will find it difficult to keep these studs satisfied.

Ideally, a cat breeder should have had at least five years experience of owning queens and rearing kittens before acquiring a stud cat. By this time the breeder will have taken his queens to various studs and will appreciate the necessity of choosing the correct 'lines' to breed together. Some lines are incompatible with each other, for many good breeding cats may carry recessive, lethal genes, which only appear from certain matings.

Having decided that the time has come to keep a stud cat, the cat breeder then has the difficult task of finding the best possible mate for his queen. Advice from other breeders will usually be offered, and should be considered carefully. Magazines for cat fanciers usually carry advertisements of most breeds of cats, but the novice breeder should be aware of possible pitfalls if the purchase of an adult stud is considered. It takes much time and money to rear a kitten to the age when it is ready to sire kittens. During this time a close bond is usually formed between male kitten and owner. Young males are incredibly affectionate, and can grow to be companions to both their owners and the queens that one day will be their mates. A potential purchaser should ask exactly why the owner wishes to sell the young male.

From the age of about a year, the stud cat will spend most of his life in his stud house and run, which should be made as comfortable and as spacious as possible. Ideally, a stud house should be constructed of cedar wood and should measure not less than 8 × 6 feet (2.5 × 1.8 metres) with a pent roof 7 feet (2 metres) high at the front sloping to 6 feet (1.8 metres) at the back. If possible, the stud quarters should be close to the owner's kitchen, so that the cat can take an interest in all that goes on during the day. A lonely, bored cat is never a good stud. Attached to the house should be a spacious run, not less than 10 × 12 × 7 feet (3 × 3.6 × 2 metres) high, consisting of 1-inch (2.5-centimetres) square wire mesh on a wooden frame. All outside wood should be treated with a wood preservative that does not contain creosote.

The entire house and run should be based on concrete, which is easily disinfected and will withstand all kinds of weather. The interior of the house should be well-insulated. This can be done by lining the walls with glass fibre, and covering them with hardboard. All joins should be sealed to prevent possible flea infestation and as a protection from infection. The walls should then be given two coats of lead-free gloss paint.

The stud house should have two or, preferably, three windows, one of which should be used for ventilation. The door of the stud house should open inwards, to prevent easy escape of the cat, and there should always be an escape-proof area between the door to the run and the exterior door. Fitted into the stud house door should be a special cat-flap to allow the stud and his queen to have access to the run. The flap should be fitted with a catch to deny entry if necessary.

The stud house floor should be of wood, covered with "Vinolay", which should extend about 9 inches (23 centimetres) up the walls. "Vinolay" is the only material that is impervious to cats' urine and the 9-inch (23-centimetre) overlap prevents spray from ruining the wall-paint.

The queen's pen should be a separate compartment within the house, measuring approximately 4 × 6 feet (1.1 × 1.8 metres). The dividing partition should be of wood and 1-inch (2.5-centimetre) square wire mesh, and fitted with a door to allow easy access for the stud-owner. Both stud and queen's quarters should be fitted with several shelves at different heights from the floor, so that

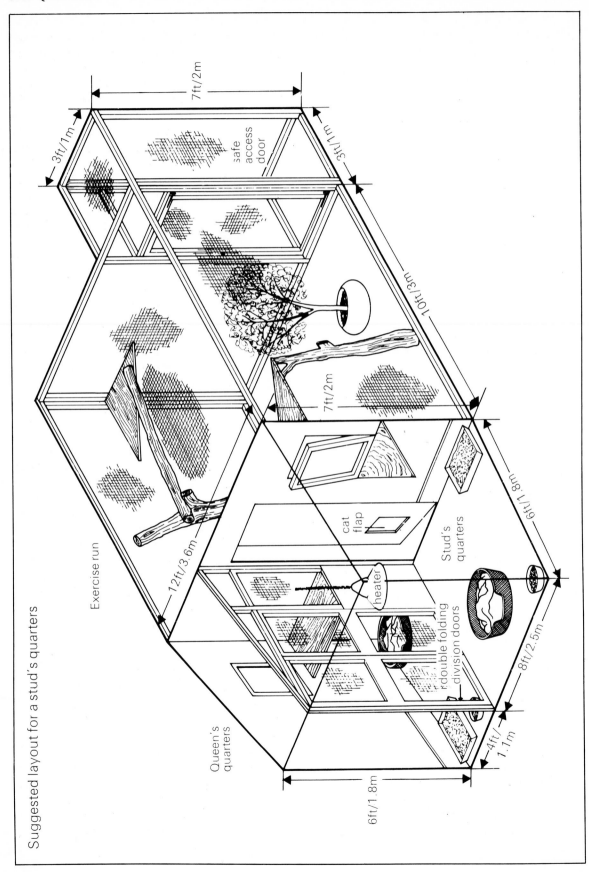

Suggested layout for a stud's quarters

Exercise run

7ft/2m

3ft/1m

safe access door

3ft/1m

10ft/3m

7ft/2m

12ft/3.6m

6ft/1.8m

cat flap

heater

Stud's quarters

double folding division doors

Queen's quarters

8ft/2.5m

4ft/1.1m

6ft/1.8m

the cats can exercise and the stud can jump away from the queen immediately after mating. Bearing in mind that a stud cat is easily bored, he should be given toys. If possible he should also have a sturdy tree branch to climb and a box of fresh-growing grass on which he can nibble.

If more than one stud is kept, it is important that each one is housed separately, with a gap of three feet between each run and house.

The most effective heating for a stud-house is electricity. A tubular heater along one wall and a dull-emitter infra-red heater over the stud's bed are ideal. The temperature at which the house should remain will vary according to the breed of cat. A longhaired cat will live happily at a temperature of about 48°F (8°C), but the house will need to be kept at 55°F (13°C) for a foreign breed.

The ideal bed for both stud and queen is a large cardboard box, lined with newspaper and a blanket. At the end of each queen's visit the box and paper can be burned. A fresh box with clean paper and a clean blanket can be supplied for the next queen. The stud and the queen will need separate toilet trays. Strong hard plastic trays are available in most pet shops and hardware stores. They are ideal because they are quickly and easily washed and disinfected. There is no doubt that commercially-made cat litter is also ideal. Plastic feeding bowls are easily disinfected too, although some breeders prefer to use disposable dishes.

Assuming that the breeder has a stud from kittenhood, the cat should be allowed to spend several hours a day in his house from the age of six months so that by the time he is sexually mature (and this age varies) he will be quite content to spend his whole day in the stud house and run. Nevertheless, he will still need human companionship, and his owner should be prepared to devote at least half an hour of every day to playing with him when he is not working.

It is very important that a young stud's first experience of mating is a happy one, and for this reason, his first queen should be an experienced brood queen who can show him the way. A bad-tempered or inexperienced queen could make the young male become a nervous and uncertain stud. Although the actual act of mating lasts only a few seconds, the courtship may take many hours. A stud's behaviour varies with every queen, and there can be no doubt that while many queens are regarded purely as 'business objects', there are some love matches, when the stud washes and cares for his queen, really grieving for her when she goes.

Most vets agree that a young stud should not be allowed more than one queen a month, but after the age of eighteen months he will need at least one queen every two weeks, and not more than two queens in one week, to keep him healthy and happy.

Every stud owner will know his cat's particular habits, but the basic mating procedure does not vary greatly. On arrival, the queen should be examined to make sure that she is in health and in oestrus; has clean ears and is free of fleas. If there is any doubt about her health, she should be kept isolated while her owner is contacted.

Assuming that she is fit, she should be placed in the queen's pen and left for at least an hour while she sniffs around her temporary home and makes the acquaintance of her new mate. It is impossible to over emphasize the importance of this introductory period, which may last for more than a day. It can be disastrous to place a queen immediately into the stud's pen, and then leave the two cats alone, as the two cats may well injure one another. Even if they do not, the queen may be so frightened that she will not accept the stud, and she may never become a reliable brood queen.

Usually, after the queen has been in close proximity to the stud for an hour or two, she will begin to call to him rubbing herself against the wire division. The stud in his turn will call back, attempt to lick her hindquarters and most probably spray close to her pen. When they both appear sexually excited, the queen should be taken from her pen and allowed to explore the stud's domain. He will immediately approach her, sniffing her and licking her. If she does not resent his advances, he will then attempt to mount her, and, if she is completely "ready", she will hold her tail to one side while he penetrates her. The act of mating is brief. The stud ejaculates very soon after penetration, and, as he withdraws from the queen, she will cry out, and then roll violently on the floor. This rolling is a sure sign that a full mating has taken place, and the queen then attempts to claw the stud, who soon learns to jump out of her reach! When she has become quiet again, the stud owner should pick her up gently, stroke her, and return her to her pen, where she should rest for a further hour.

A queen should remain with the stud for a minimum of three days, during which she should have at least three matings. If the two cats seem to be on good terms with each other, they can be allowed to run together freely after the third mating. However, a very popular stud may need to have his matings restricted.

A nervous or maiden queen might need additional manual stimulation from the stud owner before she will allow herself to be mounted, but some studs resent human interference, although the owner must remain near to ensure that all goes well.

From October to February in the northern hemisphere, and April to August in the southern hemisphere, many queens go through a period of anoestrus, and studs, particularly longhairs, appear to lose some of their sexual drive.

When the queen goes home, the stud house and queen's pen should be carefully disinfected. There are many good disinfectants on the market, but it must be remembered that any disinfectant containing phenol is lethal to a cat. Pure formalin or formaldehyde is probably the best disinfectant for cat houses and runs, as it is the only known disinfectant to destroy viruses as well as bacteriae. It is also the cheapest available, possibly because it has no added perfume. Formalin should be diluted before use, using one teaspoon per 20 fluid ounces (about .56 litres) of water, to which a little washing soda may be added.

It is inevitable that there will be occasions when a visiting queen will bring some infection to a stud. If he is fit and fully vaccinated, he should not develop the illness, but it may be necessary to fumigate the stud house. This can be carried out simply and effectively by using a formalin 'gas'. The stud must be moved to other quarters, and the windows and doors of the stud house sealed with masking tape. Two tablespoons of potassium permanganate should be placed in a deep fireproof bowl, and on to this should be poured 4 fluid ounces (about 1 decilitre) of pure Formalin. The stud owner then needs to run, closing the door, as the two substances react violently to produce a dense gas, which will destroy all known insects, viruses, and bacteria. The house should remain closed for forty-eight hours, after which the bowl should be removed and the building well aired before the stud is reinstated.

It is obvious that to keep a stud fit and happy is neither cheap nor easy, but when his progeny arrive and are later seen on the show bench, all the effort and expense seem worthwhile, and the stud will remain a fit and affectionate companion for fourteen to sixteen years.

Opposite: queen and stud sniffing each other in the first stages of courtship. Above: the queen has accepted the stud's advances and he prepares to mount her.

The queen and stud in adjoining quarters

Design and Management of Boarding Catteries

Boarding cats is a way of life, and an arduous and demanding one at that. Nevertheless, for people who *care* about cats – to love cats is not enough – it can bring satisfaction, interspersed with worry and anxiety, and a number of intangible rewards.

People considering building a boarding cattery should think very carefully indeed before committing themselves to such an undertaking. Hedged around by bureaucracy and practically strangled at every turn by red tape, even the smallest alteration or addition to one's house becomes a marathon task and a trial of patience and endurance.

Apart from the legal considerations, potential cattery proprietors must examine very carefully their own position, tastes, and physical and mental stamina. They must accept from the beginning that to run a boarding cattery properly requires capital expenditure, and produces little profit. In other words, young couples cannot expect to raise a family and educate and clothe their children on the proceeds, although a reasonable living can be made by, say, two people. Above all, they must be very sure that not only is this the type of work they wish to undertake, but that they are physically and temperamentally suited to do so. The work is hard, the hours long, and regardless of weather conditions, social attractions, or merely a disinclination to do anything, the unvaried routine must continue seven days a week. The telephone rings constantly, and generally at the most inconvenient moments, and freedom is curtailed to the extent that it becomes a problem to leave the premises even for a few hours.

The legal position in Britain

The first step is to obtain planning permission. Before purchasing the land and property that appears suitable, approach the Planning Department of the relevant Local Authority to ascertain whether or not it is likely that permission would be granted for the building of a boarding cattery. If any difficulty is encountered with the planning authority, members of the Feline Advisory Bureau can obtain advice and possible backing from the Secretary of the Bureau, who will contact the planners on their behalf.

When the long months of toil and frustration are over and the boarding cattery is finally completed, a licence to board must be obtained from the local district council in accordance with the Animal Boarding Establishments Act, 1963. The following is an excerpt from the Act, copies of which can be obtained from Her Majesty's Stationery Offices. Anyone thinking of starting a cattery is strongly advised to obtain a copy.

'No person should keep a boarding establishment for animals except under a licence granted by the Local Authority. In determining whether to grant a licence the Local Authority must have regard to the need for ensuring:

a) that animals will at all times be kept in accommodation suitable as respects construction, size of quarters, number of occupants, exercising facilities, temperatures, lighting, ventilation and cleanliness;

b) that animals will be adequately supplied with suitable food, drink and bedding material and, so far as necessary, visited at suitable intervals;

c) that all reasonable precautions will be taken to prevent and control the spread among animals of infectious or contagious diseases including the provision of adequate isolation facilities;

d) that appropriate steps will be taken for the protection of the animals in case of fire or other emergency;

e) that a register be kept containing the description of any animal received into the establishment, date of arrival and departure, name and address of the owners. Such register to be available for inspection at all times by an officer of the Local Authority, veterinary surgeon, or veterinary practitioner authorized under Section 2(i) of this Act and without prejudice to their right to withhold a licence on other grounds.'

The licence must specify such conditions as will ensure that the above named objects are secured. The local council is responsible for inspecting all boarding establishments annually. Sadly, there is a good deal of variance between local councils. Some public health inspectors are knowledgeable about animal requirements; others know little or nothing and care less.

The licence runs from 1 January to 31 December, and lays down twenty-seven conditions, starting with the maximum number of cats that may be boarded at any one time. It deals with food storage, heating, disposal of excreta, fire precautions, the maintenance of records, security, washing and lavatory facilities for staff, and requires that the licence be permanently displayed at the boarding establishment. Under the Local Government Act of 1974 individual councils are empowered to levy their own licence fee, and the amount varies greatly throughout the country.

In the event of serious complaints being made, or if the establishment is found to be incorrectly or unhygienically run, the licensing authority also has the power to withhold or withdraw a licence. Local authority annual inspections are generally notified in advance and therefore it rests with cat-owners to complain direct to the local authority if they are dissatisfied with the conditions in which their cat has been boarded. They should also notify the Feline Advisory Bureau at the same time.

The legal position in the United States

In the United States there is no single federal law governing the establishment, control and maintenance of boarding catteries. Proper laws are needed to protect not only the cats, but also property and neighbours. Before prospective cattery proprietors make any investment, they should examine all the local zoning laws to make sure they may operate a business in the location they have provisionally selected.

Boarding catteries are few and far apart in the United States, and more are certainly needed. Many people who might wish to start such a business have the national problem of finding a suitable and convenient location. The problem is particularly severe in large cities, where there is no room for the large runs required.

A row of chalets, showing the gaps between them

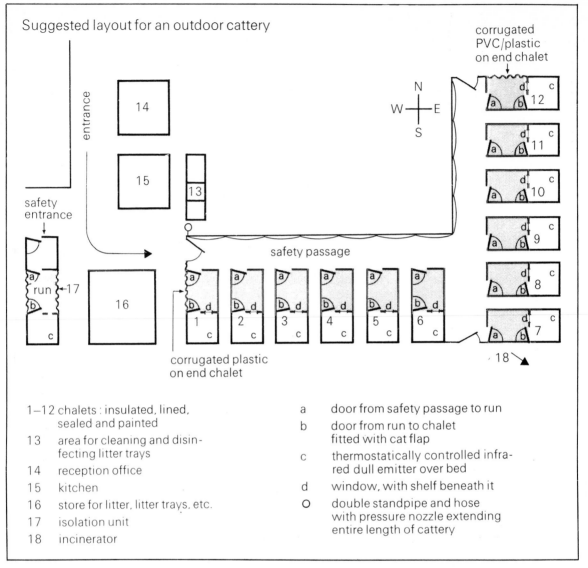

Suggested layout for an outdoor cattery

corrugated
PVC/plastic
on end chalet

entrance

safety
entrance

safety passage

corrugated plastic
on end chalet

1–12 chalets : insulated, lined,
sealed and painted
13 area for cleaning and disin-
fecting litter trays
14 reception office
15 kitchen
16 store for litter, litter trays, etc.
17 isolation unit
18 incinerator

a door from safety passage to run
b door from run to chalet
fitted with cat flap
c thermostatically controlled infra-
red dull emitter over bed
d window, with shelf beneath it
O double standpipe and hose
with pressure nozzle extending
entire length of cattery

Design

Cats who are placed in boarding catteries are domestic animals and, as such, their basic requirements are shelter, food and warmth. In their own homes, hopefully, these three vital needs are catered for, but in many boarding catteries they fall far short of the ideal. Wherever the boarding cattery is situated, certain provisions for the cat's well-being must be made, and these are listed below.

Cats from different homes must **never** share the same air space, be penned together, or ever come into contact with each other.

Adequate sleeping and exercise space must be provided. Veterinary advice is that the cubic capacity per cat should not be less than 80 cubic feet (2.3 cubic metres); roughly, this means that the chalet or cubicle should be $4 \times 4 \times 6$ feet ($1.2 \times 1.2 \times 1.8$ metres). This is more than adequate

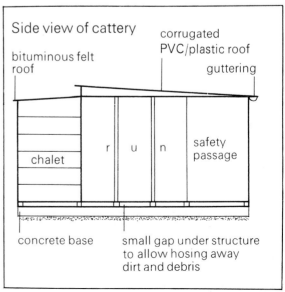

Side view of cattery

corrugated
PVC/plastic roof

bituminous felt
roof

guttering

chalet

r u n

safety
passage

concrete base

small gap under structure
to allow hosing away
dirt and debris

Suggested layout for an indoor cattery

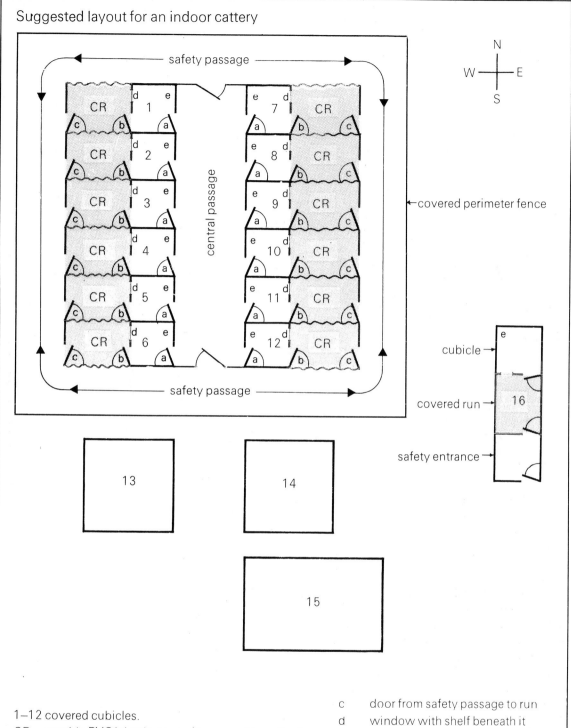

1–12 covered cubicles.

CR   outside PVC/plastic covered runs, with vertically-corrugated PVC/plastic 'sneeze barriers' at least 4 feet (1.2 metres) high between each.

a   door from central passage to cubicle should have a solid bottom and a see-through panel of glass or plastic on top

b   door from cubicle to run fitted with cat flap

c   door from safety passage to run

d   window with shelf beneath it

e   thermostatically controlled infra-red dull emitter over bed

13   reception office

14   kitchen

15   store for litter, litter trays, etc.

16   isolation unit

for one cat and sufficient for two from the same household. As some owners have more than two cats, if building a cattery from scratch, it is a good idea to incorporate one or two larger chalets or cubicles to house three or four cats from the same home.

The cat should have access to an outside covered run, but should **never** be allowed the freedom of the run at night.

Each unit should be separated from the next by a minimum of 2 feet (60 centimetres). The cattery should be mounted on a smooth concrete base. Each chalet should have a window, a shelf beneath it inside the chalet, and a close fitting cat door at the bottom of the chalet door.

All catteries must have a safety passage – minimum width 4 feet (1.2 metres) – from which there is access to all the runs. An indoor cattery with outdoor runs must be completely surrounded by a covered perimeter fence.

The entire length of runs and safety passage should be covered with a corrugated plastic roof, sloping to allow rainwater to drain off into guttering fixed to the front of the safety passage. Such a roof allows the cats to sit out in their runs comfortably, and the staff to work, whatever the weather.

In the northern hemisphere chalets should have a southern aspect, as the exposure to the sun makes the cattery much warmer and more pleasant for the cats. Heating must be provided. Electricity is the best and most acceptable form of heating for cats. Use infra-red dull emitters, which can be individually thermostatically controlled; this is important, as the heat requirements of different cats can vary considerably.

Management

No cleaning agent or disinfectant that is toxic to cats must ever be used. Wooden buildings must be regularly protected with a wood preservative that does not contain cresol (which is a derivative of coal tar and is highly toxic to cats), and no cat must be allowed anywhere near a building until the preservative is completely dry. In no circumstances must creosote ever be used.

A cat must never be placed in premises that have not been thoroughly aired, cleaned and disinfected after the departure of the last occupant.

Any veterinary treatment prescribed must be correctly and faithfully carried out.

Entire – that is, unneutered – males should not be boarded. This poses a problem for breeders, but for the boarding cattery there is too great a risk of cross-infection.

Every cattery must have an isolation unit situated some distance from the main complex.

No cattery should admit a cat whose owner cannot produce an up-to-date veterinary certificate of inoculation against feline enteritis. In the event of the owner refusing to have the animal inoculated, the cattery must refuse to admit the cat.

Inevitably, at some stage an infectious cat will be admitted, as cats can incubate infection while appearing perfectly well up to about twenty-one days. What every boarding cattery must guard against every moment of the day is the danger of cross-infection. Only constant vigilance and meticulous husbandry will prevent its occurrence. Should there be an outbreak of infection, the fault will lie fairly and squarely on the shoulders of the boarding cattery proprietor.

An outdoor boarding cattery

A regular routine of cleaning, feeding, grooming, etc. must be established. Regular meal times must be adhered to and individual diets provided. Adult cats should be fed twice daily; kittens and geriatric cats according to their needs. Many catteries administer what is popularly referred to as a 'general diet'. All cats have marked preferences and dislikes with regard to food. It is no exaggeration to say that one must reduce a cat to starvation level before it will eat the food it dislikes. Details of the cat's diet should be supplied by the owners and entered on the record card. A new menu must be prepared for all boarders daily, and note taken of whether any alterations should be made. Should a cat fail to eat at the end of three or four days after all permutations of food have been tried, make sure that there is no physical cause preventing it from eating. A very common one is neglected teeth that are in need of scaling.

Every cat must be provided with fresh water and, in most cases, fresh milk daily. There are some cats who never touch milk, and in some cases it is contra-indicated and gives rise to diarrhoea. This information should be supplied by the cat's owner.

A simple daily record should be maintained to ensure that the cats have urinated, defaecated or to note whether they have had diarrhoea. Constipation is sometimes a problem in catteries and neutered males may have urinary problems, which must be dealt with by a veterinary surgeon with little delay.

Adequate sized litter trays must be provided. Several forms of litter can be used. *Wood shavings*, obtainable from saw mills, timber merchants, furniture makers, etc., at fairly reasonable cost, are best for shorthaired cats. However, with longhaired cats these act rather like iron filings under a magnet and are wholly unsuitable. Longhaired cats must be given *manufactured litter*. All litter should be incinerated daily. *Peat* is unacceptable. It creates considerable cleaning problems, should never be composted on account of a possible health hazard, and the disposal of large quantities is impossible. *Sawdust* must never be used. It becomes clogged in the cat's paws, gets into its coat, and is ingested by the cat.

A cattery should not become too large. Employment of additional staff if the number of boarders is increased is no solution because each cat needs to become familiar with one or two people who care for it daily during its stay. It is essential that a rapport is established between each cat and its temporary guardians, who must watch it constantly and know immediately by its behaviour or mien that

perhaps all is not well, and that veterinary advice may have to be sought. It is *continuity* of care by the same people that matters enormously.

All cats should be visited at regular intervals throughout the day. There must always be a final round at night, and the time of this must depend on prevailing weather conditions. Night security must always be very carefully checked.

The best catteries are those that board cats only and undertake no other activity whatsoever, such as dog boarding, dog breeding or cat breeding.

Whether the boarding cattery is in France, America, Britain or Japan, the cats entrusted to its care must have priority over all else at all times, and a boarding cattery proprietor must never for one instant forget the immense responsibility he or she bears in caring for other people's animals.

Hygiene

No boarding cattery can hope to survive without meticulous husbandry and constant vigilance on the part of the proprietor. The best buildings in the world, with all the sophisticated equipment one can buy, are totally useless unless the highest standard of hygiene and husbandry is maintained. Each cat boarded should depart looking as well as, if not a good deal better than, when it arrived. It must be maintained in a healthy condition, well and properly fed, groomed, and, above all, cared for.

Daily record chart

Month	Date													
	1	2	3	4	5	6	7	8	9	10	11	12	13	14
Chalet 1	✓	✓	✓	✓	▮		✓	✓	✓	✓	✓	✓	✓	✓
	✓	✓	X	X	▮		X	✓	✓	✓	✓	X	X	✓
2		X	✓	✓	✓	▮	✓	✓	✓	✓				
		X	X	✓	✓	X	✓	X	✓	▮				
3	✓	✓	✓	✓	✓	✓	✓	✓	✓	✓				
	✓	✓	✓	X	X	✓	✓	D	D	X	✓			
4														
5														

Top ✓   cat has urinated
Bottom ✓   cat has defaecated
X   cat has failed to urinate or defaecate, or both
D : diarrhoea

The chart should be on a clipboard hung in the safety passage. It should be completed for each cat as the chalet or cubicle is cleaned.

While this would seem simple enough, in practice it can be arduous, time-consuming and a considerable trial of patience.

Hygiene of the highest order must be maintained throughout the premises and any disinfectant that is used must be non-toxic and tolerated by cats. The fact that a disinfectant suits sheep, horses, dogs and cattle does not necessarily mean that it is the slightest use with cats, and may even prove poisonous to them.

The cattery is generally asked to retain the carrying basket during the cat's stay. Before being stored with the other baskets, it should be very thoroughly scrubbed and disinfected.

Each chalet must have its own brush and dust pan, which remain with the cat during the entire length of its stay, after which both are thoroughly washed and disinfected.

All drinking dishes should be clearly numbered to ensure that the cat retains the same dishes throughout its stay. These dishes should be sterilized daily.

The best type of feeding dishes are disposable ones, that can be burned after every meal. If non-disposable dishes are used, they should be made of plastic, polypropylene or stainless steel, and at least four dishes, all numbered, should be allotted to each chalet, thus ensuring that a clean dish is always available. The dirty ones can be washed and sterilized at a time convenient to the staff.

It is excellent if the cat brings its own sleeping basket and bedding, because they depart with the cat. Otherwise, the boarding cattery must provide a polypropylene bed or a clean cardboard carton using wood wool as bedding. Wood wool, the very finely shredded wood often used for packing china and glass, is obtainable in large compressed bales. It is warm, cleans the cat's fur, and is easy to burn. On the cat's departure, the cardboard and wood wool should be burned, and the polypropylene bed thoroughly sterilized in a suitable disinfectant. Permanent wooden beds are not advisable, as they can constitute a health hazard however carefully they are cleaned.

Clean litter should be kept in large plastic bins, such as refuse containers. Containers used for dirty litter should also be plastic, but of a distinctive colour in order that there is no danger of the two containers becoming confused.

Litter trays, obtainable at most pet shops, must be of adequate size. The minimum requirement for a single cat is $16\frac{1}{4} \times 12\frac{1}{2} \times 3\frac{1}{2}$ inches ($42 \times 32 \times 9$ centimetres). Larger trays are required when two cats are sharing a chalet, and a chalet for three

A cat in its own sleeping basket

or four cats needs two large litter trays. Litter trays must be changed as required, and in some cases this must be done two or three times a day. Gloves should be worn when doing this and sprayed with suitable disinfectant between each change. Very thorough disinfection of litter trays is essential. If possible, this should be done outside, and when the litter tray is completely clean it should be left to dry naturally, then sprayed with a suitable disinfectant, and again left to dry naturally, thus leaving a protective film of disinfectant over the entire tray before it is stored prior to re-use.

Sprays are vital equipment in any cattery. Experience has shown that the smaller, simpler models are the most efficient. Filling a spray with disinfectant should always be done through a filter funnel. A full spray should always be available, since if a cat that could be a source of infection has been handled, the hands and clothing of the handler must be thoroughly sprayed.

The proprietor must examine all cats on arrival and reserve the right to refuse admittance to any cat whose health is obviously suspect. If it is impossible for the owners to return home with the cat, it should be put into the isolation unit immediately and veterinary advice sought. If a cat is definitely infectious and is in the isolation unit, it must virtually be barrier nursed. A special overall or lab coat, plastic gloves, and plastic bags over the shoes should be worn to help prevent any possible spread of infection. Keep any dishes or equipment used by the cat entirely separate from the remainder of the cattery.

Many cats admitted will be found to be heavily infested with fleas, particularly during the summer months. The cat should be thoroughly combed with a flea comb, and as much dirt and live fleas extracted as possible. The cat should then be dusted with a powder or sprayed with an aerosol known to be acceptable and non-toxic to cats, great care being taken not to allow the substance anywhere near its eyes. Many cats are terrified by aerosols and a powder can be used on them, but the bed and chalet can be sprayed with an aerosol. The treatment should be repeated in ten to fourteen days.

In the event of a cat coming in with a tick embedded, seek the advice of a veterinary surgeon.

The cattery should keep a supply of suitable worm tablets for both round and tape worms. These should be obtained from the cattery's regular vet, and administered only to cats *known* to have worms. In Britain a small charge may be made to the owner for this treatment. In the United States only the vet should be allowed to worm the cat, and no one except the vet is allowed to charge for medical attention.

Plastic feeding dishes are recommended

Many cats will have ear mites and skin conditions. These should be treated, but the advice of a veterinary surgeon should be sought first. Any case of hair loss should be referred to the vet immediately in case it is a symptom of ringworm.

Administration

From sheer necessity, and owing to the fact that there are only a limited number of hours in the day, it is vital that the administration of a boarding cattery be kept as simple and straightforward as possible. Whatever system of administration is adopted, it must be efficient, and it must be seen to be so. Many cat owners are very apprehensive in boarding their cat, but gain confidence in the establishment if the reception is carried out smoothly and with careful attention to detail.

Every cattery should produce a brochure, and it is helpful if this includes a directional guide. It should state clearly charges, hours, terms of business, and that no cat will be accepted unless it is vaccinated against feline enteritis – panleucopenia. Many catteries now insist on vaccination against the upper respiratory infections too, but the vaccination against panleucopenia is vital. Owners now appreciate that this is essential in order to safeguard the health of all the cats boarded. It is an

Booking chart   November 1979

Chalet number	day date	Th 1	F 2	Sat 3	Sun 4	M 5	Tu 6	Wed 7	Th 8	F 9	Sat 10	Sun 11
1												
2												
3												
4												
5												

(a)   Enter owner's name with cat's name underneath
(b)   Draw line to left of date for date of arrival
(c)   Draw line to right of date for date of departure
(d)   Enter booking on cat's record card at same time
(e)   Periodically check booking chart against cards

Keep a year's supply of monthly charts prepared, and record all bookings on them. As frequent alterations may be necessary, mark all bookings in pencil.

Cat's record card

> Owner's name
> Cat's name   Birthdate   Description
> Home address   Telephone number
> Holiday address   Telephone number
> Accommodation required
> from:
> to:
> Cat eats raw meat: cooked meat: fish:
> brand of canned/tinned food: milk:
> Food or drugs to be avoided
> Cat's own vet: Vaccination data:

excellent plan to suggest to people wishing to make a booking that they visit and inspect the cattery first, but they must be requested not to touch any of the animals boarded.

The smooth-running of the administration will depend on the correct recording of dates. This seems elementary but in practice it can lead to hideous complications and nightmare situations. People telephone their bookings at irregular times, generally at meal times on the grounds that the proprietor is bound to be in and available, and the tendency to record such bookings on the nearest scrap of paper to hand, such as the back of an envelope, can only lead to disaster. Make every effort to ensure that all bookings are correctly transcribed on to a booking sheet and record card without delay. Furthermore, check that the dates on the cards and on the booking sheet agree.

Brochures should be sent to the client confirming the booking.

Each animal should have a record card on which details of its inoculations, diet, etc. are kept, together with the name and address of the owner, and, if possible, the owner's holiday address or the name and address of some relative or friend who is *in loco parentis*. When the cat arrives at the cattery for the first time, the owner should be asked to sign an authorization for veterinary treatment.

AUTHORIZATION FORM
I agree that in the case of illness or suspected illness a veterinary surgeon will be consulted and, if necessary, called in to carry out such treatment as he considers advisable, at my expense. (While every care and precaution is taken, treatment can be carried out only at the owner's risk.)
Signature . . . . Date . . . .

On departure of the cat a release form should be signed.

RELEASE FORM

I (signature) certify that I have received my cat (name) from the (name of cattery) in apparent good health and condition after boarding. Date . . . .

This form has no particular legal significance, but it is a safeguard to the cattery and ensures that the owner inspects the cat and is satisfied that there is no evidence of injury or ill-treatment.

The cat's account and release form should be prepared before the owner arrives to collect the animal.

The cattery and grounds generally should have a well-kept, organized appearance, devoid of clutter and waste products. Houses and runs should be scrupulously clean, and free from smell. Many repairs have to be carried out throughout the year and annual maintenance is essential.

The cattery should be fully insured. Although there are various schemes whereby owners can pay so much per week against veterinary expenses, this arrangement is not completely satisfactory.

Relationships with cats and their owners

It is said that you can never please all the people all the time . . . This aphorism cannot apply to the luckless boarding cattery proprietor, who must steer an unerring course between the cats, the owners and the veterinary surgeon who usually attends the cattery. The cats present the least problem provided their conditions and treatment are correct. The domestic cat is neither vicious nor spiteful, but in strange surroundings can be very nervous and resist handling in the only way it knows. It is advisable to allow the cat to settle down on its own for about two hours; initial fussing will do no good whatsoever. The sense of security and regular routine will appeal and few cats take longer than twenty-four hours to settle.

As a species cats are selective, fastidious and sensitive. They dislike noise, and sudden and abrupt movements. Owners should restrain small children they bring with them, and not allow them to make undue noise or run up and down the safety passage. Although many cats are accustomed to co-exist with dogs very happily, it does not follow that they will take kindly to the presence of strange dogs. No dog should be allowed in the vicinity of the cattery at any time. It is also important that no one other than the staff is allowed to touch any cat except their own. As always, the fear of cross-infection lurks in the background. Too clinical an approach to the cats, however, will do nothing to gain their confidence.

Cats need affection and a degree of handling – some more than others. They are all individuals and should be talked to normally and addressed by their names. If any member of the cattery staff is afraid of a cat, the animal will become aware of this instantly and an almost impossible situation will result. Should a member of the staff be scratched or bitten, in ninety-nine cases out of a hundred, the fault lies entirely with the human being. People who work with cats, or any other animals, should be regularly protected against tetanus.

It is important that owners leave the cattery sure in the knowledge that their cat will be safe and well cared-for during their absence. They must have complete peace of mind about their cat's welfare. Generally speaking, cat owners are among the most pleasant, honest and kindly people one can hope to meet, but many are lamentably ignorant regarding the general care of their cat. If told that the cat has had fleas, they may be shocked and amazed and have not the slightest idea how to cope with the problem. Ear mites are, to many, a totally closed book. The boarding cattery owner has a definite responsibility to teach the cat-owning public as much as possible about the proper care and feeding of their cats. Most dealings with owners are perfectly straightforward and although one must state clearly and unequivocally in one's brochure the hours when cats may be admitted and collected, if for some good reason the owners are late, having been delayed by traffic, strikes, breakdowns, etc., they must always be treated with unfailing courtesy.

Most areas have two or three veterinary practices and the cattery owner should ascertain which one specializes in small animals, with particular reference to cats. There must be a clear understanding with the veterinary surgeon that the cattery owner will not call him out unnecessarily, but that he will always respond to a cry for help, no matter what time of day or night. The cattery owner must ensure that there are proper facilities in the cattery for the veterinary surgeon to wash his hands and clean and disinfect any instruments he may have used.

Emergencies can and do happen at the most unexpected and inconvenient times and it is only through constant vigilance and hygiene of the highest order that the danger of cross-infection can be averted.

Only through carelessness on the part of a member of the staff will a cat ever escape, but it is emphasized that the happily and correctly boarded cat will not make any attempt to do so.

Feline Medicine

Many cats enjoy good health for most of their lives, but problems of disease do arise, and these can range from transient, minor illnesses to severe life-threatening infections. Most owners are aware when their cat is unwell, and know that they should seek veterinary attention immediately. A veterinary surgeon will be able to carry out the necessary treatment, and will advise you on what you can do to help your cat. It is not, therefore, the purpose of this chapter to give detailed descriptions of the various cat diseases or the technique of home nursing. What follows is a brief guide to the prevention, rather than the cure, of the major cat diseases, and also a brief review of some of the new research that is being carried out in the field of feline medicine.

Vaccination

The illnesses caused by many of the viruses to which cats are prone, are either extremely serious or fatal. Because of this, any methods that help to prevent an outbreak of disease should be recommended. Infection can spread rapidly from cat to cat, and so it is in boarding catteries, breeding groups, and households where several cats are kept that the greatest problems of disease prevention and control can arise.

As cat owners and veterinary surgeons, we are fortunate that a range of useful and effective vaccines are available that can protect our cats against some diseases. In many cases vaccination can provide the first line of defence, but it is not the complete solution to disease problems.

Feline infectious enteritis (Feline panleuco-paenia/feline distemper)

Feline infectious enteritis (FIE) is a very contagious viral disease, with a high mortality rate, especially in kittens and elderly cats. Effective, safe vaccines are available in both North America and Britain. These are of two types, inactivated vaccines, and modified live vaccines. Inactivated vaccines consist of virus that has been grown in tissue culture, and then killed. Modified live vaccines consist of virus that has been grown in tissue culture until it has lost the ability to produce disease, but has retained the ability to produce immunity. In terms of the degree of protection given by the two types, there seems little to choose between them in the case of the different FIE vaccines. However, both may have advantages in particular circumstances. It is suggested that vaccination with a modified live virus vaccine shortly after exposure to the disease may have a protective effect, as the vaccine virus may interfere with the process of infection with the virulent natural or field virus. Modified live vaccines should not be given to pregnant queens, or to kittens under four weeks old, as this could result in damage to the developing kittens.

As the disease is so serious and such effective, relatively inexpensive vaccines are available, all cats and kittens should be protected by regular vaccination. The question that is often asked by cat owners is how early can a kitten be vaccinated. It has been mentioned that the use of a live vaccine in very young kittens can be hazardous, but there is no reason why a vaccine cannot be given to a kitten from four to six weeks onwards. However, it is likely to be ineffective in many kittens of this age due to passively acquired immunity. If the queen is immune to the disease, she will transfer some degree of immunity to her kittens through antibodies secreted in the colostrum, or first milk. This passive immunity lasts for varying times in different kittens, and although it is beneficial in that it protects the kittens from infection, it also can prevent effective vaccination. Most vaccine programmes try to avoid this problem by giving two or more doses of vaccine at intervals, usually of two or three weeks. This ensures that as soon as the level of the kittens passively acquired immunity begins to fall, the vaccine stimulates its immune system to produce protective antibodies against FIE. To ensure that the cat remains protected, annual booster vaccinations are recommended, although a booster every two years would probably be adequate.

As many cats are now vaccinated, disease outbreaks are less common. If an outbreak does occur, then any other possibly susceptible cat must be protected. A modified live virus may be of use for this. Alternatively, immune serum can be given. This is available commercially, and will provide temporary protection, in much the same way as the antibodies in the colostrum provide temporary protection for young kittens.

Once the disease has occurred, a further problem is that the virus is extremely resistant to destruction by many disinfectants, and can be transmitted to other cats through contact with infected bedding, food dishes, cages, and the hands and clothing of people who have been in contact with the disease. If at all possible formalin, as a 1 per cent solution, should be used to disinfect the premises. If you are using formalin, remember that it is extremely irritant: you must evacuate all buildings and pens while disinfection is in progress, and wash off the solution thoroughly after about four hours. This is obviously not practical if disease occurs in cats living in a house rather than in a cattery. In this case it is essential that any new arrivals are vaccinated before entering the potentially infected area.

Feline infectious enteritis is one of the more easily preventable cat diseases, but more complex problems are presented by other viruses.

Feline upper respiratory tract disease ('cat flu')

'Cat flu' is probably the most widespread of the cat viral diseases, most cases being caused by one of two viruses: feline viral rhinotracheitis virus (FVR), or feline calcici virus (FCV). Unlike the virus of feline infectious enteritis, the feline respiratory viruses are fairly fragile, and do not survive outside the cat for long – under forty-eight hours for FVR, under a week for FCV. They can still be transmitted, however, on feeding bowls, hands and clothing, as well as from cat to cat by sneezing.

The disease can be extremely distressing to the cat, and can be fatal, especially in young kittens. Other cats may be left with a chronic rhinitis (chronic snuffles) or chronic gingivitis (inflammation of the gums), or conjunctivitis. Once a cat has had the disease, the immunity produced does not last for very long; some cats may be re-infected with FVR after as little as six months. Due to the large number of different strains of calcici virus that exist, although a high degree of cross-protection occurs, it is possible for a cat to be infected with one strain, recover, and then be infected by a different strain. These problems of immunity have increased the difficulties of developing an effective vaccine.

Several vaccines are now available in North America and Britain. Two types are combined FVR/FCV modified live vaccines, one type being administered intramuscularly, the other intranasally. There is also an inactivated FVR vaccine, which is administered intramuscularly. Although the latter is active only against FVR, because it is a killed vaccine it can safely be given to pregnant queens.

When given to a healthy kitten that has not been exposed to the disease, vaccination is effective in most cases. There are problems, however, due to the presence of a carrier state that can follow exposure to either of the viruses. Cats can recover from the disease and appear healthy, but, in fact, may still be harbouring the virus. In the case of FVR, periods of virus shedding occur intermittantly, and during these periods the cat can infect other cats and kittens, or may itself show clinical signs of disease. These episodes of virus shedding tend to occur following some sort of stress, for example, entering a cattery, attending a cat show or, of particular importance to breeders, following giving birth and lactation. Carriers of FCV shed virus continuously and are a constant source of infection to other cats. Most carriers of this virus seem to eliminate the infection eventually, but the time taken varies considerably, and can be as long as several months. Cats that are carriers of these two viruses have been shown to be very widespread in the cat population, especially among pedigree animals. A survey of cats attending shows in Britain showed that 25 per cent of apparently healthy animals were carriers of FCV.

There is a lack of information about the effect of vaccination on carrier animals, but there is some evidence to suggest that previously healthy vaccinated animals can undergo subclinical infection with FVR virus, and then become carriers of it.

Additional problems associated with vaccination are the short duration of immunity (which may mean that boosters are needed at six monthly intervals), and the relatively high cost of the vaccine. Together, these problems may make vaccination of a large group of cats an expensive procedure. In view of these difficulties, carefully designed management procedures remain important in the prevention and control of feline respiratory disease. These procedures will vary in different circumstances.

In the case of the household pet, providing infection did not occur as a kitten, the opportunities for encountering the virus will be few. If there is a large number of cats in the area, as occurs in some urban situations, then neighbouring pets may provide a source of infection, but as cats do not usually have much contact, the likelihood of infection is low. The main times of risk for most cats will be on visiting a boarding cattery or attending a cat show. In view of this, vaccination is best used to provide protection at times of high risk – in most cases once a year before entering a cattery.

With larger groups of cats, which include some breeding queens, there are other considerations. As these groups are usually pedigree cats, some will most certainly be regularly attending shows and some may be sent away to stud. In addition, a stud may be owned, in which case queens may visit the group for stud purposes. Most owners of pedigree cats will purchase new cats and kittens as additions to their breeding group, and a regular supply of susceptible individuals, the newborn kittens, are produced. This situation obviously requires some sort of management control. All cats should be vaccinated on a regular basis. However, this will not eliminate the viruses, as some cats may be carriers, and hence there is still the risk of infecting new-born kittens. If showing and breeding (involving visits to stud cats) are to be continued, then it must be expected that sooner or later respiratory viruses will enter the colony. The main problem is likely to be infection of young kittens, and to minimize it the the following procedures should be adopted:

1) vaccinate breeding queens before mating to try to ensure that a high level of immunity is transferred to the kittens in the colostrum;
2) arrange for queens to give birth in isolation, so that the kittens are not exposed to other cats that may be carriers of the virus;
3) wean the kittens early and continue to rear them in isolation – this will help to prevent infection if their dam is a carrier;
4) vaccinate the kittens before introducing them to other cats.

These relatively simple management procedures can be applied to some of the other virus diseases, and certainly giving birth in isolation should be regarded as essential.

Feline leukaemia virus (FeLV)

Feline leukaemia virus causes one of the most widespread fatal diseases of the domestic cat. The virus is present in most areas of the cat population, and can be readily transmitted by contact between cats. It can produce various types of disease, including leukaemia, anaemia, lymphosarcoma (tumors of various organs), and reproductive disorders. A vaccine is being developed in Britain, but is not yet available commercially. Until vaccination becomes possible, the only way to prevent FeLV infection in a group of cats is to aim at avoiding contact with infected animals.

It has been shown by research in the United States that if a household has several cats and one develops feline leukaemia virus infection, then, unless the infected cat is removed, it is likely that many of the other cats will become infected. It is possible to test cats for the presence of FeLV, and this should be done if infection is suspected. There are two types of test; one is the virus isolation test, in which plasma (obtained from a blood sample) is incubated with cell cultures and the presence of FeLV recognized by its effect on the cells. This test is carried out only at Glasgow Veterinary School in Scotland. The second test is the immunofluorescence (IF) test, which is used extensively in North America and is now also being used at Glasgow. The IF test is carried out on blood smears, and involves the detection of virus within the white blood cells. In a persistently infected cat the virus is present in the blood, and so these tests are reliable indicators of whether the cat is infected or not. The only method of control is to test your cats, and when those cats that are carrying the virus have been detected, to keep them isolated from other cats or put them to sleep. It is this problem – what action to take with an infected cat – that has produced most argument among cat owners, breeders, and veterinary surgeons. The decision can be taken only by the owners, but it should be remembered that an infected cat, in addition to the likelihood of developing one of the diseases caused by FeLV, can infect other cats.

Having dealt with the detection of disease in your own cats, the next problem is the prevention of the introduction of the disease. If you are breeding cats, then any cat coming to you for stud purposes should have been tested and shown to be free of infection. If you intend to send a queen to stud, it should be to a stud cat that is known to have been tested and found free from FeLV infection. The question of cat shows remains a problem. It is possible that contact at shows is too brief for transmission to occur, but it should be considered a possibility, especially with regard to any overall plan on the part of the breed societies to attempt to reduce the severity of the problem of FeLV infection.

One other aspect of FeLV that causes great concern is the suggestion that the virus may be transmissible to man. Widespread epidemiological surveys have failed to produce any evidence to show that such transmission occurs.

Feline infectious peritonitis (FIP)

If a cat is infected with the virus of feline infectious peritonitis and becomes ill, the disease is almost invariably fatal. At present there is very little information concerning its natural transmission, or the disease process itself. There is no vaccine available, and so at present the only preventive measures that can be taken are to avoid contact with infected animals.

Work in the United States is producing some interesting new ideas about the nature of FIP. It was thought that FIP was almost always fatal, but

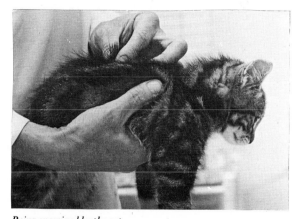

Being examined by the vet

Vaccination is an important defence against disease

serological studies have now shown that a large percentage of the cat population have antibodies to the virus, and so must have been infected and yet not developed clinical signs of disease.

An FIP test is now available in North America, which it is hoped will enable the detection of resistant, susceptible, and diseased cats. The results of such tests need to be interpreted with caution, however, as much more information is still needed concerning the significance of the various antibody levels.

Rabies

Rabies is an infectious disease of man and animals, and is usually transmitted through the bite of a rabid animal. It produces a variety of signs of nervous disturbance, and usually results in death.

Rabies is present in the United States, and most cat owners are aware of the geographical areas in which danger of infection exists. Vaccination programmes to provide protection for pets are readily available. Rabies is not yet endemic in Britain, but some people believe that it is only a matter of time before the disease becomes established. Given the constant threat posed by the illegal importation of pets, rabies remains, quite rightly, of considerable concern to veterinary surgeons, pet owners, and the general public. At present, vaccination against rabies for pets in Britain is available only for animals undergoing quarantine. This policy of not vaccinating pets has been formulated by the

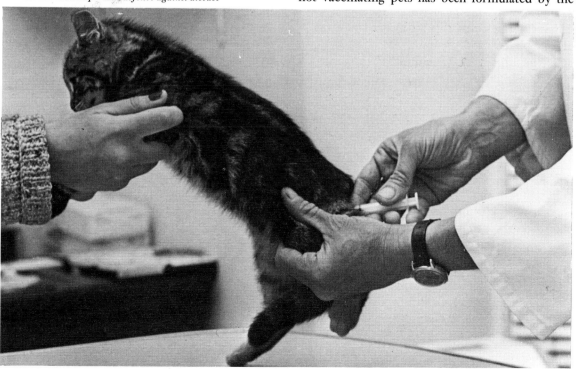

Ministry of Agriculture after careful consideration of the likelihood of disease entry, and the probable course of a disease outbreak. If a case of the disease does occur, all pets and other domestic animals within a certain distance of the outbreak probably will be vaccinated immediately. Strict control of pet animals will be required then to avoid the possibility of spread of the disease. This policy, coupled with the various measures that would be taken, will, it is hoped, result in containment and elimination of any disease outbreak.

If, during an outbreak of rabies, your pet develops signs of nervous disturbance or even a change of temperament, it is essential that you contact your veterinary surgeon immediately so that the animal can be securely housed for observation. There are many diseases that can produce similar symptoms to rabies, and it is important to rule these out. This will then allow treatment of any people who might have had contact with the disease, and so prevent any further spread of the virus.

Skin diseases

Abnormalities of the skin are quickly noticed by cat owners, particularly as their pets normally have such attractive coats, and it is worth noting some of the more important types of disorder. Whatever the nature of the disease, it is important to take your cat to a veterinary surgeon as soon as the condition is noticed, as this will enable early treatment, and, it is to be hoped, the prevention of some of the serious problems that can be caused by chronic skin disorders.

One particularly common cause of skin disease is an infestation of cat fleas. Their presence on the cat is usually readily detected by combing the coat and looking for the fleas, or their droppings, which resemble black grains of sand. If in any doubt, the cat's fur can be brushed over a sheet of damp white paper; any flea dirts that are dislodged will dissolve on the paper and produce a reddish-brown stain. Although many cats have fleas, most tolerate them and remain completely healthy; some cats, however, develop areas of hair loss with small, crusty skin lesions, often at the base of the tail. In severe cases the whole of the back may be involved, the area may become infected by bacteria, and treatment by a veterinarian will be required.

In general, treatment is aimed at controlling the flea infestation. A variety of insecticidal baths, sprays, powders, collars and tablets can be used. The safest of these contain synergized pyrethrins, but whatever the active ingredient, the manufacturer's instructions should always be followed carefully. As fleas only live on the cat for short periods, and the flea larvae can survive in dust and bedding for many months, treatment must include the cat's environment as well as its skin. Particular attention should be paid to the cat's bedding and its favourite resting places; any other cats or dogs in the household should also be treated. Regular de-fleaing of all cats will help prevent a build-up of these parasites, and help to reduce the incidence of skin problems.

Flea bites may also produce a different type of reaction, causing the cat to lick its fur and produce areas of hair loss, often on the hind legs. It is believed that this type of lesion can also be caused by hormonal imbalance, and so the type of treatment given can be very varied. This condition and others of possible hormonal origin are difficult to diagnose with confidence, as estimation of the cat's hormone levels usually is not possible. As a result, treatment may be difficult and prolonged, until the correct combination of medication is achieved.

Ringworm, a fungal disease that affects cats and other animals, including man, is another skin disorder that can be difficult to diagnose. The signs of infection can vary considerably, ranging from inapparent infections to the production of large areas of hair loss, which may become secondarily infected with bacteria. The areas of hair loss are often circular, and this appearance may help in recognizing the condition. In most cases, however, laboratory examinations of hair is needed to confirm a diagnosis. A further aid is examination under ultraviolet light, as this will cause many species of ringworm to fluoresce with a typical greenish-yellow colour. An absence of fluorescence is not an indication that ringworm is not present, and care must also be taken to distinguish ringworm from the fluorescence produced by other substances in the coat. On considering these limitations, it can be appreciated that screening of cats at shows with an ultraviolet lamp is unlikely to be a particularly effective method of detecting infected animals and preventing the spread of the disease. Microscopic examination and culture of the fungus is the only certain way of diagnosing the condition.

Effective treatment is possible with griseofulvin tablets, but medication must be continued for several weeks to eliminate the disease completely. The use of griseofulvin in pregnant cats carries a slight risk of producing abnormalities in the kittens; however, since the alternative would be a litter of infected kittens, treatment should always be recommended.

Control of an outbreak in a group of cats is very

difficult. Affected animals should be isolated and treated, and unaffected animals regularly examined for evidence of infection. As the spores of the fungus are very resistant, the cat's bedding should be destroyed, and any bowls or similar equipment sterilized.

In a group of pedigree cats, who have regular contact with other animals at shows and for stud purposes, the introduction of ringworm is almost unavoidable. Fortunately, many cats do not become affected, but some may become carriers of the disease. As an aid to prevention, cats could be shampooed when returning from shows, to remove any spores that may have lodged in the fur.

Although uncommon, ringworm can affect humans. Owners should therefore be alert for possible lesions on their own skin, and seek medical advice if these appear when a case of ringworm has been confirmed in their cat.

Reproductive failure in the cat

Most people feel that cats reproduce all too easily, and usually have their female cats neutered to prevent unwanted pregnancies. However, owners of pedigree animals sometimes experience considerable difficulties when trying to breed from their cats. Unfortunately, there is a lack of information about many aspects of normal reproduction in the cat, and this is a major impediment to solving problems when they occur.

One of the more dramatic types of reproductive failure is spontaneous abortion, but fortunately this is uncommon and tends to be sporadic in occurence. It can be due to a variety of causes and is not usually a serious problem once the immediate effects on the cat have been dealt with.

More difficult to deal with is the problem of embryonic resorption. This can affect cats in a colony, and can occur at successive pregnancies in some individuals. Typically, a queen calls, is mated, and seems to be pregnant. The owner's veterinary surgeon may be able to confirm this by feeling the cat's abdomen and detecting the swellings of the uterus that contains the developing kittens. Normally these swellings increase in size throughout pregnancy. However, in some cats, if examinations are carried out regularly, it may be noticed that the swellings begin to decrease in size; this process is called resorption. As such regular check-ups are unusual, it is only when the cat fails to produce kittens or begins to call again that most owners realize that something has gone wrong. In nearly all cases of resorption the cat appears healthy.

The main cause of resorption is infection, most commonly with feline leukaemia virus, and so all cases should be FeLV tested. If the test is positive, then it's very likely that FeLV is the causative agent, and the cat should be neutered and kept in isolation, or put to sleep. Bacterial infections do occur, and these can be recognized by microbiological examination of vaginal swabs. Such infections are usually secondary to other causes, and antibiotic treatment seems to have little effect. The chances of successful breeding following infection are very poor, as even a very low grade chronic infection of the uterus is sufficient to prevent a normal pregnancy.

Hormonal abnormalities may cause resorption, but as so very little is known of normal hormone levels in cats it is difficult to make a firm diagnosis. Work is being carried out at Bristol Veterinary School to determine the normal hormone profile during pregnancy, and the types of variation that occur. Once this has been done, it should be possible to identify and treat hormonal causes of infertility. Other causes of resorption may include stress or management and environmental factors, but at present it is not possible to assess the importance of these.

Having briefly discussed some aspects of reproductive failure, there will be occasions when a cat breeder will wish to prevent a cat becoming pregnant, but only as a temporary measure. In these cases a contraceptive drug may be considered. These are usually progestagens (progestins), and their use may result in certain side effects. The main risk is of infection of the uterus, or endometritis, or, rarely, mammary hyperplasia, inflammation and enlargement of the mammary glands. Because of these possible side effects, the use of contraceptive drugs is not recommended until satisfactory clinical trials have been carried out in cats.

There is a reasonable alternative, however; research has shown that ovulation can safely be stimulated artificially. Cats do not ovulate unless mated, and so if mating does not occur, they may keep returning to call. When ovulation is stimulated artificially, no kittens are produced, as mating has not occurred, but the queen ceases to call and accidental matings therefore are prevented. This procedure should be carried out only by a veterinary surgeon.

From this brief discussion of some aspects of cat medicine, it is obvious that much more research needs to be carried out to enable veterinary surgeons to deal successfully with the various problems encountered by cat owners and breeders.

Feline Behaviour

Social development

Cats are frequently described as 'aloof' or unsocial (usually by dog fanciers!), but they are clearly capable of forming bonds to humans, other cats, and other animals. To understand the relative independence of cats, we must appreciate their evolutionary origins. When canids and felids (animals of the dog and cat families, respectively) began to diverge from a common ancestor about 50 million years ago, they followed different paths. The ancestors of dogs became specialized for cooperative hunting of large prey. This necessitated relatively stable social groups with close ties between pack members. The felids became specialized for solitary hunting. Felid bodies soon became adapted for stalking, making leaps and striking with the forepaws. Competition with the social canids was avoided, in part, by developing adaptations allowing them to climb trees and feed on arboreal prey.

The evolution of behaviour within the cat family has been very conservative. Most wild felids show similar patterns of feeding, play, communication and sexual behaviour. The domestic cat differs little from these ancestral patterns. Selection by man has produced enormous variation among dogs, to the point where many breeds reveal little of their wolf ancestry. The variations in domestic cats are small by comparison. Domestication has produced a wide variety of coat colors, patterns and textures, but there have been few major changes in size, structure or behaviour.

Both the European wildcat *(Felis silvestris)* and the African wildcat *(Felis lybica)* have been discussed as possible ancestors of the domestic cat. Whatever the exact origins of the cat, the fact remains that cats are more socially inclined to humans and to each other than are their wild counterparts. This may have come about through

Egyptian Mau kittens playing together

evolutionary changes that exaggerate the behaviours shown by all wild felids during the three periods in their lives when they are social: kittenhood, mating and parenthood. During these periods wild cats lose many of their solitary ways. Much of the behaviour that cats direct to humans can be explained in terms of the interactions between kittens, the interactions between a mother and her young, and the interactions within a courting pair.

Early social development

A kitten's social life begins immediately after birth with its contact with mother and siblings. Although blind, the newborn kitten has good senses of touch, heat sensitivity and smell. It immediately orients to a teat, guided by odour, the higher temperature ($2-3°C/3.5-5°F$ warmer than surrounding fur) and perhaps by the orientation of fur on the mother's body. Feeding does not usually begin until after the complete litter is born.

The earliest signs of social order in kittens is the establishment of a 'teat order'. Nursing is initially random, but by the second day kittens have established distinct teat preferences. The most productive posterior teats are usually chosen first. It has been suggested that the stronger kittens get the most preferred teats, but there is little evidence associating teat order with size or strength. The likelihood that a kitten will try to push a rival away from a preferred spot is not related to who the intruder is, but simply to how hungry the kitten is. Satiated kittens will tolerate nursing from non-preferred teats.

Teat constancy is not limited to situations where there is competition for food. Even in small litters, all kittens form specific preferences that last for three to four weeks.

Kittens may use a variety of clues to identify their preferred teats. In studies using bottles with a variety of artificial nipples, kittens quickly learned the texture and odour of productive versus unproductive nipples. Odour seems to be the major clue, since kittens become disoriented in their nursing if their mothers' teats are washed. Kittens may also be misdirected by odours produced by the sweat glands on the foot pads of their mother or littermates, and may attempt to nurse from these regions. This could account for the tendency of immature cats (and even some adults) to attempt to suckle clothing stained by human perspiration.

During the first few days of life a kitten will cry if removed from its mother or littermates, but will calm down once it reaches any warm spot. In the following week it becomes more discriminating and will only relax if returned to the nest area. As with teat preferences, nest odours seem to be the major clue for identifying home areas. As their vision develops in the second week of life, kittens become able to distinguish familiar areas by sight. Even at three weeks of age, however, they still rely heavily on odours and will become disoriented if their home area is scrubbed clean.

At the age of about three weeks, kittens enter into the next major stage of socialization: play. Play serves a number of important purposes. It allows the young animals to practise and refine behaviours that will be important to them as adults, including hunting, fighting and sex. In addition, play keeps kittens together at a time when their mother is leaving them alone for longer periods while she feeds or simply rests. The onset of play also coincides with the first excursions away from the nest.

Play goes through several stages. Initially (about three weeks of age), it consists mainly of belly-up rolling, pawing and riding. Most of this early play involves only pairs of kittens. At four to five weeks of age kittens begin to introduce other patterns such as side-stepping and pouncing. Play becomes more frequent, involves more kittens at once, and is performed farther away from the mother. After six weeks of age chase play becomes the most common play activity. Some of the components of play, such as the back-arch, become more serious and it is sometimes difficult to distinguish between a play-fight and a real spat.

There are individual differences in play, with some animals preferring to play more intensely than others. There are no clear-cut sex differences except that males engage in more object play than females. Females raised in litters with at least one male also show more object play than those raised only with other females.

After ten to twelve weeks, social play begins to decline. In place of play, there is an increase in exploration and in the amount of time spent simply watching things, a behaviour at which cats clearly excel. Both social play and object play can persist throughout the life of a cat, but both decline with age and never again reach the level seen in the first twelve weeks of life.

Starting at about five to six weeks, kittens go through other important developmental changes. They begin to lose their teat preferences and spend less time nursing as a group. This is the initial step in the weaning process.

In situations where females are allowed to hunt,

they will begin to introduce their kittens to prey at about six to seven weeks. The process begins with the mother either bringing dead prey to the nest or calling the kittens to a nearby kill. Later she will introduce them to wounded prey, which will usually elicit playful pawing and biting. This is the first time the kittens show a neck-bite, which is rarely used in play with other kittens.

Cats are most likely to play with potentially noxious prey, such as stinging insects or rodents capable of delivering a painful bite. Batting and tossing the prey helps to disorient it and make it easier to manipulate. The 'catch and release' play shown by some cats is not seen in wild cats preying on birds or fish, since these prey are more likely to make a permanent escape if released.

Early experiences have a profound effect on the kittens' response to prey for the rest of their lives. Studies in the 1930s compared the behaviour of cats reared with mouse-killing mothers, cats raised with non-killers and those raised with mice or rats as early social companions. In the first group 18 of 21 became killers. In the second group, half never killed a mouse and none killed a rat. Only three of 18 kittens raised with rodent companions became killers, and none killed the type of rodent with which they had been raised. Many cats do learn to kill in adulthood, but it is a much slower process than when learned in infancy. It is unreasonable to assume that an abandoned adult will learn to fend for itself.

Prey preferences formed in infancy are very persistent. In one case a cat that had been raised with chickens was observed to pounce into the midst of a group of baby chicks. It emerged from the mass of startled birds with an invading starling in its mouth! An injured European wildcat brought to an Italian zoo was quick to kill birds, but did not seem to recognize rodents as food.

During this same period kittens rapidly learn other important aspects of their surroundings, such as possible hiding places of prey and sources

Mother cat carrying kitten

Kittens are in constant physical contact with their mother

Play fighting

of danger. Kittens are very good at learning by observation. Laboratory tests have demonstrated that they do better when learning from their own mothers than from unrelated females or males. They also learn quickly by watching animals that are just learning a new task. Under natural conditions kittens learn a great deal by watching one another.

Most kittens have been removed from mother and littermates by the age of ten weeks. Their play and learning continue in their new environments, but at a slower pace. In nature, wild kittens would remain with the mother until close to the onset of sexual maturity. At that time they would begin to disperse and begin a relatively solitary life. There have been no reports of stable groups of feral cats beyond the temporary mother–infant association.

Adult social behaviour

The social behaviour of adult cats is best described as 'tolerant'. In multi-cat households, laboratory colonies and on farms cats appear to make some friends and few enemies. Male cats have been reported to form unstable pecking-orders in laboratory colonies when they must compete for food. They do not form clear ranks in which each cat knows his place. Instead, one or two 'despots' usually feed first, with the remainder feeding in no particular order.

Cats rarely fight over food or choice sleeping spots, but may become more aggressive during breeding periods. Rival males rarely fight more than once, and the outcome of their battle is often completely unrelated to the reproductive success of combatants.

When unfamiliar male cats are introduced to one another in the laboratory, they initially show some hostility, and winners and losers can be identified. In subsequent introductions they will ignore or avoid each other and it becomes more difficult to describe any social ordering. Many cats simply refuse to get involved in such arguments and live out their lives without ever fighting.

Free-roaming cats use the space available to them in different ways. First, each cat has a 'home range' consisting of the total area over which it routinely travels. For rural cats this may be as great as 60 acres (24 hectares). Many cats may occupy the same general area amicably. Second, cats also have smaller hunting and nesting 'territories'. Several cats may use the same hunting territory, but they attempt to avoid using it at the same time as others. Intrusions into another cat's territory do not usually lead to aggression. Both

Climbing trees: an important evolutionary development

parties usually stop, sit and stare until one moves off to return later. Two studies of farm cats have reported females to be more aggressive in their defence of feeding areas than males. Neutered males also tend to become more protective of their territories, although their home ranges are smaller than those of intact males.

Individuals in multi-cat households show similar patterns. All cats may use all areas of the house, but often try to avoid using the same areas at the same time. With many cats this gives the appearance of a carousel, as cats rotate from chair to window to shelf.

Although adult cat society is characterized by relative indifference (except during breeding), familiar cats exchange a variety of social greetings such as nose bumps and mutual rubbing and licking, and will often curl up together like kittens. Pairs may form persistent partner preferences in mating, but stable pair bonds are unusual. Pairs may also hunt side-by-side, but true cooperative hunting has not been reported.

Communication

Cats use every sense available to them to exchange

Showing hostility

information. Touch is of greatest importance to the newborn kitten. The kitten is in constant physical contact with its mother and siblings. As an adult, proximity and contact signify a similar bond. There is considerable individual variation in the amount of contact cats find comfortable. Some are true 'lap-cats', who may also be inclined to curling up with other cats or familiar dogs. Others are more comfortable when close to other animals, but just out of reach. Licking is another contact behaviour associated with the close bond between mother and kitten, which is used by adults to communicate affection for another animal or person.

Cats also communicate using a rich vocabulary of vocalizations, but surprisingly little formal scientific study has been given to this area. The earliest important sounds made by kittens are distress 'mews' when they lose contact with mother or littermates. For the first thirty days of life these cries are very effective in eliciting investigation and retrieval from mothers. Even tape-recorded cries will be investigated. Evidence does not suggest that mothers necessarily recognize the individual voices of specific kittens.

About thirty years ago there was an attempt to classify cat sounds in terms of human linguistics. Cats reportedly use nine consonant sounds (f, g, h, m, r, t, w and two n sounds), two dipthongs, an umlaut and an 'ou' sound. Unfortunately, this does not provide much clarification of the meanings of cat sounds.

A problem in the study of cat vocalizations is that the same sound can have different meanings. The purr, for example, can be invoked in states of pleasure and satisfaction, but has also been noted in cats in pain. *Not* purring during a social encounter can also have meaning. Another problem is that similar messages may be conveyed by rather different vocalizations. Cats may express their curiosity using a variety of different mews, trills and meows.

Cat sounds fall into three broad categories. First are the 'conversational' calls used in everyday interactions with people and other cats. The trill or 'chirrup' sounds are commonly used as a greeting and as an invitation to play. They are similar to the calls used by nursing mothers to invite young kittens to suckle. Each cat also has a characteristic 'contact call', usually a calm, rising meow that alerts companions to its whereabouts. Other meow sounds are varied in their volume, pitch, cadence and repetition to denote inquiry, demand, complaint, excitement and submission.

Cats have a second vocabulary of sounds used primarily in sexual encounters. The caterwaul of prowling males is both an invitation to rivals to come forward and prove themselves and an announcement to females. The female has her own growl-moan courtship call. Both sexes emit a variety of kittenlike mews in the final stages of courtship. The females mating scream may be a distinct signal or may simply reflect the discomforts of feline copulation.

The cat's third vocabulary consists of sounds associated with emotions. We have indicated that purring usually denotes pleasure, but can occur in other contexts. Perhaps it is best interpreted as resignation to the circumstances at hand. For most cats these circumstances will be cosy ones. Unpleasant situations elicit a variety of displays intended to scare or startle the source of discomfort. These include growling, hissing and spitting.

Cats have two other vocalizations that do not fit into any convenient categories. First there is the 'silent meow' in which the animal gives every appearance of making a typical cry, but produces no sound. This seems to involve a combination of insistence and submission, and is common in food begging. The second unusual vocalization is the 'chatter' or clicking noise often made by cats that are pursuing prey. I have also heard this sound from cats chasing flies, soap bubbles and spots of light. It may serve as a comment to others not to interfere with the chase.

Cats also convey conversational, sexual and emotional messages through body postures. They are masters of doubletalk since different parts of the body may be signalling simultaneous conflicting messages. We have already noted that body contact is an important signal. A gentle touch, tap or lick is a sign of acceptance. A swifter tap or slap is an indicator of annoyance, which can escalate into a swipe or scratch if not heeded.

The face is also very expressive. Eyes can narrow in rage or open in excitement. Eye contact is very important. A brief stare can express mutual interest in ongoing events. Long staring contests can be used to settle questions of territorial intrusion without the need for combat.

A cat's ears contain over twenty separate muscles and can rotate through 180 degrees. In addition to aiding in locating the sources of interesting noises, this mobility provides a range of expressions. The alert, 'pricked' posture of the ears can signal to other cats that something of interest has been detected. Ears that are rotated slightly back or that are partially flattened indicate uncertainty. This posture grades into the protective, fully flattened arrangement seen in both fear and anger, as well as in play-fighting.

The posture and movement of a cat's tail is a barometer of general arousal rather than a specific indicator of mood. A twitching, elevated tail denotes excitement. The circumstances may be positive, such as play, anticipating food or spotting prey – or negative, such as annoyance with rough handling or the presence of intruders. When the disturbance is serious, the cat will make an attempt to appear as menacing as possible by fluffing the tail and raising the hind legs.

In highly emotional situations the cat will use its entire body to signal its emotions. A sexually receptive female adopts a crouching posture, called 'lordosis', with her tail drawn to the side. A cat's emotions are often in conflict, producing mixed body signals. There are often impulses to both approach and withdraw from rivals or other situations. One explanation for the 'Halloween cat' arched-back posture is that the animal is trying to approach with the rear end and withdraw with the front end, necessitating a bend in the middle!

Only recently have we begun to appreciate the importance of odours in cat communication. Male cats are well-known for their tendency to spray home areas. This tendency is not purely sexual, since many castrated males and some females, show this behaviour. In addition, cats possess scent glands along the lips, chin and eye ridges, and these are used to mark objects and companions by rubbing.

We have indicated that odours are important in allowing young kittens to identify preferred teats and home areas. Individual recognition of other cats probably relies heavily on smell as well as vision. Odours are also important in eliciting appropriate behaviours. In one account, a mother cat, upon encountering the hind end of another female's kitten, proceeded to groom it as she would her own. When the kitten turned and revealed its face, it was recognized as a stranger and swatted away!

The urine from a female in heat will elicit a chirping call from males. Oestrous females show a greater interest in male urine than do other females. Similarly, nursing mothers show more interest in the urine of kittens than that of adults.

Marking by spraying seems to be the key to

avoidance of territorial conflict in males. A urine mark can inform a cat that another has passed by, how long ago this occurred and, probably, who the intruder was. Males investigate fresh marks with more interest than old ones. They are also more interested in the marks of strange cats than those of familiar ones. Upon encountering a mark, males may show a response known as 'Flehmen' in which the tongue is extended and the nose is wrinkled up. This expression, which anthropomorphically resembles disgust, aids in getting the scent to sensitive odour receptors. Males also respond to urine marks by making fresh marks of their own, but – unlike dogs – they do not attempt to directly mark over the messages left by others.

Cats do not actively avoid areas marked by others. Fresh marks instruct the finder to pause. Older marks indicate that they should 'proceed with caution'. The oldest detectable urine marks indicate that the finder should go on after leaving a fresh 'traffic signal'. Wild felids, such as lions and cheetahs, employ the same system to avoid conflicts as that used by domestic cats.

Abnormal behaviour

We must be cautious when diagnosing psychological disturbances in cats. Behaviour that a human considers abnormal may be perfectly adaptive from the cat's point of view. In addition, behaviour changes are often a sign of underlying physical complaints, and therefore all major behaviour problems should be brought to the attention of a vet. Let us outline some of the most common problems that occur.

Depression, as indicated by listlessness and loss of appetite, is the cat's initial reaction to almost every illness. If it persists for more than a day or two a physical examination should be made. If there is no medical problem, it is possible that the symptoms can be due to some disruption of the cat's routine. Cats are creatures of habit and are very sensitive to time. They come to expect certain things at certain times and are disturbed when the routine is upset. The loss of a human or animal companion, the introduction of a new pet or new family member, or even the presence of workers in the house can trigger behaviour changes. Even a change in the owner's work schedule or a minor change in diet have been known to start problems. The most effective treatment involves restoration of something approximating the animal's old schedule or simply allowing it to adjust at its own pace. In the case of a new pet, the animal should be introduced by a neutral party and an attempt should be made not to draw attention to the stranger or force a confrontation with the cat.

Cats may develop fears analogous to human phobias. They have few innate fears, but rapidly learn stimuli associated with unpleasant experiences. One of our cats was boarded with a family with noisy children. Following this experience she would run behind the sofa and vomit at the sound of children. Such problems must be overcome slowly by introducing the stressful stimuli under non-stressful conditions. In this case the problem was solved by allowing the cat slowly to explore children who were playing quietly in an area where she felt safe.

Several behaviour problems of cats involve mating and raising young. Some cat owners are alarmed by the apparent 'homosexuality' of their young males who attempt to mount other males. This is most likely to occur when no females are available, but usually disappears at maturity. Intact mature males that do not have access to mates may attempt to mount other small animals or even objects such as soft, or stuffed, toys.

The opposite problem of disinterest in mates can be due to timidity or insufficient early experience with other kittens. Cats do not have as clear-cut a 'critical period' for socialization, as do dogs, but do require some social contact for normal development. Socially inexperienced cats may benefit from exposure to other cats that are tolerant of their lack of social skills, such as kittens. Lack of early socialization to humans or other cats may be expressed as either fear or aggressiveness. Again, a gradual process of adaptation may help.

Females sometimes show aberrations of labour. They may move from place to place and seem frenzied prior to, or during, delivery. This is usually caused by not having a safe and comfortable nest area, or by some other environmental disturbance. On the other hand, there have been several reports of well-socialized cats that waited for their owners' return to begin delivery, since they felt most comfortable with human companions around. Two of my own cats have delivered litters at the foot of my bed as I slept!

After delivery some females will refuse to care for their litters. This can have several physical causes, but the primary psychological cause is disruption of the cat's environment. In extreme cases this can result in cannibalism of the young.

Male cats occasionally eat young kittens, but for different, complex reasons. Females often enter a period of pseudo-oestrous soon after producing a litter. This can arouse resident males who might

Mating

attempt to copulate with young kittens. In this case the mating neck-grip may be sufficient to kill the kitten, whereupon it is viewed as prey. Fortunately, this combination of circumstances is rare and most adult males are perfectly safe around kittens.

Many behaviour problems in cats consist of normal behaviour carried out to excess or at inappropriate times or places. Excessive spraying is a typical response to some environmental change, such as a new cat or person in the household. The same circumstances can cause increases in eating, fighting and defecation.

Cats are noted for cleanliness, so lapses are particularly distressing to owners. If physical problems have been ruled out, it is possible that the animal is using this behaviour to bring attention to an unpleasant change in its routine. One of my cats, accustomed to regular afternoon play sessions, was apparently upset by my purchase of a backgammon game. For several days I spent my free time engrossed in the game. The cat demonstrated her feelings during the night by urinating in the centre of the board, an act requiring considerable acrobatic skill and some discomfort! Needless to say, our play sessions resumed and there were no further 'accidents'. Cat owners have reported similar reactions to overly-cherished eiderdown pillows. These lapses may also come about when the cat's litter box is too small, too soiled or if the litter material is in some way unpleasant to the cat.

Another excess that alarms some cat owners is predation. The cat is specialized to be a predator, so one should not be surprised when it follows its nature. Many studies have shown that housecats have little impact on wildlife populations, especially birds. However, this may not comfort the owner who is confronted with daily offerings of birds, moles, mice, snakes and rabbits. In this case the cat is treating its human family as it would its own young, introducing it to the local prey. The cat obviously should not be punished for its concern for the owner's welfare. Bells on a collar may work, but most cats can learn to walk silently even when belled. My own response is acceptance of the fact that I have chosen to live with a predator.

These aberrations are relatively minor compared to those seen in dogs. Given love and a few creature comforts, cats can live a long and happy life as the perfect pet.

Index

Acknowledgements

The Publishers gratefully acknowledge permission to reproduce the following illustrations:

Animal Graphics 297; *Ardea* 39*bl*,67,70*b*,79,129*br*,229; *Camera Press Ltd.* 64,236,308; *Bruce Coleman Ltd.* 38, 51,62,91,94,123*br*,208,221; *Creszentia* 3,22,26,27,86*l*, 97,102,103,106,107,110*t*,115,134*b*,135,138,139,142, 143,148,149,155,163,165,166,167,169,172,173,175, 189,191,197,204,206,207,232,242,243*tr*,*br*,249,251*t*, 306; *Anne Cumbers* 7,12,14*b*,23,36,39*tl*,*tr*,*bl*,47*b*,48,52, 55*tl*,58,59,63,65,66,68,69,70*t*,72,76,77,78,80,82*r*,84, 86*tr*,*br*,87,88,89,92,96,100,101,104,105,108,109,110*b*, 112,116,118,119,120,121,123*tl*,*tr*,*bl*,128,130*cl*,*bl*, 131*bl*,132,133,134*t*,150,154,156,157*t*,162,180*tl*,*tr*,*bl*, 182,183,187,195,196,198,199,202,203,209,210,211, 212,213,215,216,219,222,223,224,226,227,230,233, 234,235,241,252,253,257,259*b*,260,263,264,288,289*b*, 296,303,309,311,314; *Mary Evans Picture Library* 8,9; *Miss S.M. Hamilton-Moore* 291,294; *Marc Henrie* 24, 57,74,90,111,126,239; *Jane Howard* 25,136,146,174, 177,180*br*,225,243*bl*,247,251*b*,289*t*; *Illustrated London News* 10; *JAF* 258,259*t*; *Orbis Publishing Ltd.* 14*t*,46, 55*tr*,83; *Pictor International Ltd.* 35; *Radio Times Hulton Picture Library* 11; *Lew Soper* 61; *Syndication International Ltd.* 82*l*; *Sally Anne Thompson* 40,41,42, 47*t*,54,55*b*,71,127*t*,*bl*,130*tl*,*br*,131*t*,*bl*,157*b*,179,193, 201,254,256,310.

Front jacket: Pictor International Ltd.; *Back jacket*: Ardea, Bruce Coleman Ltd., Jane Howard, Beverley Jane Loo.

The line drawings and colour charts are by Peter Warner.

The Publishers wish to thank the following for their assistance and advice in the preparation of this book: The Cat Fanciers' Association Inc. of America, The Governing Council of the Cat Fancy in Britain, The Feline Advisory Bureau (London), Marna Fogarty.